D0152526

Seasonal Agricultural Labor Markets in the United States

Seasonal Agricultural

Labor Markets in the United States

EDITED BY **Robert D. Emerson**
FOOD AND RESOURCE ECONOMICS DEPARTMENT
UNIVERSITY OF FLORIDA, GAINESVILLE

The Iowa State University Press • AMES, IOWA

Printed by The Iowa State University Press, Ames, Iowa 50010

First edition, 1984

Library of Congress Cataloging in Publication Data
Main entry under title:

Seasonal agricultural labor markets in the United States.

Includes bibliographical references.
1. Agricultural laborers—United States—Congresses. 2. Seasonal labor—United States—Congresses. 3. Migrant labor—United States—Congresses. 4. Alien labor—United States—Congresses. I. Emerson, Robert D.
HD1525.S37 1984 331.12'93'0973 83-140
ISBN 0-8138-1638-6

Text in this book was printed from camera-ready copy supplied by the editor.

Contents

Foreword

The primary concern of this volume--as stated by Editor Robert D. Emerson--is the functioning of seasonal agricultural labor markets. Specific components of this functioning are identified as problems of seasonality, migration, alien labor, and peculiarities of agriculture as they relate to labor markets. Economic and social problems of the labor market are also mentioned, and they are further identified as involving several key policy issues: (1) the long persisting adverse conditions experienced by the "forgotten people" who harvest our crops will not indefinitely be tolerated by society; (2) the continued technological developments and industrialization of agriculture will not eliminate seasonal fluctuations in the demand for labor; and (3) the conflicts of interest among the goals of those involved in various aspects of seasonal labor must formally be recognized, analyzed, and resolved. This last-mentioned matter involves farm laborers' welfare as against food prices, trade, immigration, and similar national policy areas.

The perspective is that of research--the identification of research needs and the evolution of research strategy. Justification for a conference on farm labor in 1980 was based on the substantial changes that have taken place since the last counterpart conference sponsored by the Department of Labor in 1965. An up-dating is accordingly appropriate.

As a half-century attender of farm labor conferences, I have to say that although the occurrence of change is not to be denied, it is nevertheless true that samenesses and abiding similarities have not been completely overwhelmed by change. In the hands of various sponsors and organizers, farm labor conferences have taken divergent directions and emphases which, given the heterogeneous subject matter, reduce comparability but not necessarily legitimacy. The differences in approach and content of the present conference as compared with that of 1965 are as much a reflection of differing interests between C. E. Bishop and R. D. Emerson (their respective organizers) as they are reflectors of changes in intrinsic situations.

When a conference about hired farm labor can legitimately be held that is free of concerns about poverty and welfare of families and children, free of concerns about where and when and how jobs and workers can be found and whether crops will be harvested on time, and free of all the other interrelated aspects of an enduring complex shrouded in uncertainty and disadvantage, the day of change will have arrived. That day still seems to me not to be near at hand.

The first farm labor conference I ever attended was held in the early 1930s. Cotton pickers in the San Joaquin Valley of California had gone on strike. The governor had appointed a fact finding committee (the archbishop of San Francisco, a college president, a university professor). A series of hearings was being held. The "facts" to be found centered around how and why cotton growers had decided among themselves to reduce the cotton picking rate to $0.60 per hundredweight as against $0.75 in the preceding year and $1.00 as requested by workers' committees. Peripheral "facts" had to do with how much cotton an average picker could gather in a day, how many working days were in a season, the number of work days lost during the season, earnings per week, and whether growers had considered workers' cost of living when setting the wage rate. The underlying issue was whether cotton pickers had the prospect of earnings at least equal to the prevailing welfare allowance. (The state relief administration was under pressure by farmers' organizations not to give welfare to persons who refused to pick cotton.) That probable earnings might be less than welfare was considered a strong argument against the "work or starve" policy, and the argument had considerable credence even in those days.

There have been changes since 1933, most prominently the elimination of the hand cotton picker. But even if the cotton picker were still there, he would have some protections and immunities that pickers of 1933 did not: he would not be so directly confronted with a collusively set wage rate, nor with a "work or starve" public welfare policy; he would have better protection of his civil liberties and better defenses against union busting.

The President's Commission on Migratory Labor, 1950-51, and the preparation of its report constituted the first public activity concerning the status and welfare of hired farm workers in which I had a substantial role. Migrants, migratory workers, and various concepts of migratoriness had attained prominence during the depression and drought bowl years and had been sustained with an added international dimension by the emergency importation programs of the World War II era. An executive order (1950) by President Harry S. Truman specified the name of the commission and the tasks it was assigned. Only once did the executive order mention anything about agriculture and this was on the question of "whether sufficient numbers of local and migratory workers can be obtained from domestic sources to meet agricultural labor needs. . . ." Other than this, the order spoke only of migratory workers, migrants, and migration. The first of several interrelated charges to the commission was to "inquire into social, economic, health, and educational conditions among migratory workers, both alien and domestic, in the United States . . . ." (President's Commission on Migratory Labor, p. 187).

This failure to specify the inclusiveness of migrant and migratory did not seem to bother the commission members or its staff a great deal. In accord with generally held perceptions of that time, it was presumed to mean broadly the persons who seasonally harvest crops by hand. The prevailing image was that most of those doing such work were migratory, a presumption promoted by government people and academics who had a propensity to draw maps of interstate migratory flow patterns that demonstrated the magnitude, direction, and extent of such recurrent patterns. There were patterns for the Atlantic, the Pacific, the Southwest, the midcontinent, and minor subflows in between. The drawers of these maps were not given to explaining the extent to which they were depending upon data as against impressions and fertile imaginations. These migratory stream pictorials were probably useful in abating uncertainty, since they seemed to confer orderliness upon circumstances that otherwise would have given the impression of chaos. The commission's staff decided it was not our business to try to establish a taxonomic distinction between migratory and seasonal (or temporary or casual). We believed that the employment situation of those who harvested crops within a commuting area while maintaining a fixed domicile was not importantly different from that of persons not maintaining a fixed domicile. Obviously, there would be differences in family welfare but finally even these differences were not impressive compared to the similarities.

The commission's duties were "to inquire . . . to make a report of its studies . . . including its recommendations for governmental action, either legislative or administrative." The recommendations submitted were comprehensive. During the following decades there have been some changes, even a few in consequence of governmental action. Minimum wages, unemployment insurance, and on-the-job safety are areas in which degrees of action might be noted. In one area, then called "illegal alien labor," I would judge the situation to be worse. At least it is so in total magnitude and in the spread beyond farm work. The current fashion of using the more euphemistic term "undocumented worker" does nothing to relieve the intrinsic chaos in human affairs.

Largely due to the interests and influence of Commissioner William Leiserson, whose pioneer role in the development of labor relations policies in this country will long be known to students of labor history, the commission addressed itself to several aspects of orderly employment practices and labor relations. Concluding that there should be a public role in this area, the necessary question was on whom to lodge the responsibility. From his background as a state agricultural college administrator, Commissioner Noble Clark argued for the Federal-State Cooperative Agricultural Extension Service. Clark's central argument was to this effect: if farmers can be profitably advised on fertilizer, pesticide, and cultural practice expenditures, they can similarly be advised on the benefits of orderly personnel practices and employment management. Other commissioners were dubious that agricultural extension had the perspective and political independence to be effective in this subject matter; lacking an alternative, they agreed to the recommendation. Contemporary critics of the Report scoffed and sneered. So it gave me considerable satisfaction to note the evidence contained in several of the chapters in this volume to the effect that this recommendation has not proved to be as bizarre as once believed.

In my perspective, the major change that has occurred in respect to seasonal farm labor is the decline in migratoriness. Although unsettled populations and individual moving about are still notable facts in the American scene, the migratory streams following crop ripenings no longer are dominant. No less important than the decline in physical magnitude is the decline in the myth. The latter includes the propensity of citizens generally to refer to persons who harvest crops as "migrants" without knowing (or wanting to know) whether they were migratory or not. The migrancy ethos had supplied elements of certainty and absolution for farm employers as well as for relief administrators and other local government officials: migratory workers, in accordance with their patterns of movement, would appear when needed and be gone when no longer needed. This was a convenient ethos that relieved employers and communities of the burdens of recruitment and unemployment, and it sanctioned the practice of enforcing restraints against settling in by seasonal workers. That seasonal workers are becoming less migratory reflects a less hostile community attitude toward their settlement, as well as some improvement in the prospect of earning about as much in settlement as in migratory life.

The farm labor conference held in 1965 was regarded as antecedent to the present one. The 1965 meeting evolved out of the introduction of several academic agricultural economists into the manpower program orbit. This came about because the manpower development and training legislation of the 1960s did not, as had been customary, exclude farm populations from eligibility. Moreover, members of Congress had made it clear in their legislation that they expected manpower programs to benefit farm and rural people. (Parenthetically, I have to note that congressional interest in rural manpower did not derive from representations of need by rural leaders, but rather from urban government spokesmen who wanted measures to be taken against the large and chaotic inflows of poor rural migrants.)

From the several academic agricultural economists who had been invited into advisory roles in the manpower orbit, administrators and labor program specialists had received some perspectives on data and theories about rural poverty that were new to them, even though rather well known in the agricultural economics community. Mostly, it was committee meetings that provided a limited medium of communication. And, as is ever true about committees, neither communicator nor auditor was satisfied that sufficient transfers of perspective and fact had occurred. So it was decided that a conference ought to be held. C. E. Bishop, then at North Carolina State University, was asked to be the organizer.

Seven papers were invited, five of them from academic agricultural economists, one on the hired farm labor force data from a USDA demographer, and one from a labor economist who had done research on hired farm labor and was currently in manpower program administration (Bishop 1967). Among the agricultural economists were several who were readily identifiable within their community as luminaries in research and theoretical exposition on the low-farm-income syndrome. Each wrote his own familiar version, referencing freely from his own writings as well as those of graduate students and colleagues. Very little was said by any of the five that would have been news to readers of agricultural economics literature. In effect, the exercise was mostly a sort of mobility project, i.e., a transfer from the pages of agricultural economics to the pages of labor economics and manpower training. (Parenthetically again, one might note that this small collection of luminaries was not devoid of indigenous talent with respect to mobility--one went on to a Nobel Prize, another to university presidencies, another to undersecretary of agriculture.)

Low-farm income, in various forms of sloganistic and arithmetic construction, has been the central preoccupation of agricultural economists since the beginning of that specialty. Theorems about causes and cures have been divergent, ephemeral, and subject to the whims of fashion. Prior to the 1950s, parity prices, production adjustment, and marketing efficiency had been in high fashion. Following World War II, a consciousness evolved that with accelerated technological advance, fewer farms and less farm labor would be needed. More than that, farm prosperity would depend upon eliminating the redundant claimants against aggregate farm income. T. W. Schultz was the prominent leader in this line of thought and in the elaborations of it that evolved in the 1950s and came into high fashion in the 1960s. Although the linkage between off-farm mobility and farm prosperity was never formally analyzed and specified, the doctrine of "homesteads in reverse" became prosperous. There also was a wispy supposition that if farmers were more prosperous, hired farm labor would also benefit, but that linkage was likewise never specified.

Notwithstanding the fact that off-farm migration attained and maintained revolutionary high levels during the quarter-century preceding 1965--depleting the farm population by more than half--the therapeutic effect on farm income statistics was less than expected. The agricultural economist's response to this outcome was to prescribe more of the same dosage--faster out-moving. There did not seem to be much concern about the welfare of the out-movers so long as they did their bit to help sanitize farm income statistics. With acceleration in mind, attention turned to measures that might be undertaken to facilitate the transfer and absorption of erstwhile farm folk into the nonfarm world of work. This was the point at which the luminaries of the 1965 conference took up their exercises.

No startling new information was presented; no new theorems were propounded; no radical cures were proposed; no effort was made to strive toward consensus or toward conference conclusions and recommendations. Individual policy suggestions in broad general form were offered. Nobody was opposed to economic growth and full employment or to education and manpower training programs for farm people that would help to integrate them into the mainstreams of national occupational life. The Director of the Office of Manpower Policy, Evaluation, and Research of the U.S. Department of Labor somewhat divergently mentioned two approaches toward solving what he termed key manpower problems: "First, of particular value for seasonal farm workers would be a program to structure the agricultural job market and decasualize worker-employer relationships. . . . The second key area to which I would urge earnest attention is the scandalous use of the public welfare system to subsidize employers of agricultural labor. Drawing on the pool of welfare recipients, farm operators are assured an adequate labor supply when and where needed, simply returning the workers to the relief rolls for storage during lulls in labor needs." (Bishop 1967, pp. 134-35.)

From a perspective in 1980, one can observe that the off-farm mobility rubric has gone out of academic fashion. Little writing is done about it anymore. The farm population has continued to decline but only modestly through the 1970s. At least, the declines were modest until 1978, when the Bureau of Census adopted a new and less inclusive definition that reduced it by 1.5 million--from 8 million to 6.5 million or from 3.7% of the national population to 3%. Whether academic pedantry or ineffectual government intervention had any significant role in the massive farm population adjustment that occurred is not a matter on which I aspire to collect evidence.

In contrast to this notable and revolutionary change, the words of the manpower policy administrator bring me back to the realities of this conference and to the "market" for California cotton pickers in 1933 from whence my interest in these affairs began. There are bits of evidence that employment relationships for seasonal workers may be a bit more stable and less uncertain now than formerly. The decline in the migratory fraction implies this. Furthermore, as more attention is being paid to the limited information available on labor force participation by that substantial fraction of seasonal workers who are not regularly in the labor market, there has come the realization that the lack of labor market structure may not be all bad. If these persons are to be utilized and not be barred from the limited opportunities available to them, ease of entry is a necessary condition. Of course this sort of generalization does not go so far as to condone failure to provide sanitary facilities and potable drinking water and the transporting of workers in unsafe vehicles.

The situation may be quite simple and local for those seeking less than full-year employment; it seems unlikely that much in the way of market structure would be found in this instance. For full-year farm workers endeavoring to make a living from seasonal farm jobs, the situation would seemingly be more complex. Perhaps their nearest approach to an equilibrium experience is that described by the manpower policy director in his above-quoted statement, i.e., the complementarity that society may or may not provide between work and public welfare.

Whatever the contemporary true-life situation, I conclude with the hope that there is not much left of the sort of market equilibrium confronted by cotton pickers in California in 1933. Then, a broadly supported "work or starve" public welfare policy, a collusively reduced piece rate for picking cotton, and an armed constabulary with the charge to root out "communist agitators" were interactive forces in a scene in which tranquility was expected to prevail.

Varden Fuller

Preface

The institutional structure surrounding farm workers is vastly changed from what it was only a decade ago. In part this is due to a recognized social concern for farm workers and the array of governmental programs that have evolved to better serve their needs. At the very minimum, a large number of new participants have entered the institutional framework via CETA, Title III, Section 303, and other programs whose direct responsibility is the welfare of farm workers and their families. At the same time, the farm labor offices of the U.S. Employment Service have been dismantled in an effort to serve farm workers in a way that cannot be distinguished from service to other persons in the labor force. One result of the new institutional structure is the introduction of a large number of persons whose primary interest is the welfare of workers, but who have little familiarity with agriculture. This development, coincident with the advent of unionization, particularly in California, has led to an adversary

---

The material in this project was prepared under Grant No. 21-12-79-12 from the Employment and Training Administration, U.S. Department of Labor, under the authority of title III, part B, of the Comprehensive Employment and Training Act of 1973. Researchers undertaking such projects under government sponsorship are encouraged to express freely their professional judgment. Therefore, points of view or opinions stated in this document do not necessarily represent the official position or policy of the Department of Labor.

environment in which one is assumed to be for or against farm workers.

Regardless of the merits of the proponents' arguments for either point of view, such a stance has done little to further our understanding of the issues involved or to enhance public policy toward farm workers. This particular volume is an effort to set forth the operation of farm labor markets and to address the more significant issues to which public policy toward farm labor markets might be addressed.

The basic conceptualization for the project underlying this volume arose from discussions within the Northeast Agricultural Experiment Stations Consultative Committee on farm labor (NEC-21). The members of the committee recognized the dearth of information available presenting any systematic coverage of farm labor markets, and particularly those that are seasonal in nature. With the aim of correcting this deficiency, funding was obtained for the development of a set of papers addressing these issues, for presentation at a conference in January 1980 and for their compilation into this volume.

The conference served as a forum for discussion of the drafts of the papers. Revisions were then made, and most of the revised papers are included in this volume. Since most of the papers had formal discussants at the conference, the remarks of the discussants have been included. However, it should be noted that the discussant was addressing an earlier version of the respective paper than is included here. Although in most cases many of the points raised remain debatable issues, the authors have had the opportunity to modify their papers in light of the comments.

One of the advantages of including contributions from several persons in a volume such as this, rather than having a single author, is the diversity of inputs and approaches that can be gained. At the same time, of course, one sacrifices some continuity. However, in labor economics as in most other areas of work there are competing methodologies for approaching the problems. A particular effort was made to include contributions from the two predominant methodologies of labor economics. One such framework is the institutional approach, of which the dual labor markets is the more common characterization. The neoclassical approach to labor markets, on the other hand, is the more firmly embedded framework within economics, emphasizing the allocative role of markets and giving a secondary role to institutions. Papers of the latter type often tend to be highly technical, as are some in this volume.

The financial support of the U.S. Department of Labor without which such an effort could not have been undertaken, is gratefully acknowledged. Appreciation is also extended to the Florida Agricultural Experiment Station at the University of Florida for additional support in this joint effort. Ronald Jones and Ellen Sehgal of the U.S. Department of Labor have freely offered their assistance in the development of this work. James S. Holt must be singled out as the person who originally conceived a project of this type and subsequently followed through unselfishly with advice and assistance on the project. Dennis Fisher, Bernard Erven, C. D. Covey, and Thomas H. Spreen have also been helpful in various aspects of the project. The editorial assistance of Lucy Cairns and Suzanne Lowitt is gratefully acknowledged. Maureen Adams, Alice Bliss, Lori Colbert, and Shirley Harris have skillfully carried out the extensive typing for this volume.

Robert D. Emerson

Seasonal Agricultural Labor Markets in the United States

1

Introduction to the Seasonal Farm Labor Problem

JAMES S. HOLT

In 1965 the Office of Manpower Policy, Evaluation and Research, U.S. Department of Labor (USDL), commissioned a series of papers on the farm manpower problem. These were presented at a conference in Washington, D.C., in October 1965 in a setting not unlike the one in which the topics in this volume were first presented. In many respects the context of the farm labor problem has changed dramatically in the intervening fifteen years. The decades-long decline in farm employment, a recurrent theme of the 1965 conference, has slowed and may well have halted. The long-standing migration of rural residents to urban areas appears to have halted or even reversed. Many of the commodities in which labor problems were most in evidence--lettuce, tomatoes, tart cherries, wine grapes, pickles--have now been substantially mechanized. The nation was then in its first crop year without the Bracero Program (Public Law 78). And in that year two fledgling farm worker organizations, the Agricultural Workers Organizing Committee, AFL-CIO, and the National Farm Workers Association, were attempting to organize grape harvest workers and negotiate contracts with DiGiorgio Corporation and Schenley Industries, among others. In the intervening years the assistance of farm workers by the public employment service has undergone an upheaval, and a new strategy for social intervention in the farm labor market, through extension of labor legislation and such programs as CETA's Migrant and Seasonal Farm Worker Program and Migrant Legal Services, has emerged. Yet in spite of these dramatic developments of the past fifteen years, the persistence of the underlying problem is remarkable.

In his preface to *Farm Labor in the United States*, which was the product of the 1965 conference, C. E. Bishop identified the two major concerns of farm labor policy to be ". . . the improvement of the persistently low returns for labor services in farming and maintenance of an adequate supply of farm labor to carry out farm operations . . ." It is not necessary to remark upon the applicability of Dr. Bishop's diagnosis to the current farm labor scene. Thus it is appropriate to once again step back to view in perspective the farm labor problem, and to attempt to provide a comprehensive and current context for the development and implementation of future farm labor policy.

Policy cannot be established, changed, or evaluated without a context for the understanding of past events and expected future scenarios. Yet there are seldom the time, resources, or inclination to develop or reconsider the context for individual policy decisions in more than a superficial fashion. Furthermore, there are many participants in the policy process, and consequently many different perceptions of the relevant context out of which policy ultimately develops. For the most part, the context of the past is simply appropriated and modified in minor ways. But in a world of increasing speed, complexity, and specialization, there is a danger that reality will outrun its slowly modifying perception, and that the perceived contexts of the participant groups in the policy development process will be sidestepped by important developments or become irredeemably divergent.

In the papers collected in this volume the authors have sought to redefine and update the context within which farm labor policy and farm labor research for the coming decade will be developed. The purpose of this chapter, in turn, is to set the stage for the more detailed examination of the subject that follows, in an integrative and retrospective statement of the farm labor problem and its setting.

THE ROLE OF THE LABOR INPUT IN FARMING

The farming industry in the United States developed in a technological and social setting vastly different from that which exists today. In the northern states the initial motivation for the development of farm enterprise was to provide for the subsistence of the family. Land was abundant, and farming was the modal occupational pattern. For the most part, farming units were diversified enterprises of the size that could be worked by one family. Virtually all the farm's productive resources except land were supplied by the family. The farm family produced for its own needs and attempted in addition to produce a small saleable surplus to obtain those necessities and an occasional luxury that they could not produce themselves. Marketable agricultural commodities were limited to a small number of storable, transportable items. Where hired labor was used, it generally had to be resident on the farm, and the few larger enterprises that existed were essentially replications of family units.

In the southern states agricultural production was originally organized around the plantation system. These large landholdings produced for the commercial, and largely export, market as well as providing for the subsistence of those who lived on them. They required an enormous and inexpensive labor force and were dependent upon the slave trade.

Initially these two modes developed side by side, moving west as the nation expanded. However, the plantation system was plagued by erratic markets, depletion of the soil resources in the older plantation areas, increasing cost of the slave system, and finally the Emancipation Proclamation. With the collapse of the plantation system, much of the population and land that remained in agriculture reverted to the subsistence mode.

Concurrently with the demise of the planatation

system, and in the ensuing decades, technological developments in agricultural production and in transportation and marketing begin to broaden the range of commodities that could enter commercial channels, facilitate larger volumes of production by the existing labor force, and provide an incentive to specialization. The subsistence mode began to give way to the modern commercial farm.

The major impetus for the development and adoption of improved farm production technology was to enable the presumably fixed resource base on individual farms--chiefly the farm family's labor and their land--to produce more agricultural products or to produce them at lower cost, thereby increasing the income of the farm family. The result for the agricultural industry as a whole, however, was that productive capacity increased more rapidly than aggregate demand for farm products. Competitive pressures in the marketplace resulted in downward pressure on prices. Many farming units could no longer produce an adequate income for a farm family and were forced out of business. The land used by these units was absorbed by those that were expanding or reverted to less intensive uses. The labor forced out of farming was largely replaced by capital investment on the expanding units.

The total labor input in agriculture declined drastically as literally millions of farm families and hired farm workers left agriculture. Low educational levels and the lack of marketable nonagricultural skills made this transition a hardship to many and a costly process for society. Some displaced farmers and farm workers were drawn into nonagricultural occupations that promised greater returns. Many farmers reverted to small scale or subsistence farming, combined with nonagricultural employment when it was available. Other farm workers and farmers with no marketable skills and few or no other resources became wards of society.

The same trends toward commodity specialization and farm enlargement that resulted from improvements in production technology were themselves an impetus to the further development of labor-displacing technology. Mechanization increased the amount of seasonal work such as planting or harvesting that could be accomplished in a day. This permitted the farmer to expand production of his most profitable crops. Often this new production technology could not be profitably exploited unless its fixed costs could be spread over a large number of units of the product, adding further impetus to product specialization and farm enlargement. However, advances in production technology did not occur at an even rate across all steps in the production process, and in some cases increased specialization exacerbated peak labor demands for those activities that resisted mechanization. In particular, harvest activities in fruit, vegetable, and some field crop production required enormous expansion of the seasonal labor force in intensive production areas and became the focus of intense mechanization efforts.

The 1950s and 1960s saw rapid development and adoption of harvest technology and other mechanization. Agricultural labor input, which declined from 24 billion worker hours in 1918 to 15 billion worker hours in 1950, declined to less than 5 billion worker hours by the mid-1970s. The magnitude of seasonal fluctuation, as well as the overall level of employment, was reduced as additional hundreds of thousands of farm workers were displaced from agriculture. Thus changes in labor demand and utilization have been both the cause and the result of specialization and technological changes.

THE CHANGING PATTERN OF AGRICULTURAL EMPLOYMENT

Farm employment grew with the expansion of agriculture through the early part of the 20th century. Although the number of farms and land in farms continued to expand into the mid-1930s, when the number of farms peaked at about 7 million, the impact of emergent technology was already beginnning to be felt in declining farm employment (Table 1.1). Farm employment declined steadily through the 1930s and

Table 1.1. Total, family, and hired employment on farms, selected years, 1910-1978

Year	Annual average farm employment[a] Total (000)	Family (000)	Hired (000)	Percent hired	Total hired farm work force[b] (000)
1910	13,555	10,174	3,381	25	...
1920	13,432	10,041	3,391	25	...
1930	12,497	9,307	3,190	26	...
1940	10,979	8,300	2,679	24	...
1950	9,926	7,597	2,329	23	4,342
1955	8,381	6,345	2,036	24	3,292[c]
1960	7,057	5,172	1,885	27	3,693
1965	5,610	4,128	1,485	26	3,128
1970	4,523	3,348	1,174	26	2,488
1971	4,436	3,275	1,161	26	2,550
1972	4,373	3,228	1,146	26	2,809
1973	4,337	3,169	1,168	27	2,671
1974	4,389	3,074	1,314	30	2,737
1975	4,342	3,025	1,317	30	2,638
1976	4,374	2,997	1,377	31	2,767
1977	4,152	2,856	1,296	31	2,730
1978	3,937	2,681	1,256	32	...

Source: USDA, ESCS.
[a]Average number of persons employed at any one time.
[b]Total number of persons employed at any time during the year.
[c]No survey conducted in 1955: average of estimates for 1954 and 1956.

1940s, during which time farm numbers also began declining significantly, though land in crops remained relatively stable. In the decades of the 1950s and 1960s farm employment shrank drastically, as did the number of farms and land used for crops. In the 1970s the employment of hired farm workers has stabilized while family labor has continued a slow decline. The rate of decline in the number of farm units has moderated, and cropland used for crops has increased to nearly the level of the 1930s and 1940s.

Farm residence is now a distinctly atypical phenomenon in the United States. The nation's farm resident population has declined from 30% of the total in 1930, to 15% in 1950, and to about 3.7% in 1978 (under the Census of Agriculture farm definition used in 1974 and earlier). In absolute numbers, the farm population has remained stable for the past three years at about 8 million, possibly presaging an end to its long decline.

Farm residence has, however, long since ceased to be correlated with occupation. Nearly one-third of the self-employed and unpaid family workers in agriculture in 1978 did not reside on a farm, while more than three-quarters of hired farm workers did not live on a farm. Of those persons in the labor force in 1978 residing on farms, only 55% were employed in agriculture either as self-employed or hired workers. Similarly "rural" is no longer synonymous with "farm." Of the 70 million persons living outside Standard Metropolitan Statistical Areas (SMSAs) in 1978, only 7.6% lived on farms.

Employment in agriculture, which once was the nation's modal occupation, is now of minor importance as an occupational category. In 1978 agricultural employment constituted only 3.8% of average annual employment, and only half of those employed in agriculture resided on farms.

Farm operators and family members have always been and remain today the preponderant source of labor in agricultural production. Throughout the wrenching period of adjustment prior to the 1970s, the relative importance of family and hired labor remained surprisingly stable, with farm operators and family members constituting about three-fourths of annual average employment (Table 1.1). In the 1970s the absolute level of annual average hired agricultural employment remained relatively stable at about 1.3 million, while the number of operators and family workers continued to decline slowly to about 2.7 million in 1978. Consequently, the proportion of average annual employment represented by hired workers has increased somewhat, to about one-third of the total.

The role of self-employed and hired farm workers differs widely throughout the country, reflecting a variety of circumstances.[1] In the Midwest only about one-fifth of average agricultural employment is hired. In the Northeast and South about one-third is hired, and in California, which alone accounted for 15% of annual average hired agricultural employment in 1978, about 75% is hired. Hired workers are also preponderant in Florida, Arizona, and parts of the Mississippi Delta and the Rio Grande counties of Texas. In general, there tend to be more hired workers than family workers in areas of extensive irrigation where fruits and vegetables are the leading crops, in the vicinity of large metropolitan areas where horticultural operations are concentrated, and in those plantation and ranching areas where units have always been larger than could be handled by a single family.

There are racial differences related to the pattern of intensity of hired labor use. Analysis of 1970 population census data indicated that among persons identified as farm operators and farm workers by the census, non-Hispanic whites were in the great majority as farm operators in every state except Hawaii. In the areas where farm operators far outnumbered hired farm workers, the hired workers tended to be drawn from the same ethnic stock as the farmers. However, where farming employed more hired workers than operators it tended (with exceptions) to be accompanied by a shift in the background of the workers, with many more of them being drawn from the black, Mexican-American, or other ethnic minority populations. In the twelve states of the Midwest, 96% of the hired farm workers were non-Hispanic whites. However, in the 27 states where hired workers were in the majority, only about 58% were non-Hispanic whites; the remaining were blacks, Hispanics, or other ethnic minorities. Thus in most areas where the employment structure of farming has developed in a mode emphasizing intensive employment of hired labor and a limited number of entrepreneurs, the employees have come from ethnic minority groups to a substantial extent. An element of potential race and class conflict is present in these areas that is almost entirely absent among the operators and regular hired workers elsewhere.

SEASONALITY OF AGRICULTURAL EMPLOYMENT

Seasonality of employment is a phenomenon central to the agricultural labor market and at the root of both the earnings and labor supply problems to which this volume is addressed. Peak demand for seasonal labor occurs at different times for different commodities and in different regions. Consequently many more people do hired farm work at some time during the year than are at work at any given time, and the job tenure of many of them is very brief. This is abetted by high labor turnover among casual and seasonal workers.

The seasonality phenomenon has considerable impact on the measurement of farm employment and of the work force, and has often led to the misinterpretation and misapplication of farm labor force statistics. Agricultural employment can be measured as a household-based or establishment-based concept (Holt et al.). It can refer to the number of persons employed in agriculture (household based) or to the number of agricultural jobs (establishment based). The difference, other than that which might arise from definitional and methodological differences in survey designs, results from multiple job holding by individual workers within the reference period used for measurement (usually one week). While this difference arises in the employment statistics of all industries and occupational groups, it is far more prevalent in agriculture. The Bureau of Labor Statistics' multiple jobholder surveys showed that in May 1978, 905,000 persons, or 20% of all multiple jobholders, held at least one agricultural job, either hired or self-employed.

The USDA has for many years published a household-based agricultural employment series presenting estimates of characteristics of the population of all U.S. residents doing hired farm work at any time during the year. This population, referred to as the "hired farm work force," has no ready analog in nonagricultural employment statistics. The magnitude of the impact of seasonality and labor turnover in agricultural employment can be inferred by comparing USDA's estimates of establishment employment and of the hired farm work force. In 1977, the most recent year for which all the estimates are available, establishment-based farm employment was 817,000 in January and 1.87 million in July. In that year approximately 2.8 million different people did some hired farm work at some time during the year.

In 1977 only about 14% of the hired farm work force worked 250 days or more at hired farm work (Table 1.2). This group comprises the "permanent" full-time agricultural work force. The great majority of the hired farm work force works a relatively short period in agriculture, almost surely at seasonal jobs. In 1977 fully 63% of the hired farm work force worked 75 or fewer days in agriculture and about 39% worked fewer than 25 days.

A socially relevant but infrequently made distinction is that between *seasonal workers* and *seasonal jobs*. The two are not equivalent, though we cannot

Table 1.2. Percentage distribution of hired farm work force by duration of farm work, 1960-1977

Year	No. of workers (000)	Duration of hired farm work during the year, %				
		Less than 25 days	25-74 days	75-149 days	150-249 days	250 days or more
1960	3,693	41	23	13	11	12
1961	3,488	46	24	10	8	12
1962	3,622	43	26	11	8	12
1963	3,597	48	21	11	9	11
1964	3,370	41	27	12	10	10
1965	3,128	40	26	13	9	12
1966	2,763	41	26	12	8	13
1967	3,078	43	24	11	9	13
1968	2,919	45	25	11	9	11
1969	2,571	43	28	10	7	12
1970	2,488	44	25	12	7	13
1971	2,550	47	25	8	8	11
1972	2,809	40	24	13	10	13
1973	2,671	41	21	13	9	16
1974	2,737	43	23	11	10	13
1975	2,638	45	21	12	9	13
1976	2,767	41	24	13	10	12
1977	2,730	39	24	12	11	14

Source: USDA, ESCS, The Hired Farm Working Force.

distinguish between them in employment data. While the composition of the hired farm work force, which includes many students, housekeepers, and multiple jobholders, suggests that some seasonal hired farm workers are seeking only seasonal jobs, it is certain that there are also some individuals in the hired farm work force who accept seasonal employment as a fall-back because they cannot find permanent employment. Some of these workers are able to piece together several seasonal jobs into a substantial spate of employment, combining for example, citrus and deciduous tree fruit harvesting on the Eastern Seaboard. However, many are consigned to periods of intermittent employment and unemployment, and all are faced with uncertainty in their earnings stream and continous job search.

Another facet of the short tenure of workers in agricultural jobs is related to turnover--that is, workers' movement between agricultural and nonagricultural jobs or into and out of agricultural jobs. Anecdotal evidence suggests high turnover rates in agricultural employment and longer average duration of jobs than the agricultural employment tenure of many of those filling them. Worker turnover, seasonal workers, and full-time workers combining seasonal jobs are all amalgamated in our statistical picture of "seasonal" employment.

The data available with which to infer the "degree" of seasonality of farm employment shows no clear trend toward increasing or decreasing seasonality during the 1950s and 1960s, in either the proportion of the farm work force seasonally employed (Table 1.2), or the seasonal fluctuation in employment (Table 1.3). The employment data in Table 1.3 suggest some decline in the amplitude of seasonal variation in employment through the 1950s and early 1960s; however the statistical precision of the estimates for years prior to 1974 is weak. A discontinuity in the data occurred in 1974, when USDA switched from estimating farm employment based upon a voluntary crop reporter's mail survey to a probability-based enumerative survey sample of agricultural employers. The switch to the probability survey resulted in a higher estimated level of employment, particularly in January, and a lower apparent seasonal fluctuation, but still shows no distinct trend in seasonality across the country as a whole.

Table 1.3. Seasonal range in employment of hired farm workers, United States, 1950-1979

Year	Low point employment[a] (000)	Peak employment[b] (000)	Ratio of peak to low employment
1950	1,100	3,752	3.41
1951	1,069	3,510	3.28
1952	1,031	3,498	3.39
1953	945	3,315	3.51
1954	1,020	3,253	3.19
1955	1,019	3,094	3.04
1956	961	2,970	3.09
1957	1,019	2,971	2.92
1958	2,047	2,984	2.85
1959	984	2,840	2.88
1960	985	2,825	2.95
1961	947	2,847	3.01
1962	929	2,704	2.91
1963	814	2,768	3.40
1964	784	2,542	3.24
1965	770	2,350	3.05
1966	758	2,042	2.69
1967	675	1,974	2.92
1968	672	1,891	2.81
1969	659	1,856	2.82
1970	641	1,796	2.80
1971	696	1,802	2.59
1972	667	1,716	2.57
1973	683	1,797	2.63
1974[c]	848	1,887	2.23
1975	833	1,988	2.39
1976	886	2,063	2.33
1977	817	1,873	2.29
1978	764	1,848	2.42
1979	785	1,807	2.30

Source: USDA, Crop Reporting Board, ESCS, Farm Labor.

[a]December employment for years prior to 1974; January employment for 1974 through 1979.

[b]Peak monthly employment for years prior to 1974; July employment for 1974 through 1979. (July was the peak employment month in all years from 1960 through 1973.)

[c]Estimates since 1974 not methodologically comparable with prior years. See text.

Farm operators' family members are also an important source of seasonal labor. In 1979, for example, hired employment increased by 1.03 million between January and July. However, employment of farm operators and unpaid family members on farms also increased by 637,000 during this period, or by about 30% of the January level. (In interpreting these data it is significant to bear in mind that unpaid family members must work 15 hours or more in the reference week to be counted as employed, while persons working for wages or salary are counted if they work one or more hours during the reference week).

CHARACTERISTICS OF EMPLOYING UNITS

The characteristics of employing units in agriculture have been a salient issue in public attitudes and public policy toward agricultural labor. Historically, agriculture has been exempted from much labor legislation and regulation on the grounds that large numbers of small employing units would make coverage administratively impractical and a hardship for small farmers, who lacked expertise in contending with regulation and record keeping. In addition, a unique employer-employee relationship was often portrayed in which the hired-hand, living with the operator and his family or resident on the farm, was protected by the care and concern of the farmer and the rural community. More recently, concern about the welfare of the farm work force, the seemingly intractable low-income problem among farm workers, and the growth of collective bargaining and farm worker militancy have given rise to questions of relative bargaining power. The farm worker's position has been characterized as one of powerlessness against an agribusiness complex dominated by large corporate farm employers. Many farm labor policy issues involve equity questions to which the relative bargaining position of the participants is indeed relevant.

It is difficult to state precisely the number of employing units in agriculture. For 1974 the total number of farms has been variously estimated at 2.3 to 2.8 million, and the number of farms hiring labor at

830,000 to 1.1 million. However, the available data tend to confirm both, that there are a large number of small agricultural employers and that agricultural employment is heavily concentrated on large farms. The *1974 Census of Agriculture* still provides the most current detailed information about the characteristics of agricultural employers. Table 1.4 shows that a surprisingly large proportion of even the smallest farms hire some labor. However, the bulk of farm employers hire only small amounts of labor. In 1974 nearly two-thirds of agricultural employers operated farms generating gross sales of $40,000 or less, but accounted for only 13% of total hired farm labor expenditure. Fully 42% of all farms hiring labor had total hired labor expenditures of less than $500 per farm, while only 10% had a hired labor bill as high as $10,000. On the other hand the 1.3% of the largest farms--those with gross sales in excess of $500,000--accounted for more than one-third of all hired labor expenditures, and the 14% of farms with gross sales of $100,000 or more accounted for 70% of hired labor expenditures. In 1975 only about 360,000 employers reported paying agricultural wages subject to the Old-Age and Survivors Disability Insurance Program of Social Security (OASDI) tax, which is required of all employers paying wages of $150 or more to an employee.

In 1978 USDA began publishing some data on the size of employing units, drawn from their quarterly enumerative employer surveys. Although this program

Table 1.4. Farms hiring labor and hired farm labor expenditures by value of agricultural sales, 1974

	Farms with hired labor expenditures			Hired farm labor expenditures	
Total value of sales	Number (000)	Percentage of farms in sales group hiring labor	Percentage of total farms hiring labor	Millions of dollars	Percentage of total
Under $2,500	130.6	21.1	15.7	86	1.8
$2,500 to $39,999	404.2	33.2	48.6	535	11.5
$40,000 to $99,999	179.2	55.5	21.6	756	16.3
$100,000 to $499,999	106.6	75.5	12.8	1,570	33.8
$500,000 and over	10.9	95.8	1.3	1,704	36.6
Total	831.5	35.9	100.0	4,651	100.0

Source: Developed from U.S. Department of Commerce, Bureau of the Census, 1974 Census of Agriculture.

was almost immediately curtailed by funding cuts, it provided a current glimpse of regional differences in the size of employing units. In 1978 in July, the month of peak farm employment in the United States, about one-fourth of farm employment was on farms employing only one or two workers, while 41% of employment was on farms employing nine or more workers. In Federal Region 9 (California, Arizona, Nevada, and Hawaii) 77% of the workers worked on farms with nine or more employees, while this was true of only 10% of the workers in Region 7 (Nebraska, Kansas, Iowa, and Missouri).

Although sole proprietorships are still the predominant form of business organization in American agriculture, corporate farms are prominent users of hired agricultural labor. The *1974 Census of Agriculture* showed corporations accounting for fewer than 2% of all farms in 1974 and for fewer than 3.3% of farms hiring labor but accounting for 35% of total hired labor expenditures for the year. As would be expected, larger farms are both heavier users of hired labor and more likely to be incorporated.

Most corporate farms are family businesses that have elected the corporate form of ownership. According to the *1974 Census of Agriculture*, virtually all corporate farms (98.9%) were privately held and most (76%) were family owned. Publicly held corporate farms accounted for only 19% of the value of agricultural sales from corporate farms and for less than 4% of the value of sales from all farms in 1974. Furthermore, most corporations employing agricultural labor were primarily farming corporations, i.e., they derived more than half their income from agricultural production. Nearly 77% of agricultural wages paid by corporations were paid by primarily farming corporations. Thus the high incidence of agricultural labor expenditures of corporations per se does not appear to be of much consequence for the seasonal agricultural labor problem.

Hired farm labor expenses occur in all areas of the United States, though they are naturally more concentrated in areas where agriculture and particularly fruit, vegetable, and other horticultural crop production is most concentrated. California alone accounted for more than one-fifth of hired labor expenditures in 1974, and along with Texas and Florida accounted for more than one-third. More than half (53%) of hired labor expenditures occurred in the ten leading states: California, Texas, Florida, Washington, North Carolina, New York, Illinois, Pennsylvania, Iowa, and Arkansas. The Eastern Seaboard states accounted for 23%, the West Coast states for 30%, and the North Central states for 21%.

Combined hired and contract labor expenditures were almost equally divided among agronomic crop farms (31%), vegetable, fruit, nut, nursery, and other horticultural crop farms (34%), and livestock and general farms (33%). Contract labor, which accounted for $500 million of labor expenditures in addition to the $4.6 billion farmers spent directly for labor in 1974, was most heavily used on horticultural crop farms, which accounted for 53% of contract labor expenditures.

With stable employment and rising wage rates farm employers' hired labor expenditures have escalated dramatically, from $3.7 billion in 1967 to $7.4 billion in 1977. However, hired labor expenditures have not risen any more rapidly than production costs generally. They constituted only 8.5% of total production expenses in 1977, a slightly smaller proportion than a decade earlier.

The importance of hired labor expenditures as an input cost varies substantially among farm types. In 1974 hired and contract labor expenditures combined to account for more than one-third of farm production expenses on fruit, nut, and horticultural specialty farms, and for nearly one-third of production expenses on vegetable farms. They were substantially less important on all other farm types.

Only the most imprecise assessment of the impact of labor costs on farm product prices can be inferred from examining data on the proportion of total farm production expenses due to hired labor. Farm production expense data include only expenses for current inputs. Capital expenses incurred for machinery and equipment and for buildings and land are excluded, as are the return for operator and family labor and management. Since these inputs, once committed to agricultural production, incur only opportunity costs or imputed values but nevertheless represent a substantial proportion of total agricultural production inputs, a meaningful determination of the magnitude of hired labor cost relative to the total cost of production cannot be made. However, it seems reasonable to infer that on the vast majority of farms, where hired and contract labor expenditures make up only a small proportion even of expenses for current production inputs, the impact of changes in farm labor costs of the magnitude relevant to most labor policy discussions (i.e., small percentage changes) would be minor. On the other hand, for commodities such as certain fruits, vegetables, and horticultural specialties where labor expenditures are a significant proportion of current production expenses, changes in labor costs could have a significant impact on farm operators' business decisions and thus on production and consumer prices.

COMPOSITION AND CHARACTERISTICS OF THE HIRED FARM WORK FORCE

The hired farm work force--those persons who do hired farm work at some time during the year--exemplifies the classical secondary labor market profile. Its characteristics include weak labor force attachment, a disproportionate number of racial/ethnic minorities and youth, a low level of educational attainment, and low earnings. In 1977 more than half (54%) of hired farm workers were not in the labor force most of the year. In fact, more than one-third (39%) were students most of the year. Only 40% of those 25 years of age and older (largely eliminating students) had completed high school. One-quarter were racial/ethnic minorities. Only 39% were heads of households or single individuals; the remainder were spouses or other family members.

Anyone attempting to describe the economic and demographic characteristics of the hired farm work force must contend with the extreme diversity of this population. Aggregate population averages become meaningless, and a great deal of misuse and misinterpretation of such data can be found in the discourse on farm workers and agricultural labor problems. In particular, those who would describe farm work force employment and earnings, as well as demographic characteristics, must take cognizance of extraordinary variation in employment durations and attempt to distinguish between the permanent and seasonal work forces.

A seasonal worker might be roughly described as anyone who works at a job that does not offer continuing year-round employment. There are many degrees of seasonality in agriculture, from the cherry or berry harvesting job that lasts only a week or two to commercial nursery work which may continue for eight or nine months. Classification of seasonal workers by duration of their agricultural work is more or less arbitrary. One such arbitrary classification, that of "seasonal" workers as those working fewer than 150 days in agriculture and "regular" workers as those who work 150 days or more, has virtually acquired the sanction of law, though it would appear to have little real significance.

In characterizing the demographic and economic characteristics of the hired farm work force, it is far more instructive to subdivide casual and seasonal farm workers into those working fewer than 75 days in agriculture during the year and those working 75 to 250 days. There are a large number of students in the hired farm work force, and this scheme concentrates most of them (about 84%) in the under-75-day classification; otherwise they distort the demographic characteristics of the other components of the hired farm work force. This classification also tends to sort workers into those who are, and are not, in the labor force the majority of the year. This, of course, is also partly a result to the large number of students. In Tables 1.5 and 1.6 farm workers are

Table 1.5. Chief activity of hired farm workers (thousands) by duration of farm work, 1977

Chief activity	Short-term seasonal (74 days or less)	Long-term seasonal (75-249 days)	Permanent (250 days or more)
All workers	1,723	617	391
In the labor force	579	434	355
Hired farm work	57	338	340
Unpaid farm work	93	29	15
Nonfarm work	391	53	...
Unemployed	38	14	...
Not in labor force	1,144	183	37
Students	820	33	1
Housekeepers	205	126	35
Others	120	24	1

Source: USDA, ESCS, The Hired Farm Working Force of 1977, by Gene Rowe. Agric. Econ. Rep. 437.

Table 1.6. Percentage distribution of the hired farm work force by selected characteristics, and employment and earnings by duration of farm work, 1977

Selected characteristics	Short-term seasonal (74 days or less)	Long-term seasonal (75-249 days)	Permanent (250 days or more)
Race/Ethnicity			
White	77	61	73
Hispanic	8	17	8
Black	15	22	19
Sex			
Male	71	82	93
Female	29	18	7
Residence			
Farm	17	28	45
Nonfarm	83	72	55
Migratory status			
Nonmigratory	94	91	94
Migratory	6	9	6
Type of employment			
Farm work only	48	69	90
Farm and nonfarm work	52	31	10
Employment and earnings			
Average days, all paid work	93	183	317
Average earnings, all work	2,185	4,193	6,563

Source: USDA, ESCS, The Hired Farm Working Force of 1977, by Gene Rowe. Agric. Econ. Rep. 437.

classified into short-term seasonal (under 75 days of hired farm work), long-term seasonal (75 to 250 days of hired farm work), and year round (250 days or more hired farm work). In doing so, it is recognized that there is still substantial opportunity for aggregation error.

The short-term seasonal work force is comprised largely of three groups: students, persons chiefly engaged in nonfarm work who do small amounts of farm work, and housekeepers. These three groups constitute 84% of the 1.7 million short-term seasonal workers. They are young (87% under 45), primarily nonfarm residents, and about half had both farm and nonfarm employment during the year. The majority (66%) of this group is not in the labor force most of the year, most of them being students. Those short-term seasonal workers who are in the labor force most of the year are primarily nonfarm workers, presumably moonlighters, persons laid off, on vacation, and on strike. An insignificant proportion (less than 4%) are primarily hired farm workers.

Among the longer-term seasonal workers, housekeepers and persons chiefly engaged in hired farm work predominate. The great majority (70%) are in the labor force most of the year, and more than half are primarily engaged in hired farm work. This group is mostly male and is older than the short-term seasonal group. More than a quarter live on farms themselves and only about one-third did any nonfarm work. This group constitutes about one-quarter of the hired farm work force, but it is a group whose welfare is clearly identified with farm work.

Among permanent workers, nearly all are chiefly hired farm workers, with a small proportion of housekeepers presumably working at continuous part-time jobs. These workers are almost exclusively male, and nearly half are farm residents. Only about 10% did any nonfarm work during the year.

Minority workers and migratory workers are found in all three groups, though they are most heavily represented among long-term seasonal workers. The

USDA *Hired Farm Work Force Survey of 1975*, on which most of this section is based, defines members of the hired farm work force as migratory if at some time during the year in question they left home temporarily overnight to do hired farm work in a different county or within a different state with the expectation of returning home, or if they had no usual place of residence and did hired farm work in two or more counties. By this measure, migratory farm workers have numbered some 200,000 persons during the past decade and compose 6 to 8% of the total hired farm work force. Like the hired farm work force as a whole, their numbers have remained relatively stable in the 1970s after declining by about half through the 1960s. Other than the fact that a somewhat larger proportion of migrants than nonmigrants are racial/ethnic minorities, there are few demographic distinctions that can be drawn between the two groups. Migratory workers average slightly more days of work and higher annual earnings than nonmigratory workers because nonmigrants predominate among seasonal workers having the shortest tenures. Migratory workers are also less likely to combine farm and nonfarm employment.

There has been substantial confusion and contention about the role of migratory labor in agriculture, including a blurring of the distinction between migrant and merely seasonal farm workers. The vast majority of seasonal farm workers are not migrants. On the other hand, although some migrants are employed almost all year, it is likely that this employment is at a sequence of seasonal jobs. The USDA estimates count a farm worker as migratory only in a year in which that person had an instance of migratory work. Only persons actually receiving pay are counted. Other definitions differ principally in how long a person is considered a migrant after doing a stint of migratory work, and in how many persons other than the worker (i.e., other members of the worker's household) are included. The USDA estimates, which have been relatively consistent from year to year though not blessed with a high degree of statistical precision, indicate that the proportion of persons who migrate is small relative to the seasonal agricultural work force as a whole. Nevertheless, it is clear that those who migrate to do seasonal farm work face a complex of problems and circumstances different from those of nonmigratory persons commuting daily from their homes to seasonal agricultural jobs. Furthermore, migratory workers fill an indispensable need in areas where the volume of seasonal agricultural work is large relative to the indigenous work force.

Foreign workers have been legally employed in seasonal agricultural work in the United States for many decades. The most recent organized program to recruit and admit them was the Bracero Program, under which large numbers of primarily Mexican workers were admitted to work predominantly in the Western states. The program originated as a measure to alleviate wartime seasonal farm labor shortages, but continued long after the war had ended. In 1959 employment of foreign agricultural workers under the Bracero Program peaked at more than 300,000. However, the program was the target of bitter criticism by domestic farm worker groups and was terminated by Congress in 1964. Since that time, reported employment of foreign nationals has dwindled rapidly, falling below 9,000 workers in the late 1960s. In recent years the numbers have again increased somewhat, exceeding 20,000 workers in the early 1970s but falling to about 15,000 for the past few years. Legally admitted foreign workers were used in only four agriculturally related activities in 1978--apple harvest on the Eastern Seaboard, woods work in several northeastern states, sugarcane cutting in Florida, and sheepherding in several western range states. While data on undocumented alien employment in agriculture are not available, a significant proportion of those apprehended have been occupationally attached to agriculture, and anecdotal evidence suggests that they constitute a significant proportion of agricultural employment, particularly of seasonal employment in the Southwest and West Coast.

Incomes of Hired Farm Workers

Social concern about the farm work force has focused on the amount and stability of employment, the returns from it, and on the quality of the employment experience. The income of farm workers has been an overriding concern. As an occupational category, farm laborers and supervisors have for many years ranked second only to domestic household workers at the bottom of the income scale. For 1978 households headed by a farm laborer averaged a mean household income of $12,025 from all sources, only 56% of the mean for all households with an employed head. Furthermore, because farm worker households tend to be slightly larger than average, per capita household income in farm worker households was only 50% of the comparable statistic for all households with an employed head. It should also be noted that the comparisons may in fact be worse than implied here. These data, from the 1979 March Current Population Survey of Census Bureau (CPS), classify households by the employment status and occupation of heads during a reference week in March. Since that is a period of relatively slack agricultural employment, some household heads who are ordinarily farm workers would be unemployed in March. The March farm worker household income data would therefore tend to be weighted toward the more stable farm employment.

The low earnings of hired farm workers result from the short or intermittent tenure of the work as well as from low earnings on the job. The presence of many very short-term workers requires that duration of work be considered in interpreting farm worker income data. The only income data related to duration of work are from the hired farm work force survey, for which there are no comparable nonfarm statistics. However, the earnings data in Table 1.6 indicate that even the longest tenured hired farm workers had low total earnings.

Workers who did both farm and nonfarm work earned, on the average, only about 73% of their average daily nonfarm wage at farm work. Those who were primarily nonfarm workers, presumably with secondary employment in agriculture, earned only about two-thirds their average daily nonfarm wage in farm work. (In neither case is the amount of work performed known, however.) Even primarily nonfarm workers doing some farm work reported averaging only $7111 in earnings from all sources for an average of 246 days of employment in 1977. Less than 10% of their earnings was derived from agricultural work. Such data tend to support the perception that the hired farm work force is a reservoir of low-skilled manual workers.

Some of the approximately one million hired farm workers who are in the long-term seasonal and year-round farm work force, that is, those who are primarily dependent on agricultural work for their livelihood, are workers with other economic alternatives who are working in agriculture by choice. However, it is likely that many others are workers in the economy's unskilled labor pool with an economic imperative to participate in the labor market who are working in agriculture, often at seasonal jobs, because there is no other alternative for them.

Agricultural work is one of the last employment opportunities remaining for the redundant unskilled labor pool. Some of these workers, unable to obtain permanent employment, try to meet year-round economic needs by patching together a sequence of seasonal jobs, sometimes including migratory work. These jobs are of low productivity and are low paying. Only certain areas of the country with long seasons or year-round agriculture (such as California, south Texas, Florida) offer enough such seasonal work to provide even a survival-level living.

It is in these areas that the occupationally identifiable unskilled agricultural workers are most concentrated and from which most migrants come. Although it is in such situations that the low income problem among farm workers is most intense, the generic problem appears to be less that they are employed in agriculture than that they are part of a pool of low skilled or unskilled laborers who are in surplus supply throughout the economy. Their productivity is low and they are working at agricultural jobs in areas where they are available for lack of more attractive alternatives. There are ready replacements for those among the unskilled farm work force who are able to advance themselves into more stable and remunerative employment. That some areas of the country offer longer-term seasonal agricultural employment but are also close to the principal source of alien worker inflow only exacerbates the problem and complicates the solution. Meanwhile, the presence of the large potential labor supply holds down the wages of those currently employed.

There are policy issues and needs related to all groups in the farm work force, including the casual participants and those with other economic alternatives who do farm work by choice. Certainly all should receive the prevailing protections and benefits afforded to all workers in the labor market. However, the group of primary concern for farm worker policy is the group of persons trapped in agricultural work and unable to earn a minimally acceptable income there. They are low skilled and unskilled workers who have become redundant in the modern economy or are unwilling or unable to cope with the regimen and discipline imposed by our highly industrialized society. They are casualties of "economic progress," including but not limited to agricultural industrialization and mechanization.

This is not a problem unique to farm workers or to the agricultural industry. In fact, it is likely that the majority of persons in this circumstance are not occupationally attached to agriculture. In 1978, farm worker households were twice as likely to have incomes under $7,000 as those headed by persons in other occupations. But farm worker households constituted only 3% of households with employed heads with incomes under $7,000. What makes this problem especially visible in agriculture is that a far higher proportion of total hired agricultural employment still consists of these types of jobs than is the case in other occupational categories, combined with the geographic concentration and relative isolation of farm workers.

POLICY APPROACHES TO THE SEASONAL AGRICULTURAL LABOR PROBLEM

Public policy approaches to the dual problems of low income among agricultural workers and uncertainty of agricultural labor supply have had four general thrusts:

1. Aiding the transition of displaced and current farm workers out of the unskilled labor pool into more remunerative and stable employment
2. Protecting and aiding those remaining employed in agriculture through legislation, regulation, and direct services
3. Reducing seasonal labor needs through the mechanization of work having low productivity and of work that is physically difficult or unpleasant, and through restructuring production and management processes to increase productivity and stability of employment
4. Facilitating the temporary participation of local and nonlocal workers in agricultural work in areas of high short-term seasonal labor demand

Facilitating the transition of farm workers into other employment is consistent with the view that an important cause of the low-income problem is a surplus supply of unskilled labor. It is also consistent with the principal historical thrust of U.S. manpower policy of investment in human capital. However, the policy has not yet been visibly successful in alleviating the problem. Moving people out of the unskilled labor pool is a slow and painstaking process at best. It holds most promise as an intergenerational strategy--an attempt to move the presumably mobile and still trainable younger members of the farm work force and the new labor force entrants from farm worker households into other occupational paths. One of the most pervasive aspects of the low-income problem is its tendency to be self-perpetuating. Peer pressure and lack of economic opportunity tend to produce successive generations of new labor force entrants with limited education, labor market skills, and aspirations.

The policy of promoting worker mobility out of the farm work force, thereby altering relative supply, is also handicapped by the sheer magnitude of the target population. Ease of entry into agricultural work and a large redundant supply of unskilled labor in the larger economy guarantee ready replacements for those workers successfully propelled out of the farm work force. Furthermore, the gains from this strategy appear to have been swamped by the effect of the influx of immigrants, especially undocumented Mexican aliens, into the United States in recent years. The rate of Mexican inflow of both permanent immigrants and temporary migrants appears, at minimum, to be severalfold greater than the capacity of present farm worker mobility programs to move workers out of the farm work force.

Perhaps the greatest dilemma that farm worker mobility programs face is the generic labor supply/demand problem that has led to the farm worker and related labor-force problems in the first place--that is, the lack of sufficient labor market demand to absorb the supply. The inexorably rising unemployment rates of the 1970s raise questions about the efficacy of human resource investments and worker mobility schemes as an approach to low-income and low-earning problems. The difficulty, of course, is that of finding jobs for which to train workers.

The provision of labor market protection to those remaining employed in agriculture has been one notable departure from pre-1960 policy. In the period of initial enactment of most current labor legislation, agricultural employers and workers were exempted, in part as the political price of securing passage of the legislation and in part because of doubts about the need for and feasibility of implementing such protections. However, these issues eventually gave way to issues of equity. The declining political power of agriculture, the demonstrable economic problems of farm workers, and the question of equal treatment for all participants in the labor force have led to a lessening of the legislative distinction between farm workers and other workers. The telling questions in extending labor legislation to farm workers have been less the specific issues of their impacts than whether farm workers, many of whom are also in the nonfarm work force, should be treated any differently from other workers with respect to social security, minimum wage protection, unemployment insurance, and the like. The issue of equity in treatment has taken precedence over the concern that these programs could have some negative impact on the level of agricultural employment.

While agricultural mechanization has clearly displaced many farm workers and smaller farmers, it has also reduced the volume of seasonal labor demand and eliminated some very disagreeable work, replacing this with a much lower level of higher quality employment. The massive dislocations that some mechanizations caused were largely unanticipated before the fact and ignored after the fact. The more recent attempts to decasualize agricultural employment through restructuring jobs are having the same effect, namely improving the quality of a much lower level of farm employment. These developments have brought to the fore in agriculture one of the unresolved dilemmas of labor policy generally, that of how to regulate the rate at which new mechanical or managerial technology is implemented, and how to share the costs as well as the benefits of such developments among all participants in the economy.

Unquestionably, technological factors are having an effect on the structure of the agricultural industry. Agriculture is moving toward greater specialization in factor supply and away from the notion that the farm operator is the primary supplier of labor and capital as well as of management. Whether this constitutes a breakdown of the family farm is a question we will leave to the philosophers and semanticists.

We can be sure, however, that these developments will have an impact on the agricultural labor force. The "agricultural ladder" leading from hired hand to tenant farmer to farm operator is now history, if indeed it ever existed. The current reality is a permanent agricultural working class that is gradually taking over more of the labor supply function as the traditional farmer becomes more specialized in the management function. The prospect is for more rather than less hired labor in agriculture, greater demands on farm labor market channels, and increased potential for labor-management conflict compared to the time when labor and management were largely supplied by the farm operator and family members.

Many of the same technological and social developments that have had a profound effect on the farm have also affected nonfarm industry and rural society. Agriculture's rural location limited the labor force available locally, but it also insulated the labor force that was available from nonagricultural competitors. However, over the past several decades there has been a significant increase in the mobility of the rural population and a significant decentralization of industry to rural areas. These trends, coupled with the urbanizing effects of mass communication media, school consolidation, and other social developments, have thrust agriculture into direct competition for labor with a wide range of nonagricultural employment and produced an industrial labor market even in many rural areas.

At present the agricultural labor environment seems to have stabilized. The pace of mechanization has abated and employment is relatively steady. In a few commodities still marked by large requirements for manual labor, especially tree fruit harvest, major dislocations may still be produced by mechanization, though none is presently in prospect. The developments in the farm labor market and the agricultural industry generally combine to favor continued growth of large technologically and managerially efficient operations at the expense of smaller ones. Agricultural employment patterns in the 1970s were greatly influenced by production adjustments brought about by the introduction of floating exchange rates and increased export trade. This has introduced a new element of potential instability into agricultural employment. Nevertheless, changes in the next decade are likely to be less chaotic than those of the 1950s and 1960s and will reflect the gradually increasing separation of labor and management rather than the dramatic impact of technological development. Accommodations will have to be made to a labor market environment characterized by increasing use of hired labor, legislation and regulation, direct competition between farm and nonfarm employment, and the evolution of labor-management conflict.

2

Some Analytical Approaches for Human Resource Issues of Seasonal Farm Labor

WALLACE E. HUFFMAN

Labor is one of the important inputs in production. Labor services in agriculture are provided by farm operators or managers who perform allocative and decision-making functions and engage directly in production, by members of the operator's family or relatives who work without pay, and by hired workers. Hired workers are of two types: regular hired workers who live on or close to the farm and hold full-time year-round jobs, and seasonal hired workers who work only part of the year. Seasonal hired workers are workers who live within daily commuting distance of the farm, domestic migratory workers who travel from farm to farm taking up temporary residence as opportunities for employment change geographically, and aliens who cross national boundaries to work. Some aliens enter the country under special national programs and others enter illegally.

There is a definite secular trend downward in the number of farm workers (the stock) and the annual hours of farm work performed (the flow).[1] Imposed on this trend is a definite seasonal pattern that is determined by the bioclimatic nature of agricultural production and by the extent of its mechanization. The sharpness of seasonal pattern differs by crop and by type of farm worker (Chap. 3). It is less sharp for operator and regular hired labor and sharpest for unpaid family and seasonal hired workers. Seasonal farm labor is providing largely unskilled and semi-skilled services that are generally repetitive in nature (Chap. 10) so speed and physical stamina are the two main characteristics of good workers.

Seasonal labor has been important historically in both agriculture and other industries. Seasonal farm work became important in U.S. agriculture during the 19th century in grain production--the harvesting of wheat (Sosnick). Later, cotton, tobacco, and sugar beet production required large amounts of seasonal farm labor for chopping weeds and for harvesting the crop (USDL 1959). With the mechanization of much of agricultural production, the principal crops currently requiring seasonal farm labor are fruits and vegetables and, to a lesser extent, tobacco and nuts (Chap. 3). Seasonal labor is an important aspect of employment in nonagricultural industries. It results whenever there is large seasonal variation in demand for an industry's output and/or when firms must operate or be open for a longer number of hours per day or per week than regular full-time employees prefer to work. Other industries where seasonal employment is quite significant are those wholesale and retail trades in which holiday seasons cause variation in demand; construction, in which weather conditions affect the type and number of projects that can be undertaken; education, in which the institutionalized school year is shorter than a full calendar year; and some other service industries (e.g., income tax preparation).

There are individuals who supply labor services on a seasonal basis. Youth who are looking for work during school vacations and weekends provide a major source of these workers. Another source is women who are primarily engaged in household work but who respond temporarily to income-earning opportunities (USDL 1959; USDA, *The Hired Farm Working Force of 1977*, and earlier issues; Sosnick, 1978; Chap. 1).

In agriculture the spatial-seasonal nature of

earnings plus the marginal value of the nonwage characteristics of occupation 0.

Who works in occupation F? They are those individuals who place a relatively large value on nonwage aspects of F. Those individuals who choose occupation 0 will be the ones who place a relatively lower value on nonwage characteristics of F. The market forces are selective: they select workers for occupation F who perceive the largest difference between the marginal values of the positive and negative aspects of occupation F. This is the conclusion reached by Sosnick from a survey of seasonal farm workers. Most farm workers viewed favorably the nonwage characteristics of seasonal farm work. Thus individuals possessing identical skills as those in occupation F, but who do not engage in it, can be assumed to have a negative bias in their valuation of the nonwage aspects of occupation F. These individuals have by their behavior revealed that they value the nonwage characteristics of the occupation less than do all of the workers who have voluntarily chosen the occupation, given the available alternatives. The market tends to operate to select within a skill group the individuals who view relatively favorably the nonwage characteristics of any occupation, including seasonal farm work.

If the demand curve for workers in occupation F was $D_f^{\prime}D_f$ rather than D_fD_f, more workers would have to be bribed to enter occupation F. At b the compensating earnings differential is positive, d_b. The annual earnings in F are now higher than in occupation 0. The marginal worker in F now places a relatively low marginal value on the nonwage characteristics of this occupation because on balance he receives disutility from the nonwage characteristics of F. (We can make the definite statement of a negative marginal value being assigned to nonwage characteristics by the marginal worker if wage income is the only characteristic of occupation 0 that matters to workers.) The positive earnings differential is required to overcome this basic dislike for (disutility of) these characteristics. Other workers in F are, however, earning economic rents because they are receiving larger earnings than the minimum required to entice them into occupation F. They are collecting rents on their relatively scarce tastes for occupation F.

If there were a large number of workers--say immigrant farm workers or illegal aliens--who could enter occupation F but not occupation 0, say because of a language barrier, and their opportunity earnings were $E_0 - d_c$, then the new labor supply curve to F would be ABS_F'. Compensating wage differentials would be reduced to d_c and annual earnings in occupation F would fall. Now some of the workers who were previously employed in occupation F would have to seek alternative employment in occupation 0.

Occupational choice among prospective seasonal farm workers is frequently a family occupational choice rather than an individual occupational choice. In seasonal farm work little skill is required, the intensity of work can be tailored to the worker, and workers are frequently paid on a piece rate basis, so children (and wives) can be employed. Furthermore, for children of migratory workers there are frequently few alternative activities. Even if schools and day-care centers are available, the (current) opportunity cost to the family of removing children from work may be prohibitive. For many migrant families, the income of wives and children represents over half of the potential family earnings. Nonfarm occupations generally do not provide the opportunity of employing the whole family. Thus for a potential migratory farm worker and his family, the family's total earnings opportunity rather than just the husband's earnings opportunity must be considered. Although the costs of moving, housing, and caring for a family are also larger than for a single individual, my hypothesis is that households with a large family size and no skilled workers would find migratory farm work most attractive.[3] Emerson, however, finds a negative effect of the number of children on the probability of the male head of a family migrating.

Temporary Migration of Unskilled Workers

Given the changing seasonal-spatial labor market conditions, the movement of workers from one labor market to another is a rational (net) income-maximizing decision. Also, it increases the efficiency of a country's resource allocation. Moving from one labor market to another is, however, a costly process. Information must be obtained about the development of crops and potential employment in other areas. Once a decision is made to relocate, a worker must bear the direct expenses of travel--transportation and food--and the opportunity cost of time spent searching for and traveling to the next job.[4] To have this investment of time and money be rational, the migrant must anticipate that his (family's) earnings in the new location will be higher than if he stayed in the old location. Thus the investment in migration cost is in anticipation of a positive earnings differential over one or more future periods. These periods are relatively short for seasonal farm workers--a few weeks or a few months. In fact, a whole string of investment decisions is made as the workers wind their way generally northward from one local labor market to another as crops mature. Also, employers of seasonal farm labor sometimes make part of the earnings a cash bonus conditional on the worker staying until a seasonal activity is completed. This bonus changes the optimal time for moving on to another farm from that deriving from a strictly piece-rate incentive scheme.

This transient life style of migratory workers and their families has decreased the degree to which they have been able to take advantage of social services and social programs (Briggs et al.; Sosnick; Marshall). The transient life style of migrants and the high opportunity cost of not working means that the migrants' children tend to have disrupted school attendance and relatively few days of attendance per calendar year. This leads to slow progress from one grade to another and to many frustrations for the children. Many drop out of school at relatively low completion levels, and their future earnings potential is dramatically reduced from what it would be for equally able children of nonmigratory households. This has the potential for perpetuating a low income or poverty problem. Actually, we know very little about the effect of migrancy of parents on the school attendance of their children. It is possible that during the school year, children of parents who are following the crop stay in one place with friends or relatives. This is a very important issue which should be investigated further. Emerson, for example, finds that farm workers whose fathers migrated are much more likely to migrate for work themselves. Surprisingly, Duncan and Cowhig concluded in a 1966 study that the occupation of seasonal farm work was not highly "inheritable."

Establishing residence is a primary qualification for the right of voting, for attending school, and for some other social programs. Because migrants spend only a few months in one location, they do not qualify for many common privileges. The transitory nature of these workers makes it difficult to count them in censuses, which are important for targeting federal funds for special programs. Also, their transitory residence makes it difficult to provide federal assistance to governing bodies to aid migrant workers and their families (Chap. 13; Briggs et al.; Marshall).

Working Conditions:
Safety, Water, Sanitation, Food, Housing

We have seen above that workers who are attracted to an occupation place the highest marginal value on nonwage characteristics of the occupation. Thus if seasonal farm work provides below-average worker safety, quality and quantity of water, food, and housing, and poor sanitary facilities, the market's solution is to attract workers who place relatively little weight on these "negative" nonwage occupational characteristics. If jobs are available that require equal skill but offer a lower wage and better working conditions than seasonal farm work, then workers attracted to the latter occupation will be those who value its higher wage more than the better conditions of the nonfarm occupation.

Is there anything socially unacceptable about this market solution? It depends on (1) participants' knowledge about the consequences of their choices and (2) the presence of external effects arising from these actions. Workers and employers might not comprehend the implications for short- and long-run worker good health and earnings potential of different levels of worker safety, quality of food, water, housing, and sanitation. If they do not, they might underestimate the size of the marginal value of these nonwage characteristics of seasonal farm work. This causes socially inefficient decisions on occupational choice to be made.

The performance of seasonal farm work under poor working conditions might also cause negative external effects--other persons being made directly worse off. Negative external effects occur if, for example, seasonal workers spread a contagious disease to other persons because of bad working conditions. This causes other persons to lose working time and other productive time. A negative external effect also arises if, as a result of bad working conditions, seasonal farm workers or their families become partially or completely dependent on society for economic support. For example, a worker might become disabled on the job, and he and his family might require governmental transfers as a means of economic support. All taxpayers are then made worse off. Parents might not perceive the negative effect of their migrancy on their children's future earning capacity and welfare. Thus there are conditions under which it is reasonable for society to attempt to internalize these negative external effects, which means that working conditions must be improved. There are numerous schemes that might be used to accomplish this change.

Society might decide collectively that each of its citizens has a right to a certain minimum income, perhaps implemented as a negative income tax, and let individuals decide how to allocate the income to expenditures on food, housing, personal care, and other goods and services. Alternatively, society might be more paternalistic in its decisions and guarantee a minimum level of "basic needs" (Harberger). For example, individuals in society may receive an increase in their welfare or utility when one or more of the living conditions of other citizens are raised. There might be a consensus reached that some subset of all citizens should have a minimum quantity and quality of housing or nutrition, and the citizenry would allocate part of their income to attaining this objective. Contributions might be made to voluntary charities or the government could organize the collection of revenues and dispersal of expenditures for the basic needs of the target group. Under certain conditions, therefore, it is reasonable for society to establish incentives to insure some minimum standard of living or some minimum standard of consumption of a particular set of goods or services.

If improved working conditions change the quantity and quality of labor services supplied by workers, then they can be viewed as an investment in human capital. An employer would be willing to voluntarily bear the cost of this type of investment only if he were to receive the returns or if the workers were to accept compensatory reductions in their earnings. For employers of seasonal farm labor to bear the cost of this investment, the expenditures must have only a transitory effect on workers' productivity. Given the transitory nature of employee-employer relations in the seasonal farm labor market, workers (or society) would have to share in the cost of changing working conditions in ways which would result in permanent improvement in seasonal workers' health status. This is because they can anticipate receipt of the future benefit from better health whereas the employer cannot.

Formal Training

For certain occupations, formal training obtained in school, vocational-technical training, and/or on-the-job training changes the ability of workers to make a selected set of decisions or perform a selected set of tasks (Huffman 1977a; Welch 1970). This training enhances their efficiency of production. Because training is costly--direct outlays on books and tuition and indirectly on foregone earnings--individuals must expect their productivity in market and/or nonmarket activities to be enhanced by training such that a positive rate of return can be anticipated on the real resources invested. Holding nonearnings characteristics of occupations constant, occupations requiring larger investments in training must provide a higher present value of anticipated lifetime earnings than occupations requiring smaller investments. Thus for markets of different skill level and years of occupational experience to be in equilibrium, occupations requiring large investments in training must have higher earnings at least sometime in a worker's lifetime than occupations requiring less training (Becker 1971).

If, however, markets for different skill levels are in disequilibrium, the positive relationship of cost of training to earnings need not exist and the ex post rate of return on investment may be negative. For example, Chiswick cites the situation of the Jewish population in Israel in 1948. It was composed primarily of well-educated immigrants from Europe who had migrated to a country with an underdeveloped economy primarily for noneconomic considerations. These individuals found that their previous training was often of little economic value for the best jobs they could obtain. The results were low wage-skill differentials, a low return on previously obtained schooling, and low correlation between schooling and annual earnings. Also, during the 1950s and 1960s in the U.S., farm consolidation and mechanization of agricultural production occurred at such a rapid rate that farm markets were in disequilibrium. Thus one would not be surprised to find small ex post returns to schooling possessed by farm workers at this time.

Individuals face a number of occupational choices over their lifetimes because they face (1) a finite lifetime over which returns from investments in training can be obtained, so postponing investment by one period reduces the number of periods over which returns can be obtained and (2) rapidly rising marginal cost of human capital production in any period, which makes it irrational to complete large investments in a short time (Becker 1975; Ben-Porath). Thus it is optimal in the sense of maximizing lifetime satisfaction (or present value of lifetime earnings) to invest early in life but to invest over several years. As a result of this rising cost of training, academic years have been set at a length that is shorter than a calendar year.

Since training is a seasonal activity, youth are available for work in the off-school season. Wage opportunities for these youths, given that school vacations at different levels and different institutions correspond roughly to the same time period, will be best in occupations that experience a peak demand during the same period as school vacations.

Youth, while engaging primarily in training, which is seasonal, have the opportunity to choose a seasonal income-earning occupation. The number of available occupations is much smaller for these seasonal (or part-time) workers than for full-time workers (Owen). The reason is that employers are unwilling to pay search and training costs for workers expected to work relatively few total hours per year and to have a short tenure with the firm. They can obtain higher expected returns, other things being equal, by investing in full-time workers.[5] Thus seasonal workers are generally concentrated in low-skilled jobs, and seasonal farm work may be a reasonably attractive temporary occupation. Provided that youth do not permanently harm their health while engaging in such work, it seems a good choice.

When students complete their schooling, they are available for full-time employment. The combination of more skill and availability for full-time work leads to greatly expanded occupational choices. Seasonal farm work has been a transitory occupation for many youth who will eventually have other, high-paying, full-time jobs. Very few individuals who have completed high school would be expected to choose seasonal farm work as a major occupation.

Additional training for individuals who are primarily engaged in seasonal farm work seems likely to enhance occupational mobility rather than to raise the wage rate of seasonal farm workers. Seasonal farm work is and has historically been an occupation in which added training has little if any effect on the productivity of a worker's time. Cost-minimizing employers cannot rationally pay seasonal workers with more training a higher wage than that which covers their enhanced productivity.

Studies conducted at the University of Florida by Poveda and by Emerson of male hired farm workers (including migrants) drawn from the Florida Farm Labor Survey in the period November 1970 to February 1971, report estimates of multiple-regression earning functions. These results show that years of schooling completed by hired farm workers have a positive and statistically significant effect on earnings. However, the estimated rate of return to schooling for all male workers is 2.3%, which is much smaller than the 10-15% rate of return to schooling in nonagricultural occupations reported by Becker (1975) and Mincer (1974). Poveda's results also imply that for all males the rate of return for schooling at nonfarm work is about 100% higher than at farm work. Thus training is unlikely to be a rational investment of resources by individuals or society for those individuals who plan to remain in the occupation of seasonal farm work.

Additional training may open new higher-paying job opportunities, including better paying off-farm jobs in the off-season. Discrimination against women and minorities in nonfarm labor markets can blunt these incentives. For example, Briggs et al. (1977) find considerable discrimination against these groups in the rural Southwest. Thin labor markets for particular skills in sparsely populated areas and small towns can result in married women being overqualified for some jobs they hold. However, Matta (Chap. 5) finds that years of schooling have a positive and significant effect on the probability of a farm worker being engaged in off-farm work sometime during the year. Additional training will enhance a seasonal farm worker's occupational mobility and seems to be a good avenue to follow for escaping from the occupation of seasonal farm work.

Unionization and Minimum Wages

Minimum wage legislation and unionization of workers in an occupation are institutional factors that affect the performance of labor markets. Farm workers were not covered by minimum wage legislation until 1967. From 1967 to 1974 the minimum wage for farm workers was below the minimum for other workers. The Fair Labor Standards Act amendments of 1974 legislated farm-nonfarm equality, but scheduled convergence to equality was not actually achieved until 1978. Minimum wage and unionization both have the objective of raising wage rates for a certain set of workers. The minimum wage sets a floor on all nominal wage rates for covered occupations. Union efforts to raise wages apply to its members. Unions may also attempt to change working conditions and fringe benefits of workers (Sosnick; Chap. 10). But they also add to the uncertainty associated with agricultural production by introducing the potential threat of a strike. This can be especially devastating for producers, since seasonal laborers work primarily in the harvesting of highly perishable crops.

To the extent that unionization and minimum wages are effective in raising real wage rates (or employer costs) from what they would otherwise have been for farm labor, both short- and long-run effects occur. In the short run the quantity of labor services employed declines. Workers who remain employed and have their wage rate raised will receive short-run benefits, but workers who lose their jobs because of the higher wage are made worse off. (Producers' profits are also reduced because profit functions are concave in input prices.)

Of the workers who lose their jobs, not all will remain unemployed. Some may find other jobs. Research by J. P. Mattila suggests that others will enroll in school. His results show that increases in the minimum wage have had a positive and significant effect on the school enrollment of teenagers. Thus although these youth have lost low-paying jobs, some enroll in school. The additional schooling is a means of raising their skill level and wage offers so that they will be employable at a wage above minimum wage. Still other youth will turn to illegal activities as a source of income. Given positive probabilities of apprehension and conviction and the adverse effect of conviction on further employment opportunities, some of these individuals will experience further reduced job opportunities. The work history of a seasonal farm worker is, however, generally irrelevant and not obtained by employers (Sosnick), so some of these individuals may eventually reenter the seasonal farm labor occupation.

Because of exemptions and evasion, minimum wage legislation has had less direct effect on wage rates and employment in agriculture than might be expected. The intent of the legislation was that workers on small or moderate-sized family farms were to be exempt from coverage. Thus the main exclusion comes from the exemption of all employees of employers who used less than 500 man-days of hired agricultural labor during each quarter of the preceding calendar year. Other exclusions are for workers in the range production of livestock, temporary seasonal workers who commute daily from their homes, students, field workers less than 17 years of age working on the same farm as their parents, and members of farm operators' families. Gardner (1981) estimates that only 40-50% of hired agricultural workers are actually covered. Evasion seems, however, to be widespread for these covered workers (Sosnick; Briggs et al.). The reasons are (1) for low-skilled manual workers (especially illegal aliens), workers and employers are often made better off by lower wages, given that derived labor demand curves slope downward, and (2) the cost of enforcement is relatively high for seasonal workers in low-population rural areas.

The minimum wage coverage of nonfarm workers also affects indirectly the seasonal farm labor supply.

Leighton and Mincer have found that a higher minimum wage reduces the quantity of on-the-job training supplied by nonagricultural firms to their workers. This is because a higher minimum wage prevents firms from reducing the wage rate during the training period of low-wage workers to cover the cost of general on-the-job training sold to these employees (Becker 1975). Thus low-wage individuals, especially teenagers, are being forced into formal schooling and vocational-technical training programs to obtain training rather than being able to combine working with learning on the job. This has the effect of increasing school enrollments from what they would otherwise be. Some of these youth may choose seasonal farm work as a temporary off-season occupation.

As employers of seasonal farm labor have time to make full adjustment to a higher minimum wage rate and to unionization, the only rational response is further mechanization of production or a switch to less labor-intensive crops. Unionization may actually provide stronger economic incentives for further mechanization than escalating minimum wage rates. The reason is the threat of a strike at harvest time, in addition to attempts to raise real wage rates and improve working conditions (Chap. 7).

As the size of fruit- and vegetable-producing firms located largely in California and Florida grow and replace smaller family operations, the number of seasonal hired farm workers demanded and employed may rise temporarily (Chap. 3). These larger farms with a large number of workers per farm (Chap. 3) are, however, prime targets of unionization efforts. To the extent that union drives are successful, they are contributing to the ultimate demise of the unions. It seems only a matter of time until most of the unskilled seasonal farm labor in fruit and vegetable production is replaced by machines and a few skilled workers.

Poveda's study shows that major occupational classes of hired farm workers have a significant effect on worker earnings even after accounting for differences in schooling, experience, health status, and other personal characteristics. Those workers in the occupational class of vegetable worker, general farmhand, and livestock worker earn the least and managerial workers earn the most. The first group has wage rates that are about 13-15% below the wage of fruit harvesters, and managers (manager, farm operator, and foreman) have a wage 48% higher than do fruit harvesters. Most importantly for mechanization, machine operators and truck drivers have wage rates 14% higher than harvester workers and 27-30% higher than vegetable workers and general farm hands.

Unionization and higher minimum wage rates increase the expected return from further mechanization of agricultural production. Growers can be expected to demand that research on labor-saving harvesting technology be undertaken by public sector research institutions. They can also be expected to be prospective buyers of new machines developed by private industry (Huffman and Miranowski). Thus in the long run, the response to institutional changes will result in almost all unskilled labor being replaced by machines. More skilled machine operators will be demanded, fewer total labor services will be demanded, and most of the workers will have higher skill levels (Chap. 10).

Aggregate Unemployment and Seasonal Farm Labor Supply

The supply of seasonal farm labor is responsive to the national unemployment rate. When the national rate is low, a relatively small quantity of seasonal farm labor is supplied, but during a recession the pattern is reversed. Thus business cycles have a major impact on the availability of seasonal farm labor. If, over the business cycle, nonfarm wage rates fluctuated rather than employee hours of work and layoffs, then business-cycle effects on wage rates and labor availability in the farm labor market would be moderated. The issue is why wage rates tend to be rigid and employment flexible in the nonfarm labor market.

The new macroeconomics advances our understanding of business cycles. The primary focus has been on the inflation-unemployment trade-off in a world of rational expectations. The consensus is that no long-run trade-offs exist, that is, the Phillips curve is vertical at the natural rate of unemployment in the long run. The area of disagreement lies in whether there exists a short-run trade-off. Recent applications of the theory of rational expectations by Sargent and Wallace and by Lucas led to the conclusion that the public will always off-set governmental policy because they behave as if they understand the performance of the economic system. In this context, rational expectations in a deterministic model means that economic agents have perfect foresight about the predictions of economic models. In a stochastic model, rational expectations means that the subjective probability distribution used in decision making by economic agents is the same as an objective probability distribution obtained from the relevant economic model. Thus for strict rational expectationists, a short-run trade-off between inflation and unemployment cannot occur by changing macro policy. Their view is that monetary and fiscal policy cannot be used to moderate business cycles.

Other builders of rational expectational models (Pool; Fischer; Friedman) see a role for governmental policy in the short run. Advances have come by distinguishing between auction markets and labor markets. In auction markets (i.e., markets for financial assets, agricultural commodities, and primary metals) transaction and storage costs are small relative to price fluctuations. They respond instantly and efficiently to changes in circumstances that provide new information, and successive price movements in these markets are uncorrelated (Pool). Labor markets are different because labor services cannot be sold in auction markets, and the transaction costs of arbitraging between markets are sizeable.

The lengths of production and distribution cycles are significant in most firms in a technically and economically advanced economy. Firms, especially large nonfarm firms, enter into contracts to insure future delivery of products. They also enter into contracts for raw materials, to hedge their production costs. In wage contracts, wage rates are fixed temporarily, but hours of work are variable. This allows firms to meet transitory components of product demand by varying the hours worked by their employees. Transaction costs are thereby reduced since the need to continually renegotiate prices in contracts for final products is avoided (Fischer; Friedman). Unemployment results during some periods because the wages and prices used in negotiating these contracts are projected for more than one period in the future, and even though they are based upon all relevant information available at the time of the forecast, unexpected fluctuations in the economy occur more frequently than labor contracts are negotiated. Thus unemployment sometimes develops because of these temporary price rigidities in the nonfarm sector.

In this latter type of model, macroeconomic policy can affect the short-run behavior of output and employment, and it can thereby cause short-run tradeoffs between inflation and unemployment. Thus policymakers could conceivably reduce the fluctuations in national unemployment rates and thereby stabilize labor supply in the seasonal farm labor market. This would reduce the labor supply uncertainty faced by farmers.

DUAL LABOR MARKETS AND INSTITUTIONALISM

The dual labor market approach is sketchy and vague. Description, narratives, and taxonomies crowd out model development. Primary emphasis is placed on the view that the behavior of workers is determined by institutional arrangements or restrictions rather than by response to economic incentives. The dual labor market concept is important for human resource issues because it discounts heavily the importance of human capital in determining wage rates and job opportunities. Also, the assumption of a dual labor market mechanism seems to be the basis of congressional seasonal farm labor policy (Marshall, p. 89; Chap. 13). For example, consider CETA, Title III, Section

303. I think it is a fair assessment to say that this legislation is based on the belief that seasonal farm work is a "bad" job and that the Section 303 program can eliminate bad jobs by transferring the workers to better jobs.

Essential Characteristics of Dual Labor Markets

The concept of dual labor markets is a highly descriptive alternative to classical labor market analysis. According to this concept, institutional arrangements are the primary determinants of how workers are allocated among jobs, of wage rates, and of promotions. Workers are viewed as being largely homogeneous in their ability to do work, although the potential productivity of workers is considered to be largely irrelevant for hiring, promoting, and wage-determining decisions. Jobs are, however, heterogeneous: jobs are dichotomized into "good" jobs that pay high wage rates and provide opportunity for intrafirm advancement, and "bad" jobs that pay low wage rates, provide few opportunities for intrafirm advancement, and are unstable.[6] Thus the dichotomy is between good and bad jobs and not between skilled and unskilled jobs (Doeringer and Piore; Wachter; Cain).

Since workers are viewed as being largely homogeneous and wanting good jobs, there are not enough good jobs for everyone and so there are long queues for them. Many workers must take "bad" jobs if they are going to be employed. Such workers supposedly develop bad work habits--e.g., frequent absenteeism and high quit rates--as a result of holding bad jobs and are frequently unemployed. Thus because some workers must take "bad" jobs, there is a high rate of underemployment among workers in secondary labor markets.

Job performance is viewed as being based on nonefficiency considerations: seniority, being an insider, and arbitrary discrimination.[7] The view is that high wage rates adhere to certain jobs, irrespective of the ability and skill of workers. The wage structure is dominated by custom, tradition, habit, seniority, and other nonefficiency considerations.

Good jobs go to individuals who are insiders and who have put in their time waiting in lines; outsiders are arbitrarily discriminated against.

The dual labor market approach places relatively heavy emphasis on internal labor markets. These markets reallocate workers within firms among jobs, compared to intrafirm mobility of workers with a particular skill level. Entry is considered to be at a low level, and the dual labor market literature has a "work-your-way-up" perspective on the method of obtaining good jobs. Thus if workers enter at a low level, long intrafirm job ladders are required for them to have the potential for eventually reaching a high-paying job. This approach is exemplified in the petroleum industry where a gasoline station manager or tankwagon driver works his way up to a managerial position in the central office of a large petroleum company, or in a large commercial bank where an individual starts as a teller and works his way up to becoming bank president. With mobility occurring at entry levels, which are low-wage jobs, workers do not change jobs frequently because they cannot transfer to another firm for a better-paying job, but rather they must start over again at the low entry level. Other jobs, for example hired farm work, generally have a very short job ladder. Under these conditions technology is viewed as being endogenous in the sense that it is manipulated by employers to further class interests rather than firm interests.

The Primary Sector

The primary sector is described as the location of "good" jobs. They are a subset of all nonfarm jobs. However, skill is not a prerequisite for holding these jobs. The view (perhaps naive) is that this sector is composed primarily of "good" jobs that *make* highly paid workers (Doeringer and Piore; Wachter; Cain). Jobs carry particular salary levels and anyone, irrespective of skill, ability, or past experience, can fill these jobs equally well. Promotion is by institutional arrangements of insiders. Thus the concept called an internal labor market provides the pool of workers from which promotees are chosen. The primary sector is composed mainly of large nonfarm firms that have a large number of different pay levels--a long job ladder--e.g., General Motors, Standard Oil of Indiana, IBM.

The dual labor market proponents seem to fail to see that much of what they regard as institutional procedures for hiring and advancement may be less rigid than they perceive them to be, and many of the practices are rational in a neoclassical labor market framework (Fleisher and Kniesner, pp. 359-67). If working for a firm in the primary sector involves sizeable investment in firm-specific human capital (Becker 1975) and/or hiring new workers requires high job search and training costs, then much of the described behavior in the primary sector has a plausible alternative neoclassical explanation.

To reduce labor turnover among specifically trained workers, firms have an incentive to share the costs and benefits of this training with the worker in whom it is embodied. The worker's wage inside the firm is higher than his opportunity wage outside the firm because he is obtaining a return on his share of the investment in training. Workers seldom change firms or strike because of the effectiveness of this shared investment incentive scheme in reducing labor turnover. Workers would be unable to capture a return on their share of the investment in specific training if they should quit or lose working time because of union activity. Firms are reluctant to lay off or terminate a worker because they cannot then obtain a return on their share of the investment in his training.

Firms may attach a wage rate to particular jobs rather than to individuals, but they plan to fill the jobs with individuals who have the relevant skills. Recent rural development experience has provided some convincing evidence that only if new firms have primarily low-skill jobs will a significant number of low-income workers be employed (Marshall). If firms come with high-skill jobs, skilled workers will be imported and local low-skilled workers will be largely unaffected. Firms also may promote insiders because information on the performance characteristics of outsiders is relatively costly to obtain and/or because a considerable amount of firm-specific human capital is required for upper-level jobs. With workers possessing different amounts of general and specific training, they are heterogeneous and promotion seems likely to be very selective, based on training and favorable past job performance.[8] Studies of occupational mobility have found that much, rather than little, upward mobility can be gained by switching firms (Blau and Duncan; Kelley). This is especially true for young but seasoned employees.

Secondary Labor Markets

The secondary sector is described as the location of "bad" jobs. Farm hired work and many nonfarm jobs are included in this sector. Here there is minimal potential for advancement to higher paying jobs or the potential is underdeveloped. Thus job ladders are short. Vacant jobs are filled by hiring from outside the firm. Workers are paid a low wage but it is approximately equal to their opportunity wage. Workers develop bad work characteristics because of bad jobs; they do not have bad jobs because they have undesirable work characteristics. It is claimed that these workers are excluded from good jobs in the primary sector for noneconomic reasons. The view is that these individuals hold jobs as hired farm workers and other low status jobs because they are unfairly excluded from being considered for primary sector jobs.

The description of secondary sector labor markets seems to fit well (from a neoclassical view) the case of unskilled or manual labor in industries where the demand for labor is seasonal or affected significantly by business cycles. Workers receive very little on-the-job training of any type and job ladders are short. When workers have low skill and possess very little firm-specific human capital, workers and firms are basically indifferent to labor turnover, i.e., quits and terminations (Becker 1975). Homogeneous workers are available to firms in the market as replacements, and homogeneous jobs are available to workers in other secondary sector firms.

This labor turnover imposes minimal capital losses on both workers and firms because neither has invested significant amounts in job search costs or firm-specific training. Furthermore, firms may have wanted to increase the size of their labor force only temporarily, and workers may not have been seeking full-time employment. When labor demand shifts left in the off-season or in a recession, firms minimize their costs of production by terminating part of their unskilled work force. Thus unskilled workers in cyclical occupations have higher turnover rates and higher unemployment rates than do workers possessing large amounts of firm-specific training (Becker 1975).

Workers are relatively homogeneous in their ability to do manual labor. Workers are not, however, homogeneous in their ability to perform skilled tasks (Schultz 1971). Secondary-sector workers may (rightly) feel trapped in low-wage jobs because other individuals possess more relevant training for high paying primary-sector jobs or because other individuals are viewed as providing a higher expected return on the firm's share of the investment of firm-specific human capital. Thus the competition for "good" jobs among qualified applicants means that marginal candidates are never hired for them.

Dual Labor Markets and Contradictions to Principles of General Equilibrium

The dual labor market concept is primarily descriptive of the behavior of individual decision-making units. It ignores the basic warning of macroeconomics: options available to individuals and to individuals collectively are generally very different. For example, consider "good" jobs. Any one individual can obtain a good job, but unless only good jobs are supplied, not all individuals can have good jobs and be employed.

Dual labor market analysis misses the thread that ties everything together economically, which is the tendency toward general equilibrium with frequent disturbances along this path. Economic agents are faced with a wide set of choices within a basic framework of constrained optimization. Behavior is changed only as a result of new information, changed economic incentives, or perhaps institutional changes. Thus although "bad" jobs could be upgraded by changing the intensity of use of other inputs and/or nonwage job characteristics, economic incentives must exist to make the changes worthwhile. They frequently do not exist. Furthermore, in a dynamic economic environment, the demand schedules for labor services with particular characteristics are generally shifting, sometimes abruptly, because of changes in the market for final output and in the technology of production. Thus labor markets are continually in disequilibrium; some have excess demand at the old wage and others have excess supply. In either case, there are economic incentives to change the geographical location of labor services and/or to change the skill level (Schultz 1975). Both take time and the investment of other real resources.

IMPLICATIONS

This paper has analyzed human resource aspects of seasonal farm labor. One key factor in labor market analysis is homogeneity of labor services. The three main characteristics are skill level, geographical location, and point in time. Transfers of workers from one local labor market to another or from one skill level to another require investments of real resources. Resources are invested in these activities primarily with the expectation of a positive rate of return.

The low incomes of seasonal farm workers are not caused by the malfunctioning of labor markets. Market forces create economic incentives for workers to allocate themselves to their best employment opportunities (or their family's best employment opportunities). Incorrect expectations and institutional factors may distort perception of these incentives.

(We might agree that it is unfortunate that some individuals do not have better job opportunities than seasonal farm work.) Within the group of workers who voluntarily supply low-skilled manual labor, laborers attracted to seasonal farm work are the ones who place the highest value--which might be negative--on the nonearnings aspects of seasonal farm work.

Therefore, when we consider policies to increase the compensation and improve working conditions for seasonal farm labor, we must ask ourselves what is the economic rationale for the initiative? Is there excess demand for labor of seasonal farm workers because the wage rate and/or nonwage aspects of employment are too unattractive? Increased real compensation would increase the quantity of labor supplied to agriculture. If, however, there continues to be excess supply of agricultural labor, then increasing compensation will aggravate the problem by making farm work more attractive relative to other occupations. Furthermore, firms must attempt to minimize the cost of agricultural production because of competition among domestic producers and from foreign producers. This requires that firms do not provide compensation to workers higher than the *minimum required to obtain voluntary labor services*.

Are there negative external effects associated with the poor working conditions of seasonal farm workers? If so, then economic incentives need to be changed so that these external effects are internalized in the industry. This would require not only greater employer liability for accidents and for generally harmful-to-health working conditions, but *public subsidization* of housing and general health care. Alternatively there might be a consensus view that a set of "basic needs" of farm workers are not being met, and that general social welfare would be enhanced by making in-kind or tied transfers of housing, health care, or food to farm workers. If basic needs are the issue, then taxation of the general public to collect revenues for supporting these programs is appropriate. Thus it is crucial to the correct implementation of policy to identify the basic impetus for increased compensation of farm workers.

Providing further training for those individuals who plan to engage in seasonal farm work in the long run seems to be an unattractive private or social investment of resources. Additional training may, however, expand employment opportunities in other occupations where additional training is rewarded with larger wage rate increases because worker productivity is enhanced more than in seasonal farm work. Additional training may also increase the nonmarket (household) productivity of these individuals.

Given the seasonal nature of the demand for labor in agriculture, an attempt should be made to rely heavily on seasonal labor supply that is synchronized in time and location. This possibility arises when individuals are engaged in another seasonal activity. For example, students, especially in the North, and some women (ones with children in school) are sources of such a labor supply. (Using students during vacation periods to meet peak seasonal farm labor demand is not feasible in Florida, Southern California, and the Rio Grande because the peak occurs during the winter months, when students are in school.) The supply curve of labor of these individuals shifts back and forth over the year. These individuals may also be responding to the temporary rise in wage rates. Since these individuals are choosing seasonal farm work as a temporary occupation, most of them will move on to better, permanent occupations. Thus low earnings is a temporary phenomenon for many, but not all, of these workers.

3

Seasonality of Farm Labor Use Patterns in the United States

CONRAD F. FRITSCH

Major adjustments in the size of the family labor force have occurred since 1950, when an annual average of 7.6 million family workers were employed on farms. By 1979 only 2.5 million remained (USDA, ESCS, *Farm Labor*). Yet even after the consolidation of agriculture into larger, more labor-efficient units, short-term seasonal labor hirings have remained substantial and, in simple numerical terms, greatly exceed the number of family workers. The *1974 Census of Agriculture* reports 4.5 million total hirings of seasonal farm workers in 1974. Of these hirings, 3.3 million were for less than one month of farm work (vol. 2, pt. 4).

The continuing dependence of U.S. agriculture on large numbers of short-term seasonal hired workers has not paralleled the large downward adjustment in family labor use that has occurred since the 1950s. Moreover, it has been seemingly insensitive to public policy initiatives such as unemployment insurance,

---

This chapter has benefitted from comments on an earlier draft by Robert Emerson, James Holt, Paul Hurt and Steven Welch; any remaining errors are the sole responsibility of the author. Appreciation is also extended to Arnold Bollenbacher for making available special data tabulations from the *1974 Census of Agriculture*.

workers compensation, social security, minimum wage laws, and others identified by Mamer (Chap. 10) which, by internalizing social costs into employer cost schedules, provide incentives for farmers to employ fewer workers for longer periods.

The employment implications of agricultural dependence on a short-term seasonal labor force are more easily observed by annualizing seasonal labor hirings to represent an equivalent number of full-time workers. If it were possible to reorganize agricultural employment schedules in such a way that all short-term seasonal employment (workers hired for fewer than 150 days per year) could be eliminated, the 4.5 million seasonal hirings could be replaced by fewer than 350,000 full-time workers.

Regional and commodity-specific seasonal labor use patterns, including attributes of farm workers and employers, are documented in the initial sections of this analysis. Policy implications of these labor use patterns are then assessed within a simple labor market equilibrium framework that arrays seasonal farm jobs actually filled against the perceived labor market attributes of persons employed as seasonal farm workers.

DATA CONSIDERATIONS

Analysis of labor use patterns for industries with little seasonal fluctuation in labor demand can proceed with minimal bias under the simplifying assumption that all workers are employed year round. However, the sharp seasonal expansion and contraction of employer demand for labor is associated with a labor force composed predominantly of workers with short-term attachment to agricultural employment. About three-fourths of all persons with agricultural employment work at seasonal farm jobs. Of these seasonal workers, 85% indicate that they are employed in the farm sector for an average of only 10 days per year (USDA, *The Hired Farm Working Force of 1977*). The existence of (1) large numbers of employers with widely fluctuating seasonal labor needs and (2) large numbers of workers with only sporadic attachment to the hired farm working force poses insurmountable barriers to the use of any single data source as an accurate base from which to derive analysis capable of providing a comprehensive understanding of farm labor market dynamics. Accordingly, four primary data sources are used in this paper: (1) the Census of Agriculture, (2) the Quarterly Agricultural Labor Survey (QALS), (3) the December Hired Farm Working Force (HFWF) supplement to the CPS, and (4) ES-223 Department of Labor administrative data.

Each of these data series has unique attributes making it useful in the analysis of a specific type of seasonal labor use issue. As would be expected from a set of similar but not identical data sources, the definition of "total" and "seasonal" hired farm workers varies by data source. These definitional variations are primarily dependent on the combination of (1) the reference period to which the data apply and (2) the source of the information--either the employing establishment or the household unit.

Establishment data sources such as the Census of Agriculture and the QALS count workers from an employer perspective. Employment is stated as of a given time period. The QALS is a probability survey conducted by the USDA that measures employment in a specific survey week during the first month of each calendar quarter. Annual averages from this source are calculated as the sum of January, April, July, and October survey week data divided by four. Census of Agriculture counts represent total employment during the entire census calendar year.

Since establishment surveys count each worker at the work place, employees working for two or more employers during the survey period are counted once by each employer. Hence establishment survey data represent counts of employer hirings and provide an estimate of the actual number of workers employed on farm employing establishments during the survey period. Overestimation of the actual number of workers doing farm work during the survey period occurs to the extent that workers are employed by more than one employer. The overestimate of workers is not large in the QALS, which relies on a one-week survey period, but is significant in the Census of Agriculture, in which the survey period covers a full year.

Annual average employment estimates calculated from quarterly QALS data greatly underestimate the total number of workers actually employed in agriculture during the year. What is accurately estimated is the number of employees working during the survey weeks. However, the annual averages calculated from the QALS represent the best available estimate of the total number of workers that would be required if all available jobs could be filled by full-time workers.

The December hired farm working force supplement to the CPS is conducted by the Bureau of the Census for the USDA. It is the only data series providing estimates of the number of persons doing hired farm work during the year. A probability survey, it is conducted during the third week in December and is based on all persons resident in the United States during the interview week who did some farm work for wages during the current calendar year. The resulting estimate contains no worker duplication but excludes foreign workers who worked on United States farms during the year and subsequently returned home. Hence, the HFWF count is an estimate of domestic hired farm workers only. (See Appendix 3 for a more complete description of the data sources and comparisons of estimates from each.)

SEASONAL HIRED LABOR USE

Based on aggregate hired labor movement during the 1960s and 1970s, Gardner (Chap. 14) concludes that the hired labor demand curve has shifted to the right during the 1970s, reversing its leftward movement of the 1960s, when major reductions in aggregate hired labor use occurred. The evolution since the late 1940s of a labor force that is almost 80% nonfarm residents from one composed primarily of farm residents is cited as further evidence that hired farm labor is predominantly a seasonal phenomenon.

Holt (Chap. 1) attributes the declines in hired farm labor demand in the 1950s and 1960s to increasing commodity specialization and technological change. In addition to these factors, changes in farm labor demand are the result of shifting geographical location of production and increases or decreases in the level of aggregate product demand.

Direct comparison of seasonal hired labor use in the 1969 and 1974 census years suggests that the major seasonal labor use adjustments of this period were reflective of shifts in aggregate product demand. Indeed, the increase in labor use on cash grain farms noted in Table 3.1 can only be described as dramatic and illustrative of (1) the dependence of agriculture on very short-term seasonal workers and (2) the dynamic nature of farm labor market adjustment processes.

Fruit and nut farms (Standard Industrial Classification [SIC] 017) were the major users of seasonal labor, with 860,000 hirings in 1974, but only 30% were for more than 25 days on an individual farm. Total labor use by this subsector declined very little, but important regional shifts are noted in Table 3.1. The major decline in the Lake States was concentrated in Michigan and correlates with the shift to mechanical harvesting of cherries. Declines in the Corn Belt are most likely related to reduction in the quantity of apples harvested in Ohio, Missouri, and Illinois. Arkansas recorded the largest decline in the Delta States.

Labor use in the Northeast varied by state, with increased seasonal employment in Maine, New Hampshire, Massachusetts, and Vermont related to expanded apple production. Declines were concentrated in New York and Pennsylvania.

Seasonal labor use on vegetable operations (SIC 016) declined in all major growing areas over the period. About 320,000 hirings were recorded in 1974. Additionally, vegetable operations were able to provide almost 40% of their seasonal workers with employment beyond 25 days. The largest absolute and relative declines occurred in the Mountain States.

Table 3.1. Seasonal farm labor hirings, 1974 and change from 1969 (percentage from 1969 given in parentheses)[a]

Region[b]	Total	Farm type: Cash grain	Tobacco	Cotton	Other field crops	Vegetables	Fruit & Nut	Dairy	Other livestock
Northeast	321,699	15,802	20,085	0	33,705	33,666	70,164	75,082	15,437
	(-10)	(+78.1)	(-24)	0	(-0.6)	(-3.6)	(-7.7)	(-15)	(-15.7)
Lake States	352,089	70,537	2,153	0	20,665	20,031	57,830	101,588	37,214
	(-19.2)	(+54.3)	(+116.8)	0	(+14.5)	(-8.7)	(-35.4)	(-32.1)	(-39.1)
Corn Belt	640,994	288,866	5,819	1,822	7,629	14,582	15,854	52,046	197,644
	(-13.4)	(+41.2)	(+26.4)	(-58.2)	(+125.4)	(-38.7)	(-32.5)	(-35.7)	(-38.4)
Northern Plains	229,281	114,000	0	0	14,987	364	352	11,669	72,156
	(-22)	(+7.8)	0	0	(+54.8)	(+19.7)	(-56.2)	(-33.4)	(-45.3)
Appalachian	773,012	68,319	408,577	4,055	33,256	7,966	16,064	47,849	116,711
	(-9.4)	(+115.1)	(-12.1)	(-52.9)	(+112.9)	(+1.5)	(-14)	(-17.2)	(-16.3)
Southeast	373,252	38,466	77,897	8,900	37,941	33,612	45,833	8,305	52,716
	(-13.9)	(+111.2)	(-30.6)	(-31.8)	(+67.8)	(-7.3)	(+1.3)	(-22.4)	(-23.5)
Delta	197,432	58,122	c	36,932	18,482	3,726	4,007	10,912	39,469
	(-14.7)	(+9.4)	c	(-36.2)	(+51.1)	(-4.4)	(-45.5)	(-23.4)	(-7.8)
Southern Plains	257,043	61,726	0	29,100	17,829	9,456	5,214	7,302	97,450
	(-24.4)	(+21.8)	0	(-41.9)	(+24)	(-26.1)	(+40)	(-40.3)	(-30.4)
Mountain	248,560	38,772	0	9,578	58,698	19,884	25,340	12,626	60,464
	(-19.8)	(+25)	0	(+10.7)	(+42.4)	(-48.6)	(-4.7)	(-32.3)	(-36)
Pacific	1,109,087	43,292	0	28,181	80,779	174,593	617,434	18,226	30,539
	(-1.4)	(+40.1)	0	(+105.4)	(+58.8)	(-9)	(-0.8)	(-21.7)	(-42.8)
U.S.	4,502,516	797,908	514,565	118,568	323,971	317,826	858,092	345,605	719,820
	(-12.2)	(+37.4)	(-15.5)	(-24.2)	(+46)	(-2.8)	(-6.1)	(-27)	(-32.8)

Source: U.S. Department of Commerce, Bureau of the Census, 1969 Census of Agriculture. 1969 data are from vol. 2, Chap. 4; 1974 data are from unpublished Census tabulations.

[a]Farm labor hirings include only workers hired by farm employers for less than 150 days per year. Labor hirings exceed total workers to the extent that workers are employed by more than one farmer during the year.

[b]Regions include the following states:

Northeast: Maine, New Hampshire, Massachusetts, Rhode Island, Connecticut, Delaware, New York, New Jersey, Pennsylvania, Maryland, Vermont
Lake States: Michigan, Wisconsin, Minnesota
Corn Belt: Ohio, Indiana, Illinois, Iowa, Missouri
Northern Plains: North Dakota, South Dakota, Nebraska, Kansas
Appalachian: Virginia, West Virginia, North Carolina, Kentucky, Tennessee
Southeast: South Carolina, Georgia, Alabama, Florida
Delta States: Mississippi, Louisiana, Arkansas

The decline in labor use in Arizona was greater than for the region as a whole, but small increases in Colorado and New Mexico provided a slight offset. Major declines in Ohio and Illinois accounted for most of the reduction in seasonal labor use on vegetable farms in the Corn Belt states.

Declines in tobacco harvest labor use (SIC 0132) were concentrated in the Carolinas and Florida. Over 83% of all hirings in this sector were for fewer than 25 days. Tobacco harvest in this area takes place between June and early September. Students dominate as seasonal workers.

Employment on cotton operations (SIC 0131) declined in all regions except the Pacific. Although once a major user of seasonal harvest labor, cotton operations accounted for fewer than 120,000 seasonal hirings in 1974. Only 30% of these seasonal workers were employed on an individual farm for 25 or more days. The data also capture the shift in production from the traditional, nonirrigated cotton states in the South to irrigated production areas in the West. Cotton production in the West is concentrated in New Mexico, Arizona, and California.

Major declines in seasonal labor use occurred in the livestock and dairy sectors (SICs 021 and 024). Livestock farms and ranches were heavy users of seasonal hired labor in 1969, when over 1 million hirings were identified. By 1974 seasonal worker hirings dropped 33%, to fewer than 720,000. Fewer than one out of five seasonal workers were employed on a single farm or ranch for 25 days or more. Although relative declines were large in most regions, major absolute declines occurred in the Corn Belt and Northern Plains regions.

Declines occurred in seasonal labor use on dairy farms (SIC 024). Only about one-quarter of all seasonal workers were employed for 25 or more days. The Corn Belt and the Northeast accounted for one-third of the total decline in hirings on dairy farms.

Major increases in seasonal labor use occurred on cash grain farms (SIC 011) and other field crop farms (SICs 0133, 0134, 0139). Sugar beets and potatoes are the major commodities involved in the latter classification. The dramatic increase in the number of seasonal worker hirings on grain farms (37%), combined with the decline in hirings on livestock farms, is consistent with increased grain production in response to expansion of U.S. markets for grain and the relative deterioration of price levels for cattle. Wheat acreage harvested increased by 28% over the period. Almost 80% of the seasonal workers on cash grain farms and about two-thirds of those on farms classified as "other field crops" were employed fewer than 25 days on a single farm.

Although absolute increases in seasonal labor use on cash grain operations occurred in all regions, over half, or an increase of almost 110,000 hirings, were reported in the eight states included in the Corn Belt and Lake States. Iowa, with an increase of almost 42,000 hirings, Indiana with 19,000, and Minnesota with 18,300, were the three states with the greatest increases.

Attributes of Seasonal Farm Labor Employers

Overall hirings of seasonal workers (those hired by an individual employer for fewer than 150 days) declined by about 12% between census years--about 5.1 million hirings in 1969 compared with 4.5 million in 1974. Hirings of less than 25 days duration numbered 3.3 million in 1974, comprising three-fourths of all seasonal hirings.

In addition to hiring large numbers of very short-term seasonal workers, most farm employing units are small. Only 17%, or fewer than 100,000 farmers, hired more than 11 seasonal workers. Yet this generality must be viewed in the context of wide disparities across regions and commodity groups. Farms in the midwestern states defined by the Corn Belt, Northern Plains, and Lake States regions include almost half of all farm employing units (263,324), but fewer than 8% hire more than 11 workers. At the opposite extreme, the 46,000 farm employers in the Pacific region represent less than 8% of all employers, but over 40% hire 11 or more workers.

Employers in the Appalachian and Pacific regions represent over 40% of all seasonal labor hirings but contain fewer than one-quarter of all employing units.

Implications for coverage of seasonal workers and employers under labor legislation are more readily apparent from the distributions displayed in Table 3.2, which arrays the twenty leading hired-labor-using states by the number of employing units in each state. Iowa, with almost 40,000 employing units, contains the largest number of farm employers. Of the twenty leading labor use states, Florida contains the smallest number (6,763). Employers in the midwestern states including Iowa, Illinois, Minnesota, Missouri, Wisconsin, Ohio, and Indiana hiring 20 or more seasonal workers do not exceed 4.1% of all agricultural employers in these states. Similarly, these large employers only hire from one-fifth to one-third of total seasonal labor used within their respective states.

At the other extreme, California, Washington, Oregon, and Florida employers hiring 20 or more workers accounted for 80-87% of all seasonal hirings in their states. Even so, with the exception of the Pacific region, employers hiring 20 or more workers

Table 3.2. Farms hiring seasonal workers by number of workers hired, 1974[a]

State	Employers hiring seasonal workers	Seasonal hirings	Employers hiring 20 or more seasonal workers, %	Seasonal hirings by employers with 20 or more seasonal workers, %
Iowa	39,994	202,529	3.4	22.5
Texas	37,293	198,096	5.1	34.8
Kentucky	31,121	217,932	7.2	34.0
Illinois	29,258	143,989	3.3	25.8
Minnesota	28,042	123,697	3.2	26.0
North Carolina	27,209	321,845	17.6	50.6
California	25,357	725,127	33.0	86.6
Missouri	23,628	95,563	2.7	24.7
Wisconsin	23,182	100,790	3.3	29.2
Ohio	20,816	98,765	4.1	33.8
Indiana	19,720	100,148	4.0	28.5
Tennessee	18,708	114,485	5.6	31.0
Michigan	14,876	127,602	10.8	58.0
New York	13,222	90,886	8.6	49.0
Pennsylvania	12,509	73,473	6.0	43.8
Washington	11,959	229,035	23.5	79.9
Georgia	11,948	107,128	11.4	48.6
Oregon	7,935	146,849	19.9	79.8
South Carolina	7,213	81,372	16.8	57.0
Florida	6,763	125,137	19.2	79.0
Total	398,244	3,424,448		

Source: U.S. Department of Commerce, Bureau of the Census, 1974 Census of Agriculture, unpublished tabulations.

[a]The table arrays the 20 leading seasonal labor-using states by number of employers.

are a relatively small proportion of all employers of seasonal labor. One-third of all California employers of seasonal labor hire 20 or more workers, while in the other three states with high concentrations of workers hired by larger employers, these large employers account for only 19-24% of the total.

It is clear that most employers of seasonal farm labor continue to hire only small numbers of workers. However, a trend toward greater concentration of the seasonal labor force on larger employing units is evident since 1969. Only 8% of all employers hired 20 or more seasonal workers in 1974, but this is almost double the 1969 figure.

The proportion of workers hired by large employing units is generally much smaller in the agricultural sector than in most nonagricultural industries. Farms hiring 20 or more workers in 1974 represented about half of total hirings. By contrast, firms in the nonagricultural sector hiring 20 or more workers employed about three-fourths of the total work force (U.S. Department of Commerce, *County Business Patterns, 1974*). Only the Pacific region, dominated by the statistics of Washington, Oregon, and California employers, conforms closely to the hiring patterns of the nonagricultural sector. In these states almost 85% of all seasonal hirings are by employers hiring 20 or more workers.

Employment patterns vary considerably by commodity group and are consistent with the employment concentrations by states (Table 3.3). Farms with 11 or more seasonal hirings account for at least 72% of all hirings on tobacco, cotton, vegetable and melon, fruit and nut, and other field crop farms (the latter raise primarily potatoes, sugar beets, or sugarcane). At the other extreme, farms with 11 or more seasonal hirings represent only 10% of all cash grain farms hiring labor and less than half of all workers hired by them. Similar distributions occur in dairy and other livestock operations. Only vegetable and fruit operations have concentrated hirings among farms with 20 or more workers. By contrast, dairy and cash grain employers hiring *less* than 20 workers account

Table 3.3. Seasonal farm worker hirings by employer size, 1974

Commodity group	Total hirings	Total employers	Farms hiring 11 or more seasonal workers, %		Farms hiring 20 or more seasonal workers, %	
			all farms	all hirings	all farms	all hirings
Cash grain	797,908	173,544	10	45	4	28
Tobacco	514,565	48,235	33	72	14	47
Cotton	118,568	12,146	27	79	14	62
Other field crops	323,971	30,181	28	77	14	60
Vegetable & melons	317,826	9,854	47	93	32	87
Fruit & nuts	858,092	30,374	54	93	38	85
Dairy	345,605	74,369	10	42	3	25
Other livestock except poultry and dairy	719,820	161,655	9	42	3	25
All others	506,161	53,732	23	73	12	59
Total	4,502,516	594,090	17	66	8	51

Source: U.S. Department of Commerce, Bureau of the Census, *1974 Census of Agriculture*, unpublished tabulations.

for fully three-fourths of all seasonal hirings by such operations.

Attributes of Seasonal Farm Workers

During the 1970s some 2 million persons were annually employed as part of the domestic seasonal farm work force with fewer than 150 days of hired farm work per year. In 1977, the last year for which statistics are available, about 2 million seasonal workers were employed (HFWF). Although there has been a decline from the early 1960s peak of almost 2.9 million seasonal workers, hired farm work at the end of the 1970s is still a decidedly seasonal endeavor. The 2 million seasonal workers comprise three-quarters of all domestic workers employed on farms. Of these seasonal workers, those employed on a casual basis (fewer than 25 days of hired farm work per year) account for 85%, about the same as in 1967.

Farm earnings distributions provide further support for the short-term employment experiences of hired farm workers (HFWF micro data 1977). About 60% of all persons with hired farm work in 1977 earned less than $1,000, averaging about $11 per day for 27 days of farm work. Distributions of workers earning less than $1,000 while working primarily on crop farms (including grains, cotton, fruits, and vegetable farms) were close to the average for all farms.

Workers on farms growing primarily potatoes, sugar beets, or hay crops had the most seasonally intensive work experience. Almost three-fourths earned less than $1,000, while just over half averaged under $100 for 9 days of farm work. Workers employed primarily on livestock farms had a lower-than-average incidence of short-term work experiences. Only 38% of the hired workers employed primarily on dairy farms earned less than $1,000.

Three subgroups, as identified by major economic activity in Figure 3.1, constitute the major source of seasonal farm labor. First, about 1 million students have annually engaged in seasonal farm work since 1970. Second, since 1972 some 450,000 persons with primary labor force attachment as nonfarm workers have annually participated in seasonal farm work. Third, about 250,000 persons who identified "keeping house" as their primary activity have been members of the seasonal farm work force since 1973. As seen in Figure 3.1, persons with major economic activity in the nonfarm sector have increased their participation in the seasonal farm work force since the 1960s, while the number associated with "keeping house" has

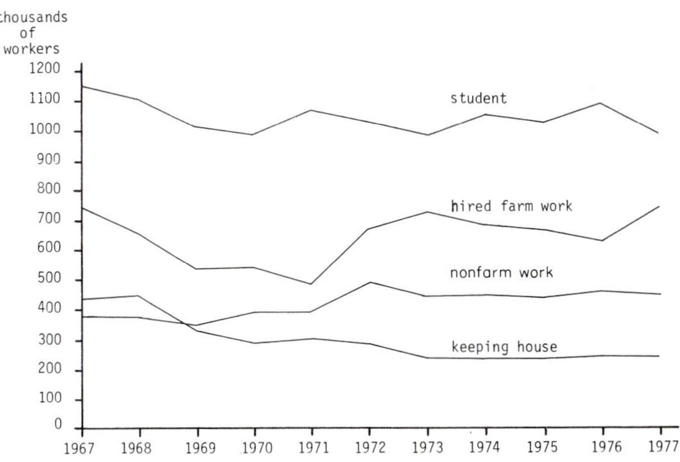

Fig. 3.1. Major activity of persons in the hired farm work force, 1967-1977. (USDA, <u>The Hired Farm Working Force</u>, various issues.)

declined. These three subgroups accounted for over 80% of the seasonal farm work force in 1977.

The national trend of relative stability in the size of the domestic seasonal farm labor force over the past decade as measured by the HFWF masks changes occurring in specific employer hirings that are consistent with changes identified in the Census of Agriculture data. Between 1967 and 1977 the number of seasonal agricultural workers remained relatively constant in the Northeast at about 150,000, but declined in the West from 650,000 to 474,000. A 25% decline took place in the South, from 1,120,000 to 841,000. The North Central region was unique in recording an increase in the number of seasonal hired workers. It peaked in 1976 at 577,000, almost 25% above the 1967 level.

The movement in the North Central states toward increased acreage and greater specialization of grain production, with its high peak seasonal labor demands, is consistent with the steadily increased employment of seasonal hired labor in the region. Although employment of long-term hired workers (over 150 days per year) in the North Central states declined through 1968, employment has increased since then. From an estimated 1968 low of 82,000, the number of long-term workers almost doubled, to 154,000, in 1977.

This pattern of hired labor use suggests that a process of partial substitution of long-term hired labor for family labor took place as farm consolidation proceeded in the 1960s and as farmers adjusted to changing relative product prices in the 1970s. Family workers still predominate in this region, but the combination of rapid expansion in crop acreage over the past few years, increased specialization of grain production, and the consolidation of farms into larger economic units requiring more hired employees probably accounts for most of the increased use of both seasonal and long-term hired labor.

Decline in seasonal labor use is most commonly associated with (1) the substitution of capital for labor or (2) substitution of full-time labor for seasonal labor as part of the mechanization process. Regional decline in seasonal labor use is also a result of diminishing farming intensity.

The increased efficiency of the agricultural labor force appears to be a contributing factor in explaining the drop in the number of domestic seasonal workers employed in western agriculture, which is dominated by California. Concurrent with the decline in domestic seasonal labor use was an increase in long-term employment (150 days or more) up through 1973. Since that time, however, longer-term domestic employment has decreased, while the level of agricultural production has continued to expand. Estimates of workers employed 150 days or more increased from 186,000 in 1967 to 227,000 in 1973. By 1977, however, the estimated number of full-time workers had fallen to 162,000.

Foreign workers are direct substitutes for seasonal domestic workers, but substitution of foreign workers for domestic workers employed more than 150 days per year in agriculture cannot be completely ruled out as an explanation of the decline in employment of long-term workers in the West. In addition, unionization of farm workers in California, which dominates the statistics for this region, combined with a climate favorable to multicrop plantings during the year, favors the development of labor management practices resulting in increased job duration for a smaller number of employees.

The decline of seasonal labor use in the South paralleled a similar decline in long-term labor use up to 1971. From a peak of 318,000 long-term workers in 1967, employment dropped to 219,000 in 1971. Since 1971, longer-term employment in this region has gradually increased to an estimated 300,000 in 1977. It appears that the major adjustments in seasonal labor use during the 1960s and 1970 were related to the substitution of mechanical harvesting processes for hand harvest workers. A more highly capital-intensive agriculture, with greater reliance on a stable longer-term labor force, is evolving in this area.

Migrant workers. Migrant workers are included in the previous discussion of seasonal workers. They compose a relatively small but regionally important segment of the seasonal hired farm work force. The number of domestic migrant workers has remained steady at about 200,000 since the early 1970s, according to HFWF estimates. ES-223 administrative reports prepared by the Department of Labor estimate the sum of 1978 peak monthly migrant labor use at 173,630, a decline of 45% from the 388,225 peak employment in 1968 (Table 3.4). Almost one-quarter of all seasonal workers identified as migrants by this source in 1978 were employed in California. Arizona and Florida each employed about 9%. The relative distribution of peak migrant labor use has decreased since 1968 in both the Northeast and the Lake states, but has increased in the Appalachia and Southeast states. The relative increase in migrant labor use in these traditional home-base states as total migrant use has declined suggests that a smaller proportion of the migrant work force is traveling long distances to do hired farm work. It appears that more of the remaining migrants

Table 3.4. Changes in use of migrant agricultural workers, 1968-1978

Region or State	Peak migrant employment, %	
	1968	1978
Northeast	13.9	9.9
Lake States	15.8	9.8
Corn Belt	9.6	8.6
Northern Plains	3.6	2.9
Appalachian	4.2	9.1
Southeast		
Florida	6.4	8.6
Other states	5.1	4.0
Delta	0.6	0.4
Southern Plains	9.7	5.5
Mountain		
Arizona	8.1	9.3
Other states	0.8	1.8
Pacific		
California	18.6	22.6
Other states	6.8	7.5
Total migrant employment	388,225	173,630

Source: USDL, Employment and Training Administration, ES-223 Rep. for 1978a; USDL, Manpower Administration, Manpower Developments, various issues for 1968.

Table 3.5. Primary employment status for persons doing migratory and nonmigratory farm work, 1975

Primary employment status during calendar year 1975	Persons with nonmigratory farm work only, %			Persons with migratory farm work, %		
In labor force	45.9			51.6		
Hired farm work		24.8			27.7	
Without nonfarm work			19.7			24.0
With nonfarm work			5.1			3.7
Other farm work		3.3			[a]	
Nonfarm work		16.2			18.6	
Looking for work		1.6			5.3	
Not in labor force	54.1			48.4		
Keeping house		9.0			5.8	
Attending school		39.0			38.3	
Other		6.1			4.3	
Total		2,449,000 (100)			188,000 (100)	

Source: USDA, ESCS, The Hired Farm Working Force, microdata tape, 1975.
[a]Less than 0.1.

work within their home state. Over 40% of the migrant workers identified in 1978 worked in Florida, Arizona, or California, compared to 33% in 1968.

The HFWF contains the only systematic evidence permitting generalizations of the demographic and labor force characteristics of migrant workers. Like the seasonal farm work force, the migrant work force is generally young. Over half of all migrant workers are under 25 years of age (55% in 1977). Less than 10% are 55 or older (HFWF 1977). The labor force status of the migrant work force also appears to be similar to that of nonmigratory farm workers, as shown in Table 3.5. Slightly less than half of the persons with migrant work in 1975 were out of the labor force most of the year. Additionally, 85% of the migrant workers who were in the labor force most of the year (24% of all migrant workers) did not supplement their farm work with nonfarm employment. They averaged 220 days of farm work per year. The remaining 15% (3.7% of all migrant farm workers) combined farm and nonfarm work. They averaged 215 days of farm work and 64 days of nonfarm work per year.

LABOR TURNOVER AND WORKER ATTACHMENT TO THE HIRED FARM WORK FORCE

The continued importance in the hired farm work force of (1) students from both high school and college, (2) workers with primary attachment to the nonfarm work force, and (3) persons whose primary activity is "keeping house" suggests that long-run attachment to the hired farm work force is weak for most workers. Nationally, almost 60% of all hired farm workers have five or fewer years of experience as hired farm workers, with 44% having three or fewer years of employment at hired farm work (HFWF 1977).

Weak attachment to the hired agricultural work force is more characteristic of white workers than of black or Hispanic workers. Only one-third of all white workers have six or more years experience as hired farm workers, while almost three-fifths of the minority group workers have six or more years of experience. The predominance of minority workers among the experienced work force is further underscored by the fact that less than 20% of all white hired workers have eleven or more years of experience, compared with 29% of Hispanic workers and 35% of black workers. However, the concentration of workers with limited job experience in agriculture, regardless of racial or ethnic origin, suggests that the domestic seasonal hired farm work force will continue to be dominated by younger, less experienced workers and by part-time workers with major attachment to the non-agricultural sector. However, exceptions, as noted below, may continue to prevail in selected local labor markets.

The relatively weak attachment of farm workers to the agricultural labor force suggested by national data is consistent with the results of a 1975 study of citrus workers in the Rio Grande valley of Texas. Over half of the sample workers, most of whom were of Hispanic origin, had three or fewer years experience in citrus harvesting. Yet even among those workers with six or more years experience, the proportion of workers over 30 years of age was not large. The report concludes that "the lack of experienced workers in the older age groups would indicate that few workers of any age can be expected to remain in this labor market" (Hicks et al.).

A case study of three California citrus employers documents similar destabilizing labor market characteristics (Hayes 1975). Turnover among crews included in the sample was high, with 70-80% of all employees remaining with a given employer for less than 14 weeks. Under improved work scheduling procedures the number of persons employed by these three employers could have been reduced by almost 75%, from 1,824 to 461, and the number of full-time workers increased from 13 to 206.

Mamer and Rosedale report the experience of the Coastal Growers Association, a cooperative of citrus growers in southern California organized for the purpose of harvesting lemons for member growers. Through concerted efforts to decasualize seasonal labor market activities, total employment over the season was reduced from 8,517 in 1965 to 1,292 in 1978. The number of boxes of fruit picked increased by over 50% during the same period.

These studies suggest that the potential for increasing the employment duration of seasonal farm workers is present, but to date has achieved success only in the context of specific local markets. The prevailing employment experience of most seasonal farm workers remains sporadic and unattractive to workers desiring long-term commitments with individual employing units.

Fairchild further confirms the mobility of hired farm workers in his study based on a 1970 sample of Florida citrus pickers. Over half of the sample workers had been with the survey employer for less than two years and 30% were in their first year of employment with the survey employer. However, unlike the weak attachment to the hired farm work force reported by Hicks et al. in their study of Texas citrus pickers, the Florida workers had, on the average, 18 years of experience as farm workers. Almost two-thirds had worked 10 or more years. However, the data base for this study is now 10 years old. A replication is needed to determine whether current seasonal farm workers have similar long-term commitments to the seasonal farm work force.

OPERATION OF SEASONAL FARM LABOR MARKETS

Agricultural labor market operations are constrained in the short run by biological phenomena in the form of weather fluctuations and in the longer run by the discipline imposed by cyclical seasonal climatic considerations. Other industries, such as construction and longshoring, seasonal recreation, and associated retail trades, also contend with weather-imposed employment variations. But agriculture is unique in that the product produced--food--is either highly perishable or must be harvested within restrictive time constraints to forestall significant reductions in yield and income loss to the farmer. Thus the combination of weather-induced short run fluctuations and cyclical seasonal variability in labor demand and the product yield uncertainties associated with the harvesting and marketing of perishable commodities identifies the paradigm within which agricultural labor markets function. Taken individually, these considerations may not pose particularly significant problems for the reduction of short-term seasonal employment experiences. But when considered jointly they complicate work load scheduling and retard progress toward providing extended employment opportunities to local workers.

Fuller and Van Vuuren characterize seasonal farm labor markets as "salvage labor markets," citing historical evidence that wages received by workers with both farm and nonfarm jobs are consistently lower in the farm sector. Subsequent review of more recent data by Matta (Chap. 5) supports the continued relevance of these observations. Doeringer and Piore, arguing from a dual labor market perspective, characterize farm jobs as less desirable from a worker point of view than certain other jobs in the nonfarm sector. These less desirable jobs are considered to be in the "secondary labor market" while better jobs are in the "primary labor market." Secondary labor market jobs are defined as low-wage, low-status jobs having easily learned skills but few, if any, firm-specific career advancement opportunities. Job attributes such as employment duration are governed by economic variables external to the firm.

By contrast, jobs in primary labor markets are viewed as an integral part of a career advancement program internal to the firm. Skill requirements are generally higher, with job duration and other conditions of employment determined by internal administrative work rules. Hence primary labor market jobs are viewed as the ideal from the perspective of workers seeking full-time employment, while jobs in the secondary labor market are considered inferior.

Huffman (Chap. 2), in a review of alternative models of labor market behavior, concludes that the dual labor market model is an inappropriate tool with which to analyze the functioning of seasonal farm labor markets, since it "misses the thread that ties everything together economically, which is the tendency toward general equilibrium with frequent disturbances along this path."

While agreeing that this model is of limited usefulness for general equilibrium analysis, I suggest that the value of the dual labor market paradigm for the analysis of seasonal agricultural labor markets lies in its explicit recognition of worker perceptions as a proper influence on the classification of jobs as either desirable or nondesirable. However, its validity in this more limited context lies in the accuracy of the implicit assumption that all workers desire full-time, year-round employment. It may be reasonably argued that, in general, creation of more full-time jobs is preferable to creation of more seasonal jobs, but it does not follow that all potential job seekers in the agricultural sector desire full-time employment.

In this more limited context, which I believe applies to the analysis of seasonal agricultural labor markets, it seems appropriate to evaluate the desirability or nondesirability of jobs from the immediate perceptions of the job holders. Equilibrium is achieved when all seasonal farm jobs are held by persons desiring such jobs. Disequilibrium occurs to the extent that seasonal farm jobs are held by persons desiring full-time employment.

Recently available data from HFWF micro data tapes provide some insights into the matching of seasonal farm jobs with persons desiring such jobs.

Almost two-thirds of all persons employed as seasonal farm workers (150 days or less) in 1977 were not in the labor force for most of the year (Table 3.6). Almost three-fourths of this group were enrolled in school when not working at either farm or nonfarm jobs. Most of the remainder were keeping house when not in the labor force. Of the remaining 37% who were in the labor force and employed as seasonal farm workers, over 70% were primarily employed as nonfarm workers or operators of their own farms. This leaves slightly over 10%, or some 215,000 seasonal workers, who desired full-time work as indicated by participation in the labor force for most of the year.

As noted earlier, seasonal farm work has traditionally been defined by labor analysts as employment on farms for 150 days or less per year. This definition, while useful for many purposes, severely restricts the scope of the seasonal work force by arbitrarily excluding other workers employed on farms on a less than full-time basis. Table 3.6 identifies an additional 149,000 domestic workers employed in agriculture for 150 to 199 days or apparently for less than ten months. This group of workers averaged $3,400 from hired farm work in 1977.

Over half or these workers (about 82,000) were in the labor force most of the year and were employed only as hired farm workers. An additional 20,000 were primarily hired farm workers but also did nonfarm work. Thus it appears that of the 734,000 persons who were primarily hired farm workers and in the labor

Table 3.6. Primary employment status and employment duration in agriculture, 1977

Primary employment status	Total workers (000)	Days worked in agriculture			
		Less than 150, %	150 to 199, %	200 to 239, %	240 or more, %
In labor force	1,367	36.8	84.9	90.0	91.0
Hired farm work only	616	5.9	54.8	62.5	79.7
Hired farm work with nonfarm work	118	2.2	12.8	21.4	8.1
Other farm work	137	5.1	10.4	3.1	3.2
Nonfarm work	444	21.2	5.4	3.0	0.0
Looking for work	52	2.4	1.5	0.0	0.0
Not in labor force	1,364	63.2	15.1	10.0	9.0
Keeping house	238	11.3	4.0	0.0	0.2
Attending school	981	45.0	9.9	8.9	8.6
Other	145	6.9	1.2	1.1	0.2
Total (000)	2,730	2,045	149	77	459

Source: USDA, ESCS, The Hired Farm Working Force, microdata tape, 1977.

force for most of 1977, up to 320,000 were substantially underemployed as seasonal workers. The employment and earnings experience of these workers is sharply contrasted with that of workers employed 200 days or more in agriculture. The latter averaged $6,200, or almost double the earnings of workers employed 150 to 199 days.

SUMMARY

The U.S. agricultural sector remains heavily dependent on hired seasonal workers even after a protracted period of farm consolidation and off-farm migration of family workers. Seasonal labor hirings--those for less than 25 days per year on a single farm--outnumbered family workers in 1974.

This continuing dependence on a short-term seasonal hired work force does not necessarily reflect a misappropriation of labor resources. Rather, it represents the efficient performance of most local farm labor markets and a meshing of workers desiring short-term jobs with employers able to offer only sporadic employment opportunities. Most short-term domestic seasonal workers are local workers. When not doing farm work many are attending school. Most of the remainder are primarily employed as nonfarm workers or are voluntarily out of the labor force when not doing farm work.

Career commitment to the hired farm work force is weak for most hired farm workers. Almost 60% of all farm workers have five or fewer years employment duration as farm workers, and almost half of the 1977 workers had three or fewer years.

The macro adjustment of seasonal farm labor markets to changing relative product prices is facilitated by a seasonal labor force composed of persons with limited career attachment to the farm sector. From 1969 to 1974, short-term seasonal hirings on grain farms increased by 37% in response to expanded acreages, while seasonal hirings on tobacco and cotton farms declined 15% and 24%, respectively.

Hired labor intensity varies greatly depending on

the major farm commodity produced and has direct implications for worker coverage under farm labor legislation designed to have differential impacts by employer size. Farms hiring 11 or more workers account for up to 93% of all seasonal worker hirings on fruit and vegetable farms, and for about three-fourths on farms raising primarily tobacco, cotton, sugarcane, sugar beets, or potatoes. At the opposite extreme, farms hiring 11 or more workers account for only 40-45% of seasonal worker hirings on cash grain, dairy, and livestock operations.

The dependence of the farm sector on domestic migrant workers has stabilized at about 200,000 during the 1970s. Only about one-third of these workers appear to have a primary attachment to hired farm work and about 20% are primarily nonfarm workers. Students account for roughly the same proportion of the migrant and nonmigrant work forces.

The job expectations of most seasonal farm workers appear to be adequately matched to the short-term needs of farmers. Yet a large proportion of the workers apparently desiring full-time employment are not able to obtain it, at least in the short run, as hired farm workers. In 1977 over 40% of the domestic farm workers who were in the labor force most of the year were employed as seasonal hired workers. Over two-thirds of these workers were employed for less than 150 days, primarily on fruit and vegetable operations. Rationalization of seasonal labor markets to provide a greater number of long-term jobs for seasonal workers desiring them has met with some success in selected labor markets, notably in the California citrus industry. Yet this positive effect appears to be due more to long-term efforts by employer groups committed to this goal than to the economic incentives created by the passage of labor legislation designed to internalize social costs. Cyclically variable farm labor demand stemming from seasonal and short-run weather fluctuations will continue to exert strong counterpressures against the consolidation of seasonal farm jobs. Only the Far West and parts of the Southwest, in which year-round cropping patterns prevail, seem immune from these forces.

The high number of youth under 25 years of age who are employed as seasonal farm workers indicates that the agricultural sector continues to serve as a "port of entry" into the labor force for many persons. With some exceptions in local markets, the seasonal labor force is composed largely of entry-level workers with high interseasonal turnover and no long-term commitment to farm work as a career option. Similarly, most seasonal farm jobs provide low levels of annual earnings due to limited job duration and few career advancement possibilities.

It is important that public policymakers consider both the attributes of the farm work force and the nature of farm demand when designing ameliorative policy initiatives. It is clear from the previous analysis that most farm jobs are in the secondary sector as defined by dual labor markets theorists. The potential for upgrading more than a small proportion to full-time status is minimal. Consequently, farm labor market research and review of policy alternatives are likely to be most productive if based on the assumption that seasonality will continue to be the dominant attribute of farm labor market operations.

Workers most in need of targeted public policy considerations are those in the labor force most of the year but working at seasonal farm jobs. How many currently possess sufficient skills or other job attributes to move into the full-time farm or nonfarm work force? How many are content to work at a succession of seasonal farm jobs and how many are able, through their own efforts, to move upward to either permanent farm or nonfarm jobs after one or two years in the seasonal work force? To date, farm labor research has not systematically addressed the policy implications of this set of questions. If it is correct to assume that (1) seasonality dominates farm labor market operations and (2) the secondary nature of most farm labor markets will extend indefinitely into the future, then optimum labor market operations would encourage a free flow of domestic workers into and out of the seasonal farm labor force. Complementary public policy measures would eliminate impediments to this flow and be designed to encourage high rates of interseasonal turnover of seasonal farm workers.

APPENDIX 3. DATA SOURCES

Establishment Surveys

Establishment surveys collect data directly from the farm employing establishment. As such they provide measures of actual labor use during the reference period. However, since the respondent is the employer the establishment surveys generally do not provide the demographic or labor market characteristics of farm workers. The two major establishment surveys providing farm employment data are (1) the QALS conducted by ESCS, USDA and (2) the Census of Agriculture. A third source of establishment-type data is collected by the U.S. Employment Service (USES) of the USDL as part of its administrative data bank (see also Holt et al.).

QALS

This major farm labor establishment survey uses a probability sample and has been conducted quarterly since 1974.[1] (Prior to 1974 reports were issued monthly but estimates were developed on a nonprobability basis. See also National Commission on Employment and Unemployment Statistics, *Counting the Labor Force*, Chap. 10.) It provides state, regional, and national estimates of labor use at quarterly intervals throughout the year. The survey reference period is the week including the 12th day of January, April, July, and October. Although questions to identify seasonal and nonseasonal employees have been asked in the past, available published data do not directly identify seasonal workers. The number of seasonal workers employed during any given week is, for most farm operations, directly related to prevailing weather conditions. Hence the quarterly estimates may overestimate or underestimate "normal" seasonal employment if there is an aberration of the weather during the given survey week. Because only current data are collected at four discrete points in time, estimates of average annual employment based on the QALS understate the total number of persons doing hired farm work during the year, while accurately measuring survey week employment.

ES-223 Monthly Farm Labor Reports

Local USES representatives assigned to areas with high levels of seasonal farm labor use are required to estimate seasonal farm employment as of the 15th of each month during the active period of seasonal labor use. Estimates are based on reports from a very high proportion of total farm employers, but statistical accuracy cannot be ascertained. Seasonal employment is counted by designated labor market areas during the active period of seasonal agricultural activity, but only if 500 or more domestic seasonal workers are hired or at least one legal foreign worker is employed. Thus coverage is incomplete and accuracy is dependent upon the knowledge of individual ES representatives. Monthly employment data are available by state and by crop within state throughout the season. The data are best suited to identifying interseasonal changes in labor use patterns and the number and geographical distribution of migrant workers.

Census of Agriculture

Census labor data collected at five-year intervals measure the total number of farm workers hired by individual farm employers during the Census year. (In the past, census years ended in 4 and 9. A Census of Agriculture was conducted for 1978 and subsequent censuses will be taken for years ending in 2 and 7, conforming with survey years for the other economic censuses.)

The Census of Agriculture is predominantly a mail survey. In the past, questions were asked of the total population of farm employers with sales of $2,500 or more. Beginning with 1978, data are collected from a *sample* of these employers. Lack of comparability between census years has typically hampered analytical use of these data. However, direct comparability exists between some 1969 and 1974 labor use questions. Seasonal hired labor estimates are defined to include only workers employed on an individual farm for fewer than 150 days during the calendar year. A subcategory of workers employed fewer than 25 days was obtained in 1974 but was not available in 1969.

Data are tabulated in published reports for state, regional, and national levels and by farm type (SIC categories). Enumeration takes place at the start of the calendar year following the census year. Since data reflect labor hired over the full year some recall bias occurs. Workers hired by more than one employer during the year are reported by each employer, leading to an overestimation of total workers.

Since the Census of Agriculture survey is conducted by mail and respondents are not required to provide further detail about individual workers, it is very likely that most foreign workers are included in the estimates. Direct estimation of total annual employer hirings makes this data source very relevant for the analysis of adjustments in labor use patterns associated with the structural change of farm operations.

HOUSEHOLD SURVEYS

Household surveys, as their name implies, collect data directly from household members. As such they provide a rich source of data regarding the labor market and demographic characteristics of individual workers but provide little information about employer characteristics. Employer information is generally limited to identification of industry classification.

CPS December Supplement

Since 1944, the USDA has sponsored the December Supplement to the CPS. It is designed to obtain an estimate of all workers resident in the United States during the December survey week who did any hired farm work during the current calendar year. The December survey date effectively excludes from the population most seasonal foreign workers who were employed on farms earlier in the year. The data provide a rich source of information on demographic characteristics of persons doing hired farm work. However, the small sample size limits the accuracy of data below national or regional levels. Data from this source are useful for the identification of changing demographic and labor market characteristics of hired farm workers. During census years it provides a complement to the establishment-based Census of Agriculture.

CPS Monthly Data

Estimates of agricultural employment from the CPS are published monthly by the USDL, Bureau of Labor Statistics. Unlike estimates from the other major sources, CPS monthly data include employment in agricultural services and, up to September 1978, included employment in the forestry, hunting, trapping, and fisheries sectors. Only workers whose major job was in the agricultural sector so defined are included in the monthly estimates. Multiple-job holders with second jobs as farm workers are excluded.

Data Comparisons

It is clear from the previous discussion that the various farm labor data sources do not measure the same population. That is to say, the concepts "total farm workers" and "seasonal farm workers" differ by data source and therefore estimates using these conceptual bases will also differ.

Both the Census of Agriculture and the HFWF provide estimates of total annual labor use, one from the perspective of the employing establishment, the other from the perspective of the worker. Comparisons of estimated worker counts from each survey are provided below for 1974.

The largest discrepancy is among workers employed for less than 25 days. The census estimate for these short-term workers exceeds the December CPS supplement by a factor of three. Comparisons of estimates for longer-term seasonal workers and workers employed for 150 days or more are considerably closer.

Data Source	Workers employed less than 25 days	Workers employed 25-149 days	Workers employed 150 days or more
Census of Agriculture	3,357,346	1,145,171	712,715
HFWF	1,169,000	927,000	641,000

Several reasons for this discrepancy exist:

1. The Census of Agriculture potentially includes both legal and illegal foreign workers employed on farms while the December CPS excludes both.

2. The Census of Agriculture double counts workers employed on more than one farm while the December CPS is an unduplicated count of persons doing hired farm work.

3. The majority of persons doing hired farm work are employed for fewer than 25 days and many live in rural areas. (Workers with less than 25 days of farm employment per year average less than 10 days of farm work per year.) It can be expected that many workers with such a weak attachment to the farm work force may respond in the negative to the screening question used by the CPS to identify persons doing hired farm work and therefore will be excluded from the sample.

The CPS monthly household survey and the QALS both have the same reference period during the months data are collected for the QALS. As developed earlier, the CPS monthly survey excludes multiple-job holders whose second job is in agriculture but includes some nonfarm workers. Second job holders are included in the QALS but the employment estimate is limited to the farm production sector. Workers with two or more agricultural employers in the survey week are included only once in the CPS but can be counted two or more times in the QALS. Also, the household area sampling frame used in collecting CPS data may introduce a downward bias in counting transient workers. These survey characteristics lead to an expected upward estimate of QALS data when compared directly with CPS monthly data during months of heavy seasonal employment, but to a slightly lower estimate during periods of little seasonal activity.

As seen below, comparisons for January 1978 are quite similar. These estimates represent the off-peak period for most seasonal agricultural work (with the exception of some southern states, notably Florida), and hence the data reflect primarily full-time workers.

Survey	January 1978	April 1978	July 1978	October 1978
CPS monthly	808,000	960,000	1,262,000	1,083,000
QALS	764,300	1,095,000	1,848,000	1,317,000

The discrepancy between the two series increases in the expected direction as the proportion of short-term and part-time seasonal employees increases in April and July. The discrepancy declines in October, as fewer seasonal workers are hired.

Appendix Table 3.1 provides a summary comparison for estimates of total and seasonal workers from each major farm labor data source.

Appendix Table 3.1. Hired farm worker populations measured by alternative data sources

Data source		Population of hired workers counted	Population estimates	Comments
Census of Agriculture	Total:	All worker hirings during the Census year by agricultural establishments with annual agricultural sales of $2,500 or more.	Total: 1969: 5,927,946 1974: 5,215,231	1. Potentially covers all hired workers including documented and undocumented foreign workers. 2. Enumeration through 1974. Probability sample in 1978.
	Seasonal:	All worker hirings by agricultural establishments with annual agricultural sales or $2,500 or more who worked for less than 150 days during the Census year.	Seasonal: 1969: 5,125,604 1974: 4,502,516	
Quarterly Agricultural Labor Survey	Total:	All wage and salary workers employed by an agricultural establishment during the survey week including the 12th of the survey month. (Annual average employment is the sum of total quarterly employment divided by four.)	1978: Jan: 764,300 April: 1,095,100 July: 1,848,000 Oct: 1,317,000 Avg: 1,255,700	1. Potentially covers all hired workers but probably does not represent undocumented foreign workers. 2. Probability survey.
	Seasonal:	Not defined.		
ES 223	Total:	Not defined.		
	Seasonal:	Workers employed at seasonal agricultural activities on the 15th of the month in areas hiring at least 500 seasonal workers or one legal foreign worker.	1978: Jan: 215,327 April: 288,430 July: 692,899 Oct: 495,220	1. Potentially covers all hired workers in high seasonal labor use areas but probably excludes undocumented foreign workers. 2. Administrative data.

Appendix Table 3.1. (Continued)

Data source	Population of hired workers counted		Population estimates		Comments
Current Population Survey (a) Monthly	Total:	All workers with primary wage or salary employment in an agricultural establishment during the survey week including the 12th of the month.	1978: Jan:	807,000	1. Excludes farm managers, undocumented foreign workers, and multiple job holders with second jobs in agriculture; includes nonfarm workers in agricultural service sector.
			April:	960,000	
			July:	1,262,000	
			Oct:	1,038,000	
	Seasonal:	Not defined.			2. Probability survey.
(b) December supplement	Total:	All persons with wage or salary farm work during the current year.	1977:	2,730,000	1. Excludes undocumented foreign workers and legal foreign workers not resident in the U.S. during the survey week.
	Seasonal:	All persons with less than 150 days of wage or salary farm work during the current calendar year.	1977:	2,045,000	2. Probability survey.
Social Security	Total:	All persons employed by an agricultural establishment for whom Social Security tax forms were filed.	1969:	2,019,000[a]	1. Excludes all workers earning less than $150 per year or employed less than 20 days per year by an individual farm employer.
			1973:	2,262,900[b]	
	Seasonal:	Not defined.			2. Probability sample of administrative data.

[a]Bertram Kestenbaum, "Social Security Farmworker Statistics," Research and Statistics Note, Note 16, HEW, Social Security Administration, (23 August 1976), Table 1.

[b]Bertram Kestenbaum, "Estimating the Number of Hired Farm Workers Covered by Social Security," Agricultural Economics Research, 2 (1978):39-40.

Discussion

G. JOACHIM ELTERICH

While summarizing selected topics of Fritsch's interesting analysis, I will discuss points of disagreement and then treat, rather sketchily, some aspects of a larger framework that I believe to be crucial in the years ahead.

Fritsch competently delineates the regional trends of seasonal labor in agriculture and the justification for it. Regionality, seasonality, and skill levels are important aspects of this analysis. Fritsch documents the characteristics of the agricultural labor force on the basis of available data sources, which he discusses briefly (USDA's annual *Hired Farm Working Force*, *Farm Labor*, the Census of Agriculture, ES-223 reports, and case studies). I would like to echo Huffman's plea that those involved in the compilation of statistics and the subsequent economic analyses concentrate more on man-days rather than simply discussing the number of workers involved in seasonal work. This would provide a more meaningful picture of the importance of different groups.

Fritsch analyzes the reasons for the differing regional development of seasonal farm employment. Aside from the reasons given--mechanization, farmstead consolidation, and regional specialization--they run the gamut from unionization and other institutional arrangements (labor legislation, etc.) to differing degrees of intensity of farming (management practices) and regional prosperity.

Youth under 25 have increased in importance in agricultural employment; however, their attachment to this sector is temporary. I too would not find it suboptimal, from society's point of view, to expect local high school pupils, regular nonfarm job holders, and housewives (70% of all domestic seasonals) to be employed in agriculture during some seasonal periods if they so desire. I found disturbing the tentative conclusion that agricultural labor markets may not hold the full-time employment aspired to by 400,000. I am not inclined to be as kind as Fritsch when he states that " . . . rural manpower policy emphasis during past decades has fostered a secular decline of individuals with primary dependence on earnings from farm work." *Much* has to do with the *benign neglect* of this labor market by the government. Perhaps it was a blessing in disguise that the government kept out of it, since this market has exhibited an uncanny ability to adjust to changing seasonal, regional, and skill requirements. This has been manifested in the increased labor efficiency of agriculture achieved through intensified capital use. Intensified capital use has led to the substitution of permanent workers for seasonal labor. Year-round employees have also been substituted for family labor, most likely for different reasons.

I agree with Fritsch that a primary labor market is superior to and desirable for all segments of the agricultural labor market. However, due to the shortcomings of people and institutions, it is not achievable tomorrow. Informal employer-employee relations will continue to exist in agriculture unless a better system is created that can actually replace the secondary market segments.

I agree with Millen that long-standing work rules can become quite dysfunctional with technological change. I firmly endorse the demands for creating job alternatives for displaced workers and for the rationalization and regionalization of labor market operations. I believe Fritsch should have given credit to the farm sector as a training ground for many youths who enter farming unskilled and leave it later with marketable skills.

My major contentions concerning agricultural labor markets are:

1. Much more information is needed on the extent of the seasonality problem and on the way in which it affects different workers, groups, and employers. With bona fide efforts from all institutions and

persons concerned, the migrant problem could be further alleviated in a few years.

2. Although not all sectors of the agricultural labor market are in the secondary labor market realm, stronger efforts to diminish the extent of this classification in agriculture are in order.

3. It is necessary to develop a forward-looking policy for the integration of farm and nonfarm sectors on a regional basis, and for the education and (re-)training of workers.

I will now take a wider approach. Although I may encroach upon topics to be treated in detail elsewhere in this volume, I feel I am justified in looking at as many facets of this complex problem as possible.

Demand and supply for seasonal labor in agriculture follow the usual economic principles. Local *supply* is forthcoming from a population base during particular times in accordance with incentives (pay and fringe benefits) or well-being aspired to by the workers. However, local supply is modified by: a generation problem; institutional factors including education and training, the business cycle, rural development, job referral systems; and alternative opportunities including commuting and migrating to or from other regions (Greenwood 1978).

Demand, on the other hand, is a derived demand for (seasonal) labor, based on the demands of the population for food and fiber products of enterprises (commodities) exhibiting pronounced seasonal activity peaks. Seasonal labor, with its accompanying problems, will continue to exist as long as the demand for such products continues and as long as (1) it is not possible or cheaper to import them and (2) it is not possible to eliminate the peaks by distributing a chain of activities over a longer season through technological or managerial means.

I will now take a look at some aspects of historical developments and speculate about the future. Studies by Hammonds et al. suggest that the U.S. demand for hired farm labor has tended over the last decade to become less inelastic in the short run and more elastic in the long run. This change is due to increased capital-labor substitution, which has been brought about by rising wage levels accompanied by technological advances and increasing elasticity of supply of capital-intensive productive inputs. The farm sector out-migration of the last few decades has slowed in recent years, leaving two groups of workers in farm employment, bringing up the *skill* dimension of agricultural labor. At one end of the spectrum are highly skilled, well-paid, and very productive machine operators with year-round employment. On the other end are manual workers who lack skills that would enable them to find alternative employment opportunities. Such workers are not likely to be employed on a permanent basis. As various policies and opportunity costs force farmers to mechanize or switch to labor-extensive enterprise configurations, total labor expenditures are cut while demand for highly skilled workers increases. During this process unskilled workers lose what may be their sole employment opportunity, at least during a displacement phase. Obviously, the problem of farm workers with lesser skills is not one of agriculture or rural areas exclusively. It is also a problem of society in general, which enjoys the fruits of mechanization in the form of low food and fiber costs.

Risks and costs attributable to migration in general should be minimized to promote desirable regional development (T. R. Smith). Age is one important factor that results in lower interindustry mobility (Steinberg). In addition, higher unemployment in the economy can be expected in view of the large proportional increase of youth and women in the work force, as well as the effects of certain social programs (Flaim).

Let us look at this in more detail from the farm operator's and worker's points of view. I submit that there is still an overinvestment of some resources--labor and some kinds of capital--in agriculture. The results are overproduction and/or excessive levels of fixed assets. The problems stemming from overinvestment could be alleviated by retraining programs or technological developments that would open up alternative opportunities in or outside of agriculture. Both of these remedies would involve public and private costs that would have to be borne by the farmer, the worker, and/or society at large. The development of the new technologies would require more investment to make the smaller resource base more efficient. This could also be accomplished with increased short-run costs of obsolete capital from the redundant technologies and agricultural workers. If the new technologies are selective in smoothing out the peaks in labor requirements, their adoption should be made swiftly if we wish to reduce the need for seasonal labor.

Higher birth rates in rural areas, coupled with an influx of workers unable to find work in urban areas, keep the supply schedule for unskilled labor further to the right. Equilibrium with the demand schedule for such labor occurs below minimum wage levels. Hence the nonfarm sector, including ultimately the government, is called upon to alleviate the labor market pressures of seasonal and migrant workers for a fuller and more continuous schedule of gainful employment. This should not be interpreted as substituting for education and retraining programs aimed at reducing structural unemployment.

I suggest the adoption of an integrated approach to enhancing regional specialization, encompassing both agricultural and nonagricultural industries. The private and social costs of seasonal and migrant labor, such as housing, schooling, health, social programs, and unemployment insurance, should be taken into account. Imagination and ingenuity in the employment of part-time and migrant workers are urgently needed. Why should not such groups perform overtime or weekend work in local industries if farm work is not available and they are capable of the job? For example, the railbeds of our railroads are in desperate shape and most of the necessary maintenance work does not require skills lacking in agricultural laborers. Job sharing may be one option for increasing employment opportunities.

The time element of the agricultural labor market stems primarily from yearly seasonal variations. Historical developments have resulted in shifts over longer periods. Analysis of this market should also be forward looking--anticipating labor demand developments derived from technological change, regional specialization, changing demand for food, and the resulting work flow patterns for seasonal workers. Greater efforts must be made to match jobs and skills with the existing local labor pool. Only after failing to reach an equilibrium in the local market should migrant labor be resorted to.

It would make a lot of sense to install a federal computerized job referral system to match demand and supply for seasonal work. Such a system would ensure that state requests are met, but would not stop at meeting local agricultural demand. Rather, it would ultimately integrate the entire national rural labor market. This integration implies that the federal referral system would cover both farm and nonfarm employment opportunities suitable for migrant or seasonal workers. For this to happen, the following must occur:

In the short run:

1. States and the agricultural sector must mobilize their own efforts to match supply and demand for rural labor of various skill levels through the seasons.

2. The states should convey information about labor shortages and excesses to a fast-moving federal coordinating center. This coordinating center would attempt to resolve imbalances on regional and national levels. The pooling of needs should result in contracts with migrants similar to those arranged for off-shore laborers that guarantee work and income for a given period in specified locations for certain skills. Employment may be in or outside of agriculture, but decent working and housing conditions should be provided in either case. If it is not economically feasible to provide decent conditions, given the prices of products locally produced, then perhaps the

products should be produced elsewhere or imported, even if loss of local jobs ensues. I do not believe that public subsidies are warranted. They obscure the true price of the products produced.

3. Unemployed people should not only have the opportunity to retrain, but should be under an obligation to be retrained if their skills place them in a chronically and structurally unemployed group.

In the long run:

1. Schooling in rural areas ought to be comparable to that in urban areas. Vocational training should be designed to enable *all age groups* to acquire skills currently in demand. People from rural communities would thereby gain greater opportunities to obtain nonagricultural jobs.

2. Rural development efforts (financing and planning) should take into account labor pool potentials, training, energy considerations, and migration. Industries should be attracted to areas experiencing persistent seasonal unemployment. Industries must demonstrate ingenuity in providing shift and seasonal employment to suit the preferences of segments of the local labor force (Bednarzik).

3. Options for part-time workers should be expanded. Agricultural workers should be encouraged to adopt a career orientation and emphasis should be placed on the development of occupational classifications that would provide the potential for participating in gainful agricultural or nonagricultural pursuits. This implies that those in agricultural labor markets do not necessarily remain trapped in a secondary market but have access without barriers to primary markets (Lowell). Less competitive groups, including the disadvantaged, should obtain employment at wage levels commensurate with their marginal productivity, which may fall below the minimum wage.

4. Public financing should be stepped up in the area of technological and managerial advances designed to smooth out seasonal peaks in labor demand.

The foregoing proposals are based on four main

considerations (in addition to private opportunity costs). One, most of these proposals have been successfully implemented in Western European countries. Two, none of the changing demand and supply dimensions in farm labor markets should be taken as fixed in their development, but rather as subject to change by dynamic, forward-looking public and private policies designed to tackle the problem of seasonal and migratory workers in agriculture. Three, the social opportunity costs per man-year of permanent employment are significantly less than those for temporary employment. Hence the permanence (i.e., quality) of jobs is as important as the sheer number of jobs created (Jenkins and Kuo). Also in this context, Dahlberg contends, on the basis of an empirical study in Sweden, that migration may necessitate considerable net investment in publicly owned social overhead capital. Four, the manpower, social, and development programs and policies of various federal agencies such as the USDL and USDA should be coordinated. They should not counter market forces but should rather support desirable developments and remove frictions such as union and administrative barriers to adjustments. Movements of workers entering into and exiting from a job, industry, or region should be facilitated if it serves well-conceived goals.

We as a nation cannot afford to act in any other way.

4

Migration in Farm Labor Markets

ROBERT D. EMERSON

Agricultural labor markets have a prominent seasonal component. This seasonal component arises predominantly in areas where fruits and vegetables are grown, due to their intensive need for labor during harvest time but minimal labor requirements otherwise. This is in contrast to livestock operations, for example, which tend to have relatively stable employment over time. The questions raised in this volume are focused on the likelihood of the continuation of this seasonal pattern and how we as a society can best deal with the consequences of either continued or diminished seasonality in farm labor markets. This chapter addresses one aspect of the seasonality, namely the seasonal mobility of labor, more commonly designated as migratory labor.

The phrase "migratory labor" conjures up an image to most persons of poverty, poor living and working conditions, and movement from place to place with the crops in search of work. Yet there is reason to believe that the decision to migrate for work is influenced by important economic considerations. The basic hypothesis is that workers migrate because the

---

The author has benefitted from the helpful comments of Daniel Sumner and Alfred Parks. Research assistance for this chapter was provided by Steven Hubbard.

alternatives to migrating are less preferable for those who do migrate. The economic choice factors affecting the decision include expected earnings and perhaps the prospect of even *less* stable employment in the home area than that which could be secured through migration. Although there are considerable differences in income levels, the same relative economic choice factors between migrating or not are undoubtedly important for such varied groups as entertainers and construction workers as well as for agricultural migratory workers.

SEASONAL MIGRATION IN U.S. AGRICULTURE

The portion of the U.S. hired agricultural labor force migrating for employment was 7% in 1977, the most current estimate available (USDA, *The Hired Farm Working Force of 1977*, p. 8).[1] This represented an estimated 191,000 workers. The number of migrants has remained in the neighborhood of 200,000 throughout the decade of the 1970s. It is, however, only half the number who were migratory in the early 1960s. The peak year was 1965, with 466,000 workers, coinciding with the termination of the Bracero Program (Public Law 78) (USDA, *The Hired Farm Working Force of 1976*, p. 10). The proportion who were migrants in 1965 was 14.9%--again just twice the current proportion. The decline to the current proportion occurred between 1965 and 1970, as illustrated in Figure 4.1.

The group designated as domestic migratory workers is clearly a minor one in terms of numerical importance. This is accentuated by the disproportionate amount of attention they have received from our society and government in contrast to other farm worker groups equally in need of services. Nevertheless, the seasonal demand for labor in agriculture continues to give rise to pressures (incentives) for individuals to migrate for agricultural work, and the surrounding conditions are such that there has been a great deal of social concern for this group. One view of the group is that it is a segment of the farm work force, however fluid it may be, composed of people who

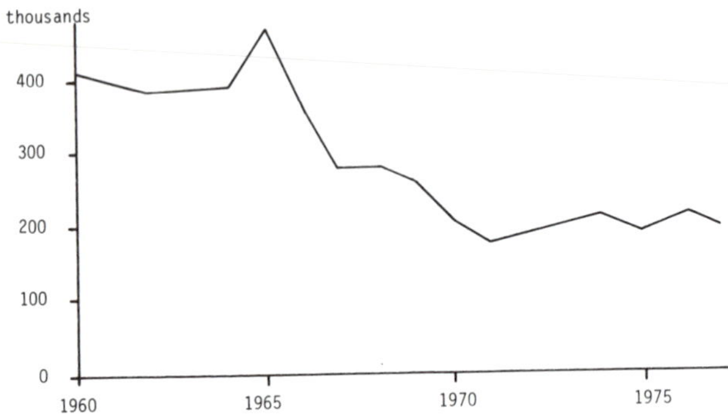

Fig. 4.1. United States migrant farm workers. (USDA, The Hired Farm Working Force of 1977, p. 10.)

have responded to employment openings away from their home location created by the apparent unwillingness of a sufficient number of local persons to work at the prevailing wage. Moreover, there is seemingly an interest in exploring means of furthering this type of activity. One particular example concerns the use of domestic migratory labor as an alternative to offshore workers.

Worker response through mobility to available employment was illustrated in 1965 by the large increase in the number of domestic migratory workers that followed termination of the Bracero Program. Other experiences following this event are also instructive. One example is the history of adoption of the tomato harvester in California, as traced out by Friedland and Barton. They suggest that the tomato harvester was commercially viable by 1961. Yet the data they compiled from the California Tomato Growers Association reveal only negligible use of the machine until 1965, when it jumped to 25% of the crop being machine harvested. The following year the figure was 60% and, for all practical purposes, it was 100% by 1970 (Friedland and Barton). California tomato growers were heavily dependent upon workers imported under the Bracero Program for their harvest labor. Although not totally unexpected, termination of the program was a shock to the system, which resulted in an excess demand for harvest labor. This demand was filled in part by increased domestic migration and by offering wages higher than presumably would have been paid for labor in the Bracero Program.

Data on regionalized migratory streams are scarce. The Public Health Service in 1965 published a map tracing three predominant migratory streams in U.S. agriculture. One consisted of a home base in Southern California and flowed up the Pacific Coast. A second emanated from the Rio Grande region of Texas with trails spreading throughout the Central part of the United States. The third started in Florida and went up the Eastern Seaboard. The extent to which these are currently valid is not readily verified with available data.

The most recent USDA data (1977) reveal that the Southwest standard federal region is the largest home base area, representing 37% of migrant farm workers (*The Hired Farm Working Force*, p. 13). The Southeast and lower Pacific Coast regions are next with 14% each while the Mountain region had 13%. Data on distances traveled for farm work reveal that just under half of the migratory workers traveled over 500 miles. Among ethnic groups, whites (58%) traveled the least and Hispanics (31%) traveled the furthest, while blacks and others (11%) were not sufficiently numerous to reveal a statistically reliable pattern (USDA, *The Hired Farm Working Force of 1977*, p. 10).

ALTERNATIVE VIEWS OF MIGRATION

The sociological and anthropological paradigms have perhaps been the most widely accepted interpretations of migratory labor. The presumption appears to have been that economics has little to say about this group. Fuller is one of the few agricultural economists providing an economic interpretation of this segment of the labor market. One approach to the study of migratory workers is illustrated by Friedland and Nelkin and a separate statement by Nelkin. Their work consisted of intensive interviewing and observation in the migrants' own environment. The framework as stated by Nelkin is as follows:

> . . . the emphasis must be placed on the isolation of a group and the relatively impermeable barriers established by the dominant society. The migrant community is marginal in that it is situated on the margins of a larger society. Economically and legally, migrants must cope with the realities of this society and they are expected to share its values. They are not accepted as belonging to a distinct and viable sub-culture, nor are they fully accepted as a part of the larger society. In this sense, marginality is a situational context in which the migrant community must minimize internal disruptions while, at the same time, it must come to terms with the larger society on which it depends. (p. 375)

There is little question that this is an insightful description of the migrant environment.

A recent stream of work in the economics of labor markets, namely the dual labor markets approach, runs nearly parallel with this argument (see Doeringer and Piore). Again, the dual labor markets approach provides a very reasonable description of the workers' environment. Most jobs that migratory workers would take would fall in the class of "bad jobs," or those for which work is irregular, working conditions are unfavorable, exploitation may be a problem, and there is little or no opportunity for advancement. Common to both of these arguments is the assumption that the individual becomes locked into this secondary market, in this case the migratory stream. The question addressed in this chapter is whether or not some of the more traditional economic factors provide any clues to the phenomenon of mobility in this environment.

There is a vast amount of economic literature relating to migration in the United States and other countries as well (see Sjaastad; Greenwood 1975). However, the migration addressed in this literature could be characterized as a single move type of mobility. It has been applied, for example, as an explanatory framework for the movement of labor out of agriculture into urban environments during the 1950s and 1960s. The mobility of migratory farm workers, however, can be viewed as having a much shorter time horizon, or as continued migration. Nevertheless, many of the factors considered to be of importance in the former case should also be important for migratory farm workers. It is to this consideration that we now turn.

ECONOMIC INTERPRETATION OF MIGRATION

The underlying hypothesis of this paper is that decisions to migrate within the farm work force are influenced by economic considerations. This is not to say that other influences are unimportant. Rather, the role of economic considerations is explored for the insights it offers regarding factors that may influence persons who have not previously migrated to migrate in the future. Similarly, an attempt is made to identify those factors that affect the likelihood of removing persons from the migratory stream.

A review of the migration literature can be found in Greenwood (1975). Among the factors treated as important in Greenwood's review are differences in wages between regions. The hypothesis is that if wages are higher in region A than region B, persons will be motivated to migrate to region A until an equilibrium is reached between the two regions. In particular, as persons leave region B there will be a tendency for wages to *rise* in region B. Conversely, as they enter region A the increased level of employment will *lower* wages in A. The extent to which they are equilibrated will depend upon a number of factors such as the monetary costs of migrating and the psychic or nonpecuniary costs of migrating. Also important are what are referred to as compensating differentials in wages that may exist between regions. The differential in this case would be due to nonpecuniary regional factors rather than to the occupational differences Huffman considers (Chap. 2).

The other main economic consideration in the

migration literature is variations in unemployment between regions. The presumption is that the higher the unemployment rate in region A relative to region B, the greater the likelihood of mobility from A to B. As pointed out by Greenwood (1975), the empirical evidence on this has not been very supportive. The more important noneconomic characteristics considered have been differences in age, education levels, and race.

The question then is whether or not this provides the rudiments of a framework for approaching migration within the farm labor market. A major difference is that the characteristic approach to migration as an investment on the part of the individual (and society) is of limited value. The duration is simply too short for this consideration to be relevant. If one focuses on a time horizon of a year, which appears consistent with migratory labor behavior, then discounting and investment decisions become relatively unimportant. The concern is the temporary differentials in wages and employment opportunities; there are seasonal variations in demand for labor providing motivation for short-term migration.

A crude piece of supportive evidence for the potential importance of employment opportunities and earnings to the decision to migrate is the substantial increase in the number and proportion of migratory workers in 1965 at the time of the termination of the Bracero Program. As noted earlier and demonstrated in Figure 4.1, there was a dramatic increase in the number of migratory workers in that year. The California market was undoubtedly the most directly affected. Data compiled by Hayes (1978, pp. 64-65) also indicate marked increases in wages at this time for crops that had utilized contract labor. Regional breakdowns in migratory labor data were not available in USDA publications covering this period. However, there is little reason to believe there were major changes in the size of the migratory stream along the Eastern Seaboard, and this group of states had not participated in any significant way in the Bracero Program. The area other than California that may have shown increases in the number of domestic migrants is Texas, and for the same reason.

With this background, we will now explore in more detail factors affecting participation in the migratory stream. Two approaches are explored: the first deals only with the effect of potential differences in earnings between migrants and nonmigrants; the second introduces additional considerations.

Earnings Differences

There is a long stream of literature emanating from the early work of Mincer (1974), Becker, and Schultz (1962) directed toward explaining earning differentials between various segments of the population.

This approach has been utilized for the analysis of a number of problems, including evaluation of returns to education, on-the-job training, migration, the existence of discrimination, and a number of other questions. The basic approach is the explanation of earnings through variations in investments that may influence earning capacity. Examples are education, on-the-job training, apprenticeship, etc. Other factors that may also influence earnings are generally controlled, as a means of isolating the effects being examined. Of course, in studies of discrimination, the latter variables become the ones of more direct interest.

If one were to accept the view that economic factors, particularly earnings, are important in influencing participation in the migratory stream, then we would expect that on the average the earnings of migrants would be less were they not to migrate. The obvious difficulty is that we cannot observe what they would have earned, only what they did earn. The alternative of comparing the earnings of migrants with those of workers who did not migrate is subject to what is referred to as self-selectivity biases. (See also Maddala; Heckman; Willis and Rosen.) This means simply that there are differences between the two groups that have led to their separation and need to be properly accounted for in the analysis. In particular, one might argue that the worker most likely to benefit from migration has chosen to do so, while an otherwise similar individual might not so benefit from migrating. The essence of this is that we cannot simply compare observed earnings of migrants and nonmigrants in order to draw unbiased conclusions on the relationship between earnings and migration.

Consider an earnings relation which we specify as

$$E = \alpha_0 + \alpha_1 EDCN + \alpha_2 EXP + \alpha_3 EXP^2 + X\alpha + \mu \qquad (4.1)$$

where E = natural logarithm of annual employment earnings, EDCN = highest grade level completed, EXP = years of farm work experience, and X = a vector of additional socioeconomic variables to be specified later (see Table 4.2). With a set of observations on farm workers one could estimate the parameters of this relation for an evaluation of factors influencing earnings. (See Poveda for such a study. The subsequent development will utilize Poveda's work as a starting point.) The question is whether or not this relationship varies between migrants and nonmigrants. A simple estimation method would be to apply least squares methods to each group separately, and then test for whether or not the relations are statistically different. The deficiency of this procedure is that it does not account for the possibility that sample selectivity has already taken place.

The problem is now reformulated to explicitly account for the migration phenomenon through the earnings relations. Let

$$E = \begin{cases} E^M & \text{if } E^M > E^{NM} \\ E^{NM} & \text{if } E^M \leq E^{NM} \end{cases} \qquad (4.2)$$

where E^M is earnings in the migratory status, E^{NM} is earnings of nonmigratory workers, and E is observed earnings. The corresponding earnings relations are

$$E^M = \beta_0^M + \beta_1^M EDCN + \beta_2^M EXP + \beta_3^M EXP^2 + X\beta^M + \varepsilon_1$$

$$E^{NM} = \beta_0^{NM} + \beta_1^{NM} EDCN + \beta_2^{NM} EXP$$

$$+ \beta_3^{NM} EXP^2 + X\beta^{NM} + \varepsilon_2 \qquad (4.3)$$

Then we can specify the probability of being a migratory worker as

$$Pr(Migrant) = Pr(E^M > E^{NM}) \qquad (4.4)$$

for any given worker, although one only observes migrant or nonmigrant earnings, not both for the same worker. Carrying through the algebra with expressions (4.3) and (4.4), the probability of migration is simply

$$Pr(\varepsilon_2 - \varepsilon_1 < Z\beta^M - Z\beta^{NM}) \qquad (4.5)$$

where Z is all explanatory variables in expression (4.3). Given the same explanatory variables for the migrant and nonmigrant earnings relations, the statistical relation collapses to a test of whether or not β^M and β^{NM} differ. If they were equal, the right-hand term in (4.5) would be zero for all levels of the explanatory variables and the probability of migration would obviously be .5 for all workers, i.e., we would have no information. A particularly important feature of the procedure to note at this point is that we have surmounted the problem of not being able to observe what migratory earnings would be for nonmigrants and vice versa.

The procedure for estimating the parameters of relation (4.5) using data on migrants and nonmigrants is quite simple using standard probit procedures (Maddala, p. 220). (The disturbances are assumed to be independently and identically normally distributed with zero means and finite variances.) While this reduces to a simple estimation procedure, the results are potentially quite rich. Most importantly, if differences in potential earnings have nothing to do with being a migrant, the relationship would not be statistically significant. Second, the factors associated with participating in the migratory stream can be directly assessed.

Modified Earnings Model

A second approach is to suppose that factors in addition to earnings differences are important in the migration decision. In the previous section, a number of characteristics such as education, experience, etc., were considered, but only indirectly through their effect on earnings. In this case, the same influence is maintained but we permit some of these to have a direct effect and, in addition, recognize that there may be factors influencing the migration decision that are not important in determining earnings.

This can be stated more succinctly in the following relations:

$$E^M = \beta_0^M + \beta_1^M EDCN + \beta_2^M EXP + \beta_3^M EXP^2 + X\beta^M + \varepsilon_1$$

if and only if $Z\gamma + \alpha(E^M - E^{NM}) > \varepsilon$.

$$E^{NM} = \beta_0^{NM} + \beta_1^{NM} EDCN + \beta_2^{NM} EXP + \beta_3^{NM} EXP^2 + X\beta_4^{NM} + \varepsilon_2 \qquad (4.6)$$

if and only if $Z\gamma + \alpha(E^M - E^{NM}) \leqslant \varepsilon$.

The set of disturbances $(\varepsilon, \varepsilon_1, \varepsilon_2)$ is assumed to be normally distributed with zero means and finite, nonzero variances and covariances. The relations with E^M and E^{NM} on the left-hand side are identical to those described in the previous section. These are merely the earnings relations for migratory and nonmigratory workers, respectively. The segment that differs is the conditioning relation determining which earning relation applies. The conditioning relation reflects the assumption of a stochastic threshold: on one side of the threshold the individual is a migrant, on the other side a nonmigrant.

The first term in the conditioning relation ($Z\gamma$) reflects the influence of factors other than the difference in earnings. Although the collection of factors in Z may include some of the same ones as are in the earnings relation, it will include additional factors as well. In the case where it does not, the specification is indistinguishable from the one described in the previous section. Examples of considerations for inclusion here are marital status and whether or not the individual's father was a migrant. There is no clear rationale for including either of these in the earnings relation, but one can argue that they are relevant determinants for the migration decision. The second term in the conditioning relation, $\alpha(E^M - E^{NM})$, reflects the influence of earnings differences on the migration decision.

Ideally, one would like to be able to sort out all of the independent effects and attribute them to either determinants of earnings or their effect on the migration decision. However, the estimation complexities for such an effort are beyond the scope of this analysis. (See Maddala for consideration of this problem.) The focus is instead limited to the migration decision. Again, this can be approached in a direct way through a probit analysis. In particular, the specification becomes:

$$\Pr(\text{Migrant}) = \Pr\left[\varepsilon + \alpha(\varepsilon_1 - \varepsilon_2) > W\delta\right] \qquad (4.7)$$

where W includes all factors in the earnings relation plus those in Z in the conditioning relation. Estimation of this relationship from observed data will yield information on how particular factors such as experience or one's father being a migrant influence participation in the migratory stream.

EMPIRICAL EFFECTS

Data

The data requirements to approach the questions of mobility are fairly stringent. Much of the literature has been based on aggregate data. An obvious difficulty raised with that type of data is the concern over whether one studies gross migration or net migration; and the results on net migration, the more useful definition, have been less encouraging than those on gross migration. More important, however, our theoretical concepts of migration are based on the individual or family unit. The difficulties created by aggregation over individuals or families are considerable.

The information required to study migration at the micro level, as in this chapter, includes factors that influence earnings levels. But we also need information on those factors that might in addition have a direct bearing on the migration decision. Examples of such factors are certain family characteristics.

One data set with information at the micro level for farm workers that approximates these requirements is the micro data file from the census--USDA, *The Hired Farm Working Force* data. While these data are reasonably current and have the additional advantage of having a national perspective, they lack some of the information needed for the migration-specific factors. An alternative data set is that which was collected as a part of the NE-58 study on unemployment insurance for agriculture (Bauder et al.; Polopolus and Emerson). These data have the advantage of being extremely detailed, including much of the information desirable for a migration analysis. A somewhat negative factor is that the data were collected in 1970-71. I would maintain, however, that this is a minor concern for the consideration of behavioral relationships on which we are focusing. The fundamental question is whether or not farm workers would be expected to demonstrate significantly different behavior then than now. While levels of earnings have changed over this time due to inflation, the only major institutional change with the potential for affecting individual behavior that has occurred is the inclusion of farm workers under unemployment insurance. (See Emerson and Arcia for an analysis of supply response to unemployment insurance.) And unlike California, the regions included in these data have not been subject to significant unionization activity.

Given these considerations, as well as earlier work on earnings determinants with this data set (Poveda) that can be directly utilized in our migration work, the data collected in Florida under the NE-58 project have been used. The data are further restricted to focus on males, to eliminate additional complications arising from potentially different behavior in the labor market by women (see Mincer [1962] or Poveda, for example). After deleting observations for which there were missing values, 559 observations remain for analysis. Characteristics of the sample as represented by the sample means are included in Table 4.1. Migratory workers represent 45% of the sample.

Earnings Relations

Poveda's earlier work has demonstrated some fundamental earnings relations that will be used as the basis for the empirical work reported here. We, however, start by estimating separate relations for migrants and nonmigrants to determine if there is a difference in the relationships for the two groups. This is fundamental to our approach since if there were no difference in earnings structures, then it would be difficult to argue that differences in earnings are important for explaining migration.

The basic earnings relation was set forth in (4.1). Estimates of the relations are specified in Table 4.2. Education and years of experience in farm work are the variables of most direct interest in explaining earnings; both are highly significant. The remaining variables are primarily control variables, including the number of weeks worked, whether or not

Table 4.1. Sample means

Item	Migrants[a]	Nonmigrants[b]	All
Education			
(highest year completed)	6.4	6.6	6.5
Experience (years)	15.8	18.6	17.3
Weeks of work	45.0	47.8	46.6
Members in household:			
Adults	1.5	1.7	1.6
Children	1.1	1.3	1.3
		Percent	
Ethnic groups			
White	14	35	25
Black	56	58	57
Other	30	7	18
Married	83	41	47
Father was a migrant	32	15	22
Own home	19	24	22
Had health problem	11	7	9
Received fringe benefits	83	64	72
Located in Central Florida	64	56	59
Located in South Florida	32	30	31
Time spent working as:			
Fruit harvester	46	28	31
Vegetable worker	21	12	16
Hand laborer	8	16	13
Machine operator	4	16	11
Livestock worker	1	5	3
Managerial work	1	6	4
Nonfarm work	16	17	16
Other	3	8	6

[a]250 workers.
[b]309 workers.

fringe benefits were received, whether or not the individual had experienced a health problem, classification by ethnic group, and adjustment for the proportion of working time spent in various types of work (hand labor is the base proportion). The overall relation explains 73% of the variation in the log of earnings.

Included in Table 4.2 are estimates of the earnings relation for migrants and nonmigrants separately. A limited inference on whether or not the earnings structures between migrants and nonmigrants differ can be drawn from a statistical test for equality of the overall relations. This test rejects equality at the 99% level of significance. (The appropriate test value is 2.53 for the statistic which is distributed as F(16,527). The critical value at the 99% level for F(16,400) is 2.04.) Recall, however, that these separate relations do not allow, for example, the prediction of earnings of nonmigrants were they to migrate or vice versa, due to the self-selectivity problem addressed above.

Table 4.2. Farm worker earnings relationships[a]

Explanatory variable	All workers (1)	Nonmigrants (2)	Migrants (3)
Education	0.01593	0.01854	0.01197
	(0.00476)	(0.00622)	(0.00723)
Experience	0.01520	0.01512	0.01623
	(0.00371)	(0.00489)	(0.00570)
Experience squared	-0.3192×10^{-3}	-0.2724×10^{-3}	-0.4166×10^{-3}
	(0.0753×10^{-3})	(0.0971×10^{-3})	(0.1215×10^{-3})
Fringe benefits	-0.1109	-0.1483	-0.01499
	(0.0316)	(0.0391)	(0.05460)
Health problem	0.01623	0.02937	0.04462
	(0.05768)	(0.09465)	(0.07044)
Ln weeks	1.1530	1.2763	1.0490
	(0.0407)	(0.0646)	(0.05102)
Blacks	-0.03821	-0.08217	0.06567
	(0.03461)	(0.04188)	(0.06112)
Other ethnic groups	0.01556	0.1283	0.02893
	(0.04763)	(0.0799)	(0.07077)
Occupational proportions			
Nonfarm work	0.2820	0.3034	0.2843
	(0.0598)	(0.0722)	(0.1107)
Fruit harvest labor	0.1658	0.1076	0.1947
	(0.0531)	(0.0708)	(0.0976)
Vegetable worker	-0.0723	-0.1013	-0.0377
	(0.0614)	(0.0780)	(0.1077)
Managerial	0.5909	0.5478	0.4957
	(0.0851)	(0.0925)	(0.2424)
Machine operator	0.2647	0.2336	0.2012
	(0.0614)	(0.0680)	(0.1507)
Livestock worker	-0.0428	-0.0404	-0.3434
	(0.0922)	(0.1003)	(0.2565)
Other	-0.2155	-0.2895	0.0423
	(0.0760)	(0.0838)	(0.1774)
Intercept	3.5637	3.1166	3.8332
	(0.1733)	(0.2707)	(0.2285)
R^2	0.73	0.76	0.73
SSE	55.44	29.94	21.55
n	559	309	250

[a]Dependent variable is the natural log of earnings; estimation is by ordinary least squares. The numbers in parentheses are estimated standard errors.

Migratory Participation

In a previous section, the examination of migration as dependent on differences in earnings structures led to a probability statement (4.5), which could be estimated through probit techniques. Our dependent variable is now a dichotomous one, taking on the value of zero for nonmigrants and unity for migrants. The relation is thus:

$$Y_i = Z_i(\beta^M - \beta^{NM}) + \varepsilon_i \tag{4.8}$$

where Y takes on the values of zero or one, Z is the set of all explanatory variables in the earnings relations, and the coefficients $(\beta^M - \beta^{NM})$ are the differences between the earnings relations for migrants and nonmigrants. By simply estimating the probit relation (4.8), β^M cannot be distinguished from β^{NM}; only the difference is estimated. However, this is sufficient for examining the influence of these factors on migration.

These estimates are specified in column 1 of Table 4.3. First note that the relation is highly significant. (The appropriate test is a likelihood ratio that yields a value of 169.1 having a $\chi^2(16)$ distribution; the critical value at the .995 level is only 34.3.) This gives a stronger confirmation to the earlier preliminary regression test of whether or not the earnings structures vary between migrants and nonmigrants. However, it has the additional interpretation that, indeed, the probability of being a migrant is influenced by the differences in earning structures.

A first observation of the results based on migration as influenced by differences in earnings structures suggests that the factors having the more statistically reliable effects are the categorical variables. Both blacks and other ethnic groups have a higher probability of being migrants. While this is not at all surprising for anyone familiar with the Eastern Seaboard migratory stream, the noteworthy

Table 4.3. Probit estimates for the probability of migration[a]

Explanatory variable	Specification		
	Earnings differences only	Expanded models	
	(1)	(2)	(3)
Education	0.03405	0.02708	0.02912
	(0.02060)	(0.02095)	(0.02096)
Experience	0.01770	0.02458	0.02039
	(0.01612)	(0.01672)	(0.01646)
Experience squared	-0.4827×10^{-3}	-0.5695×10^{-3}	-0.5092×10^{-3}
	(0.3317×10^{-3})	(0.3407×10^{-3})	(0.3371×10^{-3})
Fringe benefits	0.4081	0.3848	0.3939
	(0.1397)	(0.1424)	(0.1433)
Health problem	0.1480	0.1581	0.1500
	(0.2450)	(0.2479)	(0.2470)
ln weeks	0.0256	0.0109	0.0039
	(0.1693)	(0.1716)	(0.1716)
Blacks	0.3018	0.2980	0.3084
	(0.1542)	(0.1577)	(0.1583)
Other ethnic groups	1.2790	1.1276	1.1168
	(0.2124)	(0.2243)	(0.2235)
Occupational proportions			
Nonfarm work	0.4739	0.3358	0.3002
	(0.2581)	(0.2675)	(0.2696)
Fruit harvest labor	1.1238	1.0832	1.0924
	(0.2305)	(0.2452)	(0.2448)
Vegetable worker	0.6698	0.4309	0.3988
	(0.2637)	(0.2881)	(0.2900)
Managerial	-0.5395	-0.6714	-0.7213
	(0.4460)	(0.4731)	(0.4720)
Machine operator	-0.4170	-0.5640	-0.6002
	(0.2958)	(0.3155)	(0.3186)
Livestock worker	-0.5216	-0.6036	-0.6410
	(0.5128)	(0.5240)	(0.5260)
Other	-0.2658	-0.2377	-0.2703
	(0.3662)	(0.3798)	(0.3799)
Central Florida		0.2434	0.2010
		(0.2485)	(0.2501)
South Florida		0.4354	0.4249
		(0.2654)	(0.2654)
Own home		-0.0771	-0.1119
		(0.1661)	(0.1586)
Father migrant		0.3883	0.4329
		(0.1532)	(0.1566)
Married		0.1772	
		(0.1330)	
Adults (no.)			-0.03440
			(0.03958)
Children (no.)			-0.05195
			(0.03699)
Constant	-1.7167	-1.9991	-1.7037
	(0.7294)	(0.7781)	(0.7764)
ln likelihood	-299.76	-293.95	-293.07
-2 ln likelihood ratio	169.1	180.7	182.5

[a]Estimated standard errors are in parentheses.

consideration is that other confounding influences have been accounted for. In particular, one cannot argue that blacks and others have a higher probability because they might have less education. The influence of education has already been separately accounted for. The higher probability is simply through being in one of these groups, even if all other factors are the same.

A second factor to note is the apparent effect on the likelihood of migrating through the type of work done. The base occupation (excluded) is hand labor. The coefficients on the occupational proportions in Table 4.3 suggest that fruit harvesting is the category having the greatest likelihood of migration. Again, this is not surprising, but the extent to which these are distinct is revealing. It suggests, in particular, minimal switching between types of work.

The estimates in columns 2 and 3 of Table 4.3 are based on specifications including variables in addition to those in the earnings relations as discussed earlier under the modified earnings models. The probit relation estimated is

$$Y_i = Z_i(\beta^M - \beta^{NM})\alpha + X_i\gamma + \mu_i \qquad (4.9)$$

where again Y_i takes on the values of zero or one for nonmigrant or migrant, respectively, Z_i is the set of variables in the earnings relations, X_i is the additional variables influencing migration, and μ_i is the random disturbance. While this provides information on migration, it should be noted that α, β^M, and β^{NM} are not separately identified--only their compound effect is obtained. In fact, if some of the variables included in the earnings relation also have a direct effect on migration, i.e., are in both Z and X, then the corresponding coefficient estimate is $(\beta_j^M - \beta_j^{NM})\alpha + \gamma_j$. Nevertheless, for the purpose of considering migration alone, as we are, the combined (reduced form) estimates are informative. The coefficients on the variables entering through the earnings relations are quite comparable to those obtained with the specification based only on earnings differences (column 1 of Table 4.3).

The additional variables included household considerations, demographic factors, and the risk of unemployment. One of these factors is whether or not the worker's father was a migratory worker. It has long been argued that migratory workers are in a self-perpetuating cycle of migration from one generation to the next. To be consistent with this argument, this factor should suggest an increase in the probability of migration. Among the other factors are home ownership, marital status, and number of adults and children. Risk of unemployment is not easily captured with the type of data used here. A priori, one would expect the risk of unemployment in the local area to have a positive effect on migration. Since the risk is likely to be location specific in Florida, regions of the state are included to try to capture this effect. The central and southern regions of the state are the areas with the greatest degree of seasonality and would be expected to present the greatest risk of unemployment during the off-season.

The question of whether or not the importance of these additional factors is consistent with the data is readily verified through a statistical test. It is clear that these factors add some additional explanatory power over just looking at earnings differences, but the results are not as strong as we might expect. Statistically, the coefficients of the additional variables are significantly different from zero at just the 95% level for both specifications (columns 2 and 3 relative to column 1 of Table 4.3). The test statistic values are 11.64 and 13.40, which are respectively distributed as $\chi^2(5)$ and $\chi^2(6)$ for columns (2) and (3).

Considering these effects individually, whether or not the father was a migrant has the clearest effect, suggesting an increase in the likelihood of migration if in fact the father did migrate. Home ownership does not yield significant results. The location variables (assumed to adjust for risk of unemployment) are only marginally significant. They do, however, suggest an increase in the likelihood of migration from either of these areas as we would expect.

There are two competing views of the effects household composition might have. One is that the presence of dependent children may deter migration, other things being equal, if parents are concerned about keeping them in school. Taking this one step further, single individuals would have fewer attachments to a particular location and may be more likely to migrate. The alternative view is that the presence of additional family members would increase the likelihood of migration, since all family members may be able to work in agricultural harvest work and thus be more likely to migrate (Chap. 2). The empirical results are not particularly clear in resolving this. The number of adults in the household has, if anything, a negative effect on migration, but its statistical significance is questionable. The effect of additional children on migration is negative and has some semblance of statistical significance. When marital status is used rather than the number of household members, being married has a slightly positive effect on the likelihood of migration, although again it is not highly significant.

Probabilities of Migration

One way of succinctly summarizing these results is through the predicted probability of participating in the migratory stream, given alternative characteristics for the worker. These are demonstrated in Table 4.4. The predictions are based on the specification in the second column of Table 4.3. (The predicted probabilities have minimal variation between the two specifications. Most agree within one or two percentage points; the ordering does not change within any of the groups.) Two alternative methods for predicting the probability were used. The first

Table 4.4. Estimated probabilities of participating in the migratory stream[a]

Group	Predictions with	
	Subgroup means[b] (1)	Overall means[c] (2)
Ethnic groups		
Whites	0.22	0.40
Blacks	0.46	0.48
Other	0.81	0.81
Experience in farm work (years)		
0		0.44
15		0.53
30		0.53
Type of work (full time)[d]		
Fruit harvest		0.74
Vegetable worker		0.50
Livestock worker		0.15
Father a migrant		
Yes	0.67	0.65
No	0.40	0.50
Marital status		
Single	0.38	0.50
Married	0.56	0.57

[a]The predictions are based on the relations specified in column 2 of Table 4.3.

[b]Each probability is estimated based on the mean values within the subgroup considered.

[c]Each probability is estimated based on the mean values for all workers.

[d]All variables are at their sample means except occupational proportions which are set to one for the type of work considered, and all others are set at zero.

column of Table 4.4 is calculated on the basis of means within the group being considered. For example, in calculating the probability for whites, the mean of education of only whites was used for the education level, and similarly for the remaining explanatory variables. On the other hand, the second column is based on the mean across all groups for each variable, so that the effect of merely being within one category is isolated. Each method has its advantages. Those in the first column are closer to what we observe. The second column estimates, however, indicate how the probabilities would vary between groups if all other factors were equal.

There is a marked difference between the probabilities of migration for whites and blacks in the first column. In contrast, when all other factors are the same for each group, the probabilities are quite close: .40 versus .48. This suggests that explanatory variables other than race act to decrease the likelihood of migration for whites below that of what it is for the average farm worker.

The effect of experience in farm work has little impact on the probability of migration. The difference in the probability between no experience and considerable experience varies only from .44 to .53. This suggests a somewhat higher likelihood of migration by experienced farm workers than by someone just starting, but again the effect is not very great. In particular, the probability of a person just starting farm work entering as a migrant is lower than the probability of an experienced farm worker becoming a migrant.

There are substantial differences in the likelihood of migration by type of work. A person working solely as a fruit harvester has a probability of .75 of being a migrant (again assuming the same characteristics as all other types of workers). In contrast, working only in vegetables carries a .50 probability and working only in livestock carries a .15 probability. This result is consistent with the observation that migration is strongly influenced by the seasonality of labor demand. Should the seasonality disappear, labor supply in agriculture would be largely met by local workers.

The effect of one's father having been a migrant shows some disparity depending on whether the probability is predicted from the subgroups or the whole sample. In line with the general argument for the influence on migrants' children, those for whom the father was not a migrant have a considerably lower probability of migrating than when it is predicted over the whole sample. Again, this suggests a number of factors must be increasing the likelihood of migration for those whose father had migrated for work relative to those whose father had not migrated.

IMPLICATIONS

The results obtained in this analysis are consistent with the hypothesis that farm workers respond to potential wage differentials through migration. In particular, those for whom migration would result in higher earnings are more likely to migrate than others. The uniqueness of the approach is that it is based on the potential difference between earnings in the case of migration versus local work. The basis of the argument is that *observed* differences in migratory versus nonmigratory earnings do not give a very clear picture of the underlying decision process. We can observe only average differences. The individual has chosen to migrate or not on the basis of his perceptions of the difference in his own earnings through migrating or not, in addition to his preferences. The implication is that if potential economic gains can be realized through migration, these gains increase the likelihood of migration.

It was suggested early in the chapter that seasonality of labor demand in agriculture is the basic phenomenon giving rise to migration. While it seems trivial to raise this point, it is all too frequently overlooked. The influence of seasonality in our empirical work was reflected in part by the impact that the fruit harvesting occupational category has relative to the other categories. Were the seasonality to disappear or diminish greatly, we would expect migration to likewise decrease. We have already seen this in the context of Figure 4.1, illustrating the trends in migratory workers over the past 20 years. Further mechanization of seasonal labor-intensive crops (or elimination of those crops) would reduce the gains likely to be obtained through migration and hence decrease the number of workers migrating.

The other side of this is that consideration is only given to domestic migrants. Again, if alien workers were to enter for the purpose of harvesting seasonal crops, the potential gains by domestic workers through migration would be diminished, and we would expect fewer persons to migrate. Of course the point to keep in mind here is that, as Spreen argues, migration is only meaningful if there is seasonal work in different locations. But it is also worthy of note that if the seasonality in one home base location diminished greatly, it is not unlikely that persons would migrate from elsewhere to fill the remaining seasonal demand for labor in the other locations.

The approach strongly suggests that adjustment occurring in the demand for seasonal labor will lead to adjustments in migration. If the adjustment is in an area that had been a source of seasonal labor, fewer persons would be willing to migrate from that location on a temporary basis. The potential gains through remaining a migrant with that source location would diminish, thereby reducing the probability of migration. If the disparity in demand and supply of labor in the receiving location still existed, one would expect increased migration from alternative source areas, but presumably at a lower level than was originally the case.

The seasonality phenomenon in conjunction with the migration response suggests a policy dilemma. On the one hand, it has been perceived that the reduction of seasonality would assist in reducing migration. Yet if workers are choosing to migrate of their own accord, because they perceive potential economic gains through migrating relative to not migrating, it is not clear that efforts to reduce migration would be perceived as being in their best interest. The pertinent question is whether or not those no longer migrating can find alternative employment opportunities at least as good, and this has proved to be a rather difficult task to accomplish.

Efforts over the past several years have been extended in the direction of what is referred to as the settling out phenomenon. This is basically an effort to move workers out of seasonal and migratory employment into other presumably more stable employment. This policy is best considered under two alternative frameworks. Consider first the case in which the number of seasonal jobs is continually declining, and further that this may be happening in markets where migratory workers have typically been employed. Since many seasonal agricultural workers have difficulties finding and maintaining employment outside agriculture, efforts to enhance job skills for gainful employment are reasonable.

The alternative scenario is the one in which we are now and have been over the past decade, namely one of relatively stable migratory and seasonal employment. The value of efforts to encourage settling out is less certain here. If we assume for the moment that the program is successful in removing individuals from the migratory stream to some form of stable nonfarm employment, the question immediately raised is who must take their place. Recognizing the seasonality of employment and the fact that workers respond to incentives to migrate, it is only reasonable that for every worker removed from the stream, another will have replaced him. To assume otherwise is to assume there has been some fundamental change in the local labor market so that now local workers will supply labor sufficient for the season at the prevailing wage.

If the settling out were on a sufficiently massive scale, a slightly different result could take place. Assuming that it was being carried out on a regular basis, it is conceiveable that the supply curve for seasonal labor could be shifted far enough to the left that employers would eventually change to methods of production requiring less labor or cease growing such crops altogether. In this case, the program would actually be an endogenous force in the labor market rather than reacting to assist those who have been displaced. While it seems reasonably clear that much of the CETA 303 effort is directed to this end, the labor market has proven rather difficult to conquer. A major factor in this is that the supply of labor to seasonal agricultural labor markets is reasonably elastic (Emerson et al.), i.e., a substantial quantity of labor must be removed from this labor market to have a significant effect on wage rates.

A host of other labor policies can directly

affect migration although they are not themselves targeted for migratory workers. One of these is unemployment insurance. A recent flurry of research on unemployment insurance has raised the question of the extent to which it alters labor market behavior (Feldstein). The argument is basically that unemployment benefits are at levels such that the incentive to obtain new employment prior to the expiration of benefits is minimal. Agricultural workers have only recently come under this program. The structure of the program, however, is such that the economic incentive for migration is clearly diminished. (See Emerson and Arcia for an estimate of the impact on agricultural labor markets.) If earnings in the migratory and nonmigratory status are redefined to include potential unemployment insurance benefits, the difference in earnings between migrating and not migrating is surely diminished, and our empirical results would suggest a reduction in migration. Moreover, to the extent that migration is influenced by the risk of unemployment in the off-season, this risk is clearly diminished by unemployment insurance, and this would exert a similar depressant force on migration.

Policy toward alien workers is highly relevant for future migratory activity. Although Martin and North in Chapter 6 address the alien issue in more detail, its relation to domestic migratory workers cannot be ignored here. It is widely acknowledged that there are large numbers of undocumented workers in the United States, many of whom find work in agriculture. If one believes that labor supply curves for agriculture are upward sloping, then it follows that this influx of labor acts as a depressant on agricultural wages (Schuh 1962; Emerson 1975). If undocumented workers were, for sake of argument, no longer permitted to work, one would expect a substantial increase in domestic migration. First, it is likely that such workers are in seasonal jobs, where anonymity is easily maintained. Second, if they were removed, there would presumably be localized seasonal shortages of labor that would give rise to incentives for domestic migration. How long this would continue would depend on the dynamics of the labor market from both the supply and demand side. In particular, how long would it take for changes in technology or in the type of crops grown to adjust to the increased cost of production?

Legal aliens are equally important to future levels of domestic migration. An obvious way to eliminate domestic migration would be to automatically permit employers to contract with offshore workers for their seasonal employment. To the extent that all seasonal needs were met in this way, there would no longer be any incentives for migration for seasonal work. This raises a particularly difficult social welfare question that cannot be addressed in this chapter. Of course the opposite side of the coin is that further restrictions in offshore labor could increase domestic migration. Although legal and illegal aliens have been discussed separately, all three groups--legal aliens, illegal aliens, and domestic migrants--are highly interdependent.

Program Implications

The basic thrust of this chapter is that economics is relevant to the decision-making process of the individual worker choosing between migrating or not migrating. The results are suggestive of economic rationality on the part of farm workers who choose to migrate. If this is the case, it has very definite implications for programs directed toward migratory workers. Most importantly, it suggests that efforts to influence the migratory labor market must take into account other facets of the farm labor market. In this respect, the approach of the CETA 303 program is a step in the right direction, since the program now includes not only migratory workers but the broader group of seasonal farm workers as well.

But the presumption of economic rationality suggests programs of a much broader scope than those covering seasonal and migratory farm workers only. At the extreme, if the programs are indeed successful, the hypothesis would suggest that they might create an added incentive for persons to become seasonal and migratory workers. While there are clear limitations as to the magnitude of such a trend, it is entirely conceivable that some farm workers not meeting the seasonal and migratory criterion might find it beneficial to alter their employment pattern so that they do meet the criterion. This effect is characteristic of almost any selective program. One way of avoiding the difficulty is to continually move toward programs that do not have occupational or employment-based eligibility criteria. An example of such a program is a universal income maintenance or negative income tax program. Whether or not an individual is eligible for benefits from such a program is independent of the type of farm worker he is, or even whether or not he is a farm worker--the benefits are determined on the basis of income level.

Implications for Future Research

Although the approach utilized in this analysis is clearly exploratory, it is an initial attempt to interpret the data on migration in economic terms. As such, a number of questions are raised that require further research.

One pertinent research effort would be to carefully separate the direct impact on migration of earnings differences from the direct impact of other factors.[2] Further evidence here could provide more definitive support or denial for the importance of earnings differences on participation in the migratory stream. A clearer understanding of the role that economic incentives play in this aspect of the farm labor market is crucial to formulating effective policies. Implicit in most farm labor policy has been the presumption that migration is a noneconomic phenomenon; migration could be eliminated by removing workers from the stream. If decisions to migrate are influenced by economic considerations as suggested in this analysis, such policies are not likely to be very successful in reaching their goal.

Family considerations are a very important factor in this labor market. It is widely observed that families often travel together and work as a family unit. Although the analysis in this chapter makes some adjustment for the influence of other family members, it is short of what is needed. An analysis that properly accounted for this phenomenon would start with the household as the unit of observation and attempt to explain behavior of the various household members. This obviously requires extensive data on all household members, which is not available in the data base utilized here. Future attempts to incorporate additional family level considerations would be highly worthwhile.

One other area in which additional data could provide interesting information would be on the dynamic nature of migration in farm labor markets. For example, do individuals move in and out of the migratory stream over time, or once they enter are they permanently in the stream? The policy presumption has been the latter, yet the approach of this analysis would suggest there may be more movement in and out than is commonly thought. Again, this would suggest an alternative policy approach to one that presumes that migrants do not have the flexibility of leaving the migratory stream.

Further research on the interrelation between the use of alien workers and the migration of domestic workers could also provide needed information for policy prescriptions. To what extent are there one-for-one trade-offs in employment between domestic migratory workers and offshore or undocumented workers? Moreover, what are the magnitudes and distribution of gains and losses through these alternatives?

CONCLUSIONS

The central thrust of this chapter has been that economics can provide some insights into the migration of labor in agriculture. In particular, the case has been argued that participation in the migratory stream is in response to less favorable employment alternatives facing the potential migrant. Confrontation of this hypothesis with data on hired farm workers suggests that it is consistent with these data. The extent to which it would be replicated is, of course, unknown. However, the pertinent question is how representative is this sample of farm workers who are potential migrants.

One difference between the Florida and the U.S. farm labor force is that Florida has few students, whereas students are a major component across the United States as a whole. The Florida farm labor force is more representative of workers who have earned their livings as farm workers. A second major difference is the ethnic composition. In Florida the farm work force is largely black whereas in the other major seasonal area, the Southwest, it is largely Hispanic. The lack of students can be readily dismissed as a different issue. They tend to be there for a short time and move on to something else as they enter the labor force full time. The policy concern has generally been with those we are considering here, the nonstudent worker there for his livelihood. Results of a study using a sample more representative of Hispanic workers would be informative. However, there is no basis for assuming that such results would be substantially different. Our results indicated the higher likelihood of Hispanic workers being migrants, and this would surely be reconfirmed. There is little reason to believe that the other factors considered would show widely divergent effects.

I hasten to add that it is not argued that sociological and anthropological approaches to migration are not important. They certainly are. Our results confirm a major theme of that literature, namely, the argument of continuity of migration from one generation to the next. The effort here is in the direction of arguing that economics can provide additional insights.

A number of alternative scenarios were considered in conjunction with policy alternatives as a means of assessing potential migration in the future. The strongest influence is the demand for seasonal labor in alternative locations. Were this to substantially decline either through technological or economic changes, migration would similarly diminish. Another major factor is the interdependence with alien labor. Substantial reductions in the number of aliens admitted would undoubtedly increase domestic migration, at least in the short run. The likelihood of higher levels of migration continuing over the longer term, however, would be questionable. Conversely, increases in the use of offshore workers would be likely to reduce domestic migration.

The impact of settling out programs on reducing the migratory stream is likely to be dependent on factors quite independent of their own influence. The reason for this is that they do not alter the demand for seasonal labor. The supply of seasonal labor is sufficiently elastic that additional workers are readily available to take the place of those removed from the farm labor force or the migratory stream. This is not to say that there are no gains from such training programs to the extent that workers are able to obtain improved stable employment. The question raised is how can the limited funds available best be used. A procedure that results in the likely introduction of a new worker to the market for each one removed has not done a great deal to improve the conditions within that market. One alternative is to focus those funds on areas where there is a substantial change taking place within the labor market causing workers to be displaced. An example would be the mechanization of the Florida citrus harvest, were it to occur.

Discussion

ALFRED L. PARKS

Emerson is to be commended for the excellent analysis he has presented on labor migration in farm labor markets. The main thrust of the study is the examination of some very basic economic factors as a means of determining the decision to migrate. Unlike previous work (see Greenwood 1975 for literature review), Emerson's analysis provides new insights into labor migration and covers several key economic factors affecting the decision to migrate.

Emerson begins with some views on the definition of migration in agricultural labor markets and how it compares with labor migration in other industries, primarily entertainment. However, he fails to give a concise definition of migration. He implies that migration is more than residential relocation for employment. This notion is supported by comments from other analysts (see Holt et al. 1978). While I generally agree with this idea, I think that migration in agricultural labor markets is quite different and as such should not be compared with the entertainment industry.

The extent of seasonal farm labor migration was reviewed very briefly. It was pointed out that the portion of the U.S. agricultural labor force migrating for employment stood at about 7%. This was according to the most recent USDA estimates (USDA, *The Hired Farm Working Force of 1977*). It was further pointed out that the absolute number of workers stood at about 191,000 and has remained fairly constant at that level during the 1970s. This compares favorably with the total farm labor hired work force, which has also remained fairly constant during this period. The extent of migration in terms of the number of days that the migrant spends in the migrant stream was not determined. In other words, the question here is whether migrant laborers are migrating for longer duration (number of days per year) or for shorter duration. This may have some bearing on the total number of workers counted as migrants.

The question of the so-called domestic migratory worker was also mentioned. Emerson seemed to suggest that the group designated as domestic migratory workers has been numerically unimportant. If this is true, then it may explain why there has been so little economic attention given to migrant laborers. On the other hand, this statement seems contradictory since the statistics on migrant labor indicate that a sizeable portion of migrant workers are domestic (USDA, *The Hired Farm Working Force of 1977*, p. 10).

The main hypothesis in Emerson's analysis is centered around certain economic considerations influencing the decision to migrate. He hypothesizes that decisions to migrate are influenced primarily by economic considerations. The main economic factor that he considers is the wage difference between regions. Other related factors include unemployment, age, and education. Thus the hypothesis is based upon the theoretical notion that if wages are higher in region "A" than in region "B," persons will be motivated to migrate from region "B" to region "A."

Two approaches were used to explain the significance of participation in the migratory stream. The first approach involved looking at the potential differences in earnings between migrants and nonmigrants. In making the comparison between earnings of migrants and nonmigrants, the self-selectivity bias approach was used. This very simplified approach accounts only for the observed wage differences, which it assumes led to the separation. This seriously limits the significance of the results of this model. The deficiency of this approach is that it does not take into account the possibility that sample selectivity may have already taken place. The modeling procedure of this approach was the standard probit estimation procedure.

The second approach assumes that there are factors in addition to earnings differences that are important in the migration decision. A modified earnings model, which incorporates education, experience, and a number of other socioeconomic variables, is used. While this model is perhaps an improvement over the original model, it fails to recognize "skill" as a factor. Skill is perhaps one of the more significant factors affecting earnings of migrant workers. Whether or not skill is assumed to be included as experience is not clearly stated. However, earnings in farm labor are often paid on the basis of the amount produced, rather than by the number of hours or days worked. Therefore a very skillful or agile worker may have much higher earnings than an average worker.

The results of the model testing indicate that there is a significant difference between earnings of migrants and nonmigrants. However, the data do not take into consideration the difference in living costs or the cost of moving from one location to another. If these moving costs were included as adjustments to earnings I rather question if earnings differences would be significant.

The probability of participation in the migratory stream is much higher for blacks and other minorities than for whites. However, there are other variables having a strong influence on the decision to migrate. These include the type of work done and parental (father) participation in migration. It is not clearly specified whether migration is a one-time affair or whether it is continuous.

The conclusion Emerson suggests is that labor migration is positively correlated with the seasonal demand for labor. Even if this is true, there are still several options that must be explored. If the seasonal demand for labor continues, then the choice may be simple. Employers may simply continue with the present system. But what happens if farms become mechanized? What impact would this have on the migrant labor system? The extent to which this situation is likely to occur is not documented. The continued availability of cheap labor will perhaps be a strong determinant.

The use of alien and undocumented labor is

another critical concern. While the number of these workers is not known, Emerson suggests that it is significant. It is strongly suspected that these workers are willing to accept wages much lower than those of domestic workers. This may largely explain why the number of domestic migrant workers is low. Were this group of workers to be eliminated from the migrant stream, there would be some significant changes in wage rates, domestic migration, and seasonal labor requirements. That is, the reduced supply of labor, causing temporary shortages of labor, would lead to higher wages in the short and intermediate run, but to structural adjustments in the long run.

5

The Off-Farm Work of Hired Farm Workers

BENJAMIN N. MATTA, JR.

Students of agricultural labor markets observe that the relatively low human resource returns problem in the agricultural sector has been minimized by two means. First, persons have left farm work altogether (the process of occupational mobility); second, those remaining in the agricultural sector combine farm and nonfarm employment with varying degrees of success (the process of occupational diversification). While assiduous attention has been given by researchers to the phenomenon of occupational diversification among farm operators and farm operator families, little if any research has focused on the off-farm work of hired farm workers. (Tweeten (1978, p. 8) estimated that in 1976 self-employed and unpaid family farm workers numbered 1.66 million and 0.34 million, respectively. Wage and salary farm workers were estimated to number 1.32 million.) This chapter discusses three aspects of the off-farm work of hired farm workers: the historical magnitude of off-farm work, the earnings and employment durations of the off-farm work spells, and the determinants of the off-farm work selectivity process.

I wish to thank several persons for contributing to this chapter although blemishes of substances are those due to the author: Vernon M. Briggs, Robert Emerson, Varden Fuller, Eliot Orton, Martin E. Blake and Scott Urquhart, E. E. Liebhafsky, and Jon Peck.

RESEARCH ON OFF-FARM WORK OF FARM OPERATORS

The research on the off-farm work of farm operators and farm family members that has been published in economic journals has been both theoretical and econometric in orientation. Lee's (1965) graphical exposition provides a theoretical demonstration of the idea that the decision of farm operators to allocate a portion of their human resources to off-farm work is both rational and consistent with the global goals of efficient allocation of resources. Huffman (1977b) elaborates on the implications of off-farm employment in terms of the intersectoral integration of farm and nonfarm labor markets. He argues that the expansion of communication networks to rural areas has increased the availability of labor market information. Rising educational levels have increased not only skill levels, making the integration of farm operators into the nonfarm economy easier, but they have also increased the ability of farm operators to respond to changes in farm and off-farm economic conditions. The results are that among farm operators and farm families, the ratio of nonfarm to total income has risen

> . . . from 27% in 1950 to 50% in the 1970s, except for 1973 when net farm incomes rose dramatically. . . . The change has reduced the vulnerability of the farm population to wide swings in prices and net farm income. (Huffman 1977b, p. 1058)

The empirical work has been fashioned around cross-sectional data and labor supply models. An early attempt at fitting a labor supply equation was made by Polzin and MacDonald utilizing the *1964 Census of Agriculture* state level data. The specified model related average days worked off the farm by operators and their families (L) to: (1) the ratio of average hourly wages in manufacturing to gross realized income per farm (W/I, an index of the relative opportunity cost of farm employment); (2) the percentage of the population classified as rural-farm in 1960 (F, an index of the relative location and distance of the farm operator and his family from off-farm employment opportunities); and (3) the percentage of nonagricultural employment in manufacturing (M, to represent the availability of nonfarm jobs in the area). Recognizing that the state level of aggregation may conceal true relationships existing at the household level, they estimated a second equation with county level data for the states of Montana, North Carolina, Mississippi, and Kansas. The fitted total sample equation utilizing state level data is reported as

$$L = 34.755 + \underset{(9305)}{19655W/I} - \underset{(0.1165)}{0.7598F} + \underset{(0.0842)}{0.1598M}$$

$$R^2 = .563 \quad n = 48$$

with standard errors in parentheses. The equation supports two hypotheses about off-farm work. First, an increase in off-farm wage rates or a decrease in farm income is associated with an increased supply of off-farm work. Second, rural areas are likely to be associated with less off-farm work even after controlling for the proportion of nonagricultural employment, M.

Huffman's econometric estimates (1977c; 1980) follow from a model that has a more rigorous theoretical underpinning in the literature on household choice making. The labor supply function for farm household members (S_{0f}) is derived from a constrained optimization framework of a maximized household utility function subjected to the constraints of human time, family household income, and farm production. The labor supply function takes the form $S_{0f}(W_{0f}, P_1, P, W_2, V, Y_2, X_3, T^0)$ where the arguments are, in order, off-farm wage (W_{0f}), the prices of purchased goods (P_1), the anticipated farm output price (P), per unit cost of farm production excluding the cost of family member input (W_2), other household income (V), household characteristics such as age, education, etc. (Y_2), farm production inputs of family members (X_3), and total endowments of time (T^0).

The equation was estimated with county level *1964 Census of Agriculture* data supplemented with unpublished federal extension service and other Department of Agriculture data for 276 counties in Iowa, North Carolina, and Oklahoma (Huffman 1980) and with state level *1964 Census of Agriculture* data for the 48 contiguous states (with New Hampshire and Vermont, Connecticut and Rhode Island, and Delaware and Maryland grouped) (Huffman 1977c). The dependent variable in both studies was alternatively defined in two ways: as the proportion of farm operators reporting any off-farm work during 1964 and as the average number of off-farm days of farm operators during 1964.

The reader is directed to Huffman for a complete discussion of the results of his efforts. In the 1980 article, Huffman reports a strong inducement to enter off-farm work and to supply off-farm days in increasing amounts following an off-farm wage increase. In both the 1977 (b,c) and 1980 articles, the impact of schooling levels of head of the farm family is statistically significant and positive. The latter result leads Huffman to conclude:

> . . . the econometric evidence reported in this paper also suggest that farmers with more education, even when they have not migrated [off the farm] have reallocated their labor services from self-employed farm work to off-farm work faster than farmers with lower levels of education. Thus, part of the returns to education in agriculture arises from its effect on allocation of labor between farm and non-farm labor markets. (1980, p. 23)

The research of Hathaway and Perkins and of Hathaway and Waldo suggests that studies relying solely on aggregative data may be misleading. Utilizing the longitudinal feature of the *Social Security Continuous Work History Sample*, they found off-farm employment of a large proportion of the sample of farm operators to be short term and discontinuous. Waldo (1965) summarized the results of those studies as follows:

> . . . an investigation of multiple jobholders in the farm-operator labor force, utilizing the continuous registry feature of sample data from social security records, shows that relatively few farmers consistently hold off farm employment. Around 29 percent annually of all farmers covered by social security records were multiple jobholders over the period from 1955 through 1959, but almost half of the farmers classified as multiple jobholders in at least one of the five years worked off the farm in only one year. Less than one in ten farm operators who were multiple jobholders during the period worked off the farm in each of the five years. For most persons who remain in farming, multiple jobholding is largely sporadic and evidently the result of very limited participation in the nonfarm work force (p. 1242).

These findings led Waldo to observe that though continuous off-farm work is not possible for many farmers, the exposure to off-farm employment nevertheless provides valuable "training and experience that will lead to a permanent shift to non-farm employment" (p. 1243).

The social security sample is limited chiefly in two ways. First, it includes only workers covered by the social security system and second, it does not include information on education attainment. The findings of Hathaway and Perkins and Hathaway and Waldo must, therefore, be interpreted in light of these limitations. Nevertheless, the warning about imputing meaning to analytical results from data that exclude longitudinal information is clear.

THE OFF-FARM WORK OF HIRED FARM WORKERS

Temporal Data Tabulations

Information appearing in Tables 5.1 and 5.2 is suggestive of the aggregative magnitude of off-farm work by hired farm workers. The proportion of hired

Table 5.1. Number of hired farm workers doing farm work only and doing farm and nonfarm work combined, 1949-1977

Year	Total (000)	Farm work only (000)	Farm work only (%)	Farm and non-farm work (000)	Farm and nonfarm work (%)
1949	4140	2886	69.7	1254	30.3
1950[b]					
1951	3274	2410	73.6	864	26.4
1952	2980	b	b	b	b
1953[a]					
1954	3009	2145	71.3	864	28.7
1955[a]					
1956	3575	2544	71.2	1031	28.8
1957	3962	2947	74.4	1015	25.6
1958[b]					
1959	3577	2421	67.7	1156	32.3
1960	3693	2368	64.1	1325	35.9
1961	3488	2356	67.5	1132	32.5
1962	3622	2342	64.7	1280	35.3
1963	3597	2450	68.1	1147	31.9
1964	3370	2094	62.1	1276	37.9
1965	3128	1983	63.4	1145	36.6
1966	2763	1685	61.0	1078	39.0
1967	3078	2017	65.5	1061	34.5
1968	2919	1851	63.4	1068	36.6
1969	2571	1616	62.8	955	37.2
1970	2488	1483	59.6	1005	40.4
1971	2550	1617	63.4	933	36.6
1972	2809	1649	58.7	1160	41.3
1973	2671	1560	58.4	1111	41.6
1974	2737	1599	58.4	1138	41.6
1975	2638	1560	59.1	1078	40.9
1976	2766	1576	56.9	1190	43.1
1977	2730	1599	58.6	1131	41.4
Sample period percentages:					
1950s			71.3		28.7
1960s			64.3		35.7
1970s			59.1		40.9

Source: USDA, ESCS, The Hired Farm Working Force, various annual issues.

[a]No survey was conducted in 1953 and 1955.

[b]Data not available.

Table 5.2. Average yearly earnings of workers in farm and nonfarm jobs, 1960-1976 (dollars)

Year	Farm and nonfarm earnings combined	Farm earnings	Nonfarm earnings	Nonfarm earnings, %[a]
	Yearly	Yearly	Yearly	Yearly
1960	845	537	308	36.4
1961	788	502	286	36.3
1962	896	549	347	38.7
1963	818	483	335	40.9
1964	956	578	378	39.5
1965	1054	650	404	38.3
1966	1279	731	548	40.8
1967	1295	817	477	36.8
1968	1346	834	572	38.0
1969	1453	837	616	42.4
1970	1640	887	752	45.7
1971	1580	882	698	44.2
1972	2019	1160	859	42.5
1973	2369	1412	957	40.4
1974	2476	1447	1030	41.6
1975	2552	1488	1065	41.7
1976	2859	1652	1207	42.2

Source: USDA, ESCS, The Hired Farm Working Force, various annual issues.

[a]Yearly nonfarm earnings as a percent of combined farm and nonfarm earnings.

farm workers combining farm and off-farm work has steadily risen from 28.7% in the 1950s to 35.7% in the 1960s and to nearly 41% in the 1970s (Table 5.1). In contrast, the proportion of persons doing "farm work only" has fallen from 71.3% in the 1950s to 19.1% in the 1970s. Paucity of published tabulations for the 1950s on average nonfarm yearly earnings of farm workers does not permit a similar two-decade span comparison of the proportions of nonfarm to total earnings. Nevertheless, from the data in Table 5.2 a rising trend in the proportion of nonfarm to total earnings appears to be established.

These tabulations conceal the fact that the hired farm work force is diverse in its composition and that the intensity of off-farm work may vary in a nonrandom pattern. The structure of the *Hired Farm Working Force* data set permits classification of members of the hired farm work force according to their main employment activity through the survey year.

From this classification, it is possible to group persons by their degree of attachment to the hired farm working force as permanent or as temporary and as dual (farm and nonfarm) sector jobholders or as farm workers only. Workers who spend the greater part of the year working on their own farms, whether as owners, sharecroppers, tenants, or unpaid family members, were herein classified as the "primarily own farm" group. Those who spend most of the year engaged in nonfarm jobs but who nevertheless spend some time in hired farm work were classified as the "primarily nonfarm work" category. Some persons spend most of the year in hired farm work but also do some nonfarm work for wages, and these were grouped into the "primarily farm work" category. Unemployed workers are those who spend most of the year as job searchers in both farm and nonfarm labor markets and are grouped in the "primarily unemployed" classification. Among the temporary workers, there are those whose stay in the labor market is limited by illness, physical disabilities, or retirement. These individuals are classified in the "other" category to distinguish them from the other two types of temporary farm workers: those who are primarily in school throughout the year, and those who are primarily housewives. The classifications for these latter groups are entitled, respectively, "primarily attending school" and "primarily housewife."

Dividing the hired farm worker force in this way reveals several interesting phenomena. First, the hired farm worker market has historically been dominated by temporary workers, with students comprising the largest component (Table 5.3). Those doing farm work only, on a permanent basis, (category 1, Table 3) represent the second largest group, but it is still only about half the size of the student group--18.5% on a historical basis. On the other hand, permanent full-time farm workers have also supplied over 50% of all man-days, while students have supplied only 17%. Secondly, 14% of all hired farm workers are those doing chiefly nonfarm work throughout the year (cate-

Table 5.3. Percentage distribution of hired farm workers by chief employment status, 1963-1976, %

Category	Description	Percent of totals			Percent of man-days supplied in farm work
	<u>Permanently in farm worker market</u>	45			
	Persons doing farm work only		24		
1	Farm work only			18.5	55.0
2	Primarily unemployed			1.0	[a]
3	Primarily own farm			4.0	3.5
	Persons doing farm and nonfarm work combined		21		
4	Primarily farm work			5.0	10.0
5	Primarily own farm			1.0	[a]
6	Primarily nonfarm work			14.0	6.0
7	Primarily unemployed			1.0	[a]
	<u>Temporarily in farm worker market</u>	55			
	Persons doing farm work only		37		
8	Primarily housewife			9.0	4.0
9	Primarily attending school			24.0	12.0
10	Other (ill, disabled, retired)			4.0	2.0
	Persons doing farm and nonfarm work combined		17.5		
11	Primarily housewife			3.0	1.0
12	Primarily attending school			13.0	5.0
13	Other (ill, disabled, retired)			1.5	[a]
	Total	100	100	100	100

Source: USDA, ESCS, <u>The Hired Farm Working Force</u>, various annual issues.
[a]Data not available. Due to rounding errors, not all percentage columns total 100.

gory 6, Table 5.3). Among the group of dual sector jobholders, they constitute the largest segment. Third, by addition of those "persons doing farm work only" to dual sector jobholders who are primarily farm workers (category 4, Table 5.3), the magnitude of the group having a permanent connection to farm work is obtained.

Accordingly, on a historical basis, only 29% of the hired farm worker force is considered to have a primary dependence on agriculture. On the other hand, the size of the casual-seasonal, farm worker segment (the sum of categories 6 and 8 through 13) is 68.5% historically. Unemployment appears to be low, although this figure is not reliable as a measure of the actual burden of unemployment among hired farm workers. Omitted from the count of the unemployed are those who would engage in a job search for a longer period of the year rather than return to an out-of-the-labor-force status. Tweeten (1978, pp. 18-19) argues that the lack of job opportunities in rural areas makes the benefit of an extended job search low, relative to its costs.

Of special interest is the comparison of the sizes of categories 4 and 6 of Table 5.3. Category 6 is 2.8 times larger than category 4. This same finding resulted from the work of Fuller and Van Vuuren, who used only two years of observation from the *Hired Farm Working Force* sample. Utilizing annual tabulations for 1968 and 1969, they found that the flow of persons from nonfarm to farm work exceeded the flow of persons from farm to nonfarm work. They explained their findings by giving birth to "The Hired Farmworker Market as a Salvage Market" hypothesis wherein they proposed that, when underemployment occurs in the nonfarm economy, the farm worker market becomes a refuge for the salvage of "zero and low opportunity cost time. . . ." (p. 154). The dominant characteristic of the hired farm worker market that permits the salvage operations is that the market is open and unprotected from new competition.

Table 5.4 shows that participation in nonfarm jobs by those primarily in farm work (column 9) is limited to about two full months of the year. Also illustrated is the underemployment condition of those who are primarily doing nonfarm work (column 10). During the time interval from 1963 to 1976, this latter group has managed to be employed about 74% of a full year of work, an average (assuming a full year of work constitutes 260 days) in the nonfarm worker market. The slack is, presumably, absorbed by taking jobs in the hired farm worker market.

Attention is drawn to the distribution of daily earnings (Table 5.5). It is plausible to argue that those in the "primarily farm work" category gain by foregoing days in farm work, which on average have yielded $12.95 per day (column 5), to obtain $14.50 per day (column 9) in nonfarm work. But those in the "primarily nonfarm work" group would be irrational to give up days in the nonfarm sector at $18.50 per day (column 10) for $12.35 per day in farm work (column 6). Rather, there is some evidence of involuntariness: the time spent in the farm sector by primarily nonfarm workers should be regarded as the result of slack employment conditions in the nonfarm sector. Workers having few alternatives use the hired farm worker market as a market of last resort, a market characterized by limited barriers to entry.

Table 5.4. Average days in farm and nonfarm work of hired farm workers, by chief employment status, 1963-1976

	Workers doing farm work only				Workers doing farm and nonfarm work combined							
					Farm days				Nonfarm days			
Year	Farm work only (1)	Primarily own farm (2)	Primarily house-wife (3)	Primarily attending school (4)	Primarily farm work (5)	Primarily nonfarm work (6)	Primarily house-wife (7)	Primarily attending school (8)	Primarily farm work (9)	Primarily nonfarm work (10)	Primarily house-wife (11)	Primarily attending school (12)
1963	232	44	27	28	178	24	31	25	55	199	41	47
1964	238	44	42	39	158	33	26	25	51	194	53	60
1965	247	45	38	36	165	31	27	33	54	193	49	57
1966	269	83	36	35	174	41	27	35	59	197	52	58
1967	248	94	44	47	175	42	35	27	54	193	64	61
1968	240	66	34	37	176	36	30	31	55	204	44	53
1969	246	77	36	38	183	39	30	27	65	204	62	58
1970	249	68	34	44	176	33	27	27	83	199	55	63
1971	244	114	33	39	180	35	26	26	65	179	47	67
1972	235	135	38	42	187	38	19	33	66	191	64	66
1973	245	110	35	51	170	36	34	31	69	204	56	66
1974	240	69	41	40	166	30	25	34	63	207	70	66
1975	234	88	46	46	157	30	36	32	71	200	59	74
1976	232	87	40	51	175	35	21	36	48	206	64	73
Sample Period (1963-1976):												
Mean	243	80	37	41	173	34	28	30	61	198	56	62
Coefficient of Variation	.04	.33	.13	.15	.05	.13	.16	.12	.15	.03	.15	.11

Source: USDA, ESCS, The Hired Farm Working Force, various annual issues.

Table 5.5. Average daily earnings of hired farm workers, by chief employment status, 1963-1976 (dollars)

	Workers doing farm work only				Workers doing farm and nonfarm work combined							
					Farm days				Nonfarm days			
Year	Farm work only (1)	Primarily own farm (2)	Primarily house-wife (3)	Primarily attending school (4)	Primarily farm work (5)	Primarily nonfarm work (6)	Primarily house-wife (7)	Primarily attending school (8)	Primarily farm work (9)	Primarily nonfarm work (10)	Primarily house-wife (11)	Primarily attending school (12)
1963	6.90	5.40	4.30	4.10	7.25	7.15	4.55	4.00	8.75	12.45	4.95	5.30
1964	7.65	6.05	5.00	4.90	8.45	7.95	5.80	5.70	10.30	12.20	5.10	5.25
1965	8.45	8.05	5.30	4.70	7.55	10.05	6.40	5.00	10.25	13.30	5.90	4.45
1966	8.90	10.40	7.70	6.10	9.30	8.35	7.95	6.35	9.30	8.35	7.95	6.35
1967	10.60	9.85	7.70	6.95	12.40	16.40	7.00	5.55	12.40	16.40	7.00	5.55
1968	11.45	12.05	8.15	7.50	10.95	11.00	8.00	7.55	14.00	16.50	6.70	6.65
1969	11.55	18.90	7.15	7.95	10.60	11.10	7.50	8.45	13.05	18.85	8.80	7.05
1970	11.45	13.95	9.45	7.85	14.55	11.75	8.85	8.75	14.05	20.10	9.90	6.80
1971	12.95	13.90	9.80	7.50	12.95	12.00	8.65	7.75	17.05	20.30	9.70	8.85
1972	14.65	13.75	10.20	8.60	14.35	11.65	10.00	9.35	17.00	21.40	6.90	7.70
1973	16.50	16.05	10.40	8.95	16.40	15.35	9.90	10.50	18.80	22.80	9.15	9.55
1974	18.15	15.85	12.15	11.60	17.15	15.20	14.30	14.05	18.55	25.85	10.60	17.95
1975	19.70	22.30	11.65	11.35	18.25	16.85	12.75	13.20	21.22	27.11	15.59	11.57
1976	21.76	22.61	14.77	12.67	21.27	17.91	17.45	14.53	19.25	23.55	12.65	10.85
Sample Period (1963-1976):												
Mean	12.90	13.50	8.85	7.90	12.95	12.35	9.20	8.60	14.50	18.50	8.65	8.15
Coefficient of Variation	.359	.399	.333	.329	.329	.281	.380	.393	.276	.300	.344	.434

Source: USDA, ESCS, The Hired Farm Working Force, various annual issues.

On the average, the total yearly earnings of multiple jobholders exceed the earnings of those doing farm work only (Table 5.6). On this basis, it is clear that those who do diversify by holding farm and nonfarm jobs profit from diversification. However, the improvement, once again, is significantly greater among those with primarily nonfarm employment than among those going from the farm to the nonfarm market, as a comparision of columns 10 to 6 with columns 5 and 9 in Table 5.6 will reveal.

Cross-sectional Earnings Analyses

The impact of off-farm employment on group earnings of hired farm workers can be more clearly understood in the context of an earnings function. What is desired is to obtain an estimate of the contribution of off-farm employment to group earnings in the presence of controls for socio-demographic and socioeconomic variables. A variant of the human capital earnings function was estimated with the 1975 *Hired Farm Working Force* micro data file:

$$\begin{aligned}\ln(\text{earn}) = {} & b_0 + b_1(\text{schooling}) + b_2(\text{age}) + b_3(\text{age}^2) \\ & + \sum_{i=1}^{2} b_{4i}(\text{head of household status})_i \\ & + \sum_{j=1}^{4} b_{5j}(\text{migratory status})_j \\ & + \sum_{k=1}^{8} b_{6k}(\text{employment status})_k \\ & + \sum_{\ell=1}^{4} b_{7\ell}(\text{region})_\ell \\ & + \sum_{m=1}^{3} b_{8m}(\text{race})_m + \sum_{n=1}^{2} b_{9n}(\text{sex})_n \\ & + b_{10}\ln(\text{days}) + e \qquad (5.1)\end{aligned}$$

Table 5.6. Average yearly earnings of hired farm workers, by chief employment status, 1963-1976 (dollars)

	Workers doing farm work only				Workers doing farm and nonfarm work combined							
					Farm days				Nonfarm days			
Year	Farm work only (1)	Primarily own farm (2)	Primarily house-wife (3)	Primarily attending school (4)	Primarily farm work (5)	Primarily nonfarm work (6)	Primarily house-wife (7)	Primarily attending school (8)	Primarily farm work (9)	Primarily nonfarm work (10)	Primarily house-wife (11)	Primarily attending school (12)
1963	1606	238	118	114	1297	176	145	103	433	2495	204	250
1964	1818	267	211	195	1341	266	152	146	525	2374	271	317
1965	2089	365	206	172	1250	255	177	165	559	2574	285	253
1966	2403	871	284	219	1618	347	219	222	596	2953	274	378
1967	2632	927	338	327	1808	380	224	219	669	3170	448	340
1968	2755	795	277	326	1931	396	240	234	769	3368	295	352
1969	2840	1456	257	302	1939	433	225	228	850	3846	547	408
1970	2850	948	321	345	2562	388	239	236	1168	3996	544	429
1971	3156	1548	324	293	2335	421	225	201	1107	3637	457	593
1972	3440	1854	388	362	2681	443	190	308	1122	4089	443	508
1973	4052	1767	370	461	2789	552	341	330	1297	4649	514	631
1974	4374	1104	493	502	2852	463	364	473	1149	4889	879	717
1975	4625	1964	539	531	2864	500	457	421	1308	5157	893	780
1976	5054	1972	588	644	3713	623	370	528	1014	5582	995	847
Sample Period (1963-1976):												
Mean	3121	1151	337	321	2213	403	233	272	897	3770	503	486
Coefficient of Variation	.340	.539	.391	.534	.331	.294	.427	.460	.339	.271	.504	.404

Source: USDA, ESCS, The Hired Farm Working Force, various annual issues.

Schooling, labor market experience (proxied by age and age^2), and migratory status are taken to represent human capital variables. Schooling is indexed by the number of years an individual attended school. The reference group for the head of household status is nonhead of household. Migratory status is disaggregated into four categories: those who migrated within the county of home base, within the home base, and outside of the home base state. Those not migrating serve as the reference group. The employment status variables represent the eight categories described above with "other" as the omitted category. The presence of the employment status variables in the equation is believed to improve the precision of the coefficient estimates for the human capital variables. It also speaks to the issue of relative rate of return to earnings of persons across the several employment status categories.

Region is disaggregated into the four Bureau of the Census regions: Northeast, North Central, West, and South. These variables are included to control for differences in labor market characteristics; the Northeast census region serves as the reference category. The excluded race and sex groups are, respectively, white and female, and the coefficients of the included dummy racial variables partially measure the impact on earnings of labor market discrimination. Finally, to further control for variation in employment duration together with employment status, the natural log of the number of farm and nonfarm days of employment is included. The employment status variables, together with the natural log of the number of days worked, are assumed to capture employment variation across the sample. Employment status also represents an amalgam of other influences on earnings. First, as may be observed from Table 5.5, daily wage rates vary systematically with employment status. Further, because of the association of employment status with the type of work performed in the hired farm worker market and in the nonfarm sector, these variables also reflect cross-sectional differences in job experience. Finally, the distribution of employment status reflects the influence sex and age may have on the labor market assignment to such employment categories. Thus, it should be noted that part of the returns to human capital investment as well as to employment status are due to employment duration. Controlling for duration thus reduces the sizes of the coefficients of the human capital and status variables.

This equation was estimated with ordinary least squares methods. Additionally, to focus on two groups of persons who do hired farm work--those having a primary dependence on farm work and those primarily in nonfarm work--separate equations were also estimated with the appropriate smaller samples. The sample of those having a primary dependence on farm work excludes all seasonal farm workers as previously defined--that is, as the group of housewives, students, all, disabled, and retired workers and those primarily in nonfarm work. Equation 5.12 (Table 5.7) allows for variation among four chief employment categories: farm work only, primarily farm work, primarily own farm, and primarily unemployed. The primarily farm work category serves as the reference group. The results of the estimated equations appear in Table 5.7. Sample means and sample standard deviations of all variables for all sample groups appear in Table 5.8.

Estimated equation 5.11 confirms what was earlier uncovered with cross-tabulations. The impact on group earnings of the category primarily nonfarm work exceeds the impact on group earnings of the category primarily farm work after controlling for several socioeconomic and socio-demographic influences. Among the group of workers with primary dependence on farm work (5.12), the earnings of those combining farm and nonfarm work are not significantly larger than the earnings of the workers specializing in farm work.

Evident from (5.13) is the relative difference made in the returns to schooling and experience from nonfarm employment. It is also to be noted that ethnic minority workers are not at a relative earnings disadvantage in this group, given that the coefficient

Table 5.7. Earnings equations, hired farm workers (absolute values of t ratios in parentheses)

Dependent variable = earnings in 1975[a]

Equation / Variable	(5.11) All hired farm workers		(5.12) Hired farm workers with primary dependence on farm work		(5.13) Hired farm workers with primary dependence on nonfarm work	
Schooling	0.037	(5.94)	0.016	(1.98)	0.028	(2.20)
Age	0.055	(7.84)	0.030	(3.52)	0.095	(5.21)
Age^2	-0.001	(7.70)	-0.0004	(3.89)	-0.002	(4.63)
Head of household	0.076	(1.67)	0.112	(2.15)	0.049	(0.057)
Nonhead of household	c		c		c	
Migrated						
within home county	-0.230	(1.98)	-0.268	(2.01)	-0.344	(1.41)
within home state	0.147	(1.60)	0.138	(1.18)	0.138	(0.85)
outside home state	0.182	(2.24)	0.154	(1.41)	0.153	(0.75)
Did not migrate	c		c		c	
Farm work only	0.207	(2.67)	0.006	(0.002)	d	
Primarily farm work	0.149	(0.860)	c		d	
Primarily own farm	0.204	(1.65)	0.152	(1.04)	d	
Primarily nonfarm work	0.348	(4.22)	d		d	
Primarily unemployed	-0.131	(0.969)	-0.196	(1.27)	d	
Primarily attending school	-0.123	(1.60)	d		d	
Primarily housewife	-0.110	(1.16)	d		d	
Other employment status category	c		d		d	
North central	0.066	(1.09)	0.132	(1.40)	-0.016	(0.118)
South	-0.018	(0.298)	0.019	(0.043)	-0.217	(1.73)
West	0.007	(1.25)	0.256	(2.83)	0.021	(0.158)
Northeast	c		c		c	
Black	0.031	(0.662)	0.041	(0.359)	-0.005	(0.045)
Hispanic	0.237	(4.05)	0.019	(0.816)	-0.037	(0.275)
White	c		c		c	
Male	0.218	(4.65)	-0.684	(0.594)	0.291	(2.89)
Female	c		c		c	
Days worked[b]	0.970	(68.5)	1.013	(40.6)	1.013	(22.5)
(Constant)	1.113		2.000		0.748	
R^2	0.880		0.887		0.752	
F	552.505		187.204		52.085	
SE	0.611		0.458		0.528	
n	1598		465		256	

[a]Natural log of total farm and off-farm earnings.
[b]Natural log of total farm and off-farm days of employment.
[c]Omitted dummy category; used as the reference group.
[d]Omitted dummy category; not part of the sample.

estimates related to the racial dummy variables fail to achieve statistical significance. On the other hand, blacks and Hispanics represent 10% and 9%, respectively, of all workers in this group while representing 17.5% and 16.8%, respectively, of all workers in the primary dependence on agriculture group. The earnings difficulties confronting minority groups appear to be derived from their relative under-representation in nonfarm employment rather than from lack of earnings parity with whites in nonfarm work.

The Determinants of Nonfarm Employment Selectivity

The results of the earnings analyses suggest that a selective process is at work determining who, out of a pool of persons having a nexus with the hired farm

Table 5.8. Sample mean and standard deviation values of variables used in regression equations (standard deviations in parentheses)

Variable	All hired farm workers		Hired farm workers with primary dependence on farm work		Hired farm workers with primary dependence on nonfarm work	
Earnings (Farm and nonfarm)	$897.85	(5.81)	$2625.70	(3.60)	$3944.98	(2.80
Schooling (years attended)	11	(3.21)	10	(3.78)	12	(3.27
Age	28	(16.10)	37	(15.89)	30	(11.54
North central (%)	0.25	(0.43)	0.18	(0.39)	0.27	(0.44
South (%)	0.42	(0.49)	0.43	(0.49)	0.42	(0.49
West (%)	0.25	(0.43)	0.31	(0.46)	0.23	(0.42
Days worked (farm and nonfarm)	67	(4.18)	150	(3.10)	187	(2.18
Head of household (%)	0.32	(0.47)	0.60	(0.49)	0.59	(0.49
Male (%)	0.77	(0.42)	0.92	(0.26)	0.84	(0.37
Migrated						
within home county (%)	0.02	(0.14)	0.03	(0.17)	0.02	(0.14
within home state (%)	0.03	(0.17)	0.04	(0.19)	0.05	(0.21
outside home state (%)	0.04	(0.20)	0.04	(0.19)	0.03	(0.17
Hispanic (%)	0.11	(0.31)	0.17	(0.37)	0.09	(0.29
Black (%)	0.14	(0.35)	0.17	(0.37)	0.10	(0.30
Farm work only (%)	0.24	(0.43)	0.83	(0.37)	[a]	
Primarily own farm (%)	0.02	(0.15)	0.07	(0.26)	[a]	
Primarily farm work (%)	0.01	(0.09)	0.03	(0.17)	[a]	
Primarily nonfarm work (%)	0.16	(0.37)	[a]		[a]	
Primarily unemployed (%)	0.02	(0.13)	0.06	(0.23)	[a]	
Primarily attending school (%)	0.40	(0.49)	[a]		[a]	
Primarily housewife (%)	0.09	(0.28)	[a]		[a]	
n	1598		465		256	

Source: USDA, ESCS, Hired Farm Working Force, 1975 microdata file.
[a]Category not part of the sample.

worker market, will do nonfarm work. The socio-economic and socio-demographic determinants of that selective process can be understood by estimating the following equation:

$$Pr(NFW) = b_0 + b_1(\text{schooling}) + b_2(\text{grade completed}) + b_3(\text{age}) + \sum_{i=1}^{3} b_{4i}(\text{race})_i + \sum_{j=1}^{2} b_{5j}(\text{sex})_j + \sum_{k=1}^{2} b_{6k}(\text{migratory status})_k$$

$$+ \sum_{\ell=1}^{4} b_{7\ell}(\text{region})_{\ell}$$

$$+ \sum_{m=1}^{2} b_{8m}(\text{head of household})_{m}$$

$$+ b_{9}(\text{daily off-farm wage rate}) + e \qquad (5.2)$$

where the dependent variable is binary and has the value of one if a person in the 1975 *Hired Farm Working Force* micro data file worked at least one day in a nonfarm job and zero if the person did not engage in nonfarm work. The equation was estimated by probit methods, a nonlinear maximum likelihood technique. The methods of probit analysis are described in: Finney (1971), Goldberger (1964), Witherington and Willis (1978), Hill and Lau (1973), Hanushek and Jackson (1977), and T. C. Lee (1970). The estimated equation appears in Table 5.9.

The estimates of the probit coefficients and the asymptotic values of the *t* ratios suggest that the human capital variables of schooling and grade completed exercise statistically significant influences on the probability of off-farm work. (While a person may have enrolled for X years of schooling, the person may not have completed the X years. Thus the distinction between years attended and grade completed is important, particularly in the threshold years separating elementary and junior high school and at the end of 12 years of schooling.) Of special interest is the information appearing in column 3, wherein is reported the incremental impact on the probability of nonfarm employment evaluated at the sample mean following a unit change in the respective independent variable. Each additional year of schooling raises the probability of off-farm work by nearly 2%. Completing a year of schooling raises the probability by over 9%. These findings coincide with those of Huffman (1977b), utilizing a sample of farm operators. The finding that the migratory status variable fails

Table 5.9. The determinants of the probability of nonfarm employment (absolute asymptotic values of $\underline{t}$ appear in parentheses)

Dependent variable = 1 if hired farm worker did nonfarm work in 1975
= 0 if hired farm worker did farm work only in 1975

(1) Variable	(2) Coefficient B		(3)[b] $\partial Prob/\partial X_K = f(\bar{X}\hat{B})\hat{B}_K$
Schooling	0.0512	(2.76)	0.0190
Grade completed	0.2485	(3.02)	0.0922
Age	-0.0448	(4.03)	-0.0166
North central	0.1959	(1.50)	0.0727
South	0.0809	(0.64)	0.0300
West	-0.0334	(0.26)	-0.0124
Northeast	a		a
Head	0.2254	(2.16)	0.0837
Nonhead	a		a
Male	-0.4158	(3.79)	-0.1543
Female	a		a
Migrated	-0.0520	(0.42)	-0.0193
Did not migrate	a		a
Black	-0.3542	(3.11)	-0.1315
Hispanic	-0.3223	(2.57)	-0.1196
White	a		a
Daily off-farm wage rate[c]	0.5299	(3.11)	0.1967
(Constant)	-1.1370		
Log of the likelihood function =	-974.370		
n (Dependent var = 1) 639			
n (Dependent var = 0) 959			

[a]Omitted category: used as reference group.
[b]$\bar{X}\hat{B} = -0.3801$; $f(\bar{X}\hat{B}) \cong 0.37119$.
[c]Natural log; computed using wage equation appearing in Table 5.10.

to achieve statistical significance at conventional levels is interesting in light of the argument that migratory status promotes subcultural traits among migratory workers. Such traits are alleged to make migrants undesirable for all but menial harvest jobs. The present results do not support this argument. Migrants appear to be no worse off than nonmigrants in the selectivity process.

Being Hispanic or black reduces the chance of nonfarm employment by 11.96% and 13.15% respectively. Nonfarm employment is selective of the younger worker although the marginal impact on the probability about the sample mean due to the age variable is only 1.67%. The census regions, as measures of labor market differences, do not have statistically significant influences on off-farm employment. This is indeed surprising given that it is customarily argued that the lack of economic diversification and development in the South results in the underproduction of employment opportunities. It should be pointed out that as proxies for differential labor market characteristics, census regions are overly gross representations. A finer geographical disaggregation could produce different results.

Being a male worker reduces the probability of nonfarm employment by a factor of 15.43% around the sample mean. This result may well support the argument that many seasonal nonfarm jobs are filled by females having a strong seasonal work experience in farm work. Females are seen as allocating their time among household duties, seasonal farm jobs, and seasonal nonfarm employment. Also relevant here is the argument proposed by King (1978) in a study of the labor force participation of females. The study focuses on the influence of one demand-related variable on employment. He suggests that geographical areas having a large concentration of service sector jobs are also areas where the labor force participation of females is relatively large. He argues that the service sector and similar industries are able to offer flexible working hour schedules that are attractive to females who must accommodate household duties in their working life routine.

Finally, the influence of off-farm earnings on the probability of off-farm employment is significantly positive. The off-farm wage rate was created in a two step procedure. The sample of those employed in off-farm work in 1975 was utilized to estimate the coefficients of the daily wage equation reported in Table 5.10. In the second step, the equation was utilized to impute an off-farm wage rate to the total sample by using the reported individual values of the relevant socioeconomic and socio-demographic characteristics and the estimated coefficients. The results of the probit estimation show that the marginal impact on the probability of off-farm employment is 19.67%.

Table 5.10. Wage equation, all persons combining farm and off-farm work

Dependent variable = daily off-farm wage rate in 1975[a]

Variable	Coefficient estimate	Absolute value of t ratio
Schooling	0.006	5.07
Age	0.142	11.1
Age^2	-0.001	9.83
Head of household	0.114	1.51
Nonhead of household	b	b
Migrated	0.005	0.045
Do not migrate	b	b
North central	-0.136	1.26
South	-0.108	1.01
West	-0.028	0.251
Northeast	b	b
Black	-0.038	0.341
Hispanic	0.62	0.503
White	b	b
Male	0.470	6.29
Female	b	b
(Constant)	-0.796	
R^2	0.351	
F	30.9	
SE	0.723	
n	639	

[a]Natural log of ratio total off-farm earnings divided by total off-farm days worked.

[b]Omitted dummy category: used as the reference group.

CONCLUSIONS AND RECOMMENDATIONS

The results of this investigation suggest that off-farm employment is important to those in the hired farm worker market as a means of overcoming the conditions created by underemployment and unstable incomes. Occupational diversification is likewise important to those having a primary attachment to off-farm work. Without the ability to combine farm with off-farm employment, these parts of the U.S. labor force would find greater economic disadvantage than is presently the case.

Public policy can facilitate the process of off-farm employment by attempting to work through the variables that are most influential in increasing the probability of off-farm employment. On the supply side, the ability to combine farm and nonfarm employment has been found to be dependent upon age, sex, race, schooling, and completion of the year of schooling. Highly significant also in inducing off-farm employment is the expected return from off-farm employment, presumably because extended job search costs in nonfarm markets are offset. Moreover, the higher is the return from off-farm employment, the higher will be the opportunity cost of engaging in farm work only. Programs that act upon these variables will undoubtedly be successful in terms of minimizing underemployment and the instability of incomes in rural areas. Required of the policy makers above all is the perspective that the aim of public policy should not be limited to the facilitation of complete occupational mobility out of farm work, which I suspect has been the traditional aim in the fashioning of rural employment and training programs. Among those presently in hired farm work, there are those who prefer hired farm work. The policy perspective should, accordingly, be broadened to include the view that many of those in hired farm work can be aided by increasing their productivity in both farm and nonfarm employment situations.

Programs aimed at increasing schooling levels and at curbing attrition will undoubtedly be important in raising a young person's chance of minimizing the effects of a lifetime of unstable employment. In this regard, it should be recognized that some hired farm working youth, such as members of migrant worker families, may need special attention given through the CETA Section 303 Farmworker Youth Program. On the other hand, for the major portion of farm working youth, programs structured along the lines of the Youth Employment and Demonstration Projects (YEDP) are what is required. The success of the programs sponsored through YEDP should be gauged not only against the criterion of the number of permanent nonfarm placements made but also in terms of the number of high school diplomas awarded, the skills imparted to operate the complex machinery required in today's farm jobs, and the skills imparted to enable the person to hold nonfarm jobs.

Protection under the Fair Labor Standards Act on a parity with nonfarm workers is critical, along with programs aimed at raising the productivity of all workers in all jobs to minimum wage standards. The promotion of such programs will aid those whose primary employment is in nonfarm jobs but who currently do some farm work. Increased productivity may reduce their need to engage in such multiple-job holding. Persons whose primary employment is in agriculture but who currently do some nonfarm work as well will be helped in the same way. And if nonfarm employment remains a necessity for some farm workers, the rewards of an extended job search in nonfarm labor markets will be greater.

Programs that promote equal employment opportunity for racial minority workers are also important in enabling these traditionally excluded groups to participate in nonfarm employment. The mechanisms for outreach, job development, counseling, job referral, referral to supportive services, and job placements have been improved in the reforms of the U.S. Job Service. The continued reliance on these mechanisms will surely result in less underemployment and greater stability in incomes among minority workers. Particularly important is the outreach function as a means of overcoming the attitude among minority workers that they will not be given consideration by the Job Service except for the most menial work available. The provision of supportive services, such as child care for working mothers, is important in raising the proportion of hired farm workers holding nonfarm employment, since the probability of nonfarm employment is highest among females.

Two unanswered questions remain. It is not known whether off-farm employment is continuous in the longitudinal sense. First, it would be useful to know for the purposes of public policy programming whether a person primarily in farm work is able to obtain nonfarm employment on a continual or perpetual basis. Second, because females have a higher probability than do males of combining farm and off-farm employment, it would be useful to know more about the vector of off-farm jobs available to persons having a primary nexus with the hired farm worker market, as well as about the vector of farm jobs available to those having a primary nexus with the off-farm work market. Future research should address these two issues.

Discussion

ROBERT COLTRANE

Matta presents an interesting evaluation of the importance of nonfarm employment for hired farm workers. His review of literature reminds us that low returns to labor resources in agriculture, and particularly to hired farm labor, result in a significant income disparity between farm and nonfarm employment. The literature also suggests that the difference in income can be reduced by farm workers combining farm work with nonfarm employment. The major reasons used to explain why the income disparity declines when workers combine farm work with nonfarm work are familiar ones. Total income tends to increase due to the higher wages earned in nonfarm employment and because the combination of farm and nonfarm work provides fuller employment for workers. However, the total income of farm workers remains among the lowest of all occupational groups.

Matta recognizes the importance of the interaction between farm and nonfarm markets, but he argues that the form of the interaction is more important for public policy purposes than the degree of interaction. Specifically, he argues that it is important, for policy purposes, to be able to distinguish numerically between primarily nonfarm workers who occasionally take farm employment and primarily farm workers who do some nonfarm work. The significance of this for policy is not entirely clear to me, however.

The results of the analysis show that annually the number of primarily nonfarm workers who take farm jobs is nearly three times as large as the number of primarily farm workers who take nonfarm jobs. The income benefit of the nonfarm work is significant. The annual earnings of the predominantly nonfarm worker group are about 1.3 times the annual earnings of the predominantly hired farm worker group. Persons who primarily do nonfarm work earn daily wages for nonfarm work that are about 1.3 times the nonfarm wages earned by the primarily farm worker group, but the daily farm earnings are about the same for both groups.

The analysis suggests that the higher nonfarm earnings for the primarily nonfarm worker group are associated with a more favorable nonfarm occupational structure compared with the nonfarm occupational structure of the primarily farm worker group. That is, relatively more of the primarily nonfarm workers have higher wage jobs compared to the primarily farm worker group.

There are some conceptual problems with the occupational data used in the analysis, but even so the data are probably suggestive of the general differences in nonfarm occupational structure between the two groups of workers. The data source is USDA's *The Hired Farm Working Force*. The data reflect nonfarm employment only during the week prior to the time of the survey. Persons not working during that week but who worked at some other time during the calendar year were not assigned to an occupational group because occupational data were not collected for these persons. This deficiency was corrected in the 1979 survey of hired farm workers. Occupational data were collected for all workers who had nonfarm employment at any time in 1979. These new data should contribute to a better understanding of the composition of farm workers' nonfarm employment.

The results are suggestive and contribute to a better understanding of the duration and type of nonfarm work performed by hired farm workers. However, I must confess that I did not find the answer to a basic question in this review. Matta introduced his analysis by saying that we need to distinguish numerically between two types of multiple job holders for policy purposes. But why we need to make this distinction is not clear. Is it because the research was expected to suggest that changes need to be made in policy, programs, and regulations affecting the employment, working conditions, wages and salaries, and benefits of the two groups of farm workers? If so, what are the changes? Also, how do the results of the analysis relate to the recommendations?

Having raised these questions, let me say that I see little reason to argue with his recommendations, except that they do not say much about the nonfarm labor market. Much more could have been said about the need for research on the impact of the relatively high rates of nonfarm employment growth in many rural areas in the 1970s on the supply of farm labor. Has nonfarm employment growth resulted in local farm labor shortages? If so, how has this affected agriculture in those areas?

Nevertheless, Matta's recommendations require serious consideration by the research community and policymakers. For example, a rigorous assessment of the provisions that exclude farm workers from coverage in the Fair Labor Standards Act is long overdue. We should not continue to accept the exclusion of farm workers from minimum wage coverage because they happen to work on small farms, or on farms employing small amounts of labor, unless it can be demonstrated that the exclusion is necessary and equitable. Similarly, those regulations excluding farm workers from social security and other programs should be assessed.

It is not enough to simply demonstrate that current policy on minimum wage, social security, or any other aspect of employment or agricultural policies contribute to the inefficient use of resources or to inequity in income or employment opportunities among workers. Policymakers are often reluctant to alter policies unless they are provided estimates of the impacts of proposed changes. It is important to determine how increased coverage, in the case of the minimum wage, would affect the number of farm workers employed, duration of employment, earnings of workers, and income of small farm operators. Recommendations regarding policy changes must be specific and the effects of the changes must be estimated and evaluated if research is to have the desired impact on policy.

6

Nonimmigrant Aliens in American Agriculture

PHILIP L. MARTIN and DAVID S. NORTH

A work force is not selected to perform a particular assignment in the economy simply because it is available, has the needed skills, and will work for the wages offered. Similarly, the impact of a particular work force on a particular labor market goes beyond that which can be weighed by simply studying the supply and the demand for labor. Laws, customs, the expectations of workers and employers, and a host of cultural, political, and historical factors (including accidents) all play a role in the process. This is particularly true when one examines the role of nonimmigrant workers in American agriculture.

The discussion that follows is divided into two segments. North is responsible for an overview of the origins and the nature of the rural H-2 program and its now-deceased big brother, the Bracero Program; the second, by Martin, is an analysis of the impact on the labor market of these programs.

AN OVERVIEW OF THE BRACERO AND RURAL H-2 PROGRAMS

The Bracero Program

The Bracero Program, which Congress terminated on December 31, 1964, was the very essence of an employer-oriented, nonimmigrant worker program.[1] Memories dim, and there is now a younger generation of policymakers with little firsthand knowledge of that program. A brief look backward is in order.

The U.S.-Mexico border, though imposed by the United States on Mexico in the mid-19th century, was not a barrier to Mexican nationals seeking work in the United States until the midtwenties of this century. It was then that the U.S. Border Patrol was founded and persons crossing the border first had to present documentation at the ports of entry. Controls were lax, however, as World War II loomed, and undocumented Mexican farm workers helped harvest the crops throughout the Southwest.

The arrival of World War II changed the labor market drastically--in a few short years America moved from the loosest labor market in its history to the tightest.

Ernesto Galarza, in his elegant and understated *Merchants of Labor*, wrote that as World War II began, agricultural employers "recognized that their unmethodical labor pool would be seriously deranged by the war . . . the wetback was not an unmixed good. His shortcomings were obvious. One of the most serious was that it was impossible to maintain a uniform wage level for the illegals. . . ." (p. 58). (In other words, they might seek higher wages in the war economy.)

The growers proceeded to press the U.S. government to sign a bilateral agreement with Mexico, a wartime emergency measure, for the recruitment of Mexican nationals to work on U.S. farms and ranches. That agreement, signed in 1942, set a generalized pattern for rural nonimmigrant worker programs which largely persists to this day: (1) male workers were admitted, but their family members were not; (2) male workers were admitted temporarily, with the length of their stay dependent on the needs of the employers; (3) the work was hard and unattractive; (4) usually minimal government controls of wages and working conditions were imposed; (5) aliens who displeased their employers could be deported; and (6) aliens who pleased their employers could be invited back as "specials."

Braceros were brought into the United States to

work only as farm workers. Although they eventually spread into more than half of the states, they were concentrated in the West and, in most years, primarily in California. Texas was a major user state, as were the states in the Pacific Northwest.

The utilization of braceros generally declined in the first few years after World War II but picked up again in 1949 and then mushroomed during the Korean War. The number of admissions reached a plateau of more than 400,000 in the period 1956 through 1959 (see Table 6.1). The principal activities of the braceros were the hand harvest of fruits and vegetables, preharvest and harvest activities in cotton (e.g., chopping and picking), and preharvest work in sugar beets.

Table 6.1. Mexican contract workers (braceros) admitted for temporary work in U.S. agriculture, 1942-1964

Calendar year	Number admitted
1942	4,203
1943	52,098
1944	62,170
1945	49,454
1946	32,043
1947	19,632
1948	35,345
1949	107,000
1950	67,500
1951	192,000
1952	197,100
1953	201,380
1954	309,033
1955	398,650
1956	445,197
1957	436,049
1958	432,857
1959	437,643
1960	315,846
1961	291,420
1962	194,978
1963	186,865
1964	177,736

Source: Leo Grebler, Joan W. Moore, and Ralph C. Guzman, The Mexican-American People: The Nation's Second Minority (New York: Free Press, 1971), p. 68.

Once the bracero had been preselected by his own government (a process often scarred by corruption) and then hired by the U.S. employer, he was transported to the U.S. job site and was committed by the program to that employer. He could neither change jobs nor bargain for terms and conditions of employment. He either had to accept what was offered to him or face an involuntary trip back to Mexico. (Many chose to drop out of legal status; the President's Commission on Migratory Labor reported that the number doing so ranged from 4% to 50%, depending on the attractiveness of the employer. A couple of studies indicated that about 20% of the braceros simply walked off their jobs and into illegal status [President's Commission on Migratory Labor, p. 52].)

One way that a bracero could assure himself of continued work in the United States would be to impress the employer so thoroughly that the grower would ask for him by name the next season. Securing this status as a "special," needless to say, was extremely important to the worker and had a significant impact on his working behavior.

The impact of braceros on the labor market was a subject of widespread debate in the 1950s and 1960s, much like the current debate on the impact of illegal immigrants. The supporters of the program claimed that there was no impact on U.S. workers because they simply would not do the work that the braceros did. The opponents argued that displacement of indigenous workers did take place, as did depression of wages for farm workers.

The president's commission supported the latter point of view by citing the patterns of bracero utilization and cotton picking wages in the periods 1940-45 and 1947-50. The commission stated:

> Taking the two principal states in which the wartime and postwar Mexican contract programs were centered, California and Texas, the relations between wage changes and the presence of alien laborers in large numbers can be summarized as follows:

> **Wartime Program:**
> California got 63 percent of the contract Mexicans (1945); raised its cotton wages 136 percent [apparently from the 1949 level]. Texas got no contract Mexicans; raised its cotton wages 236 percent.
> **Postwar Program:**
> California got eight percent of the contract Mexicans (1949); raised its cotton wages 15 percent. Texas got 46 percent of the contract Mexicans (1949); lowered its cotton wages 11 percent. (p. 58)

See also Galarza (Chaps. 14 and 15) in which he documents (exhaustively) the same point for a multitude of crops, states, and years.

The Bracero Program attracted a growing number of critics, particularly in the liberal, labor, church, and Chicano communities. As a result, Congress made the law tighter and successive secretaries of labor (Republican Mitchell and Democrats Goldberg and Wirtz) wrote stricter regulations and enforced them with increasing vigor. By the early sixties the program was less attractive to growers than it had been in the past. Utilization was down, and therefore political support decreased as well. Further, the midsixties were the years of the civil rights movement, the War on Poverty, and heavy Democratic majorities in both the Electoral College (1964) and in the Congress (particularly 1965-67).

But the inherent difficulties of the program and the temper of the times might not have been sufficient to end the Bracero Program, or to end it so quickly, had it not been for two other totally unrelated factors: the development of the cotton and tomato harvesters, and the tactical posture of the bracero advocates in Congress.

The harvesters made the braceros extraneous in two of the principal bracero-using crops--Texas cotton and California cannery tomatoes--further diluting the support for the program. Meanwhile, activity in the Congress was influenced by the temporary character of the wartime statute authorizing the program (Public Law 78). Like all temporary legislation, it had an expiration date. This put the bracero supporters in the continuing, awkward posture of having to secure a new majority every couple of years to keep the program alive. Usually, the monkey is on the back of reformers to build the majority to get their way--in this situation, roles were reversed. Finally, the supporters of the Bracero Program promised their colleagues in the House that if they could just have one more year (1964), they would allow the program to die. They secured the year, kept their promise, and the program died.

The H-2 Program

The purpose of the H-2 program has been debated endlessly. Its supporters say that it is designed to permit the admission of foreign workers when employers face "labor shortages." Its detractors, stressing the negative language of the statute, say that it is designed to bar the admission of nonimmigrant workers except under unusual circumstances, when such admissions would not have an adverse impact on the resident labor force. The relevant language of the Immigration and Nationality Act, which has been in place since 1952, follows:

Immigration and Nationality Act, Section 101
(a) As used in this Act--
(15) The term "immigrant" means every alien except an alien who is within one of the following classes of nonimmigrant aliens--
(H) an alien having a residence in a foreign country which he has no intention of abandoning . . .
(ii) who is coming temporarily to the United States to perform other temporary services or labor, if unemployed persons capable of performing such services or labor cannot be found in this country.
(8 U.S.C. Sec. 1101[a] [15] [H] [ii])

Immigration and Nationality Act, Section 214.

(c) The question of importing any alien as a nonimmigrant under section 101(a) (15) (H) in any specific case or specific cases shall be determined by the Attorney General, after consultation with appropriate agencies of the Government, upon petition of the importing employer. . . .

(8 U.S.C. Sec. 1184)

Since the Department of Justice recognizes that the USDL has a better grasp of the labor market, it has issued regulations specifying that the requisite "consultation" be shown in the form of a certification from the secretary of labor stating that qualified persons are not available in this country and that the employment of the requested alien or aliens will not adversely affect the wages and working conditions of resident workers similarly employed (8 C.F.R. Sec. 214.2 [h] [3]).

The final power to determine whether or not H-2 workers can be admitted to the nation thus rests with the Department of Justice; about once every administration the attorney general overrules the secretary of labor on the subject. Despite these occasional eruptions and a flurry of court decisions in recent years (generally supporting employer positions), the USDL has the responsibility of making day-to-day decisions on certifying H-2 workers.

The total number of H-2 admissions (both farm and nonfarm) is not particularly large, as Reubens pointed out in his report to the National Commission for Employment Policy, and these totals have been declining in recent years. From a high of 70,000 in 1970 they dropped to a 37,000-41,000 plateau in the period 1971 through 1975, drifting down to 30,000 in 1976, 28,000 in 1977, and to 23,000 in 1978 (U.S. Department of Justice, *INS Annual Report*, Table 16A). Critics of the program tend to disregard its size and focus on what they contend are its severe impacts on micro labor markets.

It should be noted that during the War East Coast growers, faced with the same tightening of the labor market that led to the Bracero Program in the West, opted to bring in "offshore" workers from the British Caribbean Islands. Transportation costs were less than those associated with Mexican nationals, and the workers spoke English. The East Coast farm labor program, at first administered through the ninth proviso of Sec. 3 of the Immigration Act of 1917, later became written into the permanent immigration legislation cited earlier. (The ninth proviso authorized a waiver of exclusion to inadmissible aliens seeking temporary admission, with one category enumerated as "contract laborers.") As a result, the East Coast growers had no need to renew *their* labor legislation annually, and they argued to the USDL in 1965 that *their* program had not been repealed by the Congress. Despite this argument, the leadership of the department decided, following the termination of the Bracero Program and the overwhelming reelection of Lyndon B. Johnson, that foreign farm workers were not generally needed in the United States (cane cutters in Florida being an exception) and that their utilization should be cut back or ended. Thus 1965 became a year of decision for agricultural utilization of H-2s, and generally the patterns of utilization or nonutilization set that year have persisted. (For more on alien farm workers in 1965, see USDL, *Year of Transition*.)

There are four major rural industries in the lower 48 states and several minor ones employing H-2 workers. The most recent data (unpublished certification data, Division of Labor Certification, USDL) for the total number of workers employed is approximately as follows:

Activity	Location	Workers	Period
Sugarcane	Florida	8,700	1978-79 season
Apples	Eastern States	6,600	1979
Woods	Maine	900	1979
Sheep	Western States	700-900	1978

In addition, Mexican H-2s have been admitted to harvest row crops along the Rio Grande in Presidio, Texas in two of the last three years, and smaller groups of Mexican nationals have been admitted to work in other crops in Virginia, Arizona, and Colorado (in the fall of 1979). Descriptions of each of the four major groupings of activities follow.

Sugarcane. Sugarcane is grown in a number of American jurisdictions, but only in Florida is it harvested by hand. It is also grown in Hawaii, California, Texas, Louisiana, and Puerto Rico, and formerly was grown in the Virgin Islands. Sugarcane is a perennial, tall (12-14 feet) grass that is cut annually. Generally it is harvested by machine, but this option is avoided in Florida, at least partially because of the nature of the soil. Sugarcane in Florida is grown in the muck (peat) lands on the southern shore of Lake Okeechobee. This is the ultrarich soil that remained after the swamps of the area were drained some 40 years ago. The soil is powdery when dry and quite soft when wet; as a result, the cane tips over and continues to grow in a recumbent position (while cane in the rest of the country stands up straight). The posture of the cane discourages mechanical harvesting, as does the tendency of the harvesters to pull the cane out by the roots when the ground is muddy. With the more precise surgery of Jamaican hand harvesters, the roots are left untouched and the fields can produce cane for four or five years without reseeding.

If Florida sugarcane growers were denied access to H-2 harvesters, growers might mechanize with flotation-tired machines or cane production might shift to Louisiana and Hawaii. If Florida sugar production were halted because access to Jamaican labor were curtailed and if the lost Florida production were replaced with imported sugar, consumer prices for sugar might fall, since the world sugar price is less than the (subsidized) domestic price.

Apples. Apples are grown throughout the northern half of the United States. Most are picked by resident workers, including some illegal residents. But in ten states, running from West Virginia to Maine, Caribbean H-2s have been brought in to harvest part of the crop in recent years. A little less than 30% of the apple crop is grown in the ten states using H-2 workers. Since a substantial percentage of the crop in those states is picked by residents, we estimate that no more than 20-22% of the nation's apples are harvested by H-2s (USDA, *Noncitrus Fruits and Nuts, 1978 Annual Summary: Production, Use, and Value*, p. 8).

Throughout the 1950s and early 1960s the foreign workers came from three locations. Canadians worked in the Plattsburgh area of New York and in several New England states; Bahamians picked the crop in Virginia and West Virginia; and Jamaicans worked in the Hudson Valley of New York and in several New England locations.

In the midsixties the Bahamian government, because of the islands' prosperity, lost interest in the program. At about the same time, conversations with the then-President of the New England Apple Council revealed New England and New York growers had decided that Canadian workers "were getting to be like U.S. workers," so they switched to Jamaicans. Growers in the Virginias did likewise.

Apples are harvested for either processing or for the fresh market. In the latter instance they must be handled more carefully, and typically the piece rate for picking them is a nickel or so a bushel higher than for processing apples. Apple picking is hard work but is more attractive than (and usually better paid than) cutting sugarcane. The weather is pleasant, but picking generally involves working on a ladder and carrying a heavy sack of apples over the shoulder.

An alternative to mechanization in this industry is the introduction of dwarf fruit trees. Since they make ladders extraneous, it is possible for growers to recruit from a much broader population, including women and older people who might not be able to handle the heaviest of the ladders. There is some movement in this direction but replacing orchards is, by definition, a slow process.

Woods Work. The woods work done by foreign workers is now largely confined to Maine, although at one time

Canadian workers entered New York, Vermont, and New Hampshire as well. Further, the part of Maine where they are found has contracted in recent years; it is now generally in a band within 40 or 50 miles of the western border of that state. The workers are French Canadians, and in many cases work for Canada-based firms owned by other French Canadians. In some instances the work to be done is located in areas along the border that can only be reached from roads starting in Canada.

The work involves the felling, cutting, and moving of logs. Like cutting sugarcane, the work is difficult and dangerous, performed far from urban areas, and usually involves barracks living arrangements.

Unlike the sugarcane situation, woods work is heavily mechanized and growing more so, and there is substantial competition between U.S. and Canadian workers for these jobs. New and more elaborate cutting and hauling equipment has been introduced in recent years, and to a major extent the H-2 worker must provide his own tools. This can range from the basic gasoline-powered chain saw to $30,000 log hauling rigs. The compensation arrangements for this work, which revolve around the prevailing piece rates for man and machine, are more complex than in any other H-2 activity.

The number of Canadian woods workers declined in the mid 1970s, stabilizing recently in the 850-950 range. The decline was caused by the twin pressures of mechanization and active U.S. worker interest in this employment.

Sheepherding. Sheepherding is lonesome, isolated work, particularly in the spring, summer, and fall when the sheep are in the high pastures of the American West. The sheepherder stays with the animals, cooks his own meals, and lives in a small trailer if he is lucky or, if not, in a tent. There may be little human contact beyond a delivery every week or so of a fresh batch of food. He protects the sheep from predators, takes care of the sick, and during lambing plays midwife all hours of the day and night.

The sheep raisers of the country have relied on alien workers for many years. They are organized in a powerful lobby, the Western Range Association, which has its members strategically located throughout a number of western states (as the H-2 apple growers have their membership arrayed in the East). The ability of these two fairly slim economic interest groups, range owners and orchardists, to secure the ear of members of the United States Senate is a wonder to behold. For example, Sen. Robert Byrd, majority leader of the Senate, conducted a one-man, one-issue hearing in which the senator gave Assistant Labor Secretary Ernest Green an intense grilling on whether "his" West Virginia apple growers were going to secure their desired Jamaicans. (See "CETA Oversight Hearings" in *Labor Notes*, pp. 4-5.) As a result of this ability, the USDL is perpetually under strong political pressure to satisfy the interests of these two groups of rural employers.

As must be evident by now, the decision-making process regarding the certification of foreign farm workers is complex and often includes interventions of various kinds. Further, the regulatory framework that the department has provided for itself is convoluted at best.

The basic framework of the H-2 decision making process has grown out of the precedents set in the Bracero Program, as well as from the Department of Justice's regulations on the subject. (It should be recalled that there is no statutory role for the USDL in the program.) The Justice Department's regulations, which flow from the statutory language cited earlier, state that alien workers may be admitted when the secretary of labor certifies that "qualified persons in the United States are not available and that the employment of the beneficiary [the nonimmigrant worker] will not adversely affect the wages and working conditions of workers in the United States similarly employed. . . ." (8 C.F.R. 214.2 [h] [3] [i]).

How does one determine the availability of

workers or whether the admission of foreign workers will create an adverse impact on wages and working conditions of domestic workers? Some years ago the USDL began describing a set of conditions deemed sufficient to bring workers to the employers who needed them. If these criteria were met, and an insufficient number of workers appeared, then foreign workers could be brought in without creating an adverse effect. It sounds sensible, at first blush, but it contains a number of hidden assumptions, including the following:

1. The employers will genuinely meet the conditions and that they are genuinely seeking to hire resident workers.
2. The conditions outlined by the department, in terms of wages, housing, travel advances, meal deductions, etc., are appropriate tests of the labor market.
3. It is *not* appropriate for workers to bargain for one more penny per hour (or per work unit, if paid by piece rate) than the wages laid down by the department.
4. Domestic and foreign workers are competing on an even basis, and that there are no other factors (in law, tradition, or grower perceptions) tipping that balance.
5. The whole process will sort itself out with minimal external intervention.

These are, clearly, heroic assumptions.

What the department has done is to create a series of prospective exercises in the subjunctive. In effect it is asking whether, if Grower A follows the department's regulations, he will secure enough workers sufficiently in advance to conduct his harvest without using foreign workers. If the answer is negative, then Grower A will be rewarded for his recruiting failure by receiving the certification of the alien workers (which he probably secretly wanted all along).

This exercise is a *prospective* one, in that the

test of the labor market is made well before the harvest begins. Were it made right into the first few days of the season one might expect somewhat more vigorous recruiting of resident workers by H-2 users than is now visible.

LABOR MARKET IMPACTS

The H-2 Program

The certification procedure used in the H-2 program combines wage and recruitment tests that employers must satisfy before aliens are admitted. The wage test is a USDL attempt to establish a "fair" wage--a wage which will protect "similarly employed" domestic workers from any adverse impacts of H-2 aliens. The recruitment part of the mandated test is a USDL attempt to supplement employer searches with first local and then more distant domestic workers to fill vacancies. As noted, the procedure will work only if: (1) the department sets the "right" wage, (2) domestic workers can be recruited, and (3) employers accept the domestic workers supplied.

Since the tests are subjunctive and because the U.S. government assumes no direct supervisory functions, employers wanting to thwart the system and secure foreigners can do so in several ways. The USDL establishes an *hourly* Adverse Effect Wage Rate (AEWR) in each state (the hourly rate for any year is $[W_{t-1} - W_{t-2}] + W_{t-1})$ from which it receives petitions for H-2 farm workers "to prevent the employment of such aliens from having an adverse effect on the wages of U.S. workers similarly employed" (Table 6.2). (See 42 Fed. Reg. 40192 [1977] cited in U.S. Senate Committee on the Judiciary, *The West Indies [BWI] Temporary Alien Labor Program: 1943-1977*, p. 21.) Most harvest workers are paid piece rate or per unit wages. Some employers dutifully recruit at mandated AEWR but never change their piece rates. So long as employers are assured an excess supply of (domestic and foreign) labor, "insufficiently skilled or motivated" workers

Table 6.2. Adverse effect wages, 1979 (dollars)

State	Hourly rate
Arizona	3.67
Colorado	3.59
Connecticut	2.92
Florida (sugar cane only)	3.79
Maine	3.01
Maryland	3.01
Massachusetts	2.90
New Hampshire	3.15
New York	3.06
Rhode Island	2.90
Texas	3.25
Vermont	3.10
Virginia	2.96
West Virginia	3.10

Source: USDL, unpublished data.

are terminated and only those able to pick fast enough so that their piece rates exceed the AEWR are retained. The result, not surprisingly, is a pool of experienced and skillful aliens able to pick fast enough to earn hourly piece rates well above the AEWR. At some AEWR, even Jamaicans may not pick fast enough at current piece rates to earn the AEWR. Currently, many Jamaicans pick fast enough to earn $6 per hour, while the AEWR is $3 per hour, indicating that it may be some time before the gap is closed. It is not that domestic workers cannot pick apples--the aliens, selected by growers for their apple-picking skills, are better simply because they are selected from a large applicant pool just for their picking skills.

H-2 aliens are preferred for their picking skills not only because they require less supervision than slower pickers.[2] Their superior skills also enable growers to hire smaller crews, and since most growers provide transportation, housing, subsistence, and harvesting equipment, smaller crews lower the employer's "fixed costs" for each worker. More important, payroll taxes for social security and unemployment insurance drive a wedge between the costs of domestic workers and aliens that favors the latter. This payroll tax wedge can be substantial--up to 10%

for just two programs with mandated domestic worker coverage and H-2 exemptions. Payroll taxes are collected only on an employee's base wage; very few farm workers and virtually no seasonal farm workers earn more than the base wage. Exemptions from mandated programs and the lower expectations of H-2 workers for other fringe benefits make aliens cheaper than domestic workers even if hourly wages are equal.

In October 1979 the USDL offered five alternative methodologies for calculating agricultural AEWRs. The alternatives include:

1. A single national AEWR based on changes in the ratio of the average hourly earnings of agricultural piece rate workers and the hourly earnings of nonfarm production workers. The base wage is presumably the 1979 AEWR. Future AEWRs would be calculated from a regression of historical farm-nonfarm wages. Relating farm and nonfarm wages emphasizes that workers move between farm and nonfarm labor markets.

2. A national AEWR for each crop activity for which aliens are sought. A national crop-based wage recognizes the migratory nature of some crop activities.

3. An adjusted federal minimum wage. The suggested adjustment is the annual percentage change in the national or state USDA farm wage rate for field workers. This AEWR builds on the federal minimum wage--the already stated social "benchmark" wage.

4. A piece rate system designed to assure average work force wages at least 25% higher than the federal minimum wage. This AEWR is cognizant of the fact that farm worker wages are often higher than the federal minimum wage.

Alternatively, the USDL could retain the current system of state-by-state AEWRs calculated after employer petitions for H-2 workers are received.

Hearings on these alternative methods for establishing an AEWR were held around the United States in November 1979. As a result of these hearings the first option, a national AEWR relating farm and nonfarm wages, was adopted for 1980 to set an AEWR for areas from which petitions for alien labor are received.

The H-2 program is a nonimmigrant admissions program that allows employers to practice occupational discrimination, depressing wages and reducing job opportunities for domestic workers who might otherwise find employment with employers now hiring aliens. Employers are also permitted to discriminate on the basis of national origin, age, sex, etc., in the selection of foreign workers, since the labor certificate gives the employer the right to recruit anyone anywhere. Because the H-2 program (currently) permits the entry of alien workers to harvest two crops--apples and sugarcane--the effect is exactly the same as if the country were protecting (or failing to protect) a specific commodity or industry from foreign competition.[3] "*Regularly* to grant special entry permits to certain groups of workers, whatever the reason, is to subsidize their employers and (perhaps) the consumers of their output, at the expense of their native labor market competitors" (Reder, p. 229). This wage depressing effect is real--it is not absent even in sparsely populated rural areas, where a labor autarky policy would raise farm worker wages and/or encourage farmers to change their crop mix to require less hired farm labor. Farmers and processors may suffer losses if the alien labor supply is abruptly cut off since they have spatially-fixed investments in perennial crops and equipment.

Wage depression is not the only economic effect of H-2 workers. The availability of "extra" labor, whatever its source, promotes labor "wastage." We have already noted how piece rates lessen supervisory costs; what remains is to show how piece rate pay systems encourage employers to have more labor than is "technically" necessary. If payment were strictly on a piece rate system, if congestion did not lead to declining marginal productivity, and if turnover costs were zero, the employers would hire anyone who appeared for work. Growers attempted to pursue such a "maximum work force" strategy in the 1930s, advertising for, say, 2000 workers when only 200 were really "needed" (Jamieson). Fruit and vegetable agriculture, the most labor-intensive kind of crop growing, traditionally relies on an excess labor pool and then uses piece rates in lieu of effective supervision to discriminate among workers. Unionization, the inclusion of farm workers under more protective labor laws, and higher minimum wages have combined to increase turnover costs, gradually encouraging farmers to maintain a smaller pool of "professional" workers.[4] The H-2 program's transportation, housing, and other costs encourage growers to retain a small and professional work force. What the H-2 program does *not* do is encourage farmers to change harvest technologies or crop mixes.

The H-2 program is a selective nonimmigrant labor admissions policy that "segments" American labor markets by altering both the supply and demand parameters of impacted markets. Given the unemployment and underemployment of labor-supplying countries, the (falling) real cost of transportation, and the transferability of aliens' skills for menial work, we can assume that the supply of alien labor is perfectly elastic over the range of AEWRs established by the USDL. The tradition of alien labor availability allows apple and sugarcane growers to continue the production of perennial crops in remote locations and with labor-intensive techniques. Given continuing grower and processor investments and an increasing divergence between wages in H-2-impacted markets and others, it follows that the shock of labor autarky to employers will be more severe the longer they depend on alien workers.

The economic impacts of the current H-2 program are straightforward. The H-2 program is occupationally selective. Growers relying on alien harvest labor continue to produce in traditional growing areas at lower costs than those that would be imposed by a labor autarky policy. If the supply of aliens were abruptly ended, harvest costs (and product prices) would rise and both growers and processors would be left holding depreciated assets. Over time (or if the alien work force were gradually reduced), we would expect some apple production to move closer to urban areas for better access to both hired and "pick-your-own" labor, efforts to develop dwarf trees so that women and retired persons could be used as harvest workers, and renewed mechanization efforts for processing apples and sugarcane. In the short run, apple prices might rise, while sugar prices would fall if import quotas were enlarged.

H-2 workers also change labor market institutions and power relationships. Entering the United States as an H-2 worker is generally perceived as a privilege that permits the individual to earn income windfall as compared with home opportunities. The process puts the alien in a subservient position from the outset. Selection criteria at home depend on one's contacts with government recruitment officials. Once selected, an individual can assure his return to the United States if he so pleases his employer that he is requested by name. As a result, aliens attempt to achieve enough distinction while working to make the "request by name" list and return the following year. Given their alternative opportunities and the character of the selection process, it is little wonder that H-2 aliens are "hardworking and diligent."

If an H-2 alien is considered a malingerer in the United States, he can be deported in midseason without appeal. As temporary workers in remote areas, aliens have little interest in U.S.-based unions. Even if they did, few would be likely to escape employer suspicion and deportation. The basic *cause* of worker docility is their lack of alternative opportunities, but the recruitment and control system guarantees that H-2 workers will attempt few internally inspired labor reforms.

Other Alien Labor Systems

Most alien labor systems allow employers to select foreign nationals for domestic employment on whatever grounds they choose. For example, European employers were constrained to recruit in countries of the European Economic Community (EEC) and non-EEC countries with which their nation had labor agreements, but could specify the skills, physical attributes, sex, etc., of recruits. If the employer wanted, he could specify an applicant by name. (For an elaboration see Martin 1980.) All such selective admissions programs *concentrate* the benefits and costs of immigration, with the benefits accruing to employers (and their dependents). Regional and aggregate benefits and costs depend on the characteristics of the migrants and their employers, on trade policies, tax and transfer policies, and on whether the aliens remain and are integrated or are required to depart after a period of employment.

The United States has the world's largest single-country defacto alien labor or guest worker program, containing perhaps 5 million of the world's 20 million migrants (Martin and Houstoun). Neither the stock or flow of aliens into the United States is known with certainty, but apprehensions of those illegally present in the United States have quadrupled in the 1970s. Employers only indirectly control this influx of aliens, so the impacts of illegal immigration are different from those of the occupationally selective H-2 program.

At the outset it is important to note that most of today's aliens have industrial and service sector jobs. Although definitive estimates are impossible because illegal activities do not generate incontrovertible data, it is hard to imagine more than 1 million illegal aliens or undocumented workers among the nation's 2.5 to 3 million hired farm workers. The illegals in agriculture are believed to cluster in Texas, the Southwest, and along the West Coast.

Illegal immigration is far less employer structured than is immigration through legal programs, since both push-and-pull forces bring aliens for employment. Push forces are usually not enough to guarantee a supply of alien workers--unemployed and underemployed persons also require information and at least some resources to finance the trip. As a result, those in the United States illegally are often drawn from the "middle-ranks" of a sending country's work force (although the U.S.-Mexico land border allows a higher proportion of the very poor to enter the United States [North]). In most instances, it is the more informed and aggressive members of the sending country's work force who go abroad.

Once abroad, aliens working illegally seek jobs offering the highest expected income for their planned stay. Constrained by language, skills, information (often from relatives and friends), and apprehension probabilities, aliens face trade-offs between jobs offering higher wages but requiring English, work skills, and documents (including references), and more unstructured jobs paying lower wages but also offering a lower (apparent) risk of apprehension. Although only anecdotal evidence exists, it appears that agricultural work is viewed as a "last resort" by most aliens, especially by those with more U.S. contacts and those from urban areas in sending countries.

The aliens in agriculture work "hard and scared," whether they are rational maximizers or helpless individuals caught in incomprehensible systems. The combination of their illegal status and the fact that the Immigration and Naturalization Service does apprehend and return employed aliens helps to ensure docility. A rational migrant knows that the Border Patrol can be eluded, but at the cost of a \$200-\$400 smuggling fee. Apprehension results in lost wages while being returned and awaiting reentry and (perhaps) a period of job search. A rational migrant must weigh the potential income gain possible if his complaints produced wage increases against the more certain losses occasioned by apprehension and deportation. Given most migrants' planned short-duration stays, it is rational not to complain. The consequence of illegal status and (partial) enforcement strategies is a system that guarantees employers a docile alien work force. A Border Patrol-employer conspiracy could not have produced a better system to regulate alien labor in the employer's interest.

In the United States illegal immigrants are believed to be concentrated in small businesses which often lack the managerial expertise or access to capital that would permit job restructuring and/or establishment expansion. The concentration of illegal immigrants in small establishments means that employers often (1) know the illegal aliens on their payrolls and (2) maintain their own payroll accounting. In addition to any direct wage savings, illegal immigrants in small businesses allow employers to drive a payroll tax wedge between the costs of hiring natives and those of hiring aliens, which favors the latter. Such taxes, which can cost the employer an additional 15-30% of direct wage costs, can be deducted from all employees' wages and only forwarded to the appropriate revenue offices for natives. Since payroll tax records are verified only when individual employees claim benefits, illegal immigrants afraid to claim benefits never expose their employer's payroll tax savings.

If direct and indirect wage savings make illegal immigrants attractive to small employers, why do large employers use alien workers? If we assume that the larger hotels, factories, and construction firms "unwittingly" hire illegal immigrants, i.e., they *do* pay prevailing wages and payroll (taxes), wage rigidities still allow aliens to provide significant wage savings. A large hotel with bottom-level vacancies could raise wages for maids and busboys or recruit more widely, attracting (at least some) alien labor. If the hotel has a relatively rigid wage hierarchy required by union contract or tradition--preserving differentials between, for example, maids and clerks, the hotel benefits from the aliens' availability because aliens save the cost of job and wage restructuring. These costs could be substantial. For example, if 50 bottom-level vacancies could be filled with a $1-per-hour raise for each position at that level, the employer facing an interdependent but rigid job and wage hierarchy must raise *all* wages up the scale. His total labor costs would increase by $1 (or more) per hour times the *total* number of employees--not by just the $50 per hour he would face in a world of independent submarkets for labor. The significance of these restructuring costs can best be appreciated by recalling that many firms are willing to pay administrative fees, recruitment fees, transportation and housing costs, and translator expenses in order to import alien workers rather than restructure jobs.

Research and Data Needs

Both legal H-2s and illegal alien workers pose fundamental research and policy questions. The most basic issue is also the most controversial--do farmers (and other employers of alien labor) face "labor shortages"? What is a "labor shortage"? Is there an actual physical lack of workers (a perfectly inelastic supply curve), or rather is there an economic shortage of labor that would be curable if wages were raised and working conditions improved? Are farmers really arguing that the domestic farm labor supply function has become more inelastic over time (due to the growth of the nation's income security system and nonfarm work opportunities) while alien farm labor remains in perfectly elastic supply at prevailing wages? The first clear research and policy need is better labor market test information--exactly what are domestic labor supply elasticities?

Calculation of labor supply elasticities is only one part of the three-part research and policy puzzle:

1. How will domestic workers respond to changing wages and working conditions?
2. How can public and private agencies recruit available domestic workers?
3. Would public policy makers be wiser if they abandoned attempts to (1) establish a "fair" wage and then (2) recruit domestic workers? If so, what alternatives appear most promising?

One alternative to the current AEWR and recruitment system is a procedure for making alien labor availability contingent on unemployment rates in the germane work force (for example, on local unemployment rates for nonmigratory labor; on broader-based rates for interstate migrants). The advantage of such an unemployment-based test is that it puts the recruitment burden back on the employers. An unemployment test could simply proscribe alien labor admissions if the relevant unemployment rates exceeded predetermined levels. Alternatively, the use of unemployment rates could be combined with a variable tariff on alien labor, for example, $1000 per alien at 5% unemployment, $2000 at 6% and $3000 at 7%. The chief technical obstacle to quick adoption of such a testing mechanism is the absence of reliable local labor market data, especially in the sparsely populated rural areas where H-2 requests originate (National Commission on Employment and Unemployment Statistics).

Another alternative to a labor market testing mechanism is to simply encourage the relocation of labor short-crop production (either within the United States or abroad) and encourage more domestic and international trade. The problem is that land is a spatially fixed asset. If we assume that current landowners are already making the most profitable use of their land, then trade encouragement will result in losses to owners of spatially fixed land and processing assets. Recent imbroglios over the importation of Mexican fresh market tomatoes during the winter months testify to the reluctance of established (Florida) producers to accept any new competition.[5]

Very little is known about the local and aggregate impacts of illegal or undocumented workers. It is not clear how many (if any) farmers are truly "dependent" on such workers, in the sense that they would literally "go out of business" if illegal workers were no longer available. Research is necessary to establish what roles such illegal workers now play in agricultural labor markets, how their presence alters (or fails to change) production methods, and what the long-term implications of such patterns are.

Another Bracero Program

Could the United States better regulate its illegal immigrant population if a guest worker program were initiated? At the outset, it should be noted that a guest worker program *alone* will certainly not solve the problem of illegal immigration; a guest worker program in conjunction with better border enforcement, employer sanctions, and worker identification cards may convert illegal immigrants into legal guest workers. Before embracing the guest worker alternative, an exploration of the program's purposes is in order.

Some guest worker advocates argue that the United States needs alien labor to meet current labor market gaps or (expected) general labor shortages. Given high and persisting joblessness, how can a simple but accurate labor market test be devised to determine whether native workers are available for specific jobs or to ascertain the dimensions of a general labor shortage? Current specific labor market tests, which require a minimum period of recruitment at USDL-mandated wages, are cumbersome for both employers and government. Any assertions about future labor shortages beg an important question: what would happen to wages, working conditions, and jobs if alien labor was unavailable? It is certainly true that a "labor shortage" will inspire economic changes, but to avoid those changes is to assume that the current job and wage structure is somehow the "right" one.

If general and specific labor market tests are both cumbersome and inconclusive, a guest worker program can still be justified as a form of foreign aid which costs the United States little. This argument usually begins with the assertion that the U.S.-Mexican border cannot be closed and, since the United States has tolerated illegal immigration, it cannot suddenly act to close Mexico's "safety valve" without exacerbating tensions with an oil-rich neighbor. Several issues arise immediately. If the United States takes a lead in solving world unemployment problems by admitting alien labor, what proportion of the world's unemployed should we admit? Should we limit admissions to countries with a bargaining edge (Mexico) or should we include other nations now sending the United States illegal immigrants (Colombia, El Salvador)?

The purposes and effects of a large-scale temporary worker program should be carefully distinguished from those of granting amnesty to illegal immigrants already here. The immigrants now present in the United States have already made a labor market impact. Amnesty will improve individual welfare without radically changing the already accommodated labor market impacts of aliens. Amnesty could, however, change the economic impacts of illegal immigration if it led to family unification, if it promoted job and residence mobility, or if amnesty encouraged often poor aliens to use social services. Guest worker advocates are talking about *future* entrants, not those who have come in the past.

Any large-scale guest worker program will increase the availability of labor, increasing the (short-term) rate of return on now scarcer capital. Since guest workers typically earn below-average incomes and because profits are unequally distributed, one immediate impact of a large-scale guest worker program is more income inequality. More subtle but real is the labor availability advantage handed employers. Given an uncertain economic outlook, employers will prefer easily shed workers to capital with fixed costs. Because native workers can make some claims on employers and on society places at least some limits on the use of labor intensity to avoid fixed capital costs when output cannot be sold. The beauty of a guest worker program to employers is that everyone agrees the aliens will *not* place burdens on employers or society when they are no longer necessary, a strategem as fallacious as it is callous.

Discussion

FINIS WELCH

Philip Martin and David North have two objectives. The first is to describe the now-deceased Bracero Program and its successor, the Rural H-2 program. Since I am not familiar with the underlying data on either program, I cannot comment on the descriptive parts of the analysis. I would, however, have preferred to see more information on relative magnitudes, such as a comparison of the size of the nonimmigrant alien work force with that of the domestic work force on a commodity-by-commodity basis. Certainly the observation that admissions under the H-2 program fell from 70,000 in 1970 to 23,000 in 1978 suggests that any effects from the program must be small in the aggregate and are probably isolated with regard to crop and market area.

The second objective of the authors is to analyze the impact of these programs on the domestic labor market. From my perspective, the analytical aspects of the paper are incomplete. There are some hints of a theory that is not systematically developed, and there is no empirical support to justify the authors' expectations. The authors are not advocates of programs such as the bracero and rural H-2. They do not suggest their elimination, but it is clear that they would oppose a large-scale expansion.

I think that most of the theory regarding the effects of such programs can be summarized from the following quote: "The H-2 program . . . allows employers to practice occupational discrimination [discrimination with regard to national origin, age, sex, etc., is also mentioned], depressing wages and reducing job opportunities for domestic workers." I am unsure of the rationale for the reference to discrimination. With respect to occupation, it seems to be based on the employers' ability to specify the occupations of those they hire. But if this alone justifies a conclusion of discrimination, we are all guilty. With respect to discrimination directed toward other laborer attributes, the analysis referred to earlier goes on to say that with the H-2 program employers are free to hire anyone anywhere. Presumably this statement would be modified by "if they are willing." On this, I suppose I agree. Employers facing broader markets can use more discretion. This, of course, is not what most would view as discrimination. In particular, questions of discretion at a price are simply not raised.

The reference to wage-depressant effects is followed by a quote from Reder: "*Regularly* to grant special entry permits to certain groups of workers, whatever the reason, is to subsidize their employers and (perhaps) the consumers of their output, at the expense of their native labor market competitors." This is about as succinct a statement of the basis for objecting to such programs as you will find, and I trust that Reder will not be offended if I elaborate on his statement in the context of the H-2 program.

Before doing so, I should point out that Reder's concern with domestic labor market competitors is only one aspect of the concern often voiced regarding undocumented aliens, who are often more immigrant than temporary. In this case the concern usually extends to the costs of social services for which United States residents (documented or otherwise) are eligible, and to the question of whether the costs of social services swamp any gains associated with an expanded labor pool. These are very difficult questions, but they do not extend to the nonimmigrant guest worker programs in which residence is temporary and where eligibility for social services is, presumably, clearly defined. For such programs the question is the age-old one of whether there are gains from trade. The wrappings differ, but the substance is the same.

Before considering gains from trade per se, consider Reder's statement as it describes the distribution of the gains: ". . . to subsidize their employers and (perhaps) the consumers of their output." First, unless the imported workers are strictly inframarginal, the "perhaps" should be replaced by "surely." In a competitive industry like agriculture, the only way the price of a factor can be lowered without passing some of the gain through to consumers is if quantities of the relevant input--labor--are rationed (as seems likely for the H-2 program), in the sense that each employer may also hire additional substitute labor (domestic). For the gain not to be passed along to consumers, it is also necessary that the price (the wage) of domestic labor not fall. If and only if both conditions hold: (1) if the number of guest workers is rationed to each employer so that there is excess demand at the applicable wage and (2) if the wage of substitute labor does not fall--will the price to consumers not fall. But if the wages of substitute domestic workers do not fall, there are no losers in this trade. Thus, in general, if there are wage depressant effects "at the expense of their native labor market competitors" then there will also be subsidy to the "consumers of their output."

Are their employers also subsidized? If the program is short-run and unanticipated, the answer is yes--there is a windfall gain associated with a reduced input price. In the long-run, actual or potential entry of new firms will eliminate these rents. Aside from consumers, the most obvious winners are the specialized cooperating agents of production.

Consider, for example, the Florida sugarcane case where H-2 Jamaican workers cut the cane by hand. Free entrepreneurial entry implies zero-rent or zero-profit equilibria in which entrepreneurs earn only what they would elsewhere. Elimination of the H-2 program would probably induce negative quasi-rents for their fixed assets in the short-run, but the most pronounced effect in the long-run would be to lower land values--if this land is as specialized as the Martin-North discussion implies.

If the effects of the program have been capitalized into land values, those owning land during this process have gained. Those entrepreneurs acquiring land under the program after it has been fully capitalized have not been subsidized by it, even though they would surely be taxed if it were eliminated.

Who are the losers? I have no doubt that in a large-scale program there would be displaced native workers, and that aside from legislative constraints like minimum wages, substitute domestic worker wages would be depressed. Yet for some of the isolated cases--Florida sugarcane cutters, western states sheepherders, and woodcutters in Maine--one wonders whether the dominant effect of eliminating the H-2 program might not be to curtail production.

This is a near classic gains-from-trade problem. The usual problem involves importing a finished consumable where the winners are the consumers and the losers are the producers (and their associated employed factors) of competitive products. In the present case, a factor of production is imported. The winners are still the consumers and, possibly, the landowners. The losers are both the competitive factors and the producers of competitive products. Does it matter whether we import Jamaican workers to cut cane in Florida or simply import Jamaican sugar? Clearly, the only difference is the employment of cooperating factors in Florida versus their employment in Jamaica.

Since almost every form of international trade involves winners and losers, is there any way of comparing the gains and losses? Such a comparison involves distributional issues because winners and losers are different people. We have no good way of making this kind of comparison, but we can at least fall back on the compensation principle on which the gains-from-trade ideas are based. We know that in principle the gains of winners are sufficient for them to fully compensate losers and still have something left. In this sense gains exceed losses.

My reading of the Martin-North analysis is that attention is paid only to losers, specifically domestic workers, while gains are ignored. Even so, there is much in the paper that confuses me. For example, there is a section on piecework in which they assert that the availability of "extra" labor promotes labor "wastage"--that piece rate pay systems encourage employers to use more labor than is technically "necessary." These are strange terms to an economist. Is there something more here than a restatement of the proposition of diminishing returns?

The authors discuss other guest worker systems, especially illegal or undocumented ones, and raise the question of another bracero program. The concluding sentence is: "The beauty of a guest worker program to employers is that everyone agrees the aliens will not place burdens on employers or society when they are no longer necessary, a stratagem as fallacious as it is callous."

Why is it fallacious? And if it is callous, would it be less callous to eliminate the H-2 program, and were we not callous when we eliminated the Bracero Program? Is it the welfare of the alien guest workers that concerns Martin and North? They repeatedly assert that with existing United States conditions for H-2 workers there is excess supply. Clearly these potential H-2 workers would prefer something better, but the simple fact that they are willing to take the program as it is suggests that their welfare would not be enhanced by ending it.

Martin and North make several important points. Potential wage-depressant effects for domestic substitutes is the most important, and the point about employment tax avoidance is another. Yet, I would have preferred more structure. In particular I would have liked to see a discussion of perceptions of our responsibilities to: (1) consumers of agricultural products, (2) domestic workers, and (3) potential guest workers. All too often in discussions of this sort, there is a presumption that we have no responsibility to aliens if whatever happens to them happens outside the United States.

In closing I add that many and perhaps most of the products domestically produced by alien guest workers are traded internationally by the United States. As such, the relevant setting for an analysis of the gains from importing labor in a nonimmigrant program is against an alternative in which the product produced is exported or, if domestically consumed, the alternative is to import the final product rather than a subset of the factors that produce it. In such a context, the case for concern about the plight of domestic workers is considerably weakened.

7

Labor Supply Uncertainty and Technology Adoption

DAVID ZILBERMAN and RICHARD E. JUST

Modern agriculture has been characterized by a continuous process of mechanization, with labor being replaced by farm machinery. The theory of induced innovation is a very useful theory that has been used to explain this phenomenon by attributing the capital intensification of agricultural production to the relative cheapening of capital goods in terms of labor. The theory of induced innovation, however, has recently become a heavily researched area and is now well understood in many respects. (An enlightening presentation of the theory of induced innovation is provided by Binswanger.)

Another plausible reason for farm mechanization, which has received little or no attention, is labor supply uncertainty. Threats of strikes by farm labor unions and inconsistent enforcement of immigration laws make the availability of seasonal farm labor uncertain. Intuition suggests that risk-averse farmers would tend to adopt new machinery to replace these workers when labor supplies become more uncertain. For example, the introduction of the tomato harvester in the late 1960s may be explained, in part, by the unstable supply of workers for harvesting that resulted from the end of the Bracero Program in 1964

The authors would like to thank Daniel Sumner and the other conference participants for helpful comments and suggestions.

and the pursuit of strict control policies with regard to illegal migrants from Mexico in the 1950s and 1960s.

This chapter will attempt to examine the effects of labor supply uncertainties on the technology choices of farmers. This will be done by investigating the properties of an abstract theoretical model, the specification of which includes the essential features of the problem under consideration. By eliminating many details of specific agricultural cases that are seemingly inconsequential in determining qualitative or directional changes, it becomes possible to examine the impact of unstable labor supply analytically. That is, if the details that are eliminated are truly inconsequential in determining the directional impacts of changes in labor supply uncertainty in any particular agricultural problem, the results of this analysis are applicable.

The model specified is designed to be especially relevant for analyzing the behavior of growers of fruits and vegetables who face unstable labor market conditions during the harvest season. It assumes that harvesting at each farm can be carried out in either of two ways: by using a traditional labor-intensive technology or by adopting modern machinery that does not require the hiring of any additional labor but requires instead some fixed costs. The farmer has to choose his technology before the harvesting season, when labor availability is not clear. Since harvesting machinery is generally used over a number of harvesting seasons, this may be regarded alternatively as an uncertainty with respect to future crop years. In addition, the farmer also determines the quantity of other variable inputs, such as fertilizer, in either case.

A key factor that determines a farmer's reaction to changes in labor supply uncertainty is his aversion to risk. An individual is averse to risk if he would generally prefer a profit of $\bar{\pi}$ dollars to a 50% chance of $\bar{\pi} + \Delta\pi$ dollars and a 50% chance of $\bar{\pi} - \Delta\pi$ dollars. If he is generally indifferent to these two situations, then he is risk neutral. If all farmers are extremely risk averse, then intuition suggests that a shift from labor-using technology to modern machinery is a highly likely response to increased labor supply uncertainty. When some farmers are only mildly risk averse or risk neutral, however, the effects of increased labor supply uncertainty may not be so clear intuitively. For example, uncertain labor supply causes uncertain output supply among those farmers employing labor-using technology. With a downward sloping demand curve for output, this leads to output price uncertainty. Thus increased labor supply uncertainty may cause increased output price uncertainty also for those farmers adopting mechanical harvesting technology. For labor-using farmers, low outputs due to low labor supplies tend to be offset by high prices and vice versa, so risk considerations may not offer as great an inducement to shift to mechanized technology where profit variability definitely increases with labor supply uncertainty.

With these considerations in mind, the results of this analysis show that the introduction of labor supply uncertainty will not always reduce the well-being of farmers. Actually, when the industry faces inelastic demand, farmers may gain from uncertainty. In this case, a small labor supply and the resulting low output move an industry toward a monopoly output, and thus profits increase disproportionately relative to the opposing case. Alternatively, when the demand elasticity for output is high this offsetting effect is not realized, so that the introduction of labor supply uncertainty unambiguously encourages adoption of mechanized technology.

This chapter first formalizes these arguments in the context of risk neutrality. Then the results are extended to the case of risk aversion. In each case a midrange of farm sizes (as measured by output) is found in which labor tends to be replaced by machinery as a result of labor supply uncertainty regardless of demand elasticity. Outside this midrange, however, a tendency toward adoption is clear only in the case of elastic demand. Under more specific conditions with respect to risk aversion, results show that farmers could benefit from stabilization of the labor supply if, and only if, output demand is elastic.

THE MODEL

Consider a competitive industry with N identical farms. Each farm has a traditional technology characterized by a Cobb-Douglas production function,

$$q = A\ell^{\alpha_1} x^{\alpha_2} \tag{7.1}$$

where q is output, ℓ is labor used for harvesting, x is variable input used prior to the harvest season (i.e., water and fertilizer), and A is a scale coefficient. The output elasticities of labor and the other input, α_1 and α_2, are assumed to follow: $0 \leq \alpha_1, \alpha_2 < 1$, and $\alpha_1 + \alpha_2 < 1$.

In addition to the existing technology, the farm can adopt modern technology, which requires an annualized fixed cost of I dollars and uses only the variable input x in the production process. The production function of the new technology is given by

$$q_1 = A_1 x^{\alpha_2} \tag{7.2}$$

At harvest season, the labor and product prices are known by farmers; thus, if the traditional technology is used, the labor choice is made under complete certainty. Given the wage rate W and output price P, the optimal amount of seasonal labor chosen by the firm is derived from

$$\max_{\ell} PA\ell^{\alpha_1} x^{\alpha_2} - W\ell \tag{7.3}$$

The first-order condition for (7.3) is

$$\alpha_1 PA\ell^{\alpha_1 - 1} x^{\alpha_2} - W = 0 \tag{7.4}$$

Thus, the short-run labor use is given by

$$\ell = (\alpha_1 PAx^{\alpha_2}/W)^{1/(1-\alpha_1)} \qquad (7.5)$$

Define $\pi_0 = Pq - W\ell - sx$ as the profit under the old technology, given variable input x, labor input ℓ, resulting output, and respective prices s, W, and P. Using (7.3) and (7.5), profit can be rewritten as

$$\pi_0 = cx^{\alpha_2/(1-\alpha_1)} Z - sx \qquad (7.6)$$

where $c = (1 - \alpha_1)\alpha_1^{\alpha_1/(1-\alpha_1)} A^{1/(1-\alpha_1)}$ and

$$Z = (P/W^{\alpha_1})^{1/(1-\alpha_1)} \qquad (7.6a)$$

Labor supply uncertainty will cause the wage rate and output price to be random variables; thus, profit under the old technology, π_0, and Z will be random variables. If the output price is affected by changes in labor supply, then profit from the new technology π_1,

$$\pi_1 = Pq_1 - sx_1 - I \qquad (7.7)$$

is also a random variable. In choosing the optimal level of x and determining whether or not to adopt the new technology, the farmer considers the distributions of π_0 and π_1. Assuming that farmers are risk averse with utility function $U(\pi)$ with standard properties ($U' > 0$, $U'' \leq 0$), the longer run decision problem of the farmer is

$$\max_{\lambda}\{\lambda[\max_{x} EU(\pi_1)] + (1 - \lambda)[\max_{x} EU(\pi_0)]\} \qquad (7.8)$$

where λ is a discrete choice variable with $\lambda = 1$ when the new technology is adopted and $\lambda = 0$ otherwise.

OPTIMAL INPUT CHOICES UNDER LABOR AND OUTPUT PRICE UNCERTAINTIES

Using the definitions in (7.6) and (7.7) of profits under both technologies, the choice of the optimal level of fertilizer (x) under both technologies can be investigated within Sandmo's framework of analysis of firm behavior under price uncertainty (Sandmo; Feder).[1] To use this framework to analyze the optimal use of variable inputs other than labor under the old technology, one must treat the random variable Z as a price of an output y produced with the production function, $y = cx^{\alpha_2/(1-\alpha_1)}$. The results in Sandmo's paper indicate the following. (For some important exceptions to these results for cases where uncertainties arise from sources other than random labor supply, see Just and Pope.)

PROPOSITION 1. Under both technologies, risk-averse farmers will use less of variable inputs other than labor and have lower yield levels than risk-neutral farmers.

Sandmo used the notion of mean preserving spread (MPS) to construct random variables with different degrees of "riskiness." Let $\bar{Z}$ be the expected value of the random variable Z, and let Z_1 be another random variable with the same expected value as Z. The random variable Z can be written as

$$Z = Z_1 + \beta(Z_1 - \bar{Z}) \tag{7.9}$$

where β is a positive parameter. Note that an increase in β implies an MPS of the distribution of Z. Such an MPS represents an increase in risk in the sense that, for any given value of x, the expected utility of π_0 is monotonically decreasing with β for a risk averter. Using a similar construction for P and applying the corollaries to Theorems 1-3 in Feder to our problem yields:

PROPOSITION 2. (a) The optimal level of variable

inputs other than labor under the old technology decreases as the riskiness of Z increases, and increases as the expected value of Z increases. (b) The optimal level of nonlabor inputs under the modern technology increases with a reduction in output price uncertainty and with a rise in the expected value of output price. An increase in the fixed cost associated with the new technology reduces the optimal use of nonlabor inputs provided that absolute risk aversion is decreasing.[2] With constant absolute risk aversion, changes in the fixed cost will not affect the optimal use of nonlabor inputs under the new technology.

While Propositions 1 and 2 shed some light on input use of competitive farms subject to labor and output price uncertainty, more rigorous specification of the labor market and the resulting labor equilibrium price distribution is required to fully understand the effects of labor supply uncertainty.

OPTIMAL BEHAVIOR UNDER LABOR PRICE UNCERTAINTY WITH RISK NEUTRALITY

Assume that at each season aggregate labor supply for the industry is completely inelastic. Denote this labor supply by L. Assume, also, that L is a random variable with some distribution. These assumptions are not unrealistic in cases where the labor supply consists mainly of migrant workers who do not have many employment opportunities, once they are in the region, besides working for the agricultural industry. The number of these workers may change from year to year, depending on the enforcement of migration laws and the availability of economic opportunities in other regions. (There may be interesting dynamic patterns of aggregate labor supply where the supply at period t is negatively correlated with the wage rate at t − 1. This issue should be considered in further research.)

Given the nature of aggregate labor supply, when all the farms are using the old technology each one will use $\ell = L/N$ units of labor and produce q =

$AX^{\alpha_2}(L/N)^{\alpha_1}$ units of output (since the industry consists of N identical competitive farms). The aggregate output of the industry is thus given by

$$Q = AL^{\alpha_1}N^{1-\alpha_1}x^{\alpha_2} \tag{7.10}$$

Now assume that the industry is facing an isoelastic demand curve. Let the inverse demand curve be

$$P = DQ^{-\varepsilon} \tag{7.11}$$

where $\varepsilon = 1/\eta$ and η is the standard elasticity of demand. Note that D is a scale coefficient that declines as the demand shifts upward.

By introducing (7.10) into (7.11), output price can be presented as a function of labor supply, i.e.,

$$P = d_1 L^{-\alpha_1\varepsilon} x^{-\alpha_2\varepsilon} \tag{7.12}$$

where $d_1 = DA^{-\varepsilon}N^{-(1-\alpha_1)\varepsilon}$. Also, introducing $\ell = L/N$ into the first-order condition (7.4) yields

$$W = PAL^{-(1-\alpha_1)}N^{(1-\alpha_1)}x^{\alpha_2} \tag{7.13}$$

Thus, introducing (7.12) into (7.13) yields

$$W = d_2 L^{-(1-\alpha_1+\alpha_1\varepsilon)}x^{\alpha_2(1-\varepsilon)} \tag{7.14}$$

where $d_2 = DA^{(1-\varepsilon)}N^{(1-\alpha_1)(1-\varepsilon)}$.

Introducing (7.12) and (7.13) into (7.6) and (7.6a) obtains

$$\pi_0 = c_2 L^{\alpha_1(1-\varepsilon)}x^{\alpha_2(1-\varepsilon)} \tag{7.15}$$

$$Z = c_1 x^{-\alpha_2[\alpha_1/(1-\alpha_1)+\varepsilon]} L^{\alpha_1(1-\varepsilon)} \tag{7.16}$$

where

$$c_2 = (1 - \alpha_1)\alpha_1^{\alpha_1/(1-\alpha_1)} A^{(1-\varepsilon)} N^{-[\alpha_1+(1-\alpha_1)\varepsilon]} D$$

$$c_1 = DA^{-[\alpha_1/(1-\alpha_1)+\varepsilon]} N^{-[\alpha_1+(1-\alpha_1)\varepsilon]}$$

Using these definitions, the average outcome in the case where labor supply is stable at $L = \bar{L}$ and in the case where it is uncertain at $E(L) = L$ will be compared. The analysis relies heavily on Jensen's inequality, which states that if $g(L)$ is convex ($g'' > 0$), then

$$E[g(L)] \geqslant g(\bar{L}) \tag{7.17}$$

This type of analysis is frequently used in the economic literature on instability.

LEMMA 1. Assume a given x and complete use of the traditional labor-using technology. Then: (a) Output price is declining with the level of aggregate labor. However, the expected price level when labor supply is uncertain tends to be higher than when labor supply is stabilized at its mean. (b) Wage rates are declining with aggregate levels of labor supply. However, the expected wage rate under labor supply uncertainty tends to be higher than when wages are stabilized at the level corresponding to mean labor supply. (c) Profits are declining with aggregate labor supply if the demand for the final product is inelastic ($\eta < 1$); profits rise with labor supply when the output is relatively elastic ($\eta > 1$). Expected profits under uncertain labor supply tend to exceed profits for labor supply stabilized at its mean if demand is inelastic ($\eta < 1$), and labor supply uncertainty tends to yield less expected profit than certain labor supply when demand is relatively elastic.

PROOF. See Appendix 7.A.

The results of Lemma 1(c) are depicted graphically in Figure 7.1. In cases where output demand is elastic, a reduction in labor supply causes an increase in output that outweighs the reduction in output price; thus, revenues [and profits, which are $(1 - \alpha_1)$ times revenues] are increasing under the old technology. Marginal profit, however, is decreasing in L. For example, consider the curve π_0^1 as depicted in Figure 7.1. Suppose L has two values, L_1 and L_2, and $E(L) = \bar{L}$. The concavity of π_0^1 causes profit at the average labor supply level $\bar{L}$ (point B) to be higher than the expected profit denoted by point A. The curve π_0^2 denotes profit as a function of aggregate labor when demand elasticity is small ($\eta < 1$). This curve is declining with L and is convex. Here expected profits are given by point C. This point is higher than point D, which denotes profit at the average labor level $\bar{L}$.

When a farmer considers the adoption of modern technology, it is assumed that he takes the existing

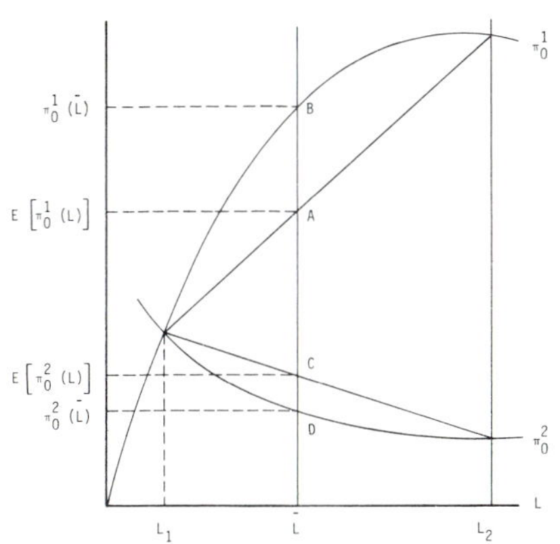

Fig. 7.1. Demonstration of lemma 1(c).

price distribution as given and ignores the effect which his adoption (and that of others) will have on labor wage rates and output prices. This assumption corresponds to the case where the industry is competitive and N is relatively large.

LEMMA 2. For a given x, the farmer's perceived profit under the new technology will decline as the aggregate labor supply increases. The perceived, expected profit under the new technology with random labor supply tends to be higher than when the supply is stabilized at its mean.

PROOF. Differentiating (7.7) yields

$$\frac{d\pi_1}{dL} = \frac{\partial P}{\partial L} q_1 = -\alpha_1 \varepsilon \frac{R_1}{L} < 0 \tag{7.18}$$

$$\frac{d^2\pi_1}{dL^2} = \alpha_1 \varepsilon(\alpha_1 \varepsilon + 1) \frac{R_1}{L^2} > 0 \tag{7.19}$$

where $R_1 = Pq_1$ is the revenue under the new technology. Using Jensen's inequality

$$E[\pi_1(L)] \geqslant \pi_1(\bar{L}) \tag{7.20}$$

Lemmas 1 and 2 are useful for deriving the following proposition.

PROPOSITION 3. Suppose farmers are risk neutral. Then: (a) They will tend to use more nonlabor inputs under the old technology and be better off when the labor supply is uncertain than when the labor supply is stabilized at its mean if the output demand elasticity is small ($\eta < 1$). When output demand is elastic ($\eta > 1$), uncertainty tends to cause a reduction in nonlabor input use and be less preferred than a stabilized labor supply (at its mean). (b) Modern technology tends to require more nonlabor input use and to yield higher expected profits when the labor supply is uncertain than when it is stabilized at its mean.

PROOF. See Appendix 7.B.

COROLLARY. When farmers are risk neutral, the introduction of labor supply uncertainty (holding mean labor supply fixed) tends to result in adoption of the new technology if output demand is elastic ($\eta > 1$).

PROOF. A risk-neutral farmer will adopt the new technology if expected profit exceeds expected profit under the old technology. When labor supply is stable at $L = \bar{L}$ the industry operates with the old technology by assumption; hence, $\pi_0(\bar{L}) > \pi_1(\bar{L})$. If $\eta > 1$, Proposition 3 indicates that destabilization of the labor supply will reduce expected profit under the old technology and increase expected profit under the new technology; hence, $\bar{\pi}_1$ may become greater than $\bar{\pi}_0$.

If demand for output is inelastic ($\eta < 1$), the introduction of labor supply uncertainty will increase the expected profit from both the new and the old technologies. Thus it is not clear whether or not uncertainty will encourage the adoption of new technology.

To better understand the nature of the adoption decision, simplify the problem by ignoring the nonlabor input choice problem and assume $x = 1$ and $s = 0$ for both technologies. Thus, the production function under the traditional technology becomes

$$q_0 = A\ell^{\alpha_1} \tag{7.21}$$

while the output level under the new technology is fixed at A_1.

Assuming that the traditional technology is preferred under complete certainty when $L = \bar{L}$, one can deduce $P(\bar{L})q_1 - I < \pi_0(\bar{L})$. If the firm adopts the new technology under uncertainty, $\bar{P}(L)q_1 - I > \bar{\pi}_0(L)$. Combining these two inequalities yields some bounds on the output levels under the new technology which will result in adoption when the labor supply is destabilized:

$$\frac{I + \pi_0(\bar{L})}{P(\bar{L})} > q_1 > \frac{I + \bar{\pi}_0(L)}{\bar{P}(L)} \tag{7.22}$$

Introducing (7.12) and (7.15) into (7.22) yields

$$\bar{q}_1 > q_1 > \underline{q}_1 \tag{7.23}$$

where

$$\bar{q}_1 = [I + c_2\bar{L}^{\alpha_1(1-\varepsilon)}]/d_1\bar{L}^{-\alpha_1\varepsilon}$$

$$\underline{q}_1 = \{I + c_2E[L^{\alpha_1(1-\varepsilon)}]\}/d_1E[L^{-\alpha_1\varepsilon}]$$

Since, by Jensen's inequality,

$$\bar{L}^{-\alpha_1\varepsilon} < E[L^{-\alpha_1\varepsilon}]$$

and since

$$\bar{L}^{\alpha_1(1-\varepsilon)} \geqslant E[L^{\alpha_1(1-\varepsilon)}]$$

for $\eta > 1$, the interval for q_1 [given in (7.23)] for which destabilization of the labor supply will result in adoption of the modern technique by risk-neutral farmers is well defined. When $\eta < 1$, a q_1 interval for which introduction of labor supply uncertainty results in adoption may not exist.

To prove that adoption is possible because of uncertainty even when the elasticity of demand is small, subtract the lower bound of the interval in (7.23) from the upper bound. The outcome of this subtraction can be rearranged to yield

$$[I + c_2\bar{L}^{\alpha_1(1-\varepsilon)}]E[L^{-\alpha_1\varepsilon}] - \{I + c_2E[L^{\alpha_1(1-\varepsilon)}]\}\bar{L}^{-\alpha_1\varepsilon}$$

$$= I\{E[L^{-\alpha_1\varepsilon}] - \bar{L}^{-\alpha_1\varepsilon}\}$$

$$+ c_2\bar{L}^{-\alpha_1\varepsilon}\{\bar{L}^{\alpha_1}E[L^{-\alpha_1\varepsilon}] - E[L^{\alpha_1(1-\varepsilon)}]\} \qquad (7.24)$$

The first element on the left-hand side of (7.24) is positive by Jensen's inequality since $L^{-\alpha\varepsilon}$ is a concave function. To determine the sign of the left-hand side of (7.24), note that

$$\bar{L}^{\alpha_1} > E[L^{\alpha_1}]$$

$$E[L^{\alpha_1}]E[L^{-\alpha_1\varepsilon}] - E[L^{\alpha_1}L^{-\alpha_1\varepsilon}] = -\mathrm{Cov}[L^{\alpha_1}, L^{-\alpha_1\varepsilon}]$$

is positive since the covariance between L^{α_1} and $L^{-\alpha_1\varepsilon}$ is negative. Thus the expression in (7.24) is positive. This proves:

PROPOSITION 4. Suppose variable inputs other than labor are used in the same quantities under both technologies. Then, under risk neutrality, the introduction of labor supply uncertainty will result in adoption of the new technology if output under the new technology is within the interval defined by (7.23).

Note that $\bar{q}_1$ in (7.23) denotes the minimal output size under the new technology which would result in adoption under complete certainty at $L = \bar{L}$. The lower bound $\underline{q}_1$ denotes the minimal output associated with a new technology which results in adoption under labor supply uncertainty, and the fact $\bar{q}_1 > \underline{q}_1$ indicates that introduction of uncertainty may result in adoption. By introducing the definition of d_1 and c_2 into (7.23), q can be rewritten as

$$\underline{q}_1 = a_1 E[L^{-\alpha_1 \varepsilon -1}] + a_2 E\{L[\alpha_1(1 - \varepsilon)]\}/E[L^{-\alpha_1 \varepsilon}] \tag{7.25}$$

where $a_1 = IA^{\varepsilon}N^{(1-\alpha_1)\varepsilon}/D$ and $a_2 = (1-\alpha_1)\alpha_1^{\alpha_1(1-\alpha_1)}N^{-\alpha_1}A$. From (7.25), one can deduce:

PROPOSITION 5. Under the assumptions of Proposition 4, the minimal output level associated with the new technology which will result in adoption of the new technology when labor supply uncertainty is introduced, declines as: (a) fixed costs associated with the new technology fall (i.e., $d\underline{q}_1/dI > 0$); (b) the scale factor of output demand increases (i.e., $d\underline{q}_1/dD < 0$); and (c) the scale factor associated with the old technology falls (i.e., $d\underline{q}_1/dA > 0$).

OPTIMAL BEHAVIOR UNDER LABOR PRICE UNCERTAINTY AND RISK AVERSION

The analysis of the outcomes under uncertainty will continue to assume that the only variable input that changes with adoption of new technology is seasonal labor (namely, x = 1 and s = 0). For the most part, the results of the previous section carry through for risk-averse farmers. Recall that a risk-averse farmer seeks to maximize his expected utility of income, $U(\pi)$, where $U' > 0$ and $U'' < 0$. There are two measures of risk aversion: (1) absolute risk aversion, $r_a = -U''/U'$, which is assumed to decline with income (Arrow) and (2) relative risk aversion, r_2

$= -U''\pi/U'$. Arrow argued that the measure of relative risk aversion, r_2, is close to 1. Following Arrow's suggestion, unity of r_2 will be assumed in deriving the following proposition.

PROPOSITION 6. Suppose farmers are risk averse with $r_2 = 1$. (a) Under traditional technology, an uncertain labor supply is preferred to a certain labor supply (stabilized at the mean) if the elasticity of demand is small. A certain labor supply is preferred when demand is elastic. (b) The mechanical technology yields higher expected utility when the labor supply is uncertain than when labor supply is stabilized at L if $\alpha_1 I/(\pi_1 \eta) < 1$.

PROOF. See Appendix 7.C.

The results of Proposition 6(a) are quite robust. It can easily be proved that they always hold when the measure of relative risk aversion is smaller than one and in many cases when it is higher than one. Note also that, using Proposition 5, the corollary to Proposition 3 can be extended to the case of risk aversion. In this case the introduction of labor supply uncertainty will raise the tendency to adopt the new technology when $\eta > 1$ and $\alpha_1 I/(\pi_1 \eta) < 1$.

One specific utility function with $r_2 = 1$ is the logarithmic function, $U(\pi) = \ln \pi$. Using this function,

$$U(\pi_0) = \ln c_2 + \alpha_1(1 - \varepsilon)\ln L \tag{7.26}$$

and $U(\pi_1) = \ln(q_1 d_1 L^{-\alpha_1 \varepsilon} - I)$. If fixed cost associated with the new technology is zero, then

$$U(\pi_1) = \ln q_1 + \ln d_1 - \alpha_1 \varepsilon \ln L \tag{7.27}$$

Thus, from (7.26) and (7.27), the conditions for farms to switch to the new technology are

$$\ln(c_2/d_1) + \ln \bar{L} > \ln q_1 > \ln(c_2/d_1) + E[\ln(L)] \qquad (7.28)$$

Introducing (7.12) and (7.15) into (7.28) yields

$$a_6 + \ln \bar{L} > \ln q_1 > a_6 + E[\ln(L)] \qquad (7.29)$$

where $a_6 = \ln(1 - \alpha_1) + [\alpha_1/(1 - \alpha_1)]\ln \alpha_1 + \ln A - \alpha_1 \ln N$. Since ln L is concave, the interval in (7.28) exists for all demand elasticities; hence, the introduction of uncertainty will result in adoption of the new technology in cases where $I = 0$, $U(\pi) = \ln \pi$, and q_1 belongs to the interval in (7.28) or (7.29).

Equation (7.29) implies that, for the special case analyzed here, the minimal output capacity of the new technology required to generate adoption of the newer technology when uncertainty is introduced increases with the scale element of the traditional production function and decreases with the number of farms in the industry. Note that the first outcome is consistent with Proposition 5(c).

CONCLUSIONS

This paper demonstrates that labor supply instability can have important implications for production, prices, and technology choices. Results show that labor supply uncertainty can be an important determinant in explaining the replacement of hand-labor technology with machine methods. Thus the effects of policies on the uncertainty of labor supply are crucial in considering the well-being of farm laborers as well as producers and, ultimately, consumers. This is especially true with regard to seasonal labor markets where labor supply uncertainties are significant.

Results show that the impacts of labor supply uncertainty depend heavily on the elasticity of demand for the final product. For example, policies that stabilize labor supply may be beneficial to the consumer through a reduction in average output price, but they will necessarily benefit farmers only if the demand for output is elastic. In the case of inelastic demand, stabilization of labor supply can make the farmer worse off. Obviously, the relevant demand elasticity for analysis of the impacts of a given change in labor supply is the elasticity of demand facing the farmers who are affected by the change. Thus stabilization of labor supply for all the growers of a crop may adversely affect producers (since the aggregate demand elasticity for most agricultural products is less than unitary). On the other hand, stabilization of the labor supply for farmers in a region with a small share of the final market may increase the welfare of farmers in that region.

If, for example, immigration policies were enforced to stabilize California's migrant labor supply at its mean, then the results of this analysis suggest that California's lettuce growers (who dominate their output market) would lose, while California's apple growers (who are a small part of their output market) may gain. Note that the consumers of both products may gain in the short run (expected price is declining), but the longer run effects are not clear since stabilization reduces the tendencies toward adoption of laborsaving technologies. Whether or not the latter situation is desirable has been a topic of controversy (Just, Schmitz, Zilberman).

The results of this analysis also emphasize that complete evaluation of any labor supply management policy must take into account not only impacts on the average scarcity of labor but also on the distribution of the labor supply about that average. For example, unionization will reduce the average labor supply and change labor supply stability.

In the early stages of unionization, when labor relationships are unstable and strikes are frequent, unionization probably increases instability. Here the effects of increased instability tend to magnify the effects of reduced mean supply of labor. That is, a reduction in mean labor supply causes a welfare loss for consumers, while producers lose (gain) depending on whether output demand is elastic (inelastic). (Similar results were derived by Carter et al. in their model of unionization of lettuce harvester growers.) Also, an increased tendency to adopt labor-saving technology by producers can cause welfare losses for workers in the long run. The results of this chapter, however, suggest that the increased instability of labor supply has these same impacts.

On the other hand, well-managed and established unions with good working relationships with farmers may ensure a more stable labor supply. In this case the increase in stabilization and the reduction in average labor supply will have contradictory effects. Reduction in average labor supply will benefit industries with low elasticity of demand and reduce the gains for industries with high elasticity of demand, while the reduction in uncertainty will have an opposite effect. Only empirical measurement can determine which effect is stronger. In the long run an increase in average output price resulting from the introduction of a union will increase the tendency to adopt new technologies; but, again, the reduction in uncertainty will operate in the opposite direction. Once more, empirical measurement is necessary to determine which effect dominates.

While this chapter investigates the effects of labor supply uncertainty on the initial introduction of new technologies, it does not take into account how partial adoption will affect the output price and labor supply distributions which, in turn, will affect the direction of the adoption process. This issue is one of many which should be pursued further in analyzing the impacts of labor supply uncertainties.

APPENDIX 7.A. PROOF OF LEMMA 1

(a) Differentiation of (7.12) with respect to L yields

$$\frac{dP}{dL} = -\alpha_1 \varepsilon \frac{P}{L} < 0 \qquad (7.A1)$$

$$\frac{d^2P}{dL^2} = \alpha_1 \varepsilon (1 + \alpha_1 \varepsilon) \frac{P}{L^2} > 0 \qquad (7.A2)$$

Thus, using Jensen's inequality in (7.A2) yields

$$\bar{P}(L) = E[P(L)] \geqslant P(\bar{L}) \qquad (7.A3)$$

(b) By differentiating (7.14) with respect to L,

$$\frac{dW}{dL} = -(1 - \alpha_1 + \alpha_1 \varepsilon) \frac{W}{L} < 0 \qquad (7.A4)$$

$$\frac{d^2W}{dL^2} = (1 - \alpha_1 + \alpha_1 \varepsilon) \cdot (2 - \alpha_1 + \alpha_1 \varepsilon) \frac{W}{L^2} > 0 \qquad (7.A5)$$

Thus, using Jensen's inequality in (7.A5) yields

$$\bar{W}(L) = EW(L) \geqslant W(\bar{L}) \qquad (7.A6)$$

(c) By differentiating (7.15) with respect to L

$$\frac{d\pi_0}{dL} = \alpha_1 (1 - \varepsilon) \frac{\pi_0}{L} \qquad (7.A7)$$

$$\frac{d^2\pi_0}{dL^2} = \alpha_1 (1 - \varepsilon)\left[\alpha_1 (1 - \varepsilon) - 1\right] \frac{\pi_0}{L^2} \qquad (7.A8)$$

From (7.A7), it is obvious that

$$\frac{d\pi_0}{dL} \begin{cases} > 0 & \text{if} \quad \eta > 1 \\ < 0 & \text{if} \quad \eta < 1 \end{cases} \qquad (7.A9)$$

and from (7.A8) that

$$\frac{d^2\pi_0}{dL^2} \begin{cases} > 0 & \text{if} \quad \eta < 1 \\ < 0 & \text{if} \quad \eta > 1 \end{cases} \tag{7.A10}$$

Thus, using (7.A10) and Jensen's inequality yields

$$E[\pi(L)] \begin{cases} \geqslant \pi(\bar{L}) & \text{if} \quad \eta < 1 \\ \leqslant \pi(\bar{L}) & \text{if} \quad \eta > 1 \end{cases} \tag{7.A11}$$

APPENDIX 7.B. PROOF OF PROPOSITION 3

(a) Under risk neutrality and uncertainty, the objective of the farmer is to

$$\max_x \; c\bar{Z}x^{\alpha_2/(1-\alpha_1)} - sx \tag{7.B1}$$

where $\bar{Z} = E(Z)$. Solving (7.B1) and introducing the value of Z from (7.16) into (7.B1) yields $s = cc_1E[L^{\alpha_1(1-\varepsilon)}]x^{\alpha_2(1-\varepsilon)-1}$. Hence, the optimal nonlabor input level under uncertainty and the old technology denoted by x_{u_0} is

$$x_{u_0} = \{ \frac{cc_1}{s} E[L^{\alpha_1(1-\varepsilon)}]\}^{1/[1-\alpha_2(1-\varepsilon)]} \tag{7.B2}$$

Solving similarly for the optimal nonlabor input level under the old technology and a stable labor supply at $L = \bar{L}$ yields

$$x_{c_0} = [\frac{cc_1}{s} \bar{L}^{\alpha_1(1-\varepsilon)}]^{1/[1-\alpha_2(1-\varepsilon)]} \tag{7.B3}$$

Since, for every $\varepsilon > 0$, $1/[1 - \alpha_2(1 - \varepsilon)] > 0$, and using Jensen's inequality for the function, $L^{\alpha_1(1-\varepsilon)}$, (7.B2) and (7.B3) imply

$$x_{u_0} \begin{cases} \geqslant x_{c_0} & \text{if} \quad \eta < 1 \\ \leqslant x_{c_0} & \text{if} \quad \eta > 1 \end{cases} \tag{7.B4}$$

Let $\bar{\pi}_0$ denote profit under the optimal solution when labor supply is uncertain and let $\bar{\pi}_0(L)$ be profit under the optimal nonlabor input level when $L = \bar{L}$. The properties of the Cobb-Douglas production function imply

$$\bar{\pi}_0 = \frac{1 - \alpha_1}{1 - \alpha_1 - \alpha_2} x_{u_0} s \tag{7.B5}$$

$$\pi_0(\bar{L}) = \frac{1 - \alpha_1}{1 - \alpha_1 - \alpha_2} x_{c_0} s \tag{7.B6}$$

Introducing (7.B4) into (7.B5) and (7.B6) implies

$$\bar{\pi}_0 \begin{cases} > \pi_0(\bar{L}) & \text{if} \quad \eta < 1 \\ < \pi_0(\bar{L}) & \text{if} \quad \eta > 1 \end{cases} \tag{7.B7}$$

(b) Considering the new technology, the optimization problem of the risk-neutral farmer under labor supply uncertainty is

$$\max_x \bar{P}(L)A_1 x^{\alpha_2} - cx - I \tag{7.B8}$$

and under $L = \bar{L}$, the objective is

$$\max_x P(\bar{L})A_1 x^{\alpha_2} - cx - I \tag{7.B9}$$

Using definitions similar to those in part (a) of the proof, one can deduce from Lemma 1(b) and (7.B8) and (7.B9) that

$$x_{u_1} \geq x_{c_1} \tag{7.B10}$$

where x_{u_1} (x_{c_1}) is the optimal nonlabor input level under uncertainty (certainty) with the new technology. Since

$$\bar{\pi}_1 = (1 - \alpha_2)\bar{P}(L)A_1 x_{u_1}^{\alpha_2} - I$$

$$\pi_1(\bar{L}) = (1 - \alpha_2)P(\bar{L})A_1 x_{c_1}^{\alpha_2} - I$$

equation (7.B10) and Lemma 1(b) indicate that

$$\bar{\pi}_1 \geq \pi_1(\bar{L}) \tag{7.B11}$$

APPENDIX 7.C. PROOF OF PROPOSITION 6

(a) Since it is assumed that x = 1 and s = 0, $EU[\pi(L)]$ is compared with $U[\pi(\bar{L})]$. Differentiating $U[\pi_0(L)]$ with respect to L and introducing (7.A9) yields

$$\frac{dU[\pi_0(L)]}{dL} = \frac{\partial U}{\partial \pi_0} \alpha_1(1 - \varepsilon) \frac{\pi_0}{L} \tag{7.C1}$$

and using (7.A8), the second derivative is

$$\frac{d^2U[\pi_0(L)]}{dL^2} = \frac{\partial^2 U}{\partial \pi_0^2} \left[\alpha_1(1 - \varepsilon) \frac{\pi_0}{L}\right]^2 \phi\left[\frac{\partial U}{\partial \pi_0}\right]$$

$$\cdot \left[\alpha_1(1 - \varepsilon)\right]\left[\alpha_1(1 - \varepsilon) - 1\right] \frac{\pi_0}{L^2}$$

$$= \frac{\partial U}{\partial \pi_0} \alpha_1(1 - \varepsilon) \frac{\pi_0}{L^2} \{\left[\alpha_1(1 - \varepsilon) - 1\right]$$

$$- r_2\left[\alpha_1(1 - \varepsilon)\right]\} \tag{7.C2}$$

The assumption that $r_2 = 1$ in (7.C2) yields

$$\frac{d^2U(\pi_0)}{dL^2} = - \frac{\partial U}{\partial \pi_0} \alpha_1(1 - \varepsilon) \frac{\pi_0}{L}$$

and, by Jensen's inequality,

$$EU[\pi_0(L)] \begin{cases} > U[\pi_0(\bar{L})] \text{ if } \eta < 1 \\ < U[\pi_0(\bar{L})] \text{ if } \eta > 1 \end{cases} \tag{7.C3}$$

(b) Differentiating $\pi_1(L)$ with respect to L and using (7.A10) yields

$$\frac{dU(\pi_1)}{dL} = \frac{\partial U}{\partial \pi_1} \left[-\alpha_1 \varepsilon \frac{R_1}{L}\right] \tag{7.C4}$$

Using (7.C4) and $r_2 = 1$, the second derivative is

$$\frac{d^2U[\pi_1(L)]}{dL^2} = \frac{\partial U(\pi_1)}{\partial \pi} \left[\alpha_1 \varepsilon(\alpha_1 \varepsilon + 1)\right] \frac{R_1}{L^2}$$

$$+ \frac{\partial^2U(\pi_1)}{\partial \pi_1^2} \left[\alpha_1 \varepsilon \frac{R_1}{L}\right]^2$$

$$= \frac{\partial U(\pi_1)}{\partial \pi} \left[\alpha_1 \varepsilon \frac{R_1}{L^2} (\alpha_1 \varepsilon + 1 - r_2 \alpha_1 \varepsilon \frac{R_1}{\pi_1})\right]$$

$$= \frac{\partial U(\pi_1)}{\partial \pi} \left[\alpha_1 \varepsilon \frac{R_1}{L^2} (1 - \alpha_1 \varepsilon \frac{I}{\pi_1})\right] \qquad (7.C5)$$

If $\alpha_1 I/(\eta\pi_1) < 1$ for all L, (7.C5) indicates $d^2U/dL^2 > L$, and, by Jensen's inequality, $EU[\pi_1(L)] > U[\pi_1(\bar{L})]$.

Discussion

DANIEL A. SUMNER

Though the initial draft title, "Agricultural Product Markets and the Demand for Seasonal Labor," was very broad and suggests general results relating conditions in the output markets to conditions in the input markets, in fact the analysis by Professors Zilberman and Just is quite specific. A more ingenuous title might be "Some Theory Concerning the Effects of Uncertainty on Firm Behavior in Models in which the Labor Supply Function to the Industry is Vertical and Random: A Cobb-Douglas Example." In this comment I will resist temptation and will discuss Zilberman and Just on their own territory rather than branch out to the more general topic. I would look forward to seeing research that begins to develop, in a simultaneous framework, the supply and demand for seasonal labor with the supply and demand for farm output. Empirical work that relates product market changes to the labor market, and labor market changes to their effects on the product markets for particular industries, is an interesting and important area for economists to explore. But that is not what Zilberman and Just do and that is not what I will be considering. Instead, I will limit myself to discussing the issue of uncertainty models and seasonal farm labor. And though I will range a bit more broadly than their analysis did, I will concentrate on comments on the methods and results of Zilberman and Just.

It is probably useful to begin by placing this chapter in some perspective by mentioning the literature to which it is closely related and to which it primarily contributes. The article by Sandmo, which they cite, has by now spawned a whole series of articles that look at the effects of product demand uncertainty on product supply and also factor demands. One might mention articles by Batra and Ullah and by my colleague Duncan Holthausen that deal directly with input demand. While several articles deal with product demand uncertainty, only a couple consider the effects of uncertainty in factor markets on firm behavior. Blair has examined the effects of random input prices on firm behavior and profits. His analysis suggests that the effects of uncertainty depend crucially on specifics of the firm's attitude toward risk and on how the uncertainty enters the problem.

In Zilberman and Just's analysis the uncertainty enters through the supply function of one input while the rest of the relationships are deterministic. As far as I know, this has not been pursued before and it is worthwhile to have had some implications derived. A limitation of the present chapter is the use of a specific functional form for the model. Further, since the authors make no mention of how robust they expected their conclusions to be, the reader is left to speculate about which results depend on the Cobb-Douglas production function and which are more general. I assume that the chapter represents an early foray into the topic and that a more general specification can be worked out using similar lines of reasoning.

A key modification to Zilberman and Just is the incorporation of an upward sloping labor supply function. Even if the supply of labor is random, its distribution surely depends, to some extent, on the distribution of wage offers. An elasticity of supply of seasonal labor will be an additional parameter in the analysis, but it is not obvious (at least to me) exactly what changes will follow in the propositions of the paper. Since hired farm labor makes up such a small part of most labor markets, and since most seasonal farm workers are local people and not migrants, a more interesting polar case than the vertical supply function might be a horizontal seasonal labor supply facing a particular agricultural industry. The industry as well as the firms would then react to a stochastic wage rate, but the quantity of labor would be determined by the derived factor demand equation. (This case is more similar to the Blair article cited above.)

I would argue that the most interesting analysis of farmer welfare in a material sense is not that of the effects of a change in the wage rate of hired labor on short-run profits from the Cobb-Douglas formulation presented in this chapter. Instead, consider a farmer who owns some managerial human capital specific to the type of farming considered and for which there is an upward sloping aggregate supply (over some intermediate length of run). Further, he may own some land that also may have an upward sloping aggregate supply. The wealth of the farmer is affected by shifting the derived demand curves for these two owned factors of production. If seasonal labor is a complement for land and the farmer's human capital, then raising its wage shifts the demand for these two inputs to the left, reduces their equilibrium rental rates, and reduces the farmer's wealth. The crucial parameters for knowing if the owners of a factor of production gain or lose are the supply elasticity of that factor and the elasticity of substitution relative to the product demand elasticity. By their formulation Zilberman and Just ignore substitution elasticities or assume that they are unity. My empirical guess is that harvest hired labor and specific human capital of a farmer are in fact complements in production for most of the crops relevant to this discussion.

Before an empirical application of the model can

be considered, we need to decide on the appropriate criterion for an "industry" in the analysis. For example, do we want to call all U.S. flue cured tobacco producers an industry or only the North Carolina producers? Or take a West Coast example--are all U.S. bartlett pear producers the relevant industry or is the industry the Lake County bartlett pear producers? Obviously the elasticity of demand we expect depends on the definition of an industry we choose and the definition depends on the problem we are considering.

For this analysis the appropriate industry is defined by labor supply conditions and the implicit *ceteris paribus* of the Zilberman and Just model. The conceptual experiment is to consider the effects on product prices, factor prices, and profits from a shift in a labor supply function, holding constant the product demand and production function. The group of producers constituting the relevant industry is that which shares a given shift in the labor supply. If, for example, a strike in the Salinas Valley lettuce fields causes a leftward shift in labor supply during the harvest, causing a higher wage to prevail there, while other production areas do not experience a significant change in labor supply, then the relevant elasticity is the elasticity of demand for Salinas lettuce. We would expect this parameter to be quite large except in the very short run. Alternatively, a change in immigration policy enforcement might affect many areas (though to varying degrees) and the relevant demand elasticity for this change is much lower.

My first reaction to the idea of looking at uncertainty for farmers is to consider not factor supply uncertainty but yield uncertainty. This also can have implications for incentives for mechanization, so it may be worth some analysis. In this case the important distinction for the firm is not between labor-intensive or capital-intensive technology. The important point for the firm is whether it must commit itself to a quantity of harvest capability before the yield is known. Stochastic yield implies stochastic demand for harvesting services. If the firm internalizes the harvesting (or vertically integrates), say by mechanization (or certain contract arrangements), then the firm bears this risk. If instead the firm buys labor only as the yield becomes known, it is the workers who are faced with the risk of uncertain demand for their services.

Take, for example, the two-technology case of Zilberman and Just. With their "old" technology the firm faces no uncertainty from its stochastic labor demand. The potential labor force bears this risk. In some years there will be high wages and much work. In other years work will be scarce and the wage relatively low. Under the "new," or mechanized, technology the firm now internally owns the supply of harvesting services and thus itself bears the risk of demand uncertainty inherent in the stochastic yields. In low-yield years the machines will be underutilized and average cost of the harvest will be high, while in very high-yield years either the machines will be overutilized (again causing high harvest costs) or additional harvest labor will be purchased.

As an aside related to the comment above, consider mechanization of harvesting as a form of vertical integration. In the labor-intensive case the farm buys a product, harvesting services, from a supplier--either the workers themselves or a contractor firm. Alternatively, it may supply harvesting services to itself through mechanization. Even if one form of harvest was not inherently more certain than another (say because of potential machine breakdowns) the fact that the firm has more control and information in the mechanized case could allow for gains. Note that the firm incorporates the uncertain supply of harvesting services into its own operations. Arrow (1975) has developed some ideas related to supply uncertainty as an incentive to vertically integrate and Carlton has examined demand uncertainty and vertical integration. Both of those papers emphasize welfare conclusions and at best are suggestive of models to be developed for the case at hand.

Even within their specific model, the example of the contradictory effects of minimum wages on firm expected profits that Zilberman and Just mention in their concluding section seems odd. We can investigate this claim with their case in which a higher expected wage lowers profits. Since the minimum wage law reduces wage variation, Zilberman and Just assert that farmers might prefer it. An analysis can proceed using the upward sloping concave profit function in Figure 7.1, which illustrates Lemma 1(c). Let labor supply (prior to the law) take the values L_1 and L_2 each half the time; $\bar{L}$ is the mean labor supply and $E[\pi_0'(L)]$ is the expected profit. Now consider a minimum wage that causes L_2 to no longer be effective. For simplicity let the wage floor be equal to the wage that would follow from $\bar{L}$ being supplied. Now on Figure 7.1 it is as though labor supply is L_1 half the time and $\bar{L}$ the rest. The new expected profit lies on the straight line connecting the L_1 point on the profit function and the $\bar{L}$ point on the profit function and is given by the point on the line directly above the point $(L_1 + \bar{L})/2$. This point must fall below the expected profit from the no-minimum-wage case. So with risk neutrality, since a minimum wage reduces labor supply variation only by chopping off the upper part of the labor supply distribution, profits must fall even though stabilization at the mean raises expected profits.

Finally, I must voice my skepticism that the effects of labor supply uncertainty is one of the major issues yet unresolved in our understanding of seasonal farm labor markets. As this book makes explicit, many of the basic empirical relationships of labor supply and demand have yet to be estimated reliably. The development of models with simple econometric specifications to estimate some of these parameters is the pressing order of business. I think that exploring uncertainty issues at this stage of our ignorance, while interesting, adds a refinement before we have the more basic knowledge in place.

8

An Intertemporal Approach to Seasonal Agricultural Labor Markets

THOMAS H. SPREEN

The existence and nature of the seasonal farm labor phenomenon has been discussed by Holt and Huffman (Chaps. 1 and 2). Briefly summarized, the nature of agricultural production and the extent of its mechanization give rise to seasonal demand for labor by agricultural producers. Mechanical harvesting has evolved for the feed and food grains, but for many fruit and vegetable crops and tobacco, labor intensive harvesting methods are utilized. Furthermore, climatic, agronomic, economic, and historical factors have resulted in regional specialization of crop production.

Particular regions tend to specialize in a single crop or a few related crops. At harvest time, local demand for farm labor increases manyfold. Seasonal labor is supplied in part by local individuals who, for various reasons, prefer seasonal rather than year-round employment (Huffman, Chap. 2). This local supply, however, may be such that wage rates for temporary farm labor in a particular region rise, providing an incentive for individuals to migrate from other regions. The result is the migratory labor phenomenon.

The objective of this paper is to propose an analytical framework to assist analysis of issues relating to seasonal farm labor markets. The term "propose" must be emphasized. The nature of local seasonal labor markets, linked by migratory workers who provide services in more than one local market, lends itself to being quantitatively analyzed through a particular methodology. In this chapter the methodology is described, a conceptual model is developed, and conjectural analysis is performed. The term "conjectural" is used because data have not been collected and an empirically specified model has not been constructed.

METHODOLOGY

As noted by Huffman (Chap. 2), labor in a market must be homogeneous in three characteristics: skill, geographic location, and point in time. Our focus is on temporary harvest labor. Several temporary labor markets throughout the United States can be delineated on the basis of location and season. In this chapter the term "temporary farm labor market" refers to a market for temporary unskilled labor utilized primarily for harvesting crops, existing in a particular region (or locale) for a specific period of time (typically, the harvest season). Embodied in this definition is the assumption that such markets can be delineated and differentiated, in that demand and supply relationships for a particular market are observable.

The existence of migratory labor explicitly links spatially and temporally separated temporary farm labor markets. The linkage is provided by the migrants themselves. As noted by Emerson (Chap. 4), the decision by persons to migrate is based in part on the earnings they expect to receive as migrant laborers. Factors which combine to determine their potential earnings as laborers are the demand and supply conditions in those temporary farm labor markets in which they participate.

Review of Literature

Analysis of seasonal farm labor markets can be viewed from the perspective of equilibrium in spatially and temporally separated markets. Samuelson first addressed the issue of equilibrium of spatially separated markets for a single commodity. Takayama and Judge (1964a, b) later extended the Samuelson formulation to multiple products. Takayama and Judge (1971), in their landmark book, showed that equilibrium in temporally separated markets and equilibrium in spatially separated markets are equivalent problems mathematically. Thus spatial and intertemporal market equilibrium models can be formulated to address issues such as optimal trade flows between regions and optimal storage over time. Duloy and Norton (1973, 1975) extended the Takayama and Judge formulation through the introduction of alternative production technologies for a given commodity. Hazell and Scandizzo (1974) introduced risk considerations into mathematical programming sector models.

The works outlined above all have dealt with equilibrium in product markets. Hazell (1979) and McCarl and Spreen have shown that such models can be extended to factor market equilibrium as well.

A MATHEMATICAL MODEL

Assume, for illustrative purposes, that there are three regions of interest. Region 1's harvest occurs in time period 1 and harvest in Region 2 and Region 3 takes place in time period 2. Thus there are three temporary farm labor markets. Assume that there is only one crop to be harvested in each region and let q_k denote the level of production of the crop in Region k, measured in acres planted.

Region 1 is the sole supplier of the crop it produces in time period 1 and the crop cannot be stored over time periods. The aggregate demand for its crop is

$$P_1 = D_1(Z_1, \theta_1) \tag{8.1}$$

where P_1 = market price of crop grown in Region 1, Z_1 = consumption of crop grown in Region 1, and

θ_1 = vector of other variables that influence the demand for crop grown in Region 1. The term θ_1 includes relevant demand factors such as consumer income, population, and prices (or quantities) of related commodities. The components of θ are of secondary interest. We assume

$$\frac{\partial D_1}{\partial Z_1} < 0 \qquad (8.2)$$

i.e., the demand function is downward sloping.

The total production from Region 2 and Region 3 is not significant relative to the total supply of those crops available in time period 2, thus the prices of those crops are assumed to be exogenously determined at P_2 and P_3.

Let the per acre yields of crops in each region be given by d_k; thus

$$Z_k = d_k q_k \quad (k = 1, 2, 3) \qquad (8.3)$$

where Z_2 and Z_3 denote total crop production in Regions 2 and 3, respectively.

The per acre temporary labor requirement for each of the three regions is c_k; thus

$$L_k = c_k q_k \quad (k = 1, 2, 3) \qquad (8.4)$$

where L_k is total temporary labor employed in Region k. Equation (8.4) assumes a fixed proportion relationship between the number of acres planted and the amount of temporary labor required in a particular region. All other costs of production such as permanent labor, fertilizer, irrigation, etc., per acre are r_k for Region k, (k = 1, 2, 3).

Let the supply of temporary labor provided by persons domiciled in Region 1 for work in Region 1 be given by

$$W_1 = S_1(L^1, \Gamma^1) \tag{8.5}$$

where W_1 = relevant wage rate in Region 1, L^1 = labor supplied by persons domiciled in Region 1, and Γ^1 = vector of other factors that influence the supply of temporary labor in Region 1. The term Γ^1 includes the opportunity wage rate or, as a proxy, the wage rate in the nonfarm sector at the equivalent skill level. Thus (8.5) is specified consistent with the usual assumption that the wage rate must attain some minimum level (i.e., the opportunity wage) before any temporary labor is supplied. It is also assumed that

$$\frac{\partial S_1}{\partial L^1} > 0 \tag{8.6}$$

i.e., the temporary labor supply function is upward sloping.

Similarly, for Region 2 and Region 3

$$W_2 = S_2(L^2, \Gamma^2) \tag{8.7}$$

$$W_3 = S_3(L^3, \Gamma^3) \tag{8.8}$$

and S_2 and S_3 are assumed to possess the properties described for S_1, above.

To simplify the exposition, assume that workers domiciled in Region 1 may migrate to Region 2 or Region 3, but workers domiciled in Region 2 or Region 3 will not migrate to Region 1. For example, if Florida is Region 1, New York is Region 2, and New Jersey is Region 3, we observe that workers domiciled in Florida migrate to New York or New Jersey for summer work, but workers domiciled in the North rarely migrate south.

The supply relationship for persons in Region 1 to migrate to Region 2 is

$$W_2 = S_{12}(L_1^2, \Gamma_1^2) \tag{8.9}$$

where L_1^2 = labor supplied in Region 2 by those who work in Region 1, and Γ_1^2 = vector of other factors which influence the decision to migrate. Emerson (Chap. 4) discusses the nature of the functional relationship S_{12} and the components of Γ_1^2, and the reader is referred to that chapter for a more detailed discussion. Note that the left-hand side of (8.9), W_2, is the same as that of (8.7). That is, workers who migrate from Region 1 to Region 2 receive the same wage rate as those domiciled in Region 2, since workers provide the same services irrespective of their origin. (If an employer provides certain perquisites, such as housing to migrant workers, these are assumed to be included in the wages.)

Similarly for Region 3

$$W_3 = S_{13}(L_1^3, \Gamma_1^3) \tag{8.10}$$

The temporary labor market in each region clears if the demand for temporary labor equals the total supply of labor, i.e., if

$$L_1 = L^1 \ : \ \text{Region 1} \tag{8.11}$$

$$L_2 = L^2 + L_1^2 \ : \ \text{Region 2} \tag{8.12}$$

$$L_3 = L^3 + L_1^3 \ : \ \text{Region 3} \tag{8.13}$$

and we restrict

$$L_1^2 + L_1^3 \leqslant L^1 \tag{8.14}$$

that is, we assume persons will migrate only if they have worked in Region 1.

Takayama and Judge (1971) have shown that a constrained optimization problem can be formulated that will determine the competitive equilibrium levels of q_k and hence Z_k, L_k, and the flows of labor L_1^2 and L_1^3. Stated mathematically the problem is:

$$\text{Maximize} \int_0^{Z_1} D_1(Z_1, \theta_1)dZ_1 + P_2Z_2 + P_3Z_3 - \sum_{k=1}^{3} r_k q_k$$

$$- \sum_{j=1}^{3} \left[\int_0^{L^j} S_j(L^j, \Gamma^j)dL^j\right]$$

$$- \int_0^{L_1^2} S_{12}(L_1^2, \Gamma_1^2)dL_1^2$$

$$- \int_0^{L_1^3} S_{13}(L_1^3, \Gamma_1^3)dL_1^3 \qquad (8.15)$$

subject to

$$Z_k = d_k q_k \qquad (k = 1, 2, 3) \qquad (8.15a)$$

$$L_k = c_k q_k \qquad (k = 1, 2, 3) \qquad (8.15b)$$

$$L_1 = L^1 \qquad (8.15c)$$

$$L_2 = L^2 + L_1^2 \qquad (8.15d)$$

$$L_3 = L^3 + L_1^3 \qquad (8.15e)$$

$$L_1^2 + L_1^3 \leqslant L^1 \qquad (8.15f)$$

where Z_k, q_k, L^k, L_k, L_1^2, $L_1^3 \geq 0$ (k = 1, 2, 3).

The constraints defined by (8.15a-e) are the input-output relationships and the market clearing requirements for each of the three temporary labor markets. The objective function (8.15) is the sum of the areas under the product demand schedule for the crop produced in each region[1] less the miscellaneous cost of production ($\sum_{k=1}^{3} r_k q_k$) less the sum of the areas under the labor supply schedules. The quantity measured by the objective function has been referred to in the literature as net social benefit (Samuelson; Takayama and Judge 1971, p. 108).

The constrained optimization model takes as data the production coefficients (r_k, c_k, and d_k), demand relations for products, and supply relations for temporary labor. The solution of the model generates equilibrium price and quantity for products and wage rates, seasonal employment, and labor flows between regions. In the product market, the exogenously specified demand relation is equilibrated with an implicit supply relation, which corresponds to the aggregate marginal cost schedule as generated by the model. In the labor market, the exogenously specified labor supply relations are equilibrated with implicit derived demand for temporary labor relations, which correspond to the marginal value product of temporary labor in each region. An important point is that the model does not require supply of products or demand for temporary labor relations. Rather, these relations are derived internally, based upon specific input-output, miscellaneous costs of production, product demand, and labor supply relationships.

Region 1's product price and the wage rates are not explicit variables in the model. The equilibrium product price for the crop in Region 1 is the dual variable (Lagrange multiplier, see Takayama and Judge 1971, p. 138) associated with (8.15a) for k = 1. The equilibrium price can also be calculated by substituting the equilibrium value for Z_1 back into (8.1). Both values for P_1 are identical (Takayama and Judge 1971, p. 138). The equilibrium wage rate in each region can be calculated in a similar manner. First, (8.15b) can be combined with equations (8.15c, d, e) to give

$$c_1q_1 = L^1 \qquad (8.16a)$$

$$c_2q_2 = L^2 + L_1^2 \qquad (8.16b)$$

$$c_3q_3 = L^3 + L_1^3 \qquad (8.16c)$$

The dual variable (Lagrange multipliers) associated with each of these constraints is the equilibrium temporary wage rate for a region. Similar to the product market, equilibrium wage rates in each region can also be calculated by substituting the equilibrium value for L^k back into the corresponding labor supply relation.

Size of Model

The model presented in (8.15) and (8.15a-f) is a skeletal model in that the only input in the crop production process that is explicitly considered is temporary labor. All other inputs have been collected in the parameter r_k. More detail can be inserted into the model by explicitly accounting for permanent labor, fertilizer, irrigation, and so on, through the addition of accounting rows and purchase activities for each input. Furthermore, if the producers constitute a significant source of demand for a particular input, such that the assumption of a fixed, exogenously determined price for that input is not tenable, then a supply relation for that input can be introduced, analogous to the supply relation for temporary labor.

The specification of (8.15) and (8.15a-f) assumes a single production technology in each region. If producers in a particular region vary widely in their production practices, then a more appropriate specification would be to identify homogeneous groups of producers within a region and estimate the appropriate parameters (d_k, c_k, and r_k) for each group. Then define q_{ik} as the level of production of the ith homogeneous group of producers in Region k. Region k is thus represented by multiple production activities. (It may be necessary to constrain the model so that each group of producers is adequately represented. Usually, one technology is more efficient for a given set of product and input prices, and so will be the only alternative represented in the optimal solution.) If more than one crop is grown in a region, but all crops compete for temporary labor, then production activities (columns) must be defined for each crop and the appropriate input-output coefficients (c_k and d_k) and miscellaneous costs (r_k) estimated.

Scope of the Model

In order to specify (8.15) and (8.15a-f) we considered only three temporary labor markets and assumed that persons would migrate from Region 1 only. More temporary labor markets could be considered by enlarging the scope of the model, specifying a production technology, product demand, labor supply, and supply of migratory labor for each additional market. Theoretically, every local temporary labor market in the United States could be modeled. The size of the resulting model, however, would be unmanageable. The practical approach is to identify those temporary labor markets that are explicitly linked by migratory labor or that may be linked given some significant structural shift. For example, the Florida winter market and the New York and New Jersey summer markets constitute linked markets. Fewer people migrate from Florida to Michigan. The need to include Michigan in the model is dictated by policy issues and research resources.

IMPLICATIONS OF THE MODEL

Equilibrium Across Temporary Labor Markets

Let us turn our attention toward equilibrium in the temporary labor markets. Since exact values for the parameters of (8.15) and (8.15a-f) are not known, we can only conjecture as to possible solutions of the model.

Consider Figure 8.1.[2] The line marked D_2D_2 represents the marginal value product of temporary labor in Region 2. (Region 1 is the trivial case since no migration is assumed to occur into it.) Both the wage rate and the demand for temporary labor are endogenous to the model, but by successively solving the model for various labor supply relations, the derived demand for labor can be "traced" out.[3] The curve labeled S_2S_2 is the local supply of temporary labor and $S_1^2S_1^2$ is the supply of migratory labor from Region 1 to Region 2; $S_2\bar{S}_2\bar{S}_2$ is the horizontal sum of S_2S_2 and $S_1^2S_1^2$. The equilibrium wage rate and temporary labor employed determined by the intersection of

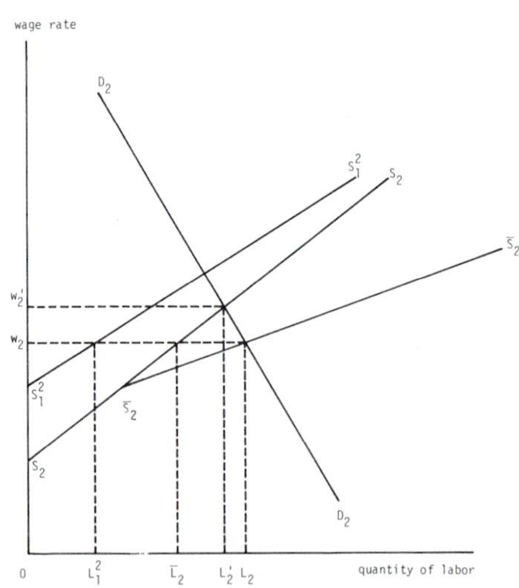

Fig. 8.1. Market equilibrium with migration.

D_2D_2 and $S_2\bar{S}_2\bar{S}_2$ occur at wage rate W_2 and level of employment L_2. The level of migration from Region 1 to Region 2 is L_1^2 and the employment of persons domiciled in Region 2 is $\bar{L}_2$. In the absence of migration, the wage rate would have been W_2' and local employment at L_2'. Thus given the position of the supply and demand schedules, the equilibrium wage rate is lower with migration and total employment is larger, but employment of persons domiciled in Region 2 is smaller.[4]

The condition that indicates whether workers will in fact choose to migrate from Region 1 to Region 2 is given by the intercept of the supply of migratory labor relation (8.9) relative to W_2'. That is, if the wage rate in Region 2 without migration is less than the opportunity cost to workers of migration from Region 1 to Region 2, then no migration between the regions will occur. This situation is depicted in Figure 8.2.

Next consider Figure 8.3. The temporary labor markets for Region 2 and Region 3 are shown. The

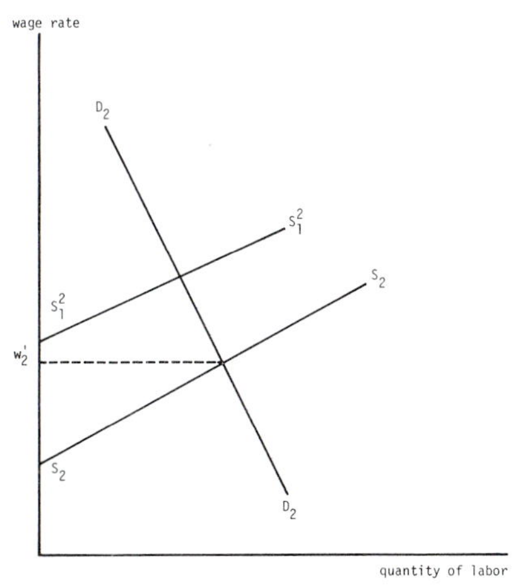

Fig. 8.2. Opportunity wage exceeds wage rate.

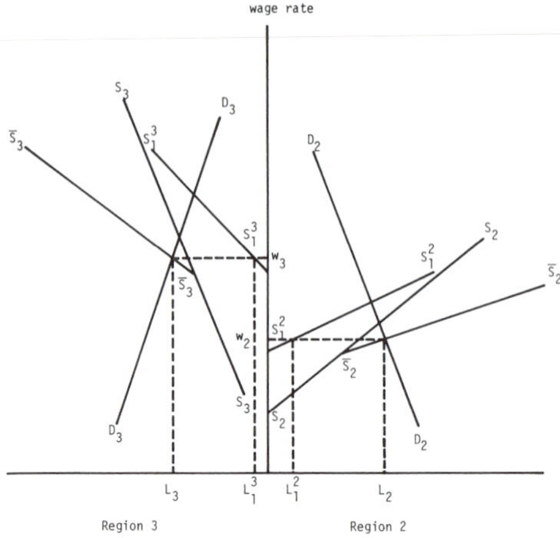

Fig. 8.3. Market equilibrium across regions with migration.

demand for labor in each region is given by D_kD_k and the supply relations are specified in a manner similar to that of Figure 8.1. Note that migration occurs from Region 1 to both Region 2 and Region 3, but a wage differential exists between Region 2 and Region 3. The magnitude of this differential may be exaggerated. It is important to point out, however, that the model will not equilibrate wage rates across regions.

In the formulation of the model, we assumed that persons based in Region 1 who may choose to migrate to Region 2 or Region 3 make two decisions. The first is the decision to supply their services to the temporary labor market in Region 1. The second decision is whether to migrate and, if so, to which region. Thus the relative magnitudes of the parameters of each labor supply relation will determine, in part, the size of wage differentials across regions. If the supplies of migratory labor relations were identical, implying that persons are indifferent towards migrating to Region 2 or Region 3, then equilibrium wage rates in Region 2 and Region 3 would be identical, assuming that migration to both of those regions occurs.

USE OF THE MODEL FOR ANALYSIS

An attractive feature of a mathematical programming model is its usefulness in the analysis of changes in the economic environment. A review of the literature incorporating a variety of modifications in a mathematical programming sector model is contained in McCarl and Spreen. In this chapter we consider two issues relevant to seasonal agricultural labor markets: the impact of the introduction of mechanical harvesting and the use of offshore labor. It is important to note, however, that a wide range of issues can be analyzed.

Mechanical Harvesting

Consider the three-region example used above. Suppose that a mechanical harvest alternative is introduced in Region 1. The model given by (8.15) and (8.15a-f) is modified by introducing a second production activity (column) in Region 1. Let q_{11} represent the existing production technology, with parameters c_{11}, d_{11}, and r_{11}, and let q_{21} represent the mechanical harvesting technology and d_{21} = yield per acre utilizing mechanical harvesting, r_{21} = all costs other than temporary labor per acre for q_{21}, and c_{21} = use of temporary labor per acre with mechanical harvesting. It is expected, of course, that c_{21} is much smaller than c_{11} but is probably not zero, since some temporary labor is required for handling, sorting, and loading.

Two questions come to mind. First, is the mechanical harvest alternative more profitable than the existing technology? The answer depends on the size of d_{21}, r_{21}, and c_{21}, relative to d_{11}, r_{11}, and c_{11}, and on the supply of temporary labor in Region 1. Second, if the mechanical harvest alternative is more profitable, what will be its impact on the temporary labor market? The model can provide answers through its solution when both alternatives are specified.

It is likely that a mechanical harvest alternative would shift the derived demand for temporary labor in Region 1 as shown in Figure 8.4 as $D_1'D_1'\bar{D}_1D_1$. The demand lies to the left at high wage rates. At w_1^*, the two alternatives are equally profitable, as is represented by the horizontal portion of the curve. At wages below w_1^*, hand harvesting is more profitable. The demand for temporary labor without mechanical harvesting is D_1D_1. Given the labor supply relation, S_1S_1, as depicted in Figure 8.4, equilibrium wage rate and employment without mechanical harvesting is w_1 and L_1; with mechanical harvesting, the equilibrium is at wage rate w_1', and employment L_1'. The effect of the introduction of mechanical harvesting in Region 1, in this situation, is a lower equilibrium wage rate and less employment. This will always be the case if the equilibrium wage level without mechanical harvesting exceeds w_1^*,

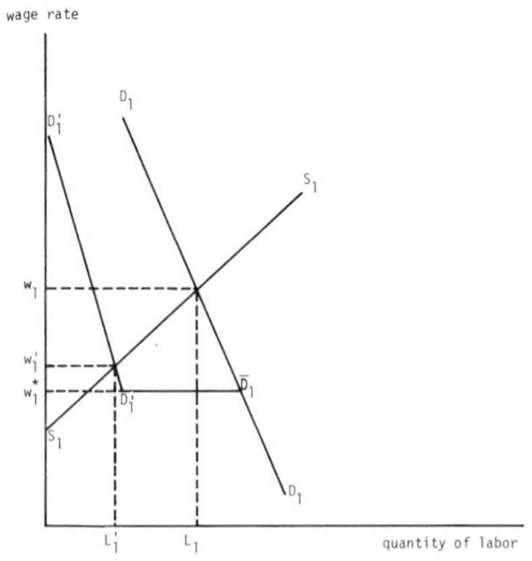

Fig. 8.4. Market equilibrium with mechanical harvesting.

the wage level at which producers are indifferent between mechanical and hand harvest.

The effect of the introduction of mechanical harvesting in Region 1 on Region 2 and Region 3 is not clear cut. This is because we assume that persons who constitute the supply side make two separate decisions. The first decision relates to supplying their services for temporary labor in Region 1. If they choose and are able to find temporary labor in Region 1, then we assume they face a decision on whether to migrate. A shift in the demand for temporary labor in Region 1 does not alter the supply of temporary labor in Region 1 nor the supply of temporary labor in Region 2 by persons based in Region 1. Thus if the number of persons migrating from Region 1 (before mechanical harvesting) did not exceed L_1', the equilibrium employment level in Region 1 with mechanical harvesting, then Regions 2 and 3 are unaffected. If total migration, however, exceeded L_1', then a different scenario evolves. Consider Figure 8.5. All lines are defined as in Figure 8.1, but now the supply of temporary labor in Region 2 from persons based in

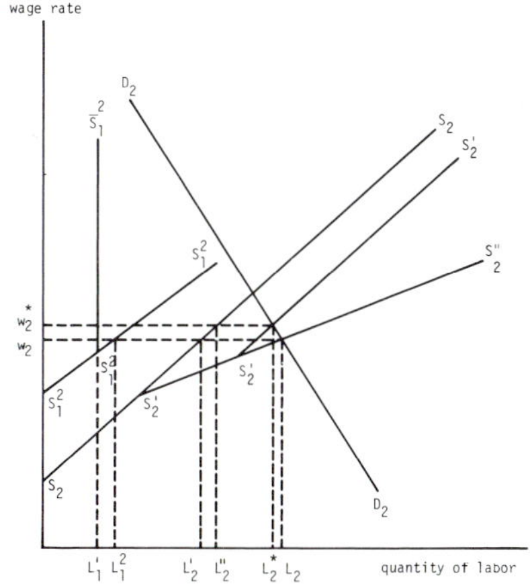

Fig. 8.5. Market equilibrium with mechanical harvesting affecting the supply of migratory labor.

Region 1 is altered. The supply relation is now $S_1^2 \bar{S}_1^2 \bar{S}_1^2$. The vertical portion results because total migration from Region 1 to Region 2 is limited by total temporary employment in Region 1, and we hypothesize that total temporary employment in Region 1 with mechanical harvesting is L_1'. The aggregate labor supply relation in Region 2 is now $S_2 S_2' S_2' S_2'$ whereas the supply relation without mechanical harvesting was $S_2 S_2' S_2''$.

The impact on wage rates and employment in Region 2 of the mechanical harvest introduction in Region 1 is that the temporary wage rate increases from w_2 to w_2^*, total employment declines from L_2 to L_2^*, migration from Region 1 to Region 2 declines from L_1^2 to L_1', but employment of persons based in Region 2 increases from L_2' to L_2''.

Implicit in the analysis above is the assumption that persons who seek but do not find temporary employment as farm laborers eventually find work elsewhere. That is, there is a "sponge" for unskilled workers, which is the reason for upward sloping supply relations with positive intercepts on the wage axis.

In addition, we should note that the introduction of mechanical harvesting changes the nature of the demand for seasonal farm labor. More skill is often required in a mechanical harvest operation. Thus it is possible that with the introduction of mechanical harvesting the demand for unskilled labor by agricultural producers in a particular region could disappear almost entirely, exacerbating the impact on other regions to which it is linked.

Use of Offshore Labor

The terms "offshore" and "alien" labor refer to foreign workers used to meet temporary needs for farm labor. Examples include the use of Jamaican nationals to hand harvest Florida sugarcane and to harvest northeastern apples.

To use offshore labor, employers must file requests with the USDL and demonstrate that domestic workers will not be adversely affected. The employers usually argue that, at prevailing wage rates, they are unable to recruit reliable domestic workers and so are forced to import foreign labor. The crux of the issue concerns the level of the appropriate prevailing wage. Economic theory suggests that workers can be recruited to perform any task, even a strenuous task such as hand harvesting sugarcane, given a sufficiently high wage level.

To illustrate the impact of alien labor, consider Figure 8.6. Assume that Region 1 is the only region directly affected. The derived demand for temporary labor is given by D_1D_1 and the local supply by S_1S_1. In the absence of alien labor, the equilibrium wage rate is W_1 and total employment is L_1. Suppose an agreement is signed which allows the importation of workers whose number is given by the line segment $L_1^{'}L_1^{''}$. The negotiated guaranteed wage is $W_1^{'}$. The result is that the total supply of temporary labor

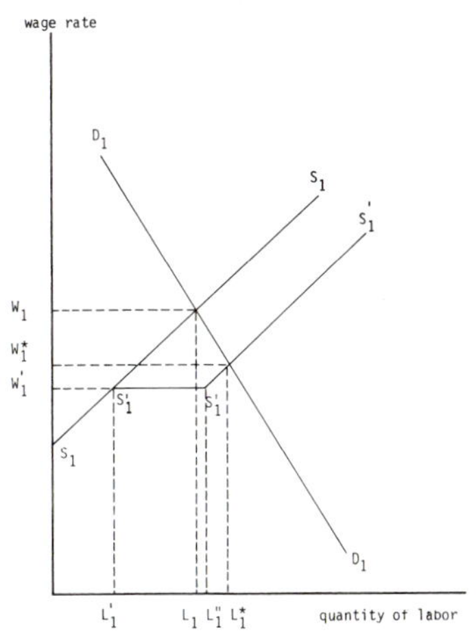

Fig. 8.6. The impact of off-shore labor.

shifts and is now given by $S_1S_1'S_1'S_1'$. In this case, the equilibrium wage drops to W_1^* and total employment increases to L_1^*. Domestic employment declines, even though total employment (and hence total crop production) is larger.

The situation depicted in Figure 8.6 is purely conjectural. The power of the proposed framework is its capacity to simulate the impact of a wide variety of scenarios relating to various levels of the negotiated wage W_2', and the absolute number of imported workers on the equilibrium wage rate, total and domestic employment, crop production, and product prices.

CONCLUDING COMMENTS

A mathematical programming model of seasonal farm labor markets has been formulated and its usefulness in the analysis of the impact of mechanical harvesting and use of offshore labor has been illustrated. If time and space permitted, other issues confronting seasonal farm labor markets could be addressed, such as illegals, minimum wages, and production technologies using lower levels of pesticides.

The incorporation of risk considerations into the model has not been shown but can be accomplished. The methods of Hazell (1971) and Hazell and Scandizzo (1974) provide a direct approach to incorporation of risk into the analysis. Seasonal farm labor is utilized primarily to harvest fresh fruits and vegetables, which are subject to yield variability. Therefore risk consideration and its attendant effect on producer response could be important and should be incorporated into the model.

Any exposition on large-scale mathematical programming models should acknowledge the data requirements of such a model. In the formulation of (8.15) and (8.15a-f), we assumed that the labor supply relations (8.5), (8.7)-(8.10) and the product demand relation (8.1) had been estimated. The estimation of the labor supply relations is no small task. Furthermore it was assumed that the production parameters (c_k,' d_k, and r_k) had been estimated. Most states routinely gather such information (e.g., Muraro and Abbitt), but the compilation of information for several regions is time consuming and resource exhausting.

Data requirements should not deter the construction of the proposed framework, which provides an integrated and, in this author's opinion, a useful approach to quantitative analysis of issues relating to seasonal farm labor markets.

Discussion

TERRY GLOVER

The apparent focus of this volume is on the likelihood of the continuation of the seasonal component of agricultural labor markets and on what can be done to modify the consequences of the continuation or alteration of seasonal and migrant employment. The seasonality of farm labor demand is the basic phenomenon giving rise to migration. If this seasonality were to diminish greatly, we would expect intertemporal migration for employment to likewise diminish.

It appears to be the purpose of Spreen's analysis to offer a framework for simulating changes on both the demand and supply sides of the seasonal farm labor market in order to provide information on this subject for review. That purpose is not clear, however, since two themes actually emerge from this chapter. One theme is a brief description of a spatial model that could be used to solve for migrant labor flows and wages. The other is an illustrative model used to trace the effects of mechanization primarily on interregional employment and earnings.

The first exposition yields no conclusion, although it is implied that the spatial model first described can be made operational and used, with modifications, to empirically represent the model presented in the second part of the chapter. There is nothing new in that development. The spatial model, with all of its modifications, has been used to obtain information on the interregional flows and returns of other commodities and factors, including the labor input. Strong, in a 1973 study of the divergence of labor earnings between the farm and nonfarm sectors, developed a theoretical dynamic framework to view the transfer of farm workers to nonfarm employment. This control theoretic framework was converted to an intertemporal spatial model to solve for optimal transfers and equilibrium wages.

The usefulness of such models for constructing simulations of interregional and intertemporal transfers and associated earnings lies in the characterization of the labor demand and supply behavior. Without this, we do not capture the market phenomenon and our simulations give us weak information. If no information is available except the levels of demand and supply, wage equations can be derived from the equilibrium and complementary slackness conditions for the Smith rent model, which relate wages in specific regions to levels of labor and output in every other region. Of course a data series is required for estimation of these relationships, whereas the spatial model offered here requires only benchmark data and previously estimated supply functions. But at least we can obtain regional wage-labor relationships which reflect the changing market structure represented in these data.

It is on the characterization of supply in both models presented in this chapter that I have reservations. The supply of products and the derived demand in the fixed proportions case represented in the spatial model are derived internally, based on the supply relationships, among other factors. Also, the assumption of a minimum wage level, or a nonmigration reservation wage, hinges on the behavior underlying the labor supply and migration decision. The labor supply and migration functions used seem to be oversimplified. In the spatial model characterization, one can solve Region 1's problem first and then turn to the other regions because of the way the supply functions are characterized.

Furthermore, it seems as though annual earnings would be the relevant factor upon which decisions to seek employment outside of the local market would depend. Annual earnings may be comprised of several different wage rates and, possibly, asset income. That is, the demand for leisure, hence labor supply in the case at hand, is derived from maximization of utility subject to a piecewise linear budget constraint comprised of different wage levels.

Obviously, this underlying supply behavior, if characterized, complicates the model and suggests that the more serious modeling work is to be done in specifying the supply and/or migration decision. Wales and Woodland have given us some insight on characterizing labor response to multiple wage levels, and there is a considerable body of literature on the derivation of labor supply from utility maximization behavior that might help us. However, linear supply functions do not generally result, and I would venture to state that linear supply functions do not represent a very interesting and useful case.

But all is not lost. The spatial model can still be used with accompanying nonlinear supply and/or demand functions. We would probably have to use some fixed point solution algorithm but, using the recent developments of MacKinnon, a fixed point algorithm has been successfully used to model interregional commodity trade with nonlinear demand and supply (Warner). I admit that these solution procedures are complex, but the virtues of and the information that can be gleaned from the spatial model are preserved.

To be fair, Spreen does imply a piecewise supply behavior in his graphical exposition. However, the migration supply function in the spatial model first offered does not adequately capture that behavior. Indeed, there are even endogenous elements implied in the migration supply function but not explicitly characterized in the specification of that function. Specifically, the minimum wage level below which no workers will migrate from the local market to another market is determined by other factors. The factors influencing that wage level are the subject of Chapter 4.

On another point, Spreen appears to argue that migration to secure temporary employment is meaningful only if there is seasonal work in different locations. However, if the seasonality in one location diminished greatly, it is not unlikely that workers would migrate from other locations. We would like to know the extent to which migration would possibly be slowed or altered interregionally. It is for this need that we would use spatial models like the one proposed to obtain information for alternative demand assumptions and seasonal patterns that might be perceived.

On still another point, Spreen suggests in his closing statements that risk considerations can be incorporated into the spatial model, and that is an important generalization. Risk and reorganization of the production plan to modify risks definitely change the demand for the labor input. However, the mean-variance approach to describing risk in the Hazell-Scandizzo framework suggested does not, for example, explain changes in quasi fixed inputs made before output price is observed and subsequent changes in the demand for variable inputs as price is observed. Representation of these effects of risk, and I would maintain they are the important ones for the issues being taken up here, would more likely follow the mean preserving-increasing risk developments of Rothschild and Stiglitz (1970, 1971).

Although I have expressed reservations about what has been characterized, or about the lack of characterization, in the models being offered, Spreen's analysis is on target in pointing out directions for obtaining information on possible changes in seasonality and their consequences. To be sure, we need this kind of information before decisions to intervene or not to intervene are made. Without such information I would opt, having more faith in the market than some, to err on the side of nonintervention.

9

Unstructured Labor Markets and Alternative Labor Market Forms

ROBERT W. GLOVER

Harvest labor markets in the United States offer perhaps the classic examples of unstructured labor markets. Workers have little job security or opportunity for advancement. There is limited attachment to particular employers and historically workers have not been covered by collective bargaining or protective labor legislation. Because workers have had little power to protect their interests and enforcement agencies have limited staffs, even modest protective legislation is frequently violated.

Employment is unstable and employers have had strong incentives to maintain labor surpluses. There has been widespread use of undocumented alien workers in competition with domestic workers. The work is seasonal and casual and work opportunities are uncertain. Employment is often of short duration and the work site is ever changing.

Harvest work has been highly competitive and wages are low. Payment for work has been mainly by the piece. Fringe benefits are nonexistent or minimal.

Indeed, farm work is often presented as the archetypical illustration of a secondary labor market. (For an analysis and comparison of primary and secondary labor markets, see Doeringer and

Piore.) All the characteristics descriptive of jobs in secondary labor markets have been present in farm work: low wages and fringe benefits, poor working conditions, high labor turnover, little chance of advancement, little training on the job, often arbitrary and capricious supervision, and the absence of work rules and processes such as seniority, formal grievance procedures, and job evaluation plans.

The key factors that distinguish secondary jobs are their instability and a lack of attachment between workers and jobs. These factors are reflected in high rates of voluntary and involuntary turnover. As Doeringer and Piore point out, in secondary labor markets "instability appears to be a characteristic of both jobs and workers" (p. 166). Workers who hold jobs in the secondary sector tend to exhibit certain characteristics including greater turnover and higher rates of tardiness and absenteeism. Indeed the instability of jobs and of workers may interact:

> Unstable and undesirable jobs may encourage workers to place low value upon job security, while a work force prone to turnover may make the costs of its reduction prohibitively high (p. 170).

In addition to *instability*, several other factors are involved in influencing labor markets to create and maintain secondary employment, according to Doeringer and Piore. These include the *lack of collective bargaining and trade union organization* that could give rise to such devices as guaranteed annual wages, formalized work-sharing arrangements, supplemental unemployment benefits and termination pay, seniority, training ladders, and pension plans (all of which tend to reduce job and employee instability). Also mentioned is the lack of labor legislation and social welfare legislation such as unemployment compensation, social security, minimum wage, and worker's compensation.

Among worker-centered influences are the behavioral patterns learned on the job and low-income lifestyles more attuned to secondary than primary sector employment. Finally, discrimination against low-income people generally isolates poor people from other social classes and perpetuates behavioral traits characteristic of low-income individuals (Doeringer and Piore, pp. 169-77).

Let us now compare the five aforementioned influences with the key factors in the California harvest market uncovered by Lloyd Fisher during the late 1940s. Fisher identified five general conditions for the existence of an unstructured market in California agriculture (pp. 7-9):

1. There must be no unions with their usual accompaniment of seniority, preference of employment, and other limitations upon access to the labor market.
2. There must be an impersonal relationship between employer and employee, lest informal obligations and various types of moral tenure develop.
3. The productive employment must be largely unskilled, so that it becomes accessible to a large and specialized labor force . . . and when division of labor is required, that the division is not a division based on hierarchy of skill.
4. The method of compensation must be by unit of product rather than by unit of time.
5. The operation must employ little or no capital or machinery.

Note that only the first factor, lack of unionization, is mentioned by both Fisher and by Doeringer and Piore. The other factors, while complementary to one another, differ significantly. Fisher focuses more on the nature of the jobs whereas Doeringer and Piore place emphasis on legal and social environmental conditions and on the people holding the jobs.

Both lists seem to describe the traditional picture of agricultural labor markets in the United States. However, the picture has changed significantly with regard to some of these factors during the past decade, especially with regard to the legal environment. At the national level, the former exclusions of farm workers have been eliminated in almost all labor standards legislation including minimum wage, social security, and unemployment insurance. Moreover, unions are no longer absent. In California, unions have a significant proportion of harvest workers under contract. In some states, worker's compensation now applies to farm workers. Also in California, labor legislation is a reality in the form of the California Agricultural Labor Relations Act of 1975.

Even though Fisher preceded Doeringer and Piore by two decades, the conditions he identified, especially those characterizing the nature of harvest work, have remained notably unchanged. One exception is the advent of extensive mechanization in selected crops, such as tomatoes. As indicated in the third column of Table 9.1, altogether six out of the nine factors or conditions mentioned have remained relatively

Table 9.1. Summary of key conditions or determinants for structureless labor markets in agricultural work

Fisher 1953	Doeringer and Piore 1971	Status of conditions 1980
	1. Instability of work	Relatively unchanged
1. Absence of unions	2. Absence of collective bargaining and union organization	Changed significantly in California only
2. Impersonal relationship between employer and employee		Relatively unchanged
	3. Lack of labor legislation and social welfare legislation	Labor legislation changed in California Social welfare legislation changed nationally
3. Work is unskilled and any division of labor is not based on hierarchy of skill		Relatively unchanged
	4. Low income life styles and behavioral traits learned on the job	Relatively unchanged
4. Use of piece rate		Relatively unchanged
	5. Discrimination against low income people which produces isolation	Relatively unchanged
5. Little or no capital or machinery		Changed in selected crops

Sources: Lloyd B. Fisher, The Harvest Labor Market in California (Cambridge, Mass.: Harvard University Press, 1953), pp. 7-9; Peter B. Doeringer and Michael J. Piore, Internal Labor Markets and Manpower Analyses (Lexington, Mass.: Heath L., 1971), pp. 169-77.

unchanged. This paper examines three factors in the unchanged category: instability of work (Doeringer and Piore), impersonal employer-employee relationship (Fisher), and use of the piece rate (Fisher).

Instability: Farm Work as a Casual Labor Market

For Doeringer and Piore, the most important determinant of secondary labor markets is the unstable attachment of workers to jobs, or the casual nature of employment. Eliminating this characteristic alone has gone a long way toward converting secondary employment into primary employment in other industries. As examples, they point to longshoring and unskilled construction work, which were transformed primarily through the use of the hiring hall (p. 181). "Decasualization," or increasing the continuity of work, is an important focus for public policy.

The chief feature of casual employment is that it is subject to significant fluctuations in demand both at the firm and industry level. Jobs in casual labor markets have been described as "uncertain and irregular, yet continual, of short duration and subject to chance" (Morewedge, p. 14). Without the benefit of structure provided by a hiring hall or other alternatives, workers in casual labor markets have little or no job security or attachment to individual employers.

Only a small core of workers have regular jobs. In agriculture the core of regular workers tend to be those who perform supervisory or skilled and technical tasks, such as spraying, irrigating, and the operation and maintenance of trucks, tractors, harvesters, and other farm equipment. Some of this work is seasonal but a significant proportion of such workers are employed on a year-round basis.

At the other extreme are temporary seasonal workers who are thought to be "students and women and youth who choose to remain in the labor force for limited periods, primarily during the summer months" (Dolp, p. 2). Also included are other temporary workers for whom agricultural work is only a part-time endeavor and not the primary source of income. Their commitment to agriculture is limited and they would likely be unavailable for temporary agricultural work if the opportunity for extended employment were offered. In between the year-round workers and temporary or short-term workers are the seasonal agricultural workers (Dolp, p. 2). (A similar classification scheme is proposed by Hayes [1975, p. 10].)

The Labor Contractor System and the Piece Rate

Two key institutions in harvest work allow agricultural labor markets to continue to operate on an unstructured basis: the labor contractor system and the piece rate.

The labor contractor system has been in existence since at least the 1860s and has been traditionally associated with the use of foreign labor. In California the system was first introduced by the Chinese, who worked under leaders who served an essential role as interpreters. Barriers of language and custom forced both worker and grower to depend upon the early contractor to act as a middleman.

But the labor contractor functions as more than a mere interpreter, and the system is strongly rooted today primarily because of the opportunity it affords growers to delegate personnel duties associated with harvest labor. Through the use of labor contractors, growers have been able to avoid the establishment of sophisticated personnel systems that would be used only during certain seasons of the year.

The labor contractor is the intermediary who brings the jobs and workers together. But he does far more than that. The labor contractor relieves the grower of many burdens. The labor contractor recruits and transports and supervises workers in the field. He also instructs workers. He keeps records and pays workers and payroll taxes. Often, he provides workers with food and lodging. He supplies drinking water and field toilets and may supply some implements of harvesting such as gloves, ladders, or clippers. He also is obligated to carry insurance. He may extend credit to workers or help them with personal problems.

Farm labor contractors usually operate on a personal basis with growers and packers. Some work for the same set of growers year after year. Although these growers delegate to farm labor contractors a large measure of responsibility, the contractors and their crews are subject to immediate dismissal should their work be found dissatisfactory.

Of course there is considerable diversity in the operations of labor contractors. Some are large and sophisticated operations whereas most are small, undercapitalized entrepreneurial ventures. Some labor contractors are family heads whose crews are composed mainly of relatives. Characterizations seem to vary somewhat by region of the country. For example, California seems to have a sizeable portion of the larger contractor operations. Registered contractors in California number only a few hundred while Florida has several thousand.

The casual nature of agricultural labor markets and the general surplus supply of workers puts the labor contractor in an advantageous position to exploit workers, much as was the case with foremen on the docks prior to the implementation of the hiring hall in the longshore industry. Under such conditions, workers simply are vulnerable. The situation places power in the hands of the labor contractor, whether or not he misuses it.

The misdeeds of unscrupulous farm labor contractors are recounted in detail elsewhere and need not be repeated here.

Although most who have studied harvest labor markets prefer a different type of intermediary than labor contractors, no alternatives have been implemented on a widespread basis. The labor contractor system is a very persistent institution in agriculture that is not likely to be abandoned or dislodged in the near future. As previously pointed out, labor contractors play important functional roles in agriculture that must be filled even if labor contractors are not used. Further, low capital requirements and small-scale operation enable the labor contractor to keep costs to a minimum and to work on a small margin and remain competitive.

As the United Farm Workers (UFW) experience in

California indicates, labor contractors are difficult to eliminate and attempts to do so often backfire. For example, the UFW was principally responsible for excluding labor contractors from the Agricultural Labor Relations Act in 1975. Under this act, labor contractors cannot be considered employers. Rather, the owner of the property being harvested is the employer. In practice, this exclusion has tended to immunize the labor contractor from unionization, and at least partly as a consequence labor contractors have thrived in California since the act went into effect.

In lieu of abolishing the labor contractor system, government has chosen to attempt to regulate the activities of the labor contractor in order to reduce the adverse impacts of the system.

However, enforcing regulations is much more difficult than making them. Labor contractors usually have few managerial skills, limited English comprehension, and low levels of education. Consequently, state and federal record-keeping requirements present a special difficulty. In addition, the fact that they work for a variety of employers in diverse localities creates an added burden for agencies charged with enforcement of legislation covering farm workers. Also, labor contractors operate informally, are numerous, and tend to be small, all of which further complicate enforcement when resources available for the purpose are limited. Thus even though the regulations, especially the Farm Labor Contractor Registration Act, are quite demanding, violations are common. Violators are seldom caught and penalties are seldom imposed on those who are caught.

It should be recognized that the labor contractor system offers special advantages for increasing the continuity of mobility. Labor contractors can move from harvest to harvest following the ripening crops. Conceptually, at least, the farm labor contractor is in a more favorable position than is an individual worker or most individual growers to facilitate steady work for crew members.

In practice, however, the contractor system has

provided neither a stable employment relationship nor steady work for the majority of crew members. Turnover rates among crew members are high and employment is more intermittent than it needs to be.

Part of the explanation for this is that contractors are paid on the basis of per worker delivered or per production unit. As Sue Hayes points out:

> The identity of the worker is not important so long as he can perform his labor without damaging the product or interfering with the work of others. There is, therefore, no reason other than altruism or a sense of family or group loyalty for the contractor to seek employment for a permanent crew so long as he has the right number of competent laborers available for the job (1975, p. 73).

The use of labor contractors is inexorably linked to the use of the piece rate. Without the piece rate, farm employers would be more reluctant to relinquish their personnel responsibilities.

As a method of payment, the piece rate offers special advantages to agricultural employers. Under the piece rate, wide variations in worker productivity can be accommodated without having much effect on cost of harvesting. Thus, as Lloyd Fisher pointed out:

> California agriculture is able to provide productive employment for men, women, and children, for the experienced and inexperienced, for alcoholic derelicts from the "slave" markets and for the skilled Filipino, at a labor cost per unit of output which does not vary widely (p. 8).

Some qualification should be added here since workers now have to earn the Federal minimum wage and growers tend to pay an hourly rate when they are concerned about quality of the pick or damage to their trees or vines or equipment.

This is an important consideration for growers who do not exercise selectivity in recruiting their work force. The piece rate also reduces the need for worker supervision. This consideration is attractive to growers who have delegated supervisory responsibilities to labor contractors who may not be able to closely monitor the performance of large crews. Viewed from this perspective, the piece rate provides the opportunity for shifting the burden of personnel management functions to the workers themselves. Piece rates can allow employers to operate effectively without devoting attention to personnel functions such as employee selection, worker training, and supervision.

Although the labor contractor system and the piece rate offer some personal advantages to growers, they also entail disadvantages from a social point of view. Chief among these is that the labor contractor system tends to isolate workers from growers and it introduces ambiguity into the employer-employee relationship in agriculture.

Further, in a labor market where workers are plentiful, where work is considered to be relatively unskilled, and where a piece rate system is used (so that the unit labor price does not vary regardless of labor practices), management has little incentive to manage workers efficiently.

Historical Lack of Attention to Labor and Personnel Issues in Agriculture

Perhaps more than any other major individual sector, agriculture has ignored personnel management. Indicators of this condition are abundant: the dearth of literature on personnel supervision in agriculture, the low participation of agricultural employers in professional personnel associations, the inattention to employer-employee issues by the agricultural extension network, and the lack of training in personnel matters provided to foremen and supervisors of harvest workers.[1] As previously pointed out, traditional employment practices in agriculture reflect the inattention to personnel. The use of the piece rate system and of labor contractors has enabled farm employers to avoid the need to give personnel functions much attention. These practices have effectively shifted the burden of personnel management to others.

This lack of concern for personnel management provides a stark contrast to the strong attention given to marketing issues.

Past employment and training efforts sponsored by the USDL to assist farm workers have not placed primary emphasis on professionalizing farm work. Rather, most employment and training programs aimed at farm workers have emphasized moving them into alternative jobs outside of agriculture. In short, the focus has been on upgrading the workers.

In contrast, the focus of this chapter is on upgrading harvest work to make it a more viable and attractive career option for those who choose it. The experience of a few employers has demonstrated that improvements can be made at reasonable, competitive costs.

The primary reason agricultural work has not been more generally upgraded and personnel issues have not received greater attention from agricultural employers is that there has been no perceived need to do so. Farm employers, by and large, have not been prodded to improve conditions sufficiently to attract American workers. With few exceptions, there has historically been a persistent surplus of domestic and immigrant workers available in agricultural labor markets. Further, when farm employers have faced scarcity of labor, the main thrust of their efforts has been to appeal for access to foreign workers, rather than to improve the jobs so that domestic workers could be attracted on a more stable basis.

As the European experience with guest worker programs testifies, temporary foreign-worker programs have permanent implications. Whether it is intended or not, the programs eventually lead to the permanent settlement of individuals who reject the jobs that they were initially imported to fill.

Employers are left to seek yet another source of fresh workers who will "work at jobs that Americans will not do." As time goes on the continuous recruitment of new workers becomes increasingly difficult and, indeed, impossible without the acquiescence, even assistance, of the government in gaining access to foreign workers. To get off the treadmill of having to constantly recruit new workers, employers can either mechanize, thereby replacing workers with capital equipment, or they can increase the attractiveness of agricultural jobs. To be more attractive farm work must gain more status and respect, improved productivity, steadier employment for higher income, and better fringe benefits and working conditions. This involves bringing greater structure to agricultural labor markets--to transform them from secondary to primary labor markets. This chapter discusses various means of pursuing this goal.

ALTERNATIVE MEANS OF COORDINATING LABOR USE TO ACHIEVE DECASUALIZATION

Since the reduction of instability is such a key factor in upgrading jobs, this section is devoted to a discussion of decasualization. Means of achieving decasualization include the public employment service, hiring halls, cooperative arrangements among employers, and a modified labor contractor system (Glover and Franklin). However, due to space limitations only hiring halls will be considered here.

Hiring Halls and Decasualization

A hiring hall is a centralized mechanism that matches workers and job openings in an industry in which there is an unstable relationship between workers and individual employers. The name "hiring hall" refers to the place where workers traditionally meet and wait to be sent out on jobs. However, in some industries the term is something of a misnomer because modern hiring halls are often not physical structures, but rather are job referral mechanisms operated entirely on paper and via computer and telephone. The hiring hall has traditionally been associated with construction and the maritime industries. It has also been used to a lesser extent in trucking and the arts and is now being implemented in portions of the agricultural harvest labor market through the efforts of the UFW.

The single most important feature common to all hiring halls is that they operate in casual labor markets that are by definition subject to severe fluctuations in employment at both the firm and industry levels. Indeed, hiring halls can be understood as attempts to lessen or equitably distribute the adverse impact of casual employment on both employers and workers. In a sense, the hiring hall is an attempt to combat some of the undesirable features of casual labor markets--a mechanism for upgrading a labor market that is adversely affected by unfavorable market conditions.

Decasualization of employment through the use of hiring halls has been the subject of several excellent studies regarding longshoring (Jensen 1964; Jensen 1971; Larrowe; Morewedge; Kahn). Similarly, the hiring hall has been used effectively by building trades unions to transform construction work from a casual job to a steady job through restructuring the labor market (USDL, Labor Management Services Administration; Ross). Success in these industries where casual labor markets formerly prevailed raises the hope that the hiring hall may be applicable to agricultural work.

Hiring halls are, first and foremost, institutions through which workers are able to share job opportunities on a basis they perceive as equitable, to reduce the number of workers competing for scarce jobs, and to obviate the need to pay kickbacks or bribes to unscrupulous foremen, harvest crew chiefs, or business agents in order to obtain work.

Hiring halls, operating in conjunction with some form of worker registration, restrict entry of those not committed to the work while allocating available job opportunities among a core group of attached workers. In this way, a form of job security is achieved by partially shielding some workers from market forces.

In casual labor markets, fluctuations in the

employment of individual employees are more severe than fluctuations in demand for workers to the whole local industry. Further, the fragmented nature of casual labor markets induces each employer, acting independently, to try to maintain access to a supply of labor sufficient to meet his peak demand for labor, so that many workers are redundant in periods of normal activity. The cost of maintaining such excess reserves is not borne by employers, but is shifted to workers in the form of high unemployment and unstable earnings. A centralized hiring facility for an industry eliminates the necessity for individual employers to maintain their own labor reserves, because a floating reserve can be dispatched to those employers with temporarily large labor requirements. This floating reserve can be much smaller than the sum of all the reserves that would be held by employers acting individually, because for the industry as a whole it is necessary to keep enough extra workers on hand to meet the peak requirements of only a few employers at any given time. Thus it is possible to guarantee employers all the labor they need while sharply reducing the number of workers necessary to make the guarantee and significantly raising the incomes of those workers remaining in the industry.

The experiences of longshoremen in New York and Seattle bear this point out. After the Seattle hiring hall was established in 1921, the resulting flexibility in the hiring system allowed the number of casual workers in the port to be reduced from 1,400 to 612, with greater year-round employment and earnings for all remaining workers (Larrowe, p. 54). As a result, by 1951 more than 70% of Seattle dock workers employed through the hiring hall had at least "adequate" incomes (as defined by the Bureau of Labor Statistics [BLS]), whereas in New York, where the shape-up still prevailed in 1950, only 22% of longshoremen's incomes could be considered adequate (Larrowe, pp. 70, 165-71). The situation in New York changed dramatically, however, with the implementation of hiring hall procedures. Between 1954, the last year of the shape-up, and 1966, the mean annual income of

New York longshoremen increased from $2,469 to $5,340 (in real terms) as the number employed in the port fell from 41,333 to 24,825. In 1954, only 1% of dock workers earned more than $7,000, while 58.5% earned less than $3,000. In 1966, 58.6% earned over $7,000, while only 14.6% earned less than $3,000 (Morewedge, p. 81).

Workers also benefit from lower costs of job search under hiring hall arrangements. Construction craftsmen who would otherwise have to travel from job site to job site inquiring about work opportunities can instead be placed on jobs by union business agents who already know where jobs exist. Dock workers' search costs have been similarly reduced, while their mobility has increased. Under the shape-up, each docker could effectively compete on only a single pier, since each morning's "shape" took place at the same time on all piers. If he was passed over in the shape-up on his own pier, he could not travel to another before all men had been engaged on that pier. The hiring hall dispatches longshoremen to piers on which they are assured of finding work; regular gangs in New York are no longer required to even be at the hall when work assignments are made.

The hiring hall has also freed workers from the necessity of paying bribes and kickbacks to grasping foremen or crooked union officials. The rules governing assignments to jobs take most of the power over those assignments away from hiring agents, whose ability to shake down workers or in other ways act capriciously is concomitantly reduced. In this light, one can understand why a principal demand of the UFW--a union representing easily exploitable workers in a highly casual industry--has been the abolition of the labor contractor system and its replacement by union-operated hiring halls. Increased utilization of hiring halls for harvest laborers could have as significant an impact on the amount of exploitation of workers in agriculture as similar hiring arrangements produced in the dock labor market in New York.

Because hiring halls offer a desirable means to upgrade the worst labor markets, producing benefits for employers, workers, and society at large, it is understandable why hiring halls have been promoted by public policy for industries such as longshoring. It should be strongly emphasized, however, that hiring halls are not a panacea for all adverse labor market conditions. In fact, if not checked they may exhibit some of the same corruption and abuses they were designed to correct. Further, since they effectively limit entry into a labor market, they are open to abuses of discrimination. This is why government has taken the policy of not only promoting hiring halls, but of also regulating their activities.

A second major note of caution is that hiring halls are hard to administer. It is very difficult to develop rules for allocating work that workers deem equitable and employers find flexible enough to meet their needs. Further, the effective administration of a hiring hall requires talented staff.

The UFW has encountered several problems in attempting to establish hiring halls. For example, some employers have complained that UFW hiring halls have not responded quickly enough to their requests for workers. Employers are also displeased that referrals are made on the basis of seniority in the union. Some workers have also been unhappy because they were referred to employers individually, occasionally even splitting up husbands and wives and other family groups that had traditionally worked together in the field.

In summary, the hiring hall does have potential as a device to decasualize some agricultural work. The establishment of hiring hall procedures for agricultural workers has been a major goal of the UFW, who hope to benefit from regularized employment and the elimination of the labor contractor system. While the reduction of excess labor supplies and the regularization of work for agricultural harvesters are clearly desirable, the seasonal and geographical aspects of farm work complicate the attainment of these goals. Moreover, the extent of the application of union-based hiring halls to agricultural work is, of course, limited to the extent of the influence of the union promoting it. Also, there is some evidence that the UFW may be retreating from its traditional demands for a hiring hall; some collective bargaining contracts recently negotiated do not mention the hiring hall.

FRESH FRUIT CITRUS HARVESTING: A GOOD BEGINNING POINT FOR UPGRADING AGRICULTURAL LABOR MARKETS

Due to certain of its features, citrus harvesting for fresh fruit offers a good point from which to begin the process of professionalizing farm work. First and most importantly, citrus has one of the longest harvest seasons of any crop. Second, the citrus industry is highly organized, especially for marketing. This means that product demand has been regularized, which in turn has steadying implications for the derived demand for harvest labor. Third, in California and Texas harvesting is generally conducted through a central institution or agent. Finally, some promising labor-management experiments have already taken place in the citrus industry. These innovations provide a base of experience upon which other efforts can be built.

Let us discuss each of these advantageous features in greater detail.

Lengthy Harvest Seasons: A Special Advantage

Unlike other crops, citrus can be harvested over a long period of time. This is because the fruit can be retained on the tree, without deterioriation of quality, pending favorable marketing conditions for picking. On-tree storage is an especially important benefit to producers for the fresh fruit market.

Harvest seasons in citrus typically last a minimum of 5 months. Moreover, because the seasons for various varieties of fruit are complementary, packinghouses handling more than one variety of fruit can easily keep harvest crews busy for 10 or more months per year. For example, in Tulare County, California, the season for naval oranges runs from early November to mid-May. The harvest season for valencia oranges begins in mid-April and extends to October (Hayes

1975, p. 93). Thus between the two varieties packinghouses can retain a group of core employees for 10 to 11 months of the year.

Lemons offer an even greater advantage. Given favorably mild weather, such as is found in the coastal areas of California, lemons can be harvested almost year round.

Under these conditions, employment in citrus can obviously differ dramatically from that in the one- or two-week season for some types of deciduous fruits, the two month season for raisin grapes, or a three-week onion harvest. The stabilization of employment and extension of the duration of work are clearly easier to achieve in citrus than in crops where harvest activity is subject to more severe seasonal constraints.

Marketing and Research in the Citrus Industry

The marketing of citrus fruit has become a well-organized and highly sophisticated operation, especially in Florida and California.

Much of the success of the Florida citrus industry can be attributed to an early recognition of the value of internal organization. The position of the Florida citrus industry, largest in the world, is at least partially the result of a long tradition of effective statewide organization and self-regulation, especially regarding marketing.

By 1934 growers of most agricultural products, including California and Florida citrus, had accepted plans to prorate shipments among the nation's markets. In the summer of 1934 Florida agreed to participate in a plan established by the Agricultural Adjustment Administration (AAA). In 1935, to meet the need for coordinated advertising as well as enforceable product quality and maturity standards, the industry convinced the state legislature to establish the Florida Citrus Commission to be funded out of taxes levied on citrus products.

In California, industry administrative committees have been established for marketing various types of citrus fruit. They have the authority to control the quantity of fruit released to the fresh fruit market during any week of the year. Under their supervision each citrus packinghouse in the state is allowed a certain share of the total tonnage, which it then distributes among its grower customers. This system was devised in response to several sales wars among California producers that resulted in bankruptcies among farmers and the dumping of harvested fruit rejected by buyers. By regulating the amount of fresh fruit available on the market in any week, the industry argues, prices can be maintained longer and more equitably among growers than under the former system, that frequently resulted in high gains to a few lucky shippers and losses to others during a short, highly competitive season.

Although Texas growers have lagged behind the citrus industry in Florida and California, they have recently taken steps toward organizing. Their primary focus has been marketing and advertising.

The marketing systems in citrus have important implications for employment. The controls on fresh fruit shipments are aimed at leveling and extending the demand over a longer period. Since the demand for harvest labor is derived from the demand for fruit products, regularizing the demand for fresh fruit results in more even employment throughout the year than would be seen if producers were scheduling their own harvest under the "boom and bust" cycle of activity that previously characterized the citrus industry.

In contrast to the enormous amounts of attention and resources allocated to the marketing and technical production facets of citrus, comparatively little effort has been devoted to research on harvest labor, beyond developing and testing technology to reduce the need for labor. For example, the termination of the Bracero Program (Public Law 78) in 1964 resulted in a considerable expenditure of effort on harvest technology research. In short, emphasis has not been placed on better utilization of existing harvest labor but rather on reducing or eliminating the need for harvest hand labor.

Centralization of Harvesting Operations in Citrus

Partly as an outcome of the highly organized marketing apparatus for citrus fruit, the packinghouse has become the central institution for harvest operations in the citrus industry. This is especially true in California and Texas. In these states almost all citrus harvesting is arranged by packinghouses, which establish picking schedules to meet orders for fruit shipments allocated by the various marketing agencies.

A packinghouse may be owned and operated by a group of growers as a cooperative, or it may be owned by an independent who buys fruit on the trees from various growers.

Labor use in citrus is arranged in various ways. Only a few growers hire the labor to pick their crop directly or through labor contractors. Most find that the packinghouse can conveniently provide picking, hauling, and packing services, eliminating the need for the growers to buy harvest equipment or to provide labor supervision.

Packinghouses typically obtain harvest labor in one of two ways: by subcontracting to a farm labor contractor on the basis of a lump sum per ton of fruit or by direct hiring and supervision of in-house harvest crews. A few packinghouses utilize both labor contractors and company crews simultaneously. In at least one case uncovered in Texas, a packinghouse used a hybrid model of the direct hire and labor contractor systems. Labor contractors were hired on a salaried basis to recruit and supervise crews, and all harvesters hired were on the payroll of the packinghouse. This system provided the packinghouse with the advantage of centralized record keeping, which helped to assure proper conformance with government regulations.

Packinghouses are not the only means for centralizing harvesting operations. A variation which has been successful on the West Coast is for growers to form harvesting cooperatives. In coastal areas of central California, harvesting operations have been performed since the early 1960s by associations established directly by growers. As an alternative to centralizing harvesting operations with packinghouses, the growers association for harvesting has inherent advantages. One of these associations, Coastal Growers, is cited in the following section regarding promising labor management experiments.

The centralization of harvest operations is a feature of the citrus industry that facilitates the adoption of innovative labor management practices.

Promising Labor-Management Experiments in the Citrus Industry

Citrus seems to have more than its share of the successful attempts to decasualize and upgrade harvest work. Developments in Florida at the Coca-Cola Minute Maid Operations, as well as the experience of Coastal Growers Association in California, offer a good illustration. (For description of the Agricultural Labor Project at Coca-Cola, see Larkin and Harris and Allen. Information regarding the Coastal Growers Association can be found in Rosedale and Mamer and in Mamer and Rosedale.) Another major advance originating in citrus has been the development of a variable piece rate system of compensation that adjusts for the difficulty of the harvest (Smith et al.).

BEYOND CITRUS: WHAT CAN BE DONE?

Without the advantage of an extended harvest season that citrus offers, the task of offering greater duration of employment is more difficult. Generally, it means that workers will have to move from one crop to the next to stay employed. This is difficult not only because an organizational sponsor for such an effort is not readily apparent, but also because it is not clear that workers are willing and able to move from crop to crop.

Nevertheless, arrangements to stabilize employment are still possible. Production schedules can be arranged to provide stable employment for a core group of workers. A single large grower under agreeable circumstances could diversify production so that different crop activities are staggered during the year, permitting the continuous employment of a versatile work force that could move from crop to crop. In California such labor use coordination has been attempted by at least a few large growers. Di Giorgio Farms in Kern County apparently followed this practice for decades. In 1946, 80% of its acreage was in vineyards, 11.3% in orchards, and 4.6% in vegetables with the remainder not planted. With this pattern of crops, Di Giorgio was able to report 91.7% of those employed during 1946 as permanent personnel, 6.8% as temporary employees from the local area and only 0.5% as transient workers. (Hayes 1975, pp. 71-72, quoting from Cecil Dunn and Philip Neff, "The Arvin Area of Kern County," report prepared for the Board of Supervisors and the Water Resource Committee of the Kern County Chamber of Commerce, Bakersfield, California, 1947. Due to rounding errors, percentages do not add to 100.)

Reportedly, other California growers have attempted to follow the same practice and at least one was still in operation in San Diego County in 1973. It is rare, however, to find a single grower of the size necessary to enable him to offer continuous employment for the bulk of his harvesters through such an arrangement. More commonly, such labor use coordination is feasible only through pooling arrangements among several employers.

One source of resistance to involvement in large-scale labor sharing programs is the fear of individual growers of increasing their exposure to unionization. Because of their size and the convenient accessibility to workers they employ, such large enterprises become attractive targets for union organization efforts.

Are farm workers willing to work more steadily? Indicators show that a significant proportion are. As Hayes notes:

> California Farm Labor Force Profile, prepared for the Assembly Committee on Agriculture, polled 4,867 workers with $100 or more in California

> farm earnings in 1963. Of these, 15.3 percent reported that they experienced more than half a year during which they were willing and able to accept agricultural employment but obtained none (Hayes 1975, pp. 10-11).

Even if cropping patterns could be arranged to yield maximum complementarity of labor demand, there remains the issue of the ability and willingness of workers to move from crop to crop. It is doubtful that the manipulative skills and dexterity required in harvesting are completely transferrable from crop to crop. Some loss in production speed is likely to result. As for the willingness of workers to move, according to some authors and industry officials workers often identify with a particular set of crops and are not agreeable to moving outside of that set. For example, workers who harvest orchard crops may be unwilling to work row crops, and vice versa. In addition, a study of citrus harvesters in South Texas indicated that farm workers attach a status distinction to harvesting various crops (Galvin). Thus these citrus harvesters would be reluctant to move to crops for which they have a lower regard.

Certainly there are restrictions on the ability and willingness of workers to move from crop to crop. The dimensions of these inhibitions to substitutability are not known, nor is it clear how deep they run. However, to reiterate, the experience of a few employers indicates that such difficulties can be overcome.

CONCLUSION

Rather than solely assisting workers to escape from farm work, public policy should address the goal of professionalizing and decasualizing farm work so that it becomes a credible career option. An essential element of upgrading farm work is the decasualization of employment for the seasonal farm worker, who performs the bulk of harvest work.

Success in decasualizing a labor market is

reflected in reduced rates of turnover and absenteeism. As a consequence of decasualization, the ratio of core workers to total workers increases and the total number of workers needed declines. Fewer jobs are available, but they are better jobs. Decasualization involves two components: regularizing the work opportunities available, and encouraging worker commitment to the job.

Decasualization in agricultural labor markets is not a new idea and many of the proposals discussed in this paper are not fresh and original. Much fine conceptual work has been done by Varden Fuller, Lloyd Fisher, and others before them. But conceptualization does not lead to implementation automatically. It seems useful at the beginning of the 1980s to revive the dialogue on means to upgrade farm work. It is appropriate because contemporary developments give cause for believing change to be possible.

Several factors can help to motivate agricultural employers to upgrade the kinds of employment they offer. These include the following:

1. Unavoidable problems of labor supply
2. Improved enforcement of legislation and regulations regarding labor standards for farm work
3. Unionization and the threat of unionization
4. Employer desire for control over the quality of work performed and over matters for which he is legally liable
5. Fringe benefit structures and record keeping requirements that increase the cost of turnover
6. Adverse publicity and the threat of adverse publicity

Currently, every one of these incentives for change is present and active in the agricultural labor market. Equally important, thanks in part to the growing size and consolidation of farm operations, employers increasingly possess the ability to change. The legal and regulatory environment has changed dramatically over the past 15 years so that farm workers are no longer considered separately from other workers for most purposes under the law. Also, for the first time in this nation's experience, unions are showing themselves to be a viable force in agriculture.

The fact that some employers have introduced improvements indicates that upgrading is possible. Pilot experiences with improved labor utilization have demonstrated that the work can be performed with far fewer workers, to the benefit of both employers and employees. Employers realize a more reliable work force and workers gain substantially in annual income.

Certainly agricultural employers have justifiable concerns about assuring that adequate work forces are available to them--especially during critical harvest periods. But major difficulties arise if public policy is aimed at guaranteeing supplies of labor to farm employers--a policy not followed toward any other industry. First, such guarantees undercut employer incentives to upgrade their labor utilization practices and to increase the attractiveness of agricultural work. Second, determining whether a labor shortage exists is not an easy judgment. Agricultural employers are in a position to manipulate their labor needs such that it is difficult to distinguish a real shortage from one that is artificially created. In addition, by definition a shortage relates to a particular wage rate.

Evidence that labor is unavailable for picking the most difficult harvest groves or fields, failure of workers to stay through an extended season without much prospect of regular work, failure to show up and wait without pay, failure to try agricultural work without a "training wage guarantee"--all these are not signs of a pervasive labor shortage, but rather of rational worker reaction to the irrationality characteristic of the unstructured market for harvest labor.

In complaining that American workers will not do farm work and in beseeching the government for access to foreign workers more tolerant of undesirable working conditions, farm employers often ignore the essential question, namely: what can be done to upgrade the work itself in order to attract American workers?

Experience in nonfarm industries reveals that

disagreeable work can be structured to attract workers. For example, as Stewart Perry points out in his book, *San Francisco Scavengers*:

> For many years, a job in the New York sanitation department has been regarded by many as a prize. The last time job openings were announced in 1974, a record of almost 69,000 men took the civil service examinations to qualify for what could be, at most, a couple of hundred slots that year (p. 188).

Harvesting food is physically demanding and disagreeable work, yet it need not be demeaning work. The dexterity and physical skill required to be a productive harvester have not been generally recognized. Nor does agricultural work need to be casual for all seasonal farm workers.

Discussion

WILLIAM H. FRIEDLAND

The utility of Robert Glover's paper in this volume is twofold: first, it reminds us of one general phenomenological fact in the examination of agricultural labor, and second, it suggests methodological possibilities and policy implications.

Let me begin with three general comments and then turn to several considerations that I believe derive from Glover's analysis.

First, Glover reminds us once again about the unusual--indeed *exceptional*--character of agriculture, and the structure of knowledge production, and governmental administration with respect to agriculture in the United States. The chapter emphasizes the differences in the treatment of labor and personnel matters in agriculture, demonstrating once again how agriculture has established an unusual place for itself. The fact that so many data sources related to labor exist within the USDA and not in the USDL is indicative of agriculture's exceptional position. An equivalent phenomenon would be the Department of Commerce maintaining an organization dedicated to producing a report on, say, *The Hired Labor Force in Manufacturing*.

While it is impossible to state what the substantive consequences are of having the USDA so thoroughly involved in agricultural labor matters, there can be little doubt that its constituent interests are different from those of the USDL. It may be that "falling between the cracks" departmentally has contributed to the weak condition of the data base on agricultural labor. While speculative, this conclusion should not simply be ignored.

Second, Glover indicates an important methodological consideration: the utility of disaggregating the "agricultural labor market" to develop a better understanding of what is going on in this marketplace.

Third, Glover reminds us of the possibilities, when disaggregating the agricultural labor market conceptually, of utilizing (for policy purposes) existing structural elements in some segments of the labor market. By showing how hiring halls and other techniques applied in other circumstances have provided structure, and by illustrating the structural features of citrus production, Glover reminds us of what might be done. The policy implications for agricultural workers could potentially be very significant.

I would particularly emphasize the possibilities, once a conceptual disaggregation of the agricultural labor market is undertaken, for introducing organizational features to improve employment possibilities for those I will discuss later as "professional farm workers." First I would note that, beyond Glover's discussion of the possibilities of introducing structure in agricultural employment, the work of Mamer and others in citrus indicates that some forms of regularization of employment are possible. Beyond citrus, however, I would note that the research we have conducted in lettuce indicates that structuring has been a feature of most lettuce harvesting since sometime in the 1950s. Indeed, since the early part of the 1970s many lettuce harvesters have been internalized as regular employees by lettuce firms (Friedland et al.). This last development is a product of unionization, but the point is that specific segments of the agricultural labor market have become highly structured. Preliminary research in grapes also indicates the possibilities of introducing greater regularity and structure of employment in some forms of grape production, table grapes in particular.

If there are possibilities for introducing greater structural coherence to the agricultural labor force, why has there been such lag and drag in this respect? In my view, the delay is related to three distinct policies of the U.S. government.

First, almost continuously in our history national policy has been designed to maintain what Fisher called the "unstructured labor market." The salient element of this policy has been to ensure a continuous and essentially unrestricted flow of labor to agriculture from whatever sources are available. This was policy during the bracero period and continues as policy, albeit unofficially, at present, with the almost unrestricted movement of *sindocumentos* from Mexico despite "heroic" and continuing efforts of the Immigration and Naturalization Service. Considering that western agriculture is based (admittedly only by "guesstimates") on somewhere between 30-50% undocumented labor, our government is telling us something about how it feels about restrictions on the flow of labor to agriculture.

Second, the USDL has had a policy orientation toward agricultural labor reflective of its constituency within U.S. society--that is, reflecting institutionalized labor (as, in my opinion, the USDA reflects institutionalized agriculture). The USDL has been concerned with the stabilization of agricultural employment by *moving workers out of agriculture*. This policy has been geared toward attempting to create a labor shortage and toward the substitution of capital for labor (i.e., agricultural mechanization). Such substitution provides stabilized labor within agriculture, on one hand, and relatively higher wages for those workers remaining in agricultural production on the other (since labor costs, as a proportion of total costs of production, drop). This has encouraged not only capital substitution but also factor substitution for labor, e.g., the use of energy-intensive herbicides as controls over weeds.

At the same time, USDL policies have drawn attention away from the considerable continuity and persistence of agricultural labor. While migrancy may have dropped, and while the total number of workers employed in agriculture continues to drop, it is now abundantly clear that it will not be feasible to eliminate seasonal agricultural labor completely. USDL policymakers, however, do not yet seem to have grasped this fact.

A third factor that has contributed to the failure to grapple with the structuring of the agricultural labor market derives from the condition of the data base that has been developed on agricultural labor. It is appalling that in 1980, despite all sorts of data collection systems, we still have only uncertain data on the numbers of agricultural workers and their characteristics. How shall we explain the poverty of the data base?

One reason, I believe, stems from the institutional aspect of data collection referred to earlier, i.e., that the USDA and USDL are both involved. Under these circumstances, with different constituent interests involved in each agency, no one has "responsibility" or accountability with respect to the quality of data concerning farm workers.

A second reason flows from the unaccountable inability to disaggregate the agricultural labor market into different kinds and types of farm workers. It is clear, leaving aside the permanently employed workers in agriculture, that there are three major categories of workers. This point has emerged in a number of analyses presented earlier in this volume. These categories include:

Racial/ethnic groups. Included in this category are what could be referred to as "professional farm workers," i.e., workers who make their living by working throughout the year in a variety of agricultural jobs. These include such workers as lettuce harvesters but also many workers in citrus, grapes, soft fruits, and other commodities. These workers are often nonmigratory but commute extensively in order to find employment for most weeks out of the year. There are also in this category a number of part-time workers who are not "professional." My estimation is that these workers provide the overwhelming bulk of workdays on an annual basis in agricultural production.

Women. This category obviously overlaps the first to some degree, since many women agricultural workers are categorized according to their racial-ethnic origins. This category is also most difficult to summarize since it is probably the most heterogeneous one in agriculture. Barton, for example, found in her study of working farm worker women in California that there were a number of women of Mexican origin who could be categorized as "professionals" but who were less successful than men in finding continuous employment. Beyond these "professionals," there are other women who would like to work longer periods but not "professionally." There are also probably numerous housewives who are willing to enter the agricultural (and related, e.g., packing shed) labor market for short periods of time, particularly at harvest peaks.

Youth. The presence of many students for relatively short harvest peaks is clearly an important factor in the harvest labor market. While lacking a firm estimate of the number of such young people, it is clear that their contribution is significant, yet qualitatively different from that of the professionals. It should also be noted that a significant number of young people in the United States would be categorized according to their racial and ethnic groups.

The inadequacies of the data base are reflected in the way in which data are collected administratively by the federal government and its related agencies. I cannot speak about this phenomenon on a national scale since I do not have details, state by state. I can note, however, that in California the system utilized has no relationship to any social reality that anyone can determine, since the determination of the numbers of farm workers working at a given time is based on synthetic data. Starting with estimates of labor requirements for different aspects of agricultural production, acreages are then used to synthesize the "numbers working." Whatever relationship these numbers have to reality is coincidental, since we have no way of establishing what constitutes social reality, i.e., how many workers are actually at work.

Another anomaly exists as a result of the exceptional history of agricultural labor, which has been left behind with respect to protective labor legislation. This has created the peculiar circumstance in which packing shed labor (covered since the Wagner Act) is treated as a phenomenon distinct from field labor. While this makes administrative and legal sense, it is hardly reflective of the fact that many workers move between packing shed activities and field labor.

It would be useful for the data collection system on agricultural labor to be more directly reflective of social realities. In the western United States, for example, there is general agreement (although it is not known just how significant this is) that migrancy has dropped substantially over the past decade or two. This would appear to be less the case in the Midwest. What is happening in the East? Would it not be useful to develop some clear conceptual categories reflecting long-distance, short-distance, and commuting movements of agricultural workers and proceed to develop a clearer picture of what really happens?

This sort of data collection process is feasible if administrative agencies become committed to conducting empirically based research that is oriented to social realities. It would involve a broader data collection process, of course, and one oriented to the realities experienced by farm workers. This indicates the importance of drawing the actors involved--the farm workers--into the actual data collection process. If we want to know the nature of social reality, why not draw the participants into the process? That social reality is surely as potent as anything that can be derived from an econometric model. Experience in other circumstances has demonstrated that people such as agricultural workers can collect data about themselves. It would be useful to produce some social data about farm workers that would have social reliability for a change.

10

Occupational Structure and the Industrialization of Agriculture

JOHN W. MAMER

This discussion centers on the occupational structure of agriculture in the United States. Of primary interest are (1) the changes in occupational structure that have accompanied the industrialization of agriculture, (2) the factors that appear to have influenced the shaping of these changes, and (3) the prospects for further change in the future.

The occupational structure of an industry refers to the distribution of jobs in that industry, arrayed on the basis of skills and responsibility exercised on the job. It is widely accepted that jobs at the upper end of the distribution--skilled, professional, entrepreneurial--offer greater opportunities for meaningful, satisfying work. In industry generally the design, definition, and structuring of jobs have been and continue to be left entirely to private decision making within the framework imposed by health, safety, and other protective legislation.

In agriculture, public intervention has taken the form of policies favorable to the family farm policies, which have been a part of agricultural policy in varying degree since the founding of this country. In agriculture, as in industry, private decision making is currently the dominant process by which the occupational structure is evolved.

The first section of this chapter is devoted to a review of the emergence of industrialized agriculture. The emphasis is on job development, major influences on labor management practices, and prospects for change contained in unionization and protective legislation. In the second section the occupational structure of agriculture (as reflected in employment data and in the agricultural jobs described in the USDL's *Dictionary of Occupational Titles*) is examined and related to some of the special problems of agriculture. The influences and changes likely to emerge from modern industrialized farming are considered in the third section. An effort to influence the occupational structure through applied research is reviewed in the fourth section, which also includes a discussion of the results of an effort to apply modern personnel recruitment and management practices to seasonal farm labor. Finally, since the essential purpose of this study is to identify problems associated with the occupational structure of agriculture, it concludes with a delineation of data and research needs.

Industrialization in general is defined as a system of production based on scientific knowledge and involving extensive use of machines, the division of labor, inanimate sources of power, and modern organizational methods (Hughes and Moore, pp. 252-53). When applied to agriculture, industrialization includes these same features; in addition, note is taken of the increased role of economic values in guiding resource allocation on the farm, as contrasted with the family farm and its emphasis on human values. It is important to observe that scale of operations is not considered as a factor in the definition of industrialized agriculture, even though relatively large-scale units have commonly been identified with such agriculture. Instead, industrialized agriculture now tends to be identified with specialization in management (Moore and Dean).

The relationship between industrialization and the patterns of skills required by the production process is complex. Some features of industrialized production, such as the division of labor (a key element), usually result in reducing the skills required by the production process. On the other hand, we commonly expect that the application of scientific knowledge and the use of machines would require an increase in skills. As we shall see in the following sections, both tendencies have been operative as the industrialization of agriculture has continued to evolve.

THE EMERGENCE OF INDUSTRIALIZED AGRICULTURE

From the colonial period onward some features of industrialized agriculture have been evident in all regions of the United States, particularly in the South (Cox). However, until the latter part of the 19th century the major forces shaping the occupational structure of American agriculture were the relative scarcity of labor and the relative abundance of land. Indeed, until the mid-1950s the dominant image of agriculture was the family farm, together with its related occupational ladder on which the worker moved from the hired worker category to the owner-operator category as he acquired the skills and capital.[1]

On the family farm, where human values took precedence over economic values, the owner's sons and the hired workers alike acquired the skills, experience, and knowledge that prepared them to become owner-operators. Accordingly, the main occupational categories were family workers (including the owner-operator) and hired workers. Use of these categories has continued to the present time, and the USDA currently reports estimates of employment on farms for all states in terms of these two categories. Many state departments of employment also use these categories in reporting estimates of employment on farms. Some states (California, for example) divide the category of hired farm workers into subgroups such as seasonal and regular.[2]

Two features of the family farm apprenticeship system deserve particular note. First, it was assumed that the hired workers as well as the sons of the operator were in a process of transition to the owner-operator category. No doubt many hired workers and many family workers never became owner-operators, but the notion of transition or mobility has always been widely accepted and continues to be the national ideal (Becket). Second, the family farm apprenticeship system required of each worker a multiplicity of skills. Since every trainee was being prepared to become an independent operator, his training tended to be extensive rather than intensive, broad rather than narrow. Success as an independent operator required and continues to demand proficiency in a great many skills, as well as the ability to exercise sound judgment with regard to many aspects of the farm enterprise.

The family farm has demonstrated a remarkable capacity for survival. In many major farming regions of this country the family farm is the dominant type of farm firm, both in numbers and in contribution to regional farm output. Perhaps the most notable change evident on these farms is the increased scale of operations, accompanied by a vast expansion in the use of farm tractors and related equipment. Nevertheless, the operator and members of his family typically constitute the dominant proportion of the labor force employed on these farms.

At the other end of the scale, the industrialization of agriculture has produced patterns of farm organization that are far removed from the family farm and its image. The pejorative term, "factories in the field," was applied to these farms by the late Carey McWilliams, who observed that the many hundreds of workers employed on these farms are "indistinguishable from our industrial proletariat. . . ." (p. 48).

Without accepting the denigration of industrial workers implied in this comment, it may be acknowledged that very often the social and economic conditions under which workers were employed on industrialized farms, both large and small, warranted the vast volume of criticism leveled at them over the years. This discussion, however, is concerned primarily with the several factors that gave rise to the factories-in-the-field system and their continued influence on the occupational structure of industrialized agriculture. Most important among these factors are (1) the dominance of economic values in farm firm decision making; (2) the tendency for new technology, particularly laborsaving technology, to evolve unevenly; and (3) the influence of labor supply conditions.

The dominance of economic values in farm firm decision making reflects the proclivity of industrialized farm firms to maximize profits--not an unusual mode of firm behavior in a market-oriented economy. Profit-maximizing behavior appears more conspicuous if the industrialized farm is contrasted with the family farm and the social values identified with that institution. Profits and anticipated profits were the primary motivation for the rapid expansion of acreage devoted to labor-intensive crops during the 1870s and subsequently, first in California and later elsewhere. Crop specialization in turn gave rise to the institution of migratory labor. The social impact and increased social costs experienced by local communities as a result of seasonality of farm employment did not enter into the profit-maximizing calculus. In recent years various programs such as unemployment insurance and other protective legislation have tended to attach a cost to seasonality of employment, thus providing farm firms with an economic incentive for stabilizing employment.

The uneven development characteristic of new technology is illustrated by the situation in California in the early 1870s. By that time advances in transportation and refrigeration technology had made it possible to ship fruits and vegetables long distances. At the same time the availability of water, large areas of good quality soil, and favorable climatic conditions made farm and regional specialization in high-value, labor-intensive crops feasible. But technological advances in transportation and refrigeration were not matched by equal technological progress on the farm. No technological substitutes were yet available for the vast and highly seasonal hand labor inputs required in the production of fruits and vegetables and other crops that were to be shipped great distances. Hence the need for large numbers of seasonal workers.

Throughout the century that has elapsed since the 1870s, this uneven pattern of development has continued. Although some technological innovations have virtually eliminated hand labor in the production of many crops, seasonal hand labor requirements nevertheless persist in sufficient volume to lead us to expect the survival of the institution of migratory labor into the foreseeable future (although continuing to decline as a proportion of total hired labor employed on farms).

The labor supply situation that evolved in California in the early 1870s, together with the then-available technology and dominance of economic values in farm organization, played a critical role in the rapid expansion of labor-intensive agriculture at that time. In his important study of agricultural labor made more than forty years ago, Varden Fuller identified and analyzed the function of labor supply conditions in the expansion of labor-intensive agriculture in California (Fuller 1942). In his analysis Fuller also traced the formation of public policy with regard to farm labor. Initiated after the 1870s, this was a policy of accommodating labor supply to demand. With only a few exceptions, this policy has prevailed to the present day.

Upon completion of the Transcontinental Railroad in 1869, thousands of Chinese who had been employed in its construction were released into the California labor market, thus providing the state with a vast surplus of labor. These Chinese workers were the first wave of seasonal and migratory farm workers in California. Their availability for seasonal farm work at that time made farm and regional specialization in labor-intensive crops economically feasible. Other groups that entered the streams of migratory farm workers in subsequent years facilitated the continuance of this pattern of farming in California and marked its appearance in other states.

Since 1869 the influence and interplay of these

factors have shaped the evolution of the occupational structure currently associated with industrialized agriculture, although the term "industrialized agriculture" did not appear until the 1930s. It was in the 1930s that patterns of labor-supply-demand adjustments, new styles of employer-employee relations, and the structure of farm jobs characteristic of industrialized agriculture emerged. Without doubt the most significant emerging pattern of labor-demand-supply adjustment was the expectation and realization that local labor supply conditions need not impose a constraint on the acreage planted to labor-intensive crops, whether tree crops or annuals. Migratory farm labor could readily be recruited to meet seasonal peak labor needs.

Ultimately, farm and area specialization in labor-intensive crops evolved to some extent in most regions of the United States. Hence migratory farm labor is currently employed at some time in the course of the year in all regions of the United States (see Fritsch, Chap. 3). Over the years the supply of labor available, its mobility, and the possibility of recruiting foreign nationals for seasonal farm work during periods of labor stringency have been the key elements in the expansion of labor-intensive agriculture to all regions of the country. They continue to be so today. Self-recruitment, either by the individual worker or by a labor contractor, has been the dominant means by which seasonal farm workers and jobs have been matched, attesting to the prevailing ample labor supply (see Emerson, Chap. 4).

Hiring and layoff policies in California consistent with the existing labor supply and demand situation emerged speedily after 1869. Appropriate policies and their advantages were described by a California farmer in 1872 in a statement extolling the advantages of employing Chinese workers. The Chinese worker, he observed, "is only employed when actually needed, and is, therefore, less expensive" (quoted in Fuller 1942, p. 19809). Given the labor surplus situation after 1869, farm operators whose labor-intensive crops required large seasonal labor inputs, particularly hand labor, found it possible to purchase such labor services as needed. Employment of hired farm workers, particularly seasonal farm workers, consequently took on features similar to the purchase of other variable factors of production stocked by local merchants and available for purchase when needed.

It is useful at this point to relate the recruitment and labor management practices to the structure of jobs that emerged. Jobs performed by seasonal and migratory farm workers tend to be narrowly defined, for they generally involve a single specific task such as harvesting fruit. The employee-employer relationship is casual, and preferences in rehiring in successive years are informal or nonexistent. The worker-job relationship also tends to be casual, as distinct from a continuing relationship that might develop in the more skilled work categories. For the most part the terms of employment are not specified in writing, but some written terms of employment, mainly wages and hours, are becoming more common.

Proficiency in the performance of the seasonal hand labor task has not typically been highly prized by employers. Payment on a piece rate basis has minimized the cost of augmenting the size of work crews in order to compensate for deficiencies in skill. This pattern also is slowly changing. However, the annual earnings commonly achieved at seasonal farm work have rarely been sufficient to induce members of the domestic labor supply to develop a continuing interest in seasonal farm work as a full-time long-term occupation. Furthermore, the relatively low annual earnings have certainly not stimulated any substantial effort among employers of seasonal and migratory farm workers to develop any complementary work that would make seasonal farm work more attractive. (Some exceptions will be discussed at a later point in this chapter.)

While seasonal farm work has attracted the dominant share of public and private attention over the years, a vast number of semiskilled, skilled, supervisory, and management jobs have evolved on industrialized farms. These jobs have their origin in the application of modern science and technology to agriculture and to the emerging management structure on industrialized farms. Although these jobs are identified and classified in the USDL's *Dictionary of Occupational Titles* (discussed in the next section), the number of workers employed in such jobs is largely unknown.

Some labor management practices that have been observed with respect to these more skilled jobs warrant comment. Very often the patterns of labor recruitment and management of seasonal farm workers have merely been extended to the semiskilled and skilled jobs on industrialized farms. Commonly a sequence of semiskilled and skilled employees are hired and laid off as their separate tasks are completed. For example, the jobs requiring some skill are likely to be performed by a sequence of workers, each of whom is laid off after the specific task is completed. As an alternative, the same workers might be employed to perform the entire sequence of tasks, assuming that such workers are appropriately trained and favor more stable employment. The problems and issues involved in this kind of adjustment are discussed in the final section of this chapter.

While many jobs have their origin in the application of science and technology to agriculture, few programs have been developed for the training of individual workers in the needed skills. Similarly, methods of verifying skills and experience remain largely informal or nonexistent. The absence of well-developed processes for the acquisition and verification of skills may very well convey to the worker the impression that employers do not truly value well-trained workers. The absence of training programs also tends to lock the seasonal and migratory workers into jobs from which they can usually exit only by leaving agriculture. No doubt there are a few reasonably well-developed training programs on some farms, but these are not an adequate substitute for a well-established industry-wide training or apprenticeship program, particularly in view of the many complaints by farm employers about the inadequate supply of skilled workers.

Running through this discussion so far has been the notion that patterns of occupational structure in agriculture are changing and yet remaining the same as the process of industrialization progresses. While this notion appears to be essentially correct, there are a number of forces for change that require more explicit recognition. These forces have their origin in legislation pertaining to the employment of hired labor on farms and in the efforts of farm workers to form unions and exert collective pressure to improve conditions of employment.

Most of the protective labor legislation of the 1930s included exemptions for agriculture, so that farm workers were initially largely excluded from coverage. By the middle 1970s, however, most of these exemptions had been removed. Social security, worker's compensation, minimum wage laws, disability insurance, and health and safety regulations now apply alike to farm and nonfarm workers. With some variation among the states, protection of the right to organize and to join unions has been extended to farm workers. It now appears that farm labor unions have established a broad foothold that promises to endure into the foreseeable future.

The coverage of farm workers under unemployment insurance, worker's compensation, social security, minimum wage laws, and other protective legislation (such as the regulation of labor contracts) tends to bring employment standards in agriculture into line with those in the nonagricultural sector. In the long run, unemployment insurance may be one of the more significant influences, since it provides some incentive for the farm firm to employ fewer workers for longer periods of time. Safety regulations and the requirement of pesticide application licensing clearly militate against a casual employer-employee relationship, as, to a lesser extent, do record-keeping requirements.

The organization of unions and the development of collective bargaining agreements tend to lead to the written specification of jobs, responsibilities, performance standards, rehiring rights, and so on. Moreover, the patterns of wages and benefits negotiated under collective bargaining tend to have an important influence on nonunion employers. The extent to which farm labor unions will develop an active interest in job restructuring and in an apprenticeship system in agriculture remains to be determined. The present interest of the UFW (AFL-CIO) in developing an apprenticeship program may provide some opportunity and some incentive for reshaping the occupational structure of agriculture.

PRESENT OCCUPATIONAL STRUCTURE OF AGRICULTURE

Ideally it would be convenient if one could relate employment data to occupational information so that farm jobs could be arrayed on the basis of skill level and so that the average number of workers employed annually could be specified for each job category. Unfortunately, this is not possible. In a very limited way, however, farm employment data can be useful in this regard.

Available farm employment data suggest that the dominant occupational categories in U.S. agriculture continue to be those of family workers (the farmer and members of his family) and hired workers. It is estimated that on an average annual basis about 2.7 million family workers and about 1.3 million hired workers have been employed on American farms in recent years. Of course the proportions of workers in these two categories vary substantially from state to state. In California and Florida, for example, the ratio of hired workers to family workers is 3 to 1 and 2 to 1 respectively. On the other hand, in Iowa, Missouri, Minnesota, and several other states, family workers outnumber hired workers by a ratio of more than 4 to 1 (USDA, *Farm Labor* Feb. 1979, p. 5).

These data do not provide us with information about the proportion of family workers who belong in the farmer-operator occupational category; we can only presume that some share of them are farmer-operators. And we know even less about the occupational status of the hired workers. In general, however, these data do indicate that the occupational structure, as reflected in the proportions of family and hired workers, varies substantially among the states.

Although we are unable to relate employment data to the agricultural occupations defined in the *Dictionary of Occupational Titles* (DOT), the array of job titles and descriptions of jobs in that compendium merits attention and comment. All of the nonmanagerial agricultural occupations as classified under "agriculture" in the DOT are listed in Appendix 10.A; the managerial jobs are listed in Appendix 10.B. Under the system of classification used, it is assumed that each job requires that a worker, in performing the tasks comprising the work responsibilities of that job, deals with data, with people, and with things. The fourth, fifth, and sixth digits assigned to each occupation are an index of the complexity of the functions performed by a worker in that occupation. The highest level of complexity is given the digit 0. The levels of complexity and corresponding digits are as follows:

Data (4th digit)	People (5th digit)	Things (6th digit)
0 Synthesizing	0 Mentoring	0 Setting Up
1 Coordinating	1 Negotiating	1 Precision Working
2 Analyzing	2 Instructing	2 Operating-Controlling
3 Compiling	3 Supervising	3 Driving-Operating
4 Computing	4 Diverting	4 Manipulating
5 Copying	5 Persuading	5 Tending
6 Comparing	6 Speaking-Signaling	6 Feeding-Offbearing
	7 Serving	7 Handling
	8 Taking Instructions-Helping	

By summing the fourth, fifth, and sixth digits for an occupation, we obtain the total level of complexity, which can range between 0 and 21, from highest to lowest. Comparing these sums, we can concisely summarize the complexity of the functions performed. As shown in Table 10.1, there are 150 nonmanagerial jobs and 15 managerial jobs in agriculture. The average complexity of functions ranges from 15 to 21. Except for one category, the range in complexity among the jobs is substantial, the highest being in the 5 to 8 range and the lowest in the 20 to 21 range.

The relative importance of supervisory and management occupations is evident in Appendix 10.A and Appendix 10.B. Among the occupations there classified, supervisory jobs account for a fourth to a third of the titles in each three-digit group. The application of science and technology to farm production is also evident in these classifications, but less so. While a substantial number of jobs of a scientific and/or technical nature are defined, they are fewer in number than the supervisory and management jobs.

If only the occupational titles and their definitions are examined, one might conclude incorrectly that skilled jobs tend to dominate the employment patterns in agriculture. Not only do we not know the number of persons employed in each occupational categ-

Table 10.1 Agricultural occupations

Job Number	Type of Agricultural Occupation	Number of Jobs in Type	Average Complexity	Complexity range	
				Low	High
40	Plant Farming Occupations				
401	Grain farming	6	14.6	21	8
402	Vegetable farming occupations	5	14.0	21	5
403	Fruit and nut farming occupations	9	11.2	21	5
404	Field crop farming occupations, NEC[a]	8	14.3	21	5
405	Horticultural specialty occupations	13	14.1	21	5
406	Gardening and groundskeeping occupations	9	13.8	21	8
407	Diversified crop farming occupations	4	12.3	21	5
408	Plant life and related service	16	14.7	21	5
409	Plant farming and related occupations, NEC	14	16.3	21	5
41	Animal Farming Occupations				
410	Domestic animal farming occupations	26	13.6	21	5
411	Domestic fowl farming occupations	17	14.9	21	5
412	Game farming occupations	5	11.8	18	5
413	Lower animal farming occupations	5	13.2	21	8
418	Animal service occupations	5	15.8	20	12
419	Animal farming occupations, NEC	1	8.0	8	8
42	Miscellaneous Agricultural and Related Occupations				
421	General farming occupations	3	15.3	21	8
429	Miscellaneous agricultural and related occupations, NEC	4	19.0	20	18
18	Agricultural Managers and Officials, NEC	15	13.3	14	8

Source: Appendix 10.A.
[a]NEC Not Elsewhere Classified.

ory, but it is also impossible to obtain, from the job identification and the description of tasks performed, any precise clues as to the amount of employment that might be realized annually in each agricultural job. Descriptions of the tasks performed provide some basis for guessing, but little more. One can deduce from the job definitions only that more workers are likely to be employed in some jobs than others--that is, there are likely to be more field workers than supervisors.

This kind of crude inference is consistent with labor force data, which suggest that highly technical jobs are not the dominant types of employment in agriculture. Estimates in the most recent issue of *The Hired Farm Working Force of 1977* (USDA, ESCS, Oct. 1979) indicate that more than half of the 2.7 million individuals who worked for wages on U.S. farms in 1977 were employed on a seasonal or casual basis. Some of these workers no doubt held jobs of a skilled nature, but it is reasonable to assume that most of them were employed in unskilled and semiskilled jobs. Data for California, a state well advanced in the industrialization process, also reflect an occupational structure in which hired workers are dominantly employed in semiskilled or unskilled jobs. On an average annual basis, farm employment in California for 1978 was as follows (California Employment Development Department, November 17, 1979):

Category	Number employed
Farmers	68,500
Total hired	218,400
Regular hired	102,400
Total seasonal	116,000

These figures reveal the importance of casual and seasonal workers. Agricultural labor inputs are not predominantly skilled labor employed on a year-round basis. The skill level at which the California regular workers are employed cannot be determined from the data. The "regular" worker is defined as a worker employed by the same employer for 150 days or more in the course of the year. It is possible to conclude that many regular workers are employed in semiskilled and unskilled jobs and that some seasonal workers are employed at jobs of a skilled nature. Despite the fragmentary evidence, it seems reasonably evident that unskilled and semiskilled jobs and short-term jobs continue to have an important, perhaps dominant, role in industrialized agriculture, particularly if fruit and vegetables figure heavily as a share of total farm output.

The continued prominence of unskilled jobs performed on a seasonal or casual basis is an outcome that was not expected or hoped for by students of farm labor. After reviewing a variety of programs and efforts to improve the wages and working conditions of seasonal farm workers, Lloyd Fisher in 1953 concluded that "The brightest hope for the welfare of the seasonal agricultural workers lies in the elimination of the jobs upon which they now depend, and the development of programs for the transfer of workers from agricultural to industrial labor markets. . . ." (p. 48).

In a paper presented at the joint meeting of the Biological Societies at the University of Colorado in 1964, Professor Fuller and I expressed the view that the future would be different from the past. Labor for the seasonal tasks would no longer be available as in the past, we hypothesized. We thought that the continued production of the then prevailing mix of fruits and vegetables would be feasible if an intensive effort to develop labor-saving technology were pursued with public support (Mamer and Fuller). Such an effort has not materialized and seasonal farm workers continue to be available.

Thus the problem of seasonality remains. However, with regard to the occupational structure of agriculture, I noted earlier that seasonality of employment has its origin not only in the annual cycle of production and harvest, but also, at least in part, in the labor management practices that prevail. The concept of prevailing practices underlies the occupational structure reflected in the DOT as well as in such publications as *Occupations in Agriculture 1979* (California Employment Development Department 1979b), the job titles of which are in Appendix 10.C, and *Functions and Activities of Agricultural Jobs in California* (Thompson and Thomas). All such compilations are lists of jobs identified and specified on the basis of careful study of prevailing practices, perhaps dominant practices.

It is important to recognize that prevailing practices are determined in part by the labor supply situation. It was noted previously that farm labor policy in the United States has tended to produce conditions of ample labor supply for agriculture. During times of war, when there were indeed prospects of a labor shortage, foreign workers were allowed to flow into agriculture. Adjustments, legal or otherwise, have continued to the present time. Further public policy has been tolerant of lower employment standards in agriculture. In 1967 Professor Fuller observed that "We share with other industrial countries the evolution of the philosophy--with some backing in explicit policy--that farmers should have incomes equal to those that prevail in comparable occupational categories, but Americans have not yet gone that far with respect to hired farm workers!" (Fuller 1967, p. 98).

It is fair to conclude that the farm labor supply situation in the United States over the years has put little pressure on the management of industrialized agriculture to make innovative efforts to minimize the seasonality of employment or to search for complementary employment for seasonal farm workers. Very few situations contradict this observation. Contrast this with the situation in Holland following World War II: in the face of labor shortages, Dutch farmers organized labor supply cooperatives that planned labor use. Farm employers were thereby assured of a labor supply and farm workers were assured of relatively full employment. In this way, agriculture was able to compete with nonagriculture for labor (Hill et al.).

When one examines thoughtfully the data and

information about the occupational structure of U.S. agriculture that has emerged with industrialization, the most striking impression is gained from what is actually not present. Given the dimensions of agriculture in the entire United States or in California, Florida, Iowa, and perhaps a dozen other states, it is surprising that neither nationally nor in any state is there established a well-developed agricultural apprenticeship system, keyed to vocational agriculture programs in local high schools, community colleges, or adult evening schools.

Even though more individuals are employed annually in seasonal farm work than in farm work of a nonseasonal nature, the breadth and depth of skills (scientific, technical, supervisory, and managerial) required on farms are sufficient to suggest that training and apprenticeship programs warrant much more attention than they presently receive. Much of the machinery for such training programs appear to be at hand in existing adult evening schools and community colleges in many states. Certainly the highly sophisticated equipment and machinery currently used on farms require a much more elaborate training program in equipment operation than any now in existence, if such equipment is to be widely operated effectively and safely.

As a corollary, it may be observed here that in U.S. agriculture today there are few well-marked paths by which a farm worker might travel from unskilled or seasonal work to more skilled jobs and more stable employment on the farm. The issues of training and career development in agriculture are discussed in detail in the following sections.

MODERN INDUSTRIALIZED AGRICULTURE AND PROSPECTS FOR CHANGE

The dominant potential for change in the emerging occupational structure of agriculture may lie in the increasingly industrialized pattern of management that oversees the recruitment, selection, supervision, and evaluation of hired farm workers. With modern management, the operation of farm firms tends to parallel the patterns of industry. In discussing industrialized farms, Charles V. Moore and Gerald W. Dean emphasize that the key characteristics of management on such farms are specialization and decentralization. The need to decentralize and specialize originates in the size of the firm. In the more fully developed form of industrialized agriculture, as in industry, management is likely to be separate from ownership and is also likely to include the usual complement of specialists in such areas as personnel, marketing, production, and advertising.

Of special interest and importance is the relationship of the professional management on the industrialized farm to the occupational structure. It is the manager and his approach to recruitment, labor management, job descriptions, job restructuring, and the legal-economic framework that most influence the evolving pattern of occupational structure. No doubt managers are as varied in their social, political, and economic views as any other group. However, implicit in the specialization of management is an orientation that brings a new element to the development of occupations in agriculture--an element not present in the more traditional management of farms.

The professional manager will see the value of an organizational chart in helping to clarify the lines of authority. He will view as routine the definition of a job, the determination of standards of performance, and the establishment of procedures for the evaluation of performance. A professional may be engaged to formulate procedures for the recruitment, employment, training, and supervision of personnel. A rational pay structure (a necessity under the Civil Rights Act) will be regarded as part of a systematic approach to compensation. Careful attention will be paid to employee relations. Collective bargaining and contract negotiation may be accepted as routine aspects of doing business, but not always.

Such matters as compliance with safety regulations will usually be incorporated into the routine system of production. If the industrialized farm is quite large, a safety engineer may be employed. By initiating a safety program that improves the safety experience of the farm, such a professional may well save the farm firm more in reduced insurance premiums than the cost of his salary. Likewise, a professional in charge of personnel may be employed to review the problems of crew turnover and its cost and to seek means of reducing both. He is likely to suggest hiring and lay-off policies designed to meet the labor force needs of the firm and reduce the percentage of the wage bill paid in unemployment insurance premiums.

All of these practices and more may be observed on industrialized farms. Many deviations from these patterns are also frequently observed by those in regular contact with industrialized agriculture. But it must be noted that none of the activities mentioned occur exclusively on industrialized farms. Although systematic information is not available, anyone who is regularly associated with agriculture is likely to have observed a substantial variety of approaches in these matters both among the industrialized and the nonindustrialized farm firms.

The main point made here is that on the industrialized farm patterns of dealing with the employment of hired workers are likely to be similar to those of industry--for better or worse. Specialized management provides a climate favorable to a systematic, though not necessarily optimal or humane, approach to the development of an occupational structure in agriculture. Where the industrialized farm is a subdivision of a larger industrial organization, it is common for the policies, practices, attitudes, and procedures of the larger organization to influence and perhaps determine the policies of the industrialized farm.

Is this modern management likely to take the initiative in restructuring jobs in agriculture as, say, a means of making farm work more attractive? Initiative or action along these lines is not an assured outcome of the industrialized management structure, particularly if the labor force needs can be met by maintaining prevailing patterns. The two most likely sources of initiative are leadership (which seems to be distributed sparsely and randomly) and outside influences. No doubt, within the agricultural sector of the economy there are many illustrations of imaginative leadership with respect to the employment of hired labor, but few of the efforts of these leaders have been the subject of research. One such effort has been studied and is briefly described in the next section; without question, there must be many others--more than any research program could hope to study.

One type of outside influence has been alluded to--the parent company. There is another, perhaps even more important, influence: the farm labor union. It is difficult to see in unionization and collective bargaining any greater potential for imaginative restructuring of jobs than one can discern in modern specialized management. Including newly organized farm workers under collective bargaining is more likely to ossify the present occupational structure, present jobs, and present hiring and lay-off policies than to stimulate any reconsideration of prevailing patterns. Specialized modern farm management, like its counterpart in industry, is motivated by profit and the desire for stability. Retaining the present job structure and related policies, but at a higher wage level, may be sufficient to meet the immediate demands of union members, while a three-year contract would promise three years of stability that both union leadership and management are likely to value most highly.

Without question the current jobs will be clearly defined, wage rates and working conditions will be specified in detail, and so on. But a thoroughgoing and critical examination of the existing occupational structure is not likely to occur. Moreover, in view of the combined influences of modern management, unemployment insurance, and collective bargaining, future prospects for a critical examination of the current job structure are hardly enhanced. The management of some modern large farm firms have reported that their employees would rather draw unemployment insurance payments than shift from one job to another--say, from tractor driving to irrigating. It is not likely that the farm labor unions will support efforts to encourage this kind of shifting of employees between what were traditionally two distinctly separate jobs. Without passing judgment on the issues involved here, it can be seen that a substantial leadership effort would be required merely to encourage a careful analysis of the issues.

THE ROLES OF RESEARCH AND LEADERSHIP

Implicit in this review of the occupational structure of agriculture and its relationship to the industrialization of agriculture is the assumption that the occupational structure of an industry can be modified by public or private efforts. This assumption also underlies the current interest in job restructuring and job enrichment efforts. Of course the possibility of job restructuring is also assumed in attempts to apply the division-of-labor principle in organizing production, whether on an industrialized farm or in a factory.

With regard to job restructuring, two important and intensive efforts to influence the nature of jobs in agriculture are discussed here briefly. First described is a recent direct endeavor to restructure jobs on operating farms with the intent of improving both the management and the employment opportunities on those farms cooperating with the project. The second program described represents an outcome that had its origin largely in the leadership provided by the manager of a specific farm labor supply cooperative.

A project to restructure jobs in agriculture, first funded by the USDL in 1971, proposed to develop a job ladder that would (1) help both year-round and seasonal workers to improve their skills and their job security and (2) help employers to utilize hired labor more effectively. All of the tasks performed on six farms were identified, analyzed, and classified according to their complexity, and an eight-step career ladder was formulated. Through a combination of job training and job restructuring it was possible to create 44 new year-round jobs on these farms, and 23 workers were moved from seasonal into year-round jobs (Baker, pp. 2-6). Both the management of these farms and the project staff agreed that these results would not have been achieved without the project research efforts.

The concept of a career ladder was developed, continuing the concept of transition, under which a worker enters the system at the unskilled farm worker level and proceeds upward as skills are acquired and opportunities arise. The project ultimately led to the development of a cooperative extension program in farm personnel management under which a personnel management farm advisor was employed as a member of the professional staff of the University of California Cooperative Extension office in Fresno County. This program is currently being expanded to other counties.

With respect to the focus of this chapter, several aspects of this project are of special interest. First, the process of cataloging all of the tasks performed on six farms and of developing a job hierarchy based on their complexity required more resources than most moderate-size farms can command. Possibly substantial economies might be achieved in successive replications of this effort, and possibly not.

Second, the difficulty of moving up the ladder was at once obvious to the project staff and to the farm management because there were relatively few jobs at the top of the ladder. A career pyramid would have been a more accurate term than ladder; there was only one owner-manager at the top. Thus if the long-term commitment of workers was to be secured, it became necessary to identify a set of tasks that would form a substantial package of skills and could provide the basis for training programs that would give each worker an opportunity to achieve his employment goals, even if only approximately.

Third, once the tasks that would more nearly facilitate year-round employment for crews were selected, training programs were established so that the workers could acquire the needed skills and knowledge. The training needs were identified by the project staff, who worked closely with the management of the farm firms. The actual training was provided entirely through the local community colleges and adult evening schools already in place. In much of the training, employees of the cooperating farm firms acted as instructors under the auspices of these institutions. The project staff made the connection between those needing training and those with the capacity and competence to offer it.

Another approach to altering and improving occupational structure in agriculture is presented by the experience of the Coastal Growers Association of Oxnard, California. This is a cooperative of several hundred citrus growers that was organized in 1964 to perform the function of harvesting lemons for its members. The association, utilizing the prevailing job categories, attempted to make the seasonal work of lemon picking sufficiently attractive to elicit the continuing interest of harvest crews. Competitive wage rates were established and a substantial package of nonwage benefits was evolved over the years.

The development of the wage and nonwage payment system was accompanied by a highly systematic approach to recruitment, selection, management, and evaluation of performance. Since 1976 the rights of workers to these jobs have been protected by a system of seniority. Between 1965 and 1978 the hourly earnings of workers increased more than twice as much as the consumer price index; production per hour increased from 3.4 boxes to 8.5 boxes, and the total cost of harvesting lemons increased by 73%--less than the increase in the consumer price index for the corresponding period.

Perhaps the most dramatic change that took place was in the number of men employed. In 1965 a total of 8,517 crew members employed at some time in the course of the year picked a total of 4.3 million boxes of lemons. In 1978 only 1,292 workers were needed to pick 6.5 million boxes. Thus as noted above, the number of boxes picked per hour increased from 3.4 in

1965 to 8.5 in 1978. The average number of days worked per man increased from 17 to 89 in the same period. As a result of the increase in productivity vastly fewer employees were required to harvest larger crops.

While the technology of picking remained unchanged, the job of picking lemons for the association was transformed from a casual seasonal job to a serious, highly skilled occupation with average hourly earnings of $5.63 in 1978 and $6.16 in 1979. Through careful selection of workers, through careful supervision, and through education of the growers about orchard conditions favorable for harvest work, it was possible to reduce substantially the underemployment implied in the relatively low productivity of workers and the employment practices that had prevailed in 1965 (Mamer and Rosedale).

With experience, the lemon harvest workers greatly improved their skills. Increasingly, crew members were hired on the basis of proficiency and a past record of remaining with the association throughout each harvest season. As a consequence, highly skilled crews returned to work year after year on the basis of seniority. Thus what once had been an unskilled casual seasonal occupation was transformed and recognized for what it is--a skilled job--one in which employees maintain a continuing interest, with rights to such work protected by a system of seniority.

The lemon pickers' interest in returning to the association year after year has been reinforced by the opportunity for upward mobility within the association, as well as by the package of nonwage benefits offered. Management of the association has consistently continued to practice internal recruitment in its selection of staff for the year-round jobs, foremen, administrative staff, and clerical workers. This is a significant departure from the more common pattern, under which seasonal farm workers tend to be isolated from opportunities to move into the year-round jobs. Of course, the opportunities to shift to year-round employment increased as the number of workers at the lemon-picking level declined--in this case a diminution of more than 80% over the 1965-78 period.

The experience of this association is an illustration of leadership, initiative, and imagination. It is not the only such illustration that one can find in the agricultural sector of this nation. Examination of others might provide additional knowledge and insights that would be helpful in determining appropriate directions for future research related to farm labor and in developing public policy related to seasonal farm workers.

CONCLUSIONS AND SUGGESTIONS FOR RESEARCH

Over the past 100 years the process of industrialization has been perhaps the most powerful force to impinge upon the occupational structure of agriculture, continuously producing changes in some features while retaining other aspects of the structure with little change. Industrialized agriculture as a system of production has undergone considerable modification over the years, responding to both external pressures, such as laws and regulations, and to internal influences, such as those arising from the application of modern management principles and organizational procedures.

Seasonal farm labor has remained an integral part of much of industrialized agriculture; yet it is clear that the additional layers of management, the application of scientific knowledge, the required technical information, and the use of sophisticated machinery--all characteristic features of industrialized agriculture--have produced an extensive array of occupations ranging from jobs that involve simple hand labor tasks to those that require a scientific education.

Because the available agricultural employment data largely fail to parallel the agricultural jobs identified in federal and state reports, it is not possible at the present time to develop an accurate statement of employment opportunities that prevail among the jobs in agriculture. This lack of correspondence between employment data and occupational information also makes it difficult to make many meaningful suggestions regarding appropriate education and training--training keyed to the array of jobs that comprise the occupational structure of agriculture. It would seem logical, therefore, that one of the first research priorities with respect to that structure should be to expand the data and information on hand regarding employment in the numerous jobs and occupational categories that have evolved in agriculture.

This research might be organized in two phases. In the first phase researchers would examine the data and information needs of individuals and groups who have an interest in the occupational structure of agriculture. These would include persons employed or contemplating employment on farms and those who are responsible for the administration of public or private job referral services. Consideration must also be given to vocational educators and to members of state and federal legislatures who are regularly called upon to legislate on matters that influence the occupational structure of agriculture.

The second phase of this research might be directed toward the identification and evaluation of the information actually on hand and toward the possibility of augmenting it to more fully serve the needs identified in the first phase.

With regard to job identification, the California publication *Occupations in Agriculture 1979* is of particular interest. This publication provides some information about job duties and working conditions in the production of food crops, together with a variety of other useful information, including patterns of advancement, wages and hours, outlook for employment, methods of entry, job search methods, and related jobs. Employment levels associated with each job are not provided, nor are jobs in the production of ornamental products. It might be appropriate to supplement job descriptions with available or improved employment data and to expand the report to include jobs in other crops and states. Obviously any changes made should be based on careful research.

Seasonality of employment remains one of the most serious and intractable problems associated with industrialized agriculture. Two approaches to reducing seasonality have been discussed here: (1) a research effort in the nature of a demonstration project, and (2) an illustration of leadership in the application of modern labor management to seasonal farm workers. The demonstration project yielded favorable results, but because of its relatively high cost it is not likely to be pursued by private firms. From the point of view of the larger society, however, the demonstration project approach may actually be a low-cost means of identifying adjustments of labor management practices on the farm that can contribute significantly to efficient utilization of labor. It can also serve to encourage cooperation, as it did in this case, among institutions functioning in the farm labor market.

By applying modern labor management principles and practices to lemon harvesting, the management of a farm labor supply cooperative was able to achieve a reduction in the number of workers recruited each year and to ease the migrancy aspect of its employment. In the process, the cooperative shifted its employment activities to a systematic basis and provided a marked contrast to the casual basis on which migratory labor is commonly employed.

In addition to these two approaches to reducing the seasonality of farm employment, there have been many other innovations or nontypical developments in the recruitment and management of seasonal farm workers in agriculture. However, most of these have received little or no attention. For example, in some areas of the country, where the growing season extends through most of the year, a few farm employers select crops, schedule planting, and otherwise arrange operations so that the crews can be employed throughout the year. Furthermore, in some specific operations, such as lettuce harvesting, relatively stable worker-job relationships have become established and some reduction in migrancy seems to be taking place. The extent to which changes have occurred is known mainly from anecdotal information. The effects of unionization, relatively high hourly earnings, and complementary employment have not yet been identified or analyzed.

It is obvious that these innovations and nontypical patterns have significant implications for the occupational structure of agriculture and that they also have an important bearing on the problems of seasonality of farm employment. In order to gain a better understanding of the occupational structure and its current unfolding, and to become aware of opportunities for constructive modification, there is clearly a need for research into existing and potential innovations and nontypical developments in the recruitment and management of hired farm labor, seasonal or otherwise. Where appropriate, demonstration projects might be undertaken to encourage desired changes that could be of benefit to both farm employers and employees but are not likely to be so perceived by either or both groups.

As expressed earlier, it is astonishing that so vast and technologically oriented an agriculture should exist without an apprenticeship system that encourages farm workers to acquire additional skills and renew previously acquired skills. Such a system would facilitate the development of a labor force with the competencies required by modern industrialized agriculture, and it would confer on the existing occupational structure a stature appropriate to the multitude and complexity of skills exercised on the farm.

At present the career aspirations of the U.S. farm workers are largely unknown and hence cannot be properly encouraged. Only vaguely known, also, are the precise dimensions of the existing need for skilled workers on farms. But it is known that much of the apparatus for skill training in agriculture already exists in programs that can be organized and offered through adult evening schools and community colleges. Many of these institutions offer technical training of professional quality in a wide range of skills for young people who enter the labor market through conventional educational channels. However, for the employed farm worker who wishes to update or augment his complement of skills, there are serious gaps in the system. If he is continually employed, a worker may very well be able to acquire additional skills and to sharpen others, but in the absence of a well-developed apprenticeship system, his work experience is often a slow and uncertain process for advancement toward more ambitious career goals. Without a formal system to identify and specify needed skills, to provide training, and to verify skills, unskilled farm workers will continue to find it extremely difficult to shift from unskilled to more skilled jobs in agriculture.

Three specific areas of research are suggested by this situation. First, there is need for an assessment of the knowledge and skills required on modern farms, with special attention given to the knowledge and skills having their origin in unique local conditions. Second, there is need for a comprehensive examination of the existing avenues by which farm workers currently acquire knowledge and new skills and renew previously acquired skills. Such an examination will probably furnish some insight into the career aspirations of farm workers and provide valuable information about desirable changes. Third, before any apprenticeship system is formally established, there is need for an evaluation of alternative systems for training farm workers. It is possible that the apprenticeship model, shaped so successfully in industry, might very well be adapted to industrialized agriculture and its many occupations, but this should not be assumed without careful study. Several advanced industrial nations, particularly Great Britain and West Germany, have mounted well-developed systems that merit examination. Since the development of a comprehensive system of training has been so long delayed in U.S. agriculture, it would seem wise to profit by the delay, utilizing as far as possible the desirable features of systems that have already been operative for several decades or more.

APPENDIX 10.A. AGRICULTURAL OCCUPATIONS: UNITED STATES

PLANT FARMING OCCUPATIONS

401 Grain Farming

401.137-101 Supervisor, Area (Agric.)
401.137-014 Supervisor, Detasseling Crew (Agric.)
401.161-010 Farmer, Cash Grain (Agric.) Cash Grain Grower; Grain Farmer
401.683-010 Farm Worker, Grain (Agric.) I
401.683-014 Farm Worker, Rice (Agric.)
401.687-010 Farm Worker, Grain (Agric.) II

402 Vegetable Farming Occupations

402.131-010 Supervisor, Vegetable Farming (Agric.) Field Supervisor
402.161-010 Farmer, Vegetable (Agric.) Garden Farmer; Vegetable Grower
402.663-010 Farm Worker, Vegetable (Agric.) I
402.687-010 Farm Worker, Vegetable (Agric.) II Garden Worker; Laborer, Vegetable Farm; Vegetable Worker
402.687-014 Harvest Worker, Vegetable (Agric.)

403 Fruit and Nut Farming Occupations

403.131-010 Supervisor, Tree-Fruit-and-Nut Farming (Agric.) Supervisor, Grove; Supervisor, Orchard
403.131-014 Supervisor, Vine-Fruit Farming (Agric.)
403.161-010 Farmer, Tree-Fruit-and-Nut Crops (Agric.) Orchardist
403.161-014 Farmer, Vine-Fruit Crops (Agric.) Berry Grower
403.683-010 Farm Worker, Fruit (Agric.) I
403.687-010 Farm Worker, Fruit (Agric.) II
403.687-014 Fig Caprifier (Agric.)
403.687-018 Harvest Worker, Fruit (Agric.) Fruit Picker
403.687-022 Vine Pruner (Agric.)

404 Field Crop Farming Occupations, NEC

404.131-010 Supervisor, Field-Crop Farming (Agric.)

404.131-014 Supervisor, Shed Workers (Agric.) Shed Boss
404.161-010 Farmer, Field Crop (Agric.)
404.663-010 Farm Worker, Field Crop (Agric.) I
404.685-010 Seed-Potato Arranger (Agric.)
404.686-010 Seed Cutter (Agric.) Cutter; Potato-Seed Cutter
404.687-010 Farm Worker, Field Crop (Agric.) II
404.687-014 Harvest Worker, Field Crop (Agric.)

405 Horticultural Specialty Occupations

405.131-010 Supervisor, Horticultural-Specialty Farming (Agric.)
405.137-010 Supervisor, Rose-Grading (Agric.) Head Rose Grader
405.161-010 Bonsai Culturist (Agric.) Dwarf Tree Grower
405.161-014 Horticultural-Specialty Grower, Field (Agric.)
405.161-018 Horticultural-Specialty Grower, Inside (Agric.)
405.361-010 Plant Propagator (Agric.)
405.683-010 Farm Worker, Bulbs (Agric.)
405.683-014 Growth-Media Mixer, Mushroom (Agric.)
405.684-010 Budder (Agric.)
405.684-014 Horticultural Worker (Agric.) I
405.687-010 Flower Picker (Agric.)
405.687-014 Horticultural Worker (Agric.) II
405.687-018 Transplanter, Orchard (Agric.)

406 Gardening and Groundskeeping Occupations

406.134-010 Supervisor, Cemetery Workers (Real Estate)
406.134-014 Supervisor, Park Workers (Gov. Serv.; Museum; Waterworks)
406.137-010 Greenskeeper (Any Ind.) I Greenskeeper, Head
406.137-014 Superintendent, Greens (Amuse. & Rec.)
406.381-010 Gardener, Special Effects and Instruction Models (Motion Pict.; Museum)
406.683-010 Greenskeeper (Any Ind.) II Laborer, Golf Course

406.684-010 Cemetery Worker (Real Estate)
406.684-014 Groundskeeper, Industrial-Commercial (Any Ind.) Caretaker, Grounds; Gardener; Yard Laborer
406.687-010 Groundskeeper, Parks and Grounds (Gov. Serv.) Park Worker

407 Diversified Crop Farming Occupations
407.131-010 Supervisor, Diversified Crops (Agric.)
407.161-010 Farmer, Diversified Crops (Agric.)
407.663-010 Farm Worker, Diversified Crops (Agric.) I
407.687-010 Farm Worker, Diversified Crops (Agric.) II

408 Plant Life and Related Service Occupations
408.131-010 Supervisor, Spray, Lawn and Tree-Service (Agric.) Crew Manager
408.137-010 Supervisor, Insect and Disease Inspection (Agric.) Disease-and-Insect-Control Boss
408.137-014 Supervisor, Tree-Trimming (Light, Heat, & Power)
408.161-010 Landscape Gardener (Agric.) Landscaper
408.181-010 Tree Surgeon (Agric.)
408.381-010 Scout (Agric.) Pest-Control Worker
408.381-014 Weed Inspector (Agric.)
408.662-010 Hydro-Sprayer Operator (Agric.)
408.664-010 Tree-Trimmer (Light, Heat, & Power; Teleph. & Telegr.) Tree-Trimmer, Line Clearance, Tree-Trimming-Line Technician
408.667-010 Tree-Trimmer Helper (Light, Heat, & Power) Tree-Trimmer Helper, Line Clearance
408.684-010 Lawn-Service Worker (Agric.)
408.684-014 Sprayer, Hand (Agric.)
408.684-018 Tree Pruner (Agric.)
408.687-010 Field Inspector, Disease and Insect Control (Agric.)
408.687-014 Laborer, Landscape (Agric.)
408.687-018 Tree-Surgeon Helper (Agric.) II

409 Plant Farming and Related Occupations, NEC

409.117-010 Harvest Contractor (Agric.) Farm-Labor Contractor
409.131-010 Supervisor, Picking Crew (Agric.) Harvest Supervisor
409.137-010 Irrigator, Head (Agric.) Supervisor, Irrigation
409.137-014 Row Boss, Hoeing (Agric.)
409.667-010 Airplane-Pilot Helper (Agric.)
409.683-010 Farm-Machine Operator (Agric.)
409.683-014 Field Hauler (Agric.)
409.684-010 Irrigator, Valve Pipe (Agric.)
409.685-010 Farm-Machine Tender (Agric.)
409.685-014 Irrigator, Sprinkling System (Agric.) Irrigator, Overhead
409.686-010 Farm Worker, Machine (Agric.)
409.687-010 Inspector-Grader, Agricultural Establishment (Agric.)
409.687-014 Irrigator, Gravity Flow (Agric.)
409.687-018 Weed Thinner (Agric.)

ANIMAL FARMING OCCUPATIONS

410 Domestic Animal Farming Occupations

410.131-010 Barn Boss (Any Ind.) Corral Boss; Hostler; Lot Boss; Stable Manager
410.131-014 Supervisor, Artificial Breeding Ranch (Agric.)
410.131-018 Supervisor, Dairy Farm (Agric.)
410.131-022 Supervisor, Stock Ranch (Agric.)
410.134-010 Supervisor, Livestock-Yard (Any Ind.)
410.134-014 Supervisor, Wool-Shearing (Agric.)
410.137-010 Camp Tender (Agric.)
410.137-014 Top Screw (Agric.) Lead Rider; Ramrod; Top Waddy
410.161-010 Animal Breeder (Agric.)
410.161-014 Fur Farmer (Agric.)
410.161-018 Livestock Rancher (Agric.) Livestock Breeder; Livestock Farmer
410.357-010 Milk Sampler (Agric.) Sampler
410.364-010 Lamber (Agric.)
410.664-010 Farm Worker, Livestock (Agric.) Laborer, Livestock; Ranch Hand, Livestock

	410.674-010	Animal Caretaker (Any Ind.) Animal Attendant; Farm Worker, Animal
	410.674-014	Cowpuncher (Agric.) Puncher; Ranch Rider; Rider
	410.674-018	Livestock-Yard Attendant (Any Ind.)
	410.674-022	Stable Attendant (Any Ind.) Barn-worker, Groom
	410.684-010	Farm Worker, Dairy (Agric.) Laborer, Dairy Farm
	410.684-014	Sheep Shearer (Agric.) Sheep Clipper; Stock Clipper; Wool Shearer
	410.685-010	Milker, Machine (Agric.) Milking-Machine Operator
	410.687-010	Fleece Tier (Agric.)
	410.687-014	Goat Herder (Agric.)
	410.687-018	Pelter (Agric.) Skinner, Pelts
	410.687-022	Sheep Herder (Agric.) Herder; Mutton Puncher; Shepherd
	410.687-026	Wool-Fleece Sorter (Agric.)
411	Domestic Fowl Farming Occupations	
	411.131-010	Supervisor, Poultry Farm (Agric.)
	411.137-010	Supervisor, Poultry Hatchery (Agric.)
	411.161-010	Canary Breeder (Agric.)
	411.161-014	Poultry Breeder (Agric.) Chicken Fancier
	411.161-018	Poultry Farmer (Agric.)
	411.267-010	Field Service Technician, Poultry (Agric.)
	411.364-010	Blood Tester, Fowl (Agric.)
	411.364-014	Poultry Tender (Agric.)
	411.384-010	Poultry Inseminator (Agric.) Artificial Insemination Technician
	411.584-010	Farm Worker, Poultry (Agric.) Helper, Chicken Farm; Poultry Helper
	411.684-010	Caponizer (Agric.)
	411.684-014	Poultry Vaccinator (Agric.)
	411.687-010	Chick Grader (Agric.) Poultry Culler
	411.687-010	Chick Sexer (Agric.)
	411.687-018	Laborer, Poultry Farm (Agric.)
	411.687-022	Laborer, Poultry Hatchery (Agric.) Hatchery Helper; Incubator Helper
	411.687-026	Poultry Debeaker (Agric.) Debeaker

412 Game Farming Occupations

412.131-010 Supervisor, Game Farm (Agric.)
412.137-010 Animal Keeper, Head (Amuse. & Rec.) Keeper, Head; Superintendent, Menagerie
412.161-010 Game-Bird Farmer (Agric.)
412.674-010 Animal Keeper (Amuse. & Rec.) Animal Caretaker; Menagerie Caretaker; Zoo Caretaker
412.684-010 Game-Farm Helper (Agric.) Laborer, Game Farm

413 Lower Animal Farming Occupations

413.161-010 Beekeeper (Agric.) Apiarist; Bee Farmer; Bee Raiser; Bee Rancher; Honey Producer
413.161-014 Reptile Farmer (Agric.)
413.161-018 Worm Grower (Agric.) Fish-Worm Grower
413.687-010 Worm Picker (Agric.) Fish-Bait Picker
413.687-014 Worm-Farm Laborer (Agric.) Worm-Bed Attendant; Worm Raiser

418 Animal Service Occupations

418.381-010 Horseshoer (Agric.) Plater
418.384-010 Artificial Inseminator (Agric.) Inseminator
418.384-014 Artificial-Breeding Technician (Agric.) Breeding Technician
418.674-010 Dog Groomer (Pers. Serv.) Dog Beautician; Dog-Hair Clipper
418.667-010 Dog Bather (Pers. Serv.)

419 Animal Farming Occupations, NEC

419.224-010 Horse Trainer (Agric.)

42 MISCELLANEOUS AGRICULTURAL AND RELATED OCCUPATIONS

421 General Farming Occupations

421.161-010 Farmer, General (Agric.)
421.683-010 Farm Worker, General (Agric.) I Hired Worker
421.687-010 Farm Worker, General (Agric.) II Chore Tender; Farm Laborer

429 Miscellaneous Agricultural and Related Occupations, NEC

429.387-010	Cotton Classer (Agric.; Textile) Cotton Grader
429.685-010	Ginner (Agric.)
429.685-014	Thresher, Broomcorn (Agric.)
429.686-010	Press Feeder, Broomcorn (Agric.)

SOURCE: USDL, *Dictionary of Occupational Titles*, 4th ed. (Washington, D.C.: U.S. Government Printing Office, 1977).

APPENDIX 10.B. AGRICULTURAL OCCUPATIONS: UNITED STATES

MANAGERS AND OFFICIALS, (NEC)

180 Agriculture, Forestry, and Fishing Industry Managers and Officials

180.117-010	Manager, Christmas-Tree Farm (Forestry)
180.161-010	Manager, Production, Seed Corn (Agric.) Manager, Regional
180.167-010	Artificial-Breeding Distributor (Agric.)
180.167-014	Field Supervisor, Seed Production (Agric.)
180.167-018	General Manager, Farm (Agric.; Wholesale Trade)
180.167-022	Group Leader (Agric.) Crew Boss; Crew Leader; Row Boss
180.167-026	Manager, Dairy Farm (Agric.)
180.167-030	Manager, Fish Hatchery (Fish.) Superintendent, Fish Hatchery; Fish Culturist
180.167-034	Manager, Game Breeding Farm (Agric.)
180.167-038	Manager, Game Preserve (Agric.)
180.167-042	Manager, Nursery (Agric.; Retail Trade; Wholesale Trade)
180.167-046	Manager, Poultry Hatchery (Agric.)

180.167-050 Migrant Leader (Agric.) Crew Leader; Farm-Crew Leader
180.167-054 Superintendent (Agric.; Cann. & Preserv.)
180.167-058 Superintendent, Production (Agric.) Grove Superintendent; Manager, Production

SOURCE: USDL, *Dictionary of Occupational Titles*, 4th ed. (Washington, D.C.: U.S. Government Printing Office, 1977).

APPENDIX 10.C. OCCUPATIONS IN AGRICULTURE: CALIFORNIA

Livestock
- Ranch Hand (Cowboy)
- Cattle Rancher (Ranch Foreman)
- Cow Washer
- Milker
- Ranch Hand
- Dairy Manager (Owner-Manager)

Poultry
- Poultry Worker
- Field Service Representative
- Supervisor, Poultry Workers
- Poultry Farm Manager

Deciduous Tree Fruit and Nuts
- Pruner
- Tier (Fruit)
- Thinner (Fruit)
- Picker (Fruit)
- Equipment Operator
- Irrigation
- Crew-Leader (Fruit)
- Harvest Machine Operator (Nuts)
- Pruner
- Equipment Operator
- Irrigator
- Harvest Supervisor

Grapes
- Vineyard Worker
- Irrigator
- Equipment Operator
- Supervisor, Vineyard Workers
- Vineyard Manager

Field Crops (Hay, Cotton)
- Weeder-Thinner (Cotton)
- Equipment Operator (Cotton)
- Cutter-Baler (Alfalfa)
- Irrigator

Vegetables and Melons
- Foreman
- Equipment Operator
- Furrow Irrigator
- Mechanic
- Field Worker
- Sprinkler Irrigator
- Sorter (Tomato)

Citrus Fruit
  Pest Control Operator
  Weed Controller
  Picker

SOURCE: California Employment Development Department, *Occupations in Agriculture 1979* (Sacramento, 1979).

Discussion

CHARLES D. COVEY

The structure issue has provided Mamer the opportunity to touch upon many of the basic issues facing farm workers and agricultural employers today. He tells us that industrialization in agriculture will increasingly involve the separation of ownership and management, and as a consequence the degree of professionalism in management will be enhanced. His conclusion is that this professionalism will result in a more receptive attitude to improved management procedures for recruiting, defining jobs, and developing standards of performance and evaluation than would be possible under an owner/manager system. Professional managers are also expected to view collective bargaining and contract negotiations as a further refinement of their managerial skills, to be viewed in nonemotional, economic terms.

Implicitly Mamer seems to assume that professional management will be favorably inclined toward the restructuring of jobs and occupational categories in agriculture. However, he stops short of this conclusion by indicating that it is not a foregone conclusion.

This inconclusiveness seems to agree with what

has been observed on a limited basis with agricultural managers who deal with labor unions. Two basic professional management philosophies emerge from these observations. The first is more traditional and reflects a desire on the part of management to always maintain complete flexibility in the assignment of work tasks to individual employees.

These managers maintain that complete job descriptions inhibit management's prerogative to exercise control over the work of an employee. Taken to its extreme, these managers feel that job descriptions provide workers with the opportunity to refuse work assignments when they are not spelled out in the job description.

The second management philosophy is one that considers job descriptions as useful and sufficiently explicit and well-constructed to serve as the key factor in dealing with grievance and disciplinary procedures. Management makes this possible by allocating sufficient resources to develop realistic, complete job descriptions for all levels of responsibility, including management. In this situation, labor is often given the opportunity to provide input in developing job descriptions for workers. This type of management is usually relatively innovative in restructuring jobs and occupational categories.

Mamer indicates that industrialization of agriculture is proceeding with varying degrees of rapidity throughout the United States, with California probably leading the nation. One interesting observation that seems to indicate industrialization in agriculture is proceeding at a relatively slow pace in most of the nation is made by Daberkow and Fritsch on the incidence of accidents in the various sectors of the United States economy. When examined by firm size based on the number of employees, accident rates for nonagricultural firms are low for small firms, increase for medium-size firms, and then decline again for large firms. This is explained in small firms by a closer employee-employer relationship, and in large firms, which presumably have more professional management, by a lower turnover, fewer young workers, lower production-jobs-to-clerical-jobs ratios, and more safety personnel and resources.

In agriculture, on the other hand, accident rates increase with the size of firm over all sizes considered, with the large agricultural firms having the highest accident rates of all industries. Additionally, the accident rate for large agricultural firms increased from 1974 to 1975 while rates for similar size firms in other industries either declined or remained the same. This data tends to suggest either small gains in the professionalism of agricultural management or that the degree of turnover in employment and the ratio of production jobs to clerical jobs in agriculture is sufficiently large to offset any gains in professional management. These data appear somewhat incongruous in a discussion of agricultural industrialization and worthy of some further analysis.

One would assume that as the industrialization of agriculture continues, with increased professional management and an improved occupational structure, conditions for improving the quality of data on the U.S. agricultural labor force would be enhanced. Given the present farm labor data base, which appears to be less than adequate for current research needs, the increasing industrialization of agriculture can be viewed as a positive step toward improving the quality and quantity of these data. It appears, however, that various agencies having farm-labor-related programs continue to talk about, but do relatively little, adopting common definitions that would improve the quality of the farm labor data base.

Mamer indicated that labor unions are not interested in the development of innovative occupational structures for agriculture. Undoubtedly this is true with the current level of maturity of labor unions in agriculture. Less mature unions will bargain hardest for bread and butter issues, while more mature unions will place less mundane issues on the bargaining table. Experienced labor relations specialists indicate that as unions mature and become more sophisticated, the issue of job descriptions and occupational structure may emerge as a bargaining issue.

Despite our progress toward industrialization in agriculture, the seasonal demand for agricultural labor has not been eliminated. The biological nature of agricultural production essentially precludes the complete elimination of seasonal labor needs as long as production is continued in the United States. Given a continuing demand for seasonal farm labor, how this demand is to be satisfied, and at the same time provide for the economic and social well-being of those who supply the hands and backs to meet this demand, is a problem of national concern. In *Farm Labor in the United States*, edited by C. E. Bishop and published in 1967, Fuller reviewed the failure of past government programs to diversify farm and nonfarm employment opportunities for seasonal farm workers. He also supported the inclusion of farm workers under the unemployment insurance program, which has now been accomplished.

Times change but the need for seasonal farm workers continues. If this need is to be met we must be innovative or at least reexamine some of those ideas that were tried in earlier days and did not work. Perhaps they were ideas before their time. In view of the dimensions of the problem, it seems reasonable to suggest that funding agencies with responsibilities for farm labor programs solicit proposals for pilot projects to reexamine the feasibility of developing alternative off-season employment through cooperative arrangements with nonfarm enterprises. Initial costs might be significant but the tax incentive philosophy, as evidenced by the Work Incentive Program and the Targeted Jobs Program, has been established.

Another alternative, which could follow the pilot project format, would be the establishment of a quasi-governmental agency, perhaps similar in structure to the Farm Credit Banks under the Farm Credit Administration, to supply, manage, transport, house, and administer a seasonal farm worker-program. Agricultural employers would belong to the organization and could draw workers in the same manner that farmers obtain credit from the Farm Credit System. It might be possible to organize the system so that workers could also be members and share in the decision-making process of the organization. Workers would have the advantage of working for the same employer for essentially the entire year or season, while farmer members would be assured of an adequate seasonal labor supply at fair and equitable costs.

Initially, such an agency might be viewed as just one more ineffectual bureaucracy. It might be successful, however, if the innovative techniques pioneered by labor cooperatives such as Coastal Growers at Oxnard, California, and others were incorporated into the proposal.

In 1967 Fuller outlined the dilemma facing agricultural labor at the time when he said:

> Whether deliberately or by default, most of the turning points other than those in labor standards that commit farming to be a component of the industrial society have already been passed. What remains to be done are some finishing and polishing of occupational status within commercial farming and the clarification of complementary employment relations between commercial farming, non-farming, and other rural industries. (p. 101)

We do not seem to have progressed very far in the intervening fourteen years. Fuller's insight seems amazingly clear, but it would be interesting to know what his timetable would have been for completing the job.

Mamer pointed out that progress toward industrialization in agriculture tends to create labor surpluses. This seems to be at the crux of efforts to deal with seasonal labor problems. The general health of the total U.S. economy determines whether there is a surplus or deficit supply situation in agricultural labor. If one were to speculate on the general health of the total U.S. economy within the current energy environment, the outlook at best seems to be one of only moderate growth. Such an environment indicates that the changes proposed by Mamer, while inevitable, will be tortuous and slow in coming.

11

The California Agricultural Labor Relations Act and National Agricultural Labor Relations Legislation

SUE EILEEN HAYES

California is the largest agricultural state in the United States. It is also, by far, the largest source for employment of farm labor. Almost 20% of all regular farm worker employment episodes in the United States take place on California ranches.[1] California has four times the episodes of employment of seasonal workers and 80% more hirings of casual workers than the next largest state, North Carolina. The *1974 Census of Agriculture* reports that almost 40% of contract farm worker hirings in the United States also occurred on California farms.

Although California was not the first state to have agricultural labor relations legislation, the magnitude of the labor force that it encompasses and the publicity that has accompanied the organizing efforts of agricultural labor unions in the state have focused national attention on California and its Agricultural Labor Relations Act.

The discussion that follows is an attempt to evaluate the California Agricultural Labor Relations Act (CALRA) as it has affected labor relations in the state since its passage. The applicability of similar legislation in other agricultural states will be examined. In addition, the hypothetical adoption of the National Labor Relations Act (NLRA) in California will be considered, with particular emphasis on the differences between the NLRA and the CALRA in worker enfranchisement and the ability of unions to organize and exert power in collective bargaining. Finally, the potential for extending the coverage of the NLRA to include agriculture, and the relative advantages and disadvantages of national versus state-by-state agricultural labor relations legislation will be discussed.

CALIFORNIA AGRICULTURAL LABOR RELATIONS PRIOR TO CALRA

In 1965 the National Farm Workers Association, led by Cesar Chavez, joined a strike of grape workers in Delano, California, which had been called by the Agricultural Workers Organizing Committee, sponsored by the AFL-CIO. The two merged in August 1965 to form the United Farm Workers Organizing Committee, which became in February 1972 the United Farm Workers Union, AFL-CIO. Although other unions were also active in California agriculture, it was the activities of the UFW and its frequent rival, the Western Conference of Teamsters, which brought California agricultural labor relations to national attention through the decade prior to passage of the CALRA. (Before August 1975, the major unions involved in organizing California agricultural workers were the UFW, the Teamsters, AFL-CIO unions such as the Amalgamated Meat Cutters and Butcher Workmen of North America, the Christian Labor Association and the International Brotherhood of Teamsters [both in the dairy industry], and some other independent associations.)

Historically, labor unions have never represented a substantial percentage of the California agricultural labor force. Prior to approximately 1970, they never represented more than 2-3% of the workers. Their impact on agricultural labor relations legislation has been much greater than the size of their membership or their voting power might indicate.

One reason for this impact was the coincidence of

the rise of the UFW with a period when national attention was focused on civil rights. The UFW capitalized on the public image of the California farm worker to attract financial and political support for its campaign. Further, the use of the consumer boycott permitted UFW supporters across the nation to attempt to influence employers at a relatively small personal cost. Although it has not been conclusively demonstrated that the UFW-sponsored boycotts of grapes or lettuce resulted in extensive adverse economic impacts on producers, it is clear that they complicated the production and distribution process.

The Teamsters and the UFW clashed repeatedly throughout the early 1970s, beginning in the lettuce industry and later moving into grapes. It became clear that unregulated labor relations in California agriculture were not going to result in stability. Employers and unions frequently resorted to the courts, but much of their litigation was unproductive and inconclusive, lacking an appropriate legal framework.

Although California agricultural employers had historically opposed any kind of legislative intrusion into agricultural labor relations, employer attitudes began to shift in the 1970s, first leading to sponsorship of national legislation, then to an attempt to pass a special law through the direct voter initiative process (Proposition 22 in 1972), and finally, when this was defeated in a state election, by proposing agricultural labor relations legislation in the state legislature. In both 1973 and 1974 a state assemblyman carried grower-sponsored bills in the legislature. In 1974 the grower bill competed with bills sponsored by the state AFL-CIO on behalf of the UFW, the Teamsters, and several independent prolabor assemblymen.

The major concerned unions had also taken several positions on labor relations legislation. The Teamsters appeared comfortable working under the NLRA, but the UFW, due to its use of the boycott as an organizing tool, felt that the NLRA was too restrictive. The union would have preferred, it appears, legislation more like the Wagner Act, which would have permitted it greater tactical flexibility. When national legislation of this type seemed unobtainable, the union accepted the bill sponsored by the California state AFL-CIO in the 1974 Assembly. Although this legislation failed to pass, it was the basis for the 1975 bill that was passed, with modifications, as the CALRA.

CALRA

The CALRA is a compromise measure, passed in June 1975 after several years of effort on the part of labor and employer groups to obtain some legislative structure in the chaotic politics of labor in California agriculture. The law is modeled after the NLRA with special provisions made necessary by the seasonal nature of agricultural employment. The act provides for secret ballot elections for union representation. It established an Agricultural Labor Relations Board (ALRB) to develop regulations, supervise elections, hear complaints, and certify the validity of bargaining agents, much in the manner of the National Labor Relations Board (NLRB).

Although in its general language and provisions it resembles the NLRA, the CALRA contains features specifically addressed to the unique employment pattern of California agriculture. The authors of the CALRA recognized the importance of seasonal work by providing for elections to be held during the periods of peak employment, when seasonal workers would have the greatest opportunity to participate. The act provides that petitions be signed by 50% or more of the workers employed during a period when employment is greater than 50% of that at the employer's peak employment. Elections are to be held within seven days. If employees are on strike, the period is 48 hours, which takes into account the particular requirements for handling perishable crops in short, critical activity periods. Because there may be a change of crews or high turnover due to different job requirements even with such a short period, eligibility to vote is based on the worker's presence on the payroll during the period prior to the filing of the petition.

We can compare the relevant features of the national and California acts in Table 11.1:

The CALRA specifically exempts farm labor contractors from employer status, making farm operators responsible for labor-management relations. The "access" regulation, adopted almost immediately after passage of the act by the ALRB permits union representatives to enter employers' property before and after working hours and during the normal lunch hours to speak to workers.

CALRA: IMPACT AND EFFECTIVENESS

The Labor Market: Employer and Worker Response

Until the late 1960s agricultural employment in California was grower dominated. Wages were set by consensus, with most growers following the lead of neighbors, labor contractors, or producer association recommendations. Seasonal agricultural labor was in a generally surplus condition, so workers accepted what was offered. They were price takers, since they could be so easily replaced.

It was felt by many, particularly union supporters, that the passage of the CALRA signalled the end of the farm labor contractor system in California agriculture. The law prohibited labor contractors from participating in elections as employers. The grower, they argued, forced to deal directly with his workers, would dispose of the contractor once his principal function--labor management--was taken from him. This process might eventually occur except that most employers have as yet been unaffected by the election process under the CALRA. The 799 elections conducted by July 1979 represent approximately 2% of the employers and about 30% of the farm workers in the state (based on the CALRB, *Third Annual Report*, as discussed in Hayes 1979). This figure for farm workers may seem high, but it should be noted that in

Table 11.1. Comparison of features of the NLRA and the CALRA

	NLRA	CALRA
Representation petition	May be filed by employees or employer	May be filed by employee group only
Bargaining unit	To be determined by NLRB	All agricultural employees of an employer
Show of interest	30% of those currently employed	50% of those currently employed when employment is not less than 50% of peak employment for the year
Election period	Not specified	Within 7 days of filing; if currently on strike, within 48 hours
Election protests	To be resolved prior to election	To be resolved after election has been held
Eligibility to vote	Workers included on payroll period just before an election; economic strikers within 12 months from beginning of strike and their permanent replacements	Workers included on payroll period prior to filing of petition; economic strikers within 12 months from beginning of strike and their permanent replacements or up to 36 months in certain cases at the discretion of the Board (now obsolete)
Union membership as condition of employment	Workers required to join union on or after 30th day, excepting construction, where membership is required on or after the 7th day of employment	Workers required to join union on or after 5th day of employment
Double payment of dues	No provision	No employee required to pay dues to more than one labor organization during single month
"Make Whole" provision	No provision	Employees may be made whole for loss of pay resulting from the employer's refusal to bargain
Secondary Boycotts	Publicity to inform of existing dispute with primary employer; picketing of secondary employer prohibited	Publicity, including picketing, of secondary employer permitted; "do not patronize" publicity and picketing of secondary employer permitted if organization is certified as representative of primary employer's employees
Decertification	No similar provision	Unions that discriminate on the basis of race, color, national origin, sex, religion, or other arbitrary classification shall be decertified

general the UFW and Teamsters concentrated on large employers in the fresh vegetable, citrus, grape, and processing tomato industries. Thus one election, in which several hundred workers might vote, could represent a thousand or more farm workers. Only about 200 of these elections have actually resulted in the signing of a contract, and of these, some are on dairy farms where employment is through direct hire, and some are renewals of previous UFW contracts. Thus far only a very few employers have been forced to change their employment practices from contractor to hiring halls as a result of elections held under the act.

The delay in obtaining collective bargaining agreements after the UFW has won a representation election has several explanations. Immediately after the CALRA became effective a large number of elections were held but many were contested. Certification was delayed, retarding the bargaining process. The number of elections won exceeded the capability of the few experienced negotiators to meet quickly with all employers. Worker participation in the collective bargaining process required extensive education of workers in contract writing and negotiation. The volunteers who assisted with negotiating changed frequently. One group of southern California employers reported to the author during private discussions that after representation elections were won on their farms by the UFW in the early months after the CALRA became effective, contract negotiations extended for more than a year and a half. They dealt with three successive union bargaining teams during this period. Each team appeared to start its discussions without knowledge of the progress achieved by its predecessor. During the last major UFW organizing drive, which occurred in the citrus industry in the spring of 1978, the UFW negotiating teams seemed, both to observers and to the employers with whom they were dealing, to demonstrate a much higher degree of skill and organization. Favorable contracts were signed quite rapidly in the Oxnard-Ventura lemon district. The negotiators, who were judged most competent by the employers, were experienced organizers for the local area; volunteer workers were not given prominence in the negotiations.

One result of the CALRA has been a change in union behavior since its passage. The UFW has adopted a more professional negotiating stance, utilizing experts from other unions to help establish better patterns for negotiation. It has already accepted an important modification of its hiring hall requirement in contracts negotiated since the effective date of the act. Contracts now allow employers to rehire previous employees prior to submitting remaining jobs to the hiring hall for filling, rather than requiring the processing of all hires through the hall. Most recently it has dropped the hiring hall provision entirely from some contracts. It is also granting seniority by employer, rather than through union membership, for tenure and promotion. Employers now are obtaining union agreement to a five-day probationary period for new workers during which unsatisfactory workers can be eliminated. At the same time, the UFW has adopted a policy requiring volunteers to spend a longer period working for the union, which should reduce the turnover rate in vital positions such as negotiating teams.

The Teamsters appear to be withdrawing from the organization of seasonal farm workers. They signed a jurisdictional agreement on March 10, 1977, with the UFW in which they agreed to drop new organizing activities among field workers. They will administer current contracts until the expiration date, but state no interest in negotiating beyond that point. They retain jurisdiction over cannery and packing employees, as well as certain truck drivers and mechanics. Some local Teamsters have not accepted the national union policy gracefully. In Santa Maria, a leading Teamster business agent organized the International Union of Agricultural Workers, an independent union that has won several elections. While he retained his post with the Teamsters he openly criticized the union for abandoning farm workers.

Eight unions have been certified as collective bargaining representatives as a result of representation elections during the years since passage of the CALRA. The UFW has received the largest number of votes, followed by the Western Conference of Teamsters. Smaller numbers of votes were received by the Fresh Fruit and Vegetable Workers, Local 78; the Christian Labor Association; The International Brotherhood of Teamsters, Local 63; and the Lumber and Sawmill Workers, Local 3019. Two new independent unions, the Independent Union of Agricultural Workers and the International Union of Agricultural Workers, each won several elections in fiscal 1977-78. Employer representatives estimate that the highest percentage of farm workers are under union contract in the fresh vegetable industry, with 80-90% in the Monterey-Salinas district, 40% in the San Joaquin Valley, and 30% in Imperial-Blythe. The Teamsters are reported to have more fresh vegetable contracts, but the UFW has more fresh vegetable workers due to several contracts with very large employers. A high percentage of dairy employers also have contracts, but the number of workers on each dairy is generally small. In other crops, such as wine and table grapes, apples, citrus, nurseries, and tomatoes, probably well below 20% of workers are covered by union contracts.

Employer organizations have grown in size and activity since passage of the act. The demand for labor relations information and counseling has also affected public agencies. The University of California Cooperative (formerly Agricultural) Extension, the California Employment Development Department, and the ALRB itself have all responded with expanded public information programs.

Impact on Wages

The impact of the CALRA on agricultural wages and fringe benefits must be examined in relation to the history of changes in worker compensation over the last three decades. Wages for hired farm workers in California and the United States have increased more rapidly than the consumer price index since 1948. Wage changes for California farm workers paralleled the changes for the price index, but at about double the rate during one period, 1965-69. In the base year, 1969, average hourly wages for California agricultural workers were $1.80 per hour, according to USDA surveys (Table 11.2). The average hourly wage, increasing from $1.00 in 1948, demonstrated the greatest change, 44%, in the period 1969-74.

The U.S. average hourly agricultural wages,

Table 11.2. Average hourly wages for hired farm workers (dollars)

	California		U.S.	
Year	Hourly Wage	Index	Hourly Wage	Index
1948	1.00[a]	56	0.78	49
1949	0.91	51	0.74	47
1950	0.89	49	0.73	46
1951	0.98	54	0.82	52
1952	1.03	57	0.87	55
1953	1.08	60	0.89	56
1954	1.06	59	0.87	55
1955	1.07	59	0.88	56
1956	1.13	63	0.91	58
1957	1.13	63	0.93	59
1958	1.14	63	0.94	59
1959	1.14	63	1.00	63
1960	1.22	68	1.02	65
1961	1.25	69	1.04	66
1962	1.28	71	1.06	67
1963	1.32	73	1.09	69
1964	1.35	75	1.13	72
1965	1.40	78	1.17	74
1966	1.54	86	1.26	80
1967	1.64	91	1.36	86
1968	1.69	94	1.45	92
1969	1.80	100	1.58	100
1970	1.90	106	1.66	105
1971	1.96	109	1.74	110
1972	2.05	114	1.85	117
1973	2.29[b]	127	1.82	115
1974	2.60	144	1.99	126
1975	2.59	144	2.24	142
1976	2.88	160	2.37	150
1977	3.20	178	2.56	162
1978	3.28[c]	182	2.74	173
1979	3.60	200	3.05	193

Source: USDA, ESCS, Farm Labor, 1948-1979.
[a]Earnings per hour without room and board or housing as of July 1.
[b]By hourly pay only. Field workers and livestock.
[c]Earnings per hour. Field workers only.

beginning with an average of $0.78 in 1948, increased at a faster rate than California agricultural wages. They also demonstrated a different pattern of change, with the greatest increase occurring since 1974, and less change occurring in 1970-74 than in the 1965-69 period. The period 1975 to 1979 demonstrated a similar pattern of wage increases for California and U.S. farm workers. Although the wages of California hired farm workers increased by a slightly greater magnitude (56 index points) than the wages of U.S. hired farm workers (51 index points), both groups had 1979 hourly earnings almost double those of 1969. The gain between 1975 and 1976 was twice as large for California farm workers as for U.S. workers, which might indicate some effect from initial contracts or from employer efforts to forestall union organizing activities. In the period 1976-79, however, the national average increased faster than the California average.

It appears that most of the increase in wages and fringe benefits offered to California farm workers cannot be the direct result of union contracts. The UFW at its preact peak held approximately 300 contracts covering employers of approximately 60,000 workers; Teamster coverage was of similar magnitude several years later. Total coverage, however, involved many less than 600 contracts, since many of the contracts were held sequentially, first by the UFW and later by the Teamsters as growers signed "sweetheart" contracts.

Unions may affect the wage and benefit level in an industry or geographic area in two ways other than as a direct result of union contracts. One is through the wage competition, which occurs as nonunion employers who are competing with employers under contract must meet union scale in order to attract or retain labor. The other effect is the "union threat," which causes employers to meet wage and benefit competition in order to avoid unionization drives among their employees.

Competition for workers implies a shortage or a

barely adequate labor supply. Since the California agricultural labor force is in a generally surplus condition, the only areas where competition for labor might drive wages upward would be those with local labor shortages or a high percentage of unionized employment. The low concentration of union contracts in most of the state does not exhibit the potential for large wage gains due to competition for workers between organized and nonunion employers. Therefore, part of the explanation for the rapid rise in agricultural wages must lie elsewhere.

Labor shortage can be easily dismissed as an objective reason for increasing California agricultural wage rates. There does not appear to have been a shortage of available labor in the state at any time since the end of World War II. Even the termination of the Bracero Program of temporary Mexican labor in 1964 caused only a few spot labor shortages, principally in tomatoes and strawberries, in 1965. The labor "shortage" was certainly not of a magnitude to trigger the sizeable wage increases that occurred in some crop activities. Subjectively, however, the situation may have been interpreted differently by some employers. They may have perceived the absence of a type of worker that they commonly used (the bracero contract worker) as constituting a general labor shortage. If so, they may have then overreacted and raised wages more than would have been necessary to attract adequate supplies of labor.

By 1966, however, most employers could be expected to have adjusted their perceptions of the available labor supply, based on their postbracero experience, so that further wage increases would reflect conditions other than presumption of a labor shortage.

Using these assumptions, the pattern of wage increases that occurred in the last half of the period 1965-69 and throughout 1970-74 can be attributed at least in part to the union threat effect in major California crop areas. It appears that employers in crops that were subject to intensive organizing activity, such as table and wine grapes, particularly in key areas such as Delano and the Coachella Valley, reacted strongly to the threat of unionization.

As target employers reacted to union pressure by raising wages, the wage relationship among various crops within the immediate area would be changed. The attempt to compete with wages offered by growers of crops in which unions are obtaining representation rights could account for wage increases in other crops where union activity was minimal.

It is thus reasonable to conclude that most of the increase in wages and fringe benefits offered to California farm workers, even those not directly involved in union organizing activity, is a result of employer reaction to labor unions in California agriculture.

Other factors must be considered as well. During the period 1960-77, California average hourly wages for hired farm workers rose 110%. United States average hourly hired farm worker wages rose somewhat less, 97%, but actually increased at a faster rate during all of the period except 1970-74, when California wages increased 44% compared to 26% for the United States as a whole (Table 11.2). For the United States, aside from some UFW activity in Texas and Florida, there was little reason for employers to change pay rates due to union threat. One possibility is that minimum wage levels, gradually rising in various states, caused agricultural wages to increase. The California minimum wage in agriculture does not seem to have had this effect. Until 1974 it applied only to women and minors, and even when it was extended to men it was well below prevailing wage rates.

Effectiveness of the CALRA

Analysis of the effectiveness of some provisions of the CALRA that differ from the NLRA indicates that:

1. Representation elections within 7 days of petition are possible and achieve generally orderly elections with high levels of worker participation.

In highly seasonal activities such as deciduous fruit harvest workers could be disenfranchised if election periods were substantially longer. Other workers, on dairy, poultry, livestock, and fresh vegetable farms, might not require those provisions. In California, just over a third of the farms employ seasonal workers for 25 days or less during the year. The large number of workers involved, however, and the migrant status of many of these workers, makes speedy election clauses necessary to enable these workers to participate in representation elections.

2. Potential election protests and unit determination are in most cases clarified by the NLRB prior to setting an election date. Due to the short time between filing of the petition and election provided by the CALRA, many disputes over voter eligibility, election procedures, and appropriateness of unit are not resolved until after the election. This tends to extend the uncertainty of employer-employee representative relations beyond the election date, since certification of election results may be delayed for some weeks or months, particularly when challenged ballots can determine election results. It appears that there is a necessary trade-off of election speed for decisiveness of results.

3. Fifty percent show of interest when employment is 50% of peak is designed to ensure enfranchisement of seasonal workers. Unions have had little difficulty obtaining enough signatures. Employers object that seasonal worker votes may overwhelm year-round workers with different loyalties; they would prefer separate representation of year-round and seasonal workers. Differences of interest have not emerged in the representation process to date. On many operations that have slight or no seasonal peaks of employment, elections can be conducted at the workers' convenience throughout the year. This provision primarily protects the interests of seasonal workers.

4. Protection against double assessment of union dues is important to low income seasonal workers who may be employed on several ranches, each time possibly

under contract with a different union, during the same month. The CALRA provides that only the first union under whose contract a worker is employed during the month is entitled to collect dues. The effectiveness of this provision cannot be measured at this time due to poor employment records in California agriculture. It would appear, however, that although it would apply only to a minority of California farm workers, the provision would reduce potential hardship.

5. The five-day period to join the union, similar to the short time period specified for building trades under the NLRA, is designed to ensure dues collection from seasonal workers. No increase in turnover to avoid union membership has been reliably reported.

6. Disqualification of farm labor contractors from employer status was designed to discourage use of the contractor system by employers. It seems to have had no effect. Thus far, existing federal regulations that affect them seem to have had more impact than the CALRA on farm labor contractors.

7. Secondary boycott clauses were strongly advocated by the UFW as necessary to balance the power of "agribusiness." It is not clear that the union boycott rights have been useful to the union organization negotiating efforts since passage of the act. Some union supporters feel they may dilute efforts to strengthen organizing programs. Growers involved in the recent lettuce dispute do not report an adverse effect from a boycott.

8. "Make whole" powers enable the ALRB to compensate employees for employer refusal to bargain in good faith. The first board orders were issued in April 1978; it is too soon to determine the impact.

9. Access to employer property, a board regulation rather than part of the original legislation, has definitely enhanced union organizing efforts among seasonal workers. Many workers commute long distances to work, change jobs frequently, or live in camps on employer property. The work site may be the only feasible location to contact workers. There has been

no significant disruption of farming activities as a result of this regulation.

Applicability of the CALRA to Agricultural Labor Relations in Other States

For the several other states in the United States with a higher level of agricultural employment in such crop activities as tree fruit, vegetables and melons, cotton, sugar beets, and possibly tobacco, the seven day election provisions of the CALRA would probably provide a better opportunity for achieving collective bargaining representation than would be available if no such rapid election procedure were possible. Requiring a 50% show of interest during employment peak protects the rights of short-term workers. According to the Bureau of the Census, *1974 Census of Agriculture*, an estimated 1,169,000 employment episodes in agriculture during the year lasted an average of only 10 days. While it is probable that many of these workers were employed in activities of much longer duration, and therefore their employment might have coincided with the election process in any case, there is also a possibility that a short tree fruit or berry harvest with a single employer was their only agricultural employment. Also, although there may be considerable duplication of the count, many of the 3,357,346 employment episodes of less than 25 days must have been in short-term crop activities which might not have lasted long enough to permit an extensive bureaucratic process prior to a representation election. For other crop activities in which there is little fluctuation in number of workers throughout the year, the 7-day and "peak" provisions do not seem particularly useful and might create unnecessary stress by postponing questions of eligibility and scope of the unit, which could otherwise have been resolved prior to the election.

The high number of casual worker contacts reported to the *1974 Census of Agriculture*, compared again to the estimate of workers employed less than 25 days on farms during the year, indicates that protection against double assessment of union dues may be important to a large number of mobile workers. It should reduce the financial penalty for changing employment.

The 10-day average duration of employment reported by farm workers employed on farms less than 25 days in 1974, and the large number of casual and seasonal farm worker episodes of employment reported in the *1974 Census of Agriculture*, indicate that in many cases the 5-day period to join the union would be very important in enabling farm worker unions to collect dues.

Disqualification of farm labor contractors from employer status could have an important impact on employer perspective in some states, particularly Idaho, Arizona, and Missouri, where contractors are more heavily utilized in relation to the size of the labor force than in other states where there is lower dependence on contractors and crew leaders. Employers of contract labor on a regular, relatively long-term basis may hire labor contractors as their foremen during the period of labor use and thus institutionalize an existing arrangement. As it has been interpreted in California, the law appears to permit designation of a custom harvester, who provides equipment and perhaps additional services to growers, as an employer. This arrangement might be possible among smaller employers in other states.

It is difficult to determine how secondary boycott provisions of the CALRA have affected employers in California, let alone to predict how workers' organizations other than the UFW might utilize them in other states.

"Make whole" has not yet had a measurable effect on employer willingness to bargain. It might be hypothesized that monetary penalties would encourage employers and labor organizations to engage in good faith bargaining, but negotiation to impasse may occur under any circumstances.

Access to employer property is an extremely inflammatory issue in agriculture. In those states with widespread on-farm housing or considerable utilization of migratory labor, unions might find work site access extremely valuable. In such areas as North Carolina and Oregon, where it appears that a considerable portion of the tobacco and berry harvest labor, respectively, is recruited from local residents, work site access would seem to be much less necessary, although it would still provide a more effective way of contacting farm workers. Obviously, concentrations of casual and seasonal workers would be the primary targets of work site organizing activities.

A final aspect of the CALRA is that there is no minimum size of employer to whom it applies. From a study of the distribution of labor on farms by number of employees (Appendix Table A.10) it is clear that most U.S. farms employ a single worker or only a few. Although these employers are generally not the most cost efficient for a union to organize and service, the act provides the opportunity, should workers and unions wish it.

Applicability of the NLRA to Agriculture in California

The principal effect of adoption of the NLRA in California agriculture would appear to be the disenfranchisement of workers in employment of short duration. This would occur primarily as a result of the NLRB's practice of resolving issues such as bargaining unit and eligibility of potential voters prior to scheduling a representation election. Speed of election is not a vital concern for dairies, poultry or egg producers, livestock operations, citrus, multiple-cropped fresh vegetables, or many employers with few or no short-term workers. Even some deciduous fruit growers who raise fruit maturing at different times have a long enough harvest season to permit workers to organize, petition for, and vote in representation elections under existing NLRA provisions. The majority of California farms that hire seasonal labor could probably be accommodated by these provisions.

While the NLRB, in scheduling elections, considers seasonal drops in employment or changes in operations that would prevent a normal work force from being present, the case of an agricultural employer with a short and high seasonal labor peak may present problems in election scheduling. In this situation there may be 10 or 11 months of minimal employment and 2 months or less when payrolls may treble or quadruple. It would appear that the 10 months of lower employment would be the appropriate period, under existing NLRB practices, in which to conduct a representation election.

This raises the possibility of differing allegiances between regular and seasonal or casual farm workers. If workers employed on a permanent, year-round basis are influenced by association with the employer or other workers to favor a union different from that supported by the majority of shorter-term workers, and if their union is selected and certified during the lower employment period, shorter-term workers will be disenfranchised. Conversely, seasonal workers, during their short period of employment, could petition for and obtain a decertification election against the other workers' choice--an election they could win due to their greater numbers during the high activity period. One solution--a NLRB determination that there is enough difference of interest to justify separate bargaining units for year-round and seasonal employees--may be more representative of worker interests but complicates the collective bargaining relationship and multiplies the paperwork.

This entire discussion presupposes a division of interests, frequently claimed by agricultural employers, between year-round and seasonal workers in California. Experience to date has not demonstrated this division of interests. A number of ALRB unfair labor practice decisions have concerned the discipline or discharge of long-term employees (some of whom had obviously previously been among the employer's favorites) who had been active union advocates and had assisted in organizing seasonal workers.

The greater length of the "grace period" (under the NLRA) during which a person can work before being required to join the union having a contract with the employer may create considerable hardship for a union active among California casual and seasonal farm workers. A 30-day grace period would permit most harvest workers in deciduous tree fruits--an important segment of California seasonal employment--to avoid payment of union dues. Another significant activity for seasonal workers, raisin grape harvest, has a peak period of 6-8 weeks, which would also provide scant opportunity for unions to collect dues from many workers.

A procedural question is raised by the NLRB's jurisdictional standards. Under existing guidelines some California farms appear to be exempt from board supervision. Since the NLRA does not presently cover agriculture, no specific jurisdictional standards exist. To measure the possible coverage of the act, the two categories with the lowest sales volumes covered by present standards might be used--nonretail business and radio, telegraph, television, and telephone enterprises. The board's standards for nonretail business require a volume of sales of at least $50,000 per year; the standards for radio and other electrical communications enterprises require a minimum volume of $100,000 per year.

Using these criteria, approximately 8,000-10,000 hirings of regular farm workers would occur on California farms with too small a sales volume for a $40,000 jurisdictional standard; an additonal 9,227 would not be covered if jurisdiction began at $100,000. An even greater number of seasonal farm worker hirings would fall outside NLRB coverage. Over 22,000 would be excluded with the $40,000 minimum standard; 50,000 at the $100,000 level. Casual workers would be severely disadvantaged. Data on episodes of employment in the *Census of Agriculture* are reported according to farms with sales over $40,000 to $99,999 as follows:

	On All Farms	On Farms with Sales over $40,000	On Farms with Sales over $100,000
Casual	460,346	331,329	250,433
Seasonal	264,781	242,177	214,565
Regular	136,216	128,258	119,131

Setting a $40,000 minimum sales volume for California farms would leave 129,000 employment episodes uncovered, and over 200,000 would be outside board jurisdiction with a $100,000 level.

It would appear that many workers on smaller farms, particularly those with few casual or seasonal workers, would remain unrepresented in almost any case, due to the expense and effort required to organize them relative to the low returns in dues or political power which a union could expect. On the other hand, it is clear that almost half the casual farm labor force in California could be disenfranchised should standards such as those currently in use by the NLRB be applied to California.

POTENTIAL FOR EXTENDING THE NLRA TO AGRICULTURAL LABOR RELATIONS IN OTHER STATES

Most of the comments in the previous section regarding application of the NLRA in California can be reiterated for the rest of the United States. In some cases, particularly in those states where activities such as dairy, livestock, cash grains, and poultry farming predominate, there is little of the extreme fluctuation in seasonal labor use that would raise the issue of "normal" work force size or speed of elections. However, in New York, Florida, the Northwest, Arizona, Michigan, and the tobacco-producing states, it appears that short, sharp seasonal activity peaks might create some of the same complicated situations described for California.

Of even greater concern is the matter of jurisdictional standards. California has a very high average farm income compared to the rest of the major agricultural states. As a result, there are fewer farms as a percentage of total farms in the rest of the United States that have gross sales of $40,000 and above or $100,000 and above. More than 12% of regular farm worker employment episodes would be outside NLRB coverage under the 540,000 standard; for example, approximately 30% would not be covered at the $100,000 level (Table 11.3). The situation is even more

Table 11.3. Number of hirings on farms, by sales level of farm and category of worker

Sales[a]	Number of hirings[b]		
	Regular	Seasonal	Casual
$100,000 and over	491,236	364,720	829,250
$ 40,000 and over	627,903	882,246	1,604,028
Over $ 2,500	712,715	1,145,171	3,357,346

Source: U.S. Department of Commerce, Bureau of the Census, 1974 Census of Agriculture.

[a]Census of Agriculture does not separate sales at $50,000. Category is $40,000 to $99,999.

[b]Hirings refers to episodes of employment. Note that the Census of Agriculture uses the term "hired workers." However, in its compilation of data it is describing episodes of employment rather than enumerating the workers employed.

extreme in the case of seasonal and casual worker hirings, for example, where it appears that three-quarters would be outside NLRB jurisdiction at the $100,000 level.

One advantage of extending coverage of the NLRA to agriculture in the United States would be that the basic administrative framework is in place and could be adapted and expanded to absorb the greater work load generated by the new population being covered. Given the experience of the existing bureaucracy in resolving jurisdictional issues and establishing election procedures, it might be possible to accelerate the preelection process in cases of short employment fluctuations to obtain high levels of worker enfranchisement. If this does not appear feasible, unions might attempt to invoke provisions of Section 8(b)(f)(c) of the NLRA to obtain an expedited election, although there would certainly be resistance if unions utilized this approach frequently.

The NLRA contains no provisions similar to the "access" regulation adopted by the CALRB but there are precedents established under the NLRA that appear to permit access to employer property for the purposes of communicating with or organizing employees. It would appear, therefore, that agricultural labor unions could utilize existing case law to establish rights of access, particularly when workers were housed on employers' property and off-site access was unlikely.

NATIONAL VS. STATE-BY-STATE AGRICULTURAL LABOR RELATIONS LEGISLATION

The principal advantage of national agricultural labor relations legislation is that, whether it is a newly created specialized law or an extension of the NLRA, it is uniform across state lines, permitting agricultural labor unions to educate organizers and workers and to develop guidelines and tactics that can be adopted in all areas of similar production. Organizers of seasonal migratory workers might find national legislation particularly helpful in obtaining certification and in negotiating contracts along the migrant pathways from Florida to the Northeast or Texas to the Northwest or North-central states, for example (see the USDL ETA, *Guide to Farm Jobs*, which was prepared for the use of migrant farm workers on these pathways). National legislation also affords employers certainty of the operating rules they face in all states. It further permits establishment of an administrative structure that can be flexible in allowing the concentration of personnel in areas of higher activity. The body of case law that develops in such a situation provides a basis, over time, for uniform decision rules.

On the other hand, national agricultural labor relations legislation, by its broad nature, cannot be constructed in the detail that would allow for consideration of the special circumstances of one or several states. It has been demonstrated, for example, that jurisdictional standards based on nonagricultural business, which may seem to provide a reasonable compromise between a manageable work load and relatively minor disenfranchisement of workers in California, eliminate from coverage as many as three-quarters of casual farm worker hirings in the country as a whole. Also, a provision such as the seven-day election requirement in the CALRA may be almost entirely superfluous in Iowa or another state with predominantly year-round activities.

State-by-state agricultural labor relations legislation meets the objection to the overly generalized national law. It can treat the special circumstances of each state's particular mix of employers and farm workers more accurately than broader legislation. On the other hand, state legislation is more sensitive to political pressure and more susceptible than national legislation to continuing efforts at alteration to meet demands of special interests. The same is true of the agencies developed to administer state laws, as the California experience clearly demonstrates. Separate state laws would require the establishment of separate bureaucracies, each operating under a different legal framework and a set of procedures that would have to be developed. An economist would have questions about the diseconomies of scale inherent in establishing the 50 sets of regulatory boards, hearing officers, legal staffs, field offices, and clerical support that separate legislation implies. The fact that most other aspects of men's lives are managed in this manner is not a convincing argument for expanding the practice.

Another possibility might be adoption of national guidelines or "floor" legislation similar to the Fair Labor Standards Act and social security legislation. Under this approach certain minima could be established, such as a statement of employee rights, an antidiscrimination provision, and the requirement that there be some sort of procedure for conducting and certifying collective bargaining elections. Other details, such as the size of units to be covered, timing of elections, types of proscribed action for employers and employee groups or penalties for illegal activity, could be established by individual states based on their special needs and the concerns of state legislative power groups. In this situation, although considerable variation might be expected among states, just as there are presently state minimum wages at or significantly above the federal minimum, the individual states could exercise their choice within a constrained environment.

FARM WORKER UNIONIZATION: WHO PAYS THE PRICE?

In the foregoing discussion only the technical aspects of hired farm worker unionization have been considered. However, a primary policy concern is with the economic impacts of collective bargaining in agriculture. There are two dimensions to the problem of ascertaining the economic impact of a labor union: the industry structure faced by the union and the product demand curve for the industry. In the case of agriculture there may be several distinct subgroups into which agricultural products fall, and each may have a different industry structure.

First is the model presented by products such as field crops and cash grains, where it is possible to have a large number of producers existing in a competitive environment close to the economist's definition of perfect competition, with each firm producing a nondifferentiated product and facing a perfectly elastic demand for its product--being, in effect, a price taker. Contrasted to this are the producers of fresh vegetables, many of whom find themselves, particularly in Arizona, California, Florida and Texas, in a more integrated but still competitive market organization that deals in highly perishable products. Finally, there are producers who operate under marketing orders, in an environment where some control can be exercised over market price through supply limitation or timing of crop marketing (see Chap. 14).

It is likely, given labor union experience in most highly competitive industries, that employers in the first category of producers would be highly resistant to organizing efforts, realizing that their profit margins would be reduced or eliminated by higher wages or fringe benefits added to their costs as a result of union contracts. Should a producer in such an industry be organized, given that he is a price taker the incidence of the additional costs could not be passed along to consumers through higher prices. The producer would bear the brunt of the wage settlement himself.

Employers of the second type, if they were well-enough organized within their industry, might have enough power to pass along increased labor costs to consumers through higher prices. It is also with these employers that one might see either a shift to a geographic area with less union activity, for example from California to either Texas or to Mexico, or possibly a shift to a higher ratio of capital to labor, as in mechanization of fresh vegetable crops.

Finally, in the case of producers who can control to some extent the supply of their product being marketed at any one time, and therefore can exercise more control over price, higher labor costs would potentially fall on consumers as well as producers, depending on the price elasticity of demand for the product.

If it is assumed that in general the demand for most U.S. agricultural products is relatively inelastic, then the eventual increase in product prices that would result from generalized unionization of agricultural workers should be passed on, in large part, to consumers. If wage and fringe benefit increases are equalled or surpassed by increased productivity of farm workers, however, these price consequences are not necessary. As employer experience in the lemon industry has demonstrated, it may well be possible, even without increased investment in capital, for a group of workers given greater stability in employment than has been available in most seasonal agriculture in the United States to increase their productivity enough to offset any increase in labor costs (Rosedale and Mamer).

Another cost of unionization of agricultural workers will be likely to fall most heavily on seasonal hired workers. As the cost of employing a worker increases, and particularly as the fringe benefits to be paid each worker increase in cost, there is an incentive for employers to utilize each worker as fully as possible and to eliminate part-time workers whenever feasible. Since much seasonal agricultural work is characterized by irregular and intermittent scheduling of work and the tendency to use larger crews than necessary, working shorter hours or completing in a short period work which could be performed by a smaller crew working for a longer period, employers could possibly change their employment pattern to reduce fringe benefit costs. The full utilization of smaller crews working for a longer duration would be of benefit to those workers hired--their income potential would be enhanced by this change in employment patterns. On the other hand, the workers who would be eliminated by this shift in labor utilization would then have no employment, or would find work only at the peak of seasonal agricultural activities, causing them significant disadvantage.

It can be argued that making the existing conditions of underemployment of seasonal hired farm workers explicit is valuable in forcing policy decisions about the direction and magnitude of rural development and incomes programs. It is probably also true, given the average age of most seasonal hired farm workers, that a shortage of available employment in agriculture would eventually result in surplus workers moving to other types of employment, should they exist. Nevertheless, in the short run the burden of unemployment would fall on the workers left out, and for older workers the possibility of movement to any alternative employment is extremely limited.

It is not employers alone who contribute to limited employment opportunities in an occupation. If the use of hiring halls is extended to large numbers of agricultural employers through collective bargaining contracts, and if agricultural labor unions limit membership to provide the desired level of employment to union members, there will be some farm workers who will be denied union membership, just as has occurred in other industries (Chap. 9). Those workers with access to jobs through hiring halls will gain income; those without access will either exist as part of a surplus labor pool, obtaining marginal employment, or will be unemployed.

POTENTIAL EXTENT OF AGRICULTURAL UNIONIZATION

It does not appear likely that there will be widespread organization of hired farm workers in the United States, any more than the nonagricultural labor force in the United States is unionized. For the same reasons that collective bargaining is limited to certain areas and industries, agricultural labor unions are likely to have variable success and demonstrate differing levels of enthusiasm for organizing in different parts of the country and among different types of producers.

It would be expected that there would be more vigorous union organizing activities in states with large populations of hired farm workers. This is not the only reason for concentration of union efforts, however. Another important factor in union organizing effort is the size of employer. It may be more efficient for a union to organize several large employers than to recruit the same number of supporters among employees of a large number of small employers. Thus even though a state such as Iowa, which has a large number of seasonal farm workers, might appear to be a prime target for union organizing efforts, the dispersion of these workers among thousands of small employers would make union activity much more costly in time and manpower than an effort of similar magnitude in Florida.

An additional factor is the type of agricultural operation that predominates in an area. The techniques of organizing seasonal farm workers and the unions they are willing to support may differ from those most acceptable to year-round employees. Dairy workers may not wish to support unions with primary strength among vegetable workers; machine operators may not ally comfortably with unskilled laborers.

Given all these differences, not to mention the structural and market constraints mentioned in the earlier section, a broad prediction of the potential extent of agricultural worker unionization in the United States can be made. It may be useful to consult Appendix 11, which contains selected data about the distribution of hired farm workers among states and types of farms. From these data, as well as from experience to date, one can safely conclude that California has a high potential for agricultural labor union activity.

In California the greatest level of union activity has been among fruit and vegetable farms and on dairies. Fruit and fresh vegetable ranches are among the types of farms that hire the largest numbers of seasonal and casual workers (Appendix Table 11.7). Their employees form the core of both the UFW and Teamster memberships. The dairy workers have been organized by two different unions. The Christian Labor Association has been active in California for over 30 years; the International Brotherhood of Teamsters, also with a long history in California, entered the dairies as a by-product of organizing milk truck drivers. Some poultry and egg workers or employees of horticultural specialty and nursery operations have also been active in collective bargaining, but there is little union activity among livestock or field crops.

Other states that have a large number of employers with 10 or more employees are Texas, Florida, North Carolina, and Washington (Appendix Tables 11.2-11.5). In three of those states tree fruit and fresh vegetables are important crop activities. At least one agricultural labor union is active in each of Texas, Florida, and Washington, even though these states do not yet have legislation overseeing collective bargaining in agriculture. Other states that appear to have a high potential for union organizing activity are New York, Oregon, Michigan, and Minnesota.

Some states that provide employment for a substantial number of hired farm workers have few large employers. Wisconsin, Iowa, Illinois, and Ohio fall into this category. In these states some activity among dairy workers or other specialty groups might be expected, but any organizing of seasonal fruit and vegetable workers would probably only occur as a supplement to activities in other states on a migrant stream. Similarly, in states where field crops or livestock raising are the primary agricultural activity and where there are few crops employing workers among whom existing unions are accustomed to organizing, future expansion of collective bargaining is unlikely. An exception might arise if specialty organizations were to develop and organize among livestock or cash grain workers. There have been unions of sheep shearers and cowboy associations in western history, but at present there are no organizations that appear ready to become active in this area of collective bargaining.

At the present time, the West Coast and Southwest, including Texas, Florida, and perhaps a few states in the North Central area, appear most likely to be the focus of union activity. Even in these states, to judge from the California experience and from union history in U.S. industry, the eventual level of organization will probably not exceed a third of the potential membership.

CONCLUSION

Experience to date indicates that the CALRA in general has met the needs of the workers it was designed to serve. It has provided a procedure for timely, orderly representation elections, has allowed the enfranchisement of even relatively short-term farm workers, and has given workers a means of obtaining collective bargaining contracts. It has not, apparently, changed the nature of the farm labor contractor system, and it remains unclear whether it has allowed, through collective bargaining, the negotiation of wage and fringe benefit rates beyond those that might have existed in the absence of such legislation. Other features of the act, such as the five-day grace period before workers must join the union, the prohibition of double assessment of dues during a single month, and the "make whole" remedy for refusal to bargain in good faith, are assumed to be favorable to the climate of collective bargaining but have not yet been thoroughly analyzed. Access to employer property, a highly controversial ALRB regulation, appears to have enhanced union organizing efforts among seasonal farm workers. Despite employer protests of work site contacts by union organizers, no significant disruption of farming activities has occurred.

The chief problem encountered in the administration of the CALRA has been the short period allowed between filing the petition for a representation election and the election itself--a maximum of seven days. As a result, many disputes over voter eligibility, election procedures, and unit determination are not resolved until after the election. Certification of election results may be delayed weeks or even months, prolonging the uncertainty of employer and union status. This delay in resolution appears to be a necessary trade-off to obtain rapid representation elections. The alternative--delay of elections until all issues are resolved--would cause difficulties in obtaining short-term seasonal worker participation in the election process.

In some other states where large numbers of seasonal farm workers are employed for relatively short periods of time, the seven-day election period, bar to multiple assessment of dues, the five-day grace period, and the 50% of peak employment show-of-interest requirement would all be advantageous to farm worker unions. In states where much agricultural employment is of longer duration, the seven-day election requirement might create unnecessary stress by postponing certification beyond the election date. The other three provisions would appear to have no particular usefulness for longer-term farm workers.

The disqualification of farm labor contractors as employers for purposes of collective bargaining does not appear to have had much effect on California employment practices to date. Farm labor contractors appear to be relatively active in only a few states (Appendix Table 11.5), particularly Texas and Florida. In some states smaller employers might utilize a custom harvesting contractor, who provides labor in addition to other services, to replace a labor contractor.

Although the "make whole" penalty provision of the act may be assumed to encourage good faith bargaining, there is not enough experience to support a prediction of its effect. It would be equally applicable to bargaining in any state.

Access to employer property would be useful for

unions organizing in states with large numbers of intrastate or interstate migrants and in crops with very short activity periods. In states where seasonal labor is primarily provided by local workers, or where most employment is of longer duration, work site organizing would presumably be preferred by, but not essential for, unions.

Since the CALRA has no legislative or administrative lower limits on size of employers, all employers theoretically fall under its jurisdiction. It is unlikely, however, that many very small employers would be organized, due to the cost to potential organizers.

The NLRA would serve most year-round or longer-term seasonal farm workers in California and the United States in most respects as the CALRA does. Its chief disadvantages would be in the case of short-term seasonal workers and migrants, who might miss voting opportunities under current NLRB procedures. If election preliminaries could be accelerated and if the NLRB interpretations of "normal" work force could be redefined to include workers of relatively short annual employment duration, these objections might be met.

The 30-day grace period might place agricultural unions with many short-term contracts at a disadvantage, but the shorter grace period permitted for building-trades unions demonstrates that exceptions permitting shorter grace periods are possible. It would appear that inclusion of agricultural workers under the building-trades clause would aid seasonal worker unions without adversely affecting other workers.

There is no access provision in the NLRA. However, sufficient precedents exist among board decisions appearing to permit access to justify the contention that a specific access provision is unnecessary.

If existing jurisdictional standards of the NLRB are applied to U.S. agricultural employers, as many as three-quarters of seasonal and casual farm worker hirings would be outside board jurisdiction at the

$100,000 level of employers' income. Over half of seasonal and casual agricultural worker hirings would not be covered at the $40,000 level. Many of these workers would have been unlikely subjects for union organizing in any case, since many are employed on farms with three or fewer workers, but they would have no opportunity at all unless jurisdictional standards are lowered.

The principal advantage of national agricultural labor relations legislation is that it is uniform across state lines, permitting unions to develop standard organizing guidelines and tactics across areas of union activity. National legislation equalizes labor relations rules among employers, who may operate in more than one state. The administrative structure and case law that develop can be broadly utilized.

The chief disadvantage of national legislation is that it cannot be expected to meet special circumstances in the various states. If it is constructed comprehensively enough to meet all needs, it is cumbersome and any provisions will be superfluous; if it provides broad guidelines, workers in specific states or crops may be disadvantaged.

State-by-state legislation can be tailored to fit local conditions, but it is more sensitive to political pressure than a national law would be. The bureaucratic proliferation involved in administering 50 separate agricultural labor laws raises a cost argument.

Another approach might be a hybrid, with national "floor" legislation similar to the Fair Labor Standards Act. Individual states could then choose either to govern agricultural labor relations under the federal minima or to add to the federal law with state legislation designed to meet the special circumstances or needs of the state. Although considerable variation might be expected among states, just as is observed among state minimum wage laws, the existence of the national law would provide some uniform substructure.

The economic impacts of collective bargaining in

agriculture will vary widely. In general, the more inelastic the demand for an agricultural product and the greater the control producers are able to exercise over product price, the more likely consumers will be to pay the majority of production cost increases due to collective bargaining. If producers are atomistic price takers, however, increased labor costs will reduce or eliminate their profit margin. These producers can be expected to strongly resist unionization of their workers. Other employers with sufficient capital might choose to substitute increased investment in equipment for higher labor costs; some producers might move ranches to lower wage areas of the United States or to other countries. If farm worker productivity grows to match increases in wage and fringe benefit costs, then workers may be better off in real terms, producers will face the same real labor costs per unit, and consumer welfare is not diminished.

If employers react to higher per capita costs of seasonal workers by reducing the number of workers and extending the duration of their employment throughout the year, the employed workers will be better off. Unions could accomplish the same effect by restricting membership and coordinating the movement of union workers among available seasonal jobs to provide each with more days of work per year. In either case, the workers who cannot obtain employment are made worse off, and the underemployment characteristic of seasonal agricultural work is made more explicit. It may be that younger and weakly attached workers will be encouraged to leave the agricultural labor market if this occurs, but older or less adaptable workers would be significantly disadvantaged.

Although the percentage of workers unionized in agriculture is growing in California and there are organizing efforts among farm workers in a number of other states, in the long run, assuming a favorable legislative climate, most farm workers will probably remain unorganized. This is partly due to the nature of agricultural employment. Most U.S. workers are employed on farms with less than four workers. These are generally uneconomic for unions to organize. Many other workers are employed in crops where there is, to date, little worker interest in unions.

Judging from the California experience, fresh fruit and vegetable workers and dairy employees are the most likely candidates for organizing efforts. The West Coast and the Southwest (including Texas), Florida, and perhaps some North Central states, appear the most probable areas for union activity. Even in these states, to judge from industrial experience, the eventual level of organization will probably not exceed a third of the potential membership.

APPENDIX 11. AGRICULTURAL LABOR MARKETS: CALIFORNIA AND OTHER STATES

California agricultural employers account for more farm worker employment episodes than employers in any other state, for all four of the categories of farm workers--casual, seasonal, regular, and contract workers (Appendix Table 11.1). According to employment data compiled for the *1974 Census of Agriculture*, California also ranks first in the nation with respect to number of employers hiring larger numbers of workers--over 10 for regular workers (Appendix Table

Appendix Table 11.1. Comparison of ten states with highest numbers of episodes of agricultural employment in four categories[a]

Ranking	Casual	Seasonal	Regular	Contract
1	California	California	California	California
2	North Carolina	North Carolina	Texas	Texas
3	Kentucky	Texas	Florida	Florida
4	Iowa	Washington	Pennsylvania	Idaho
5	Washington	Florida	New York	Arkansas
6	Texas	Michigan	Wisconsin	Arizona
7	Illinois	Oregon	Mississippi	Washington
8	Oregon	New York	North Carolina	Minnesota
9	Tennessee	Minnesota	Illinois	Missouri
10	Minnesota	Wisconsin	Arkansas	Mississippi

Source: U.S. Department of Commerce, Bureau of the Census, 1974 Census of Agriculture.

[a]Casual: employed 24 days or less
Seasonal: 25-149 days
Regular: 150 or more days
Contract: employed through labor contractor or crew leader

11.2), and more than 20 or 50 for seasonal, casual, and contract workers (Appendix Table 11.3, 11.4, and 11.5). Among other states, however, ranking and magnitude of employment vary widely from one category of worker to another. North Carolina, for example, is second nationally in the numbers of episodes of employment for workers hired less than 25 days and for 25-149 days, eighth in the number of regular farm worker hirings (Appendix Table 11.1), and is not represented among the 10 states employing the most contract labor (Appendix Table 11.5). Texas, conversely, is sixth in employment episodes of casual workers, third in seasonal worker hirings, and second in number of hirings of both regular workers and contract workers.

Variations in magnitude of employment among the different states and by type of employment episode are substantial. California has more than twice the number of regular worker employment episodes (136,216)

Appendix Table 11.2. Twenty states with highest number of episodes of employment of workers employed 150 days or more

State	Number of hirings[a]	Ranking by number of employers having more than 10 employees
California	136,216	1
Texas	53,106	3
Florida	47,443	2
Pennsylvania	20,654	8
New York	20,227	7
Wisconsin	19,259	
Mississippi	18,641	4
North Carolina	18,424	9
Illinois	17,803	
Arkansas	17,687	10
Washington	17,227	5
Iowa	16,849	
Georgia	16,756	
Ohio	14,971	
Minnesota	14,097	
Louisiana	13,619	
Arizona	12,755	6
Colorado	12,553	
Virginia	12,293	
Michigan	12,273	

Source: U.S. Department of Commerce, Bureau of the Census, <u>1974 Census of Agriculture</u>.

[a]See note [b], Table 11.3.

Appendix Table 11.3. Twenty states with highest number of episodes of employment of workers employed 25-149 days

State	Number of hirings[a]	Ranking by number of employers: Having more than 20 employees	Having more than 50 employees
California	264,781	1	1
North Carolina	65,751	3	
Texas	55,205	7	7
Washington	54,024	2	3
Florida	50,785	4	2
Michigan	35,966	5	4
Oregon	32,735	6	5
New York	32,136	8	8
Minnesota	27,381		
Wisconsin	26,349		
Iowa	26,220		
Ohio	26,041	9	
Pennsylvania	22,662		
Georgia	21,728		
Idaho	20,159		6[b]
Kentucky	20,146		
Arizona	18,984		6[b]
South Carolina	18,055		
Arkansas	17,647		
Louisiana	17,510		

Source: U.S. Department of Commerce, Bureau of the Census, _1974 Census of Agriculture_.

[a]See note [b], Table 11.3.

[b]Idaho and Arizona have the same rank.

Appendix Table 11.4. Twenty states with highest number of episodes of employment of workers employed under 25 days

State	Number of hirings[a]	Ranking by number of employers: Having more than 20 employees	Having more than 50 employees
California	460,346	1	1
North Carolina	256,088	2	4
Kentucky	197,786	4	7
Iowa	176,309	5	11
Washington	175,011	3	2
Texas	142,891	6	9
Illinois	117,650	13	19
Oregon	114,114	7	3
Tennessee	103,424	11	16
Minnesota	96,316		
Michigan	91,636	8	5
Virginia	85,988	10	14
Georgia	85,400	9	8
Indiana	84,327		
Missouri	79,470		
Wisconsin	74,441		
Florida	74,352	14	6
Ohio	72,724		
South Carolina	63,317	12	10
New York	58,750		12

Source: U.S. Department of Commerce, Bureau of the Census, _1974 Census of Agriculture_.

[a]See note [b], Table 11.3.

Appendix Table 11.5. Twenty states with highest number of contract hirings

State	Number of hirings[a]	Ranking by number of employers: Having more than 20 employees	Having more than 50 employees
California	281,704	1	1
Texas	92,140	2	2
Florida	46,828	3	3
Idaho	21,911	4	4
Arkansas	17,630	5	5
Arizona	15,620	6	6
Washington	15,281		9
Minnesota	14,518		
Missouri	14,509		
Mississippi	14,245	10	8
Oregon	13,127	8	7
North Carolina	12,426	7	
Colorado	11,467	9	
Michigan	9,560		10
New Mexico	8,253		
Virginia	7,809		
Oklahoma	7,779		
South Carolina	7,586		
Louisiana	7,553		
Ohio	6,981		

Source: U.S. Department of Commerce, Bureau of the Census, 1974 Census of Agriculture.

[a]See note [b], Table 11.3.

as the next highest state, Texas (53,106). The fourth highest state, Pennsylvania, reports only 20,654 (Appendix Table 11.2). The difference is even more evident in the reported episodes of employment of seasonal farm workers, in which California (264,781) exceeds the second state, North Carolina (65,751), by four times. After this point, however, the decline in the number of hirings is much more gradual than among regular workers--14 states each account for more than 21,000 employment episodes (Appendix Table 11.3).

Episodes of employment of workers employed less than 25 days are more numerous and, in all probability, involve a large degree of duplicate counting for some states, such as California, which have a large number of seasonal activities of short duration occurring through many months of the year. There appears to be no source that can clarify the possible degree of duplication. The USDA's *The Hired Farm Working Force of 1974*, (*HFWF*) reports the average number of days of farm work for workers who did less than 25 days of farm work as 9. The total number of workers who did less than 25 days of hired farm work was estimated at 1,169,000 (*HFWF* 1974, Table 22). The *1974 Census of Agriculture* reports 3,357,346 employment episodes of less than 25 days duration (Table 23). The majority of employment contacts could be by workers who have individual employment contacts, none of which exceed 24 days in duration, but which cumulatively fall outside the USDA "less than 25 days hired farm work" criterion. California employers alone report 460,346 casual worker contacts in the 1974 census; nine states report more than 100,000 contacts each (Appendix Table 11.4).

Of particular interest is the distribution of reported use of contract workers among agricultural states. If the answers to this census question, which received less than a 50% rate of response, are representative of the national distribution of contract labor, it is clear that only a few states utilize contract labor as a significant percentage of their agricultural labor force. California (281,704) reported three times the number of employment episodes of Texas (92,140), which in turn reported almost twice the hirings of Florida (46,828). Three states, which do not appear among the top ten labor employers in any other category, report a significant number of contract worker hirings. These are Idaho (21,911), Arizona (15,620), and Missouri (14,509) (Appendix Table 11.4). An investigation of labor market organization in these states might be useful for future policy formulation.

It is difficult to determine from published data at which tasks California and U.S. farm workers are employed. California data are available from the state Employment Development Department by crop activity and number of workers on a county basis, but do not include employment estimates for some types of employers, such as livestock and poultry (California Employment Development Department, *Farm Labor Report* and *Agricultural Employment in California*). Some other states (Florida, for example) have reports that give estimated employment by crop categories (Florida

Department of Commerce, *1977 Florida Annual Rural Manpower Report*), but not all have the same degree of specialization. National statistics have been aggregated into two main categories, "field workers" and "livestock workers," in the USDA Crop Reporting Board *Farm Labor* letter. The best method for estimating utilization of farm workers by crop activity is the breakdown in the Census of Agriculture by SICs of the number of farms employing hired farm labor. If the number of workers per farm were multiplied by the number of farms in each SIC category, a rough distribution of workers among different types of farms could be obtained.

In the United States more cash grain farms hire labor than any other single category of activity, followed by livestock farms and dairies (Appendix Table 11.6). Beyond the three top-ranked activities, the number of hiring farms varies according to the

Appendix Table 11.6. Comparison of SIC (codes[a]) of farms using hired labor in four categories

Ranking by number of farms	Category of hired labor			
	Casual	Seasonal	Regular	Contract
1	011	011	011	021
2	021	021	021	011
3	024	024	024	017
4	0132	017	0133	0133
5	017	0133	017	024
6	0133	0132	0131	0131
7	0191	0191	025	0132
8	025	018	018	0191
9	0131	0131	0191	016
10	016	016	0132	025

Source: U.S. Department of Commerce, Bureau of the Census, 1974 Census of Agriculture.

[a]Key to SIC codes:

011 Cash grains
0131 Cotton
0132 Tobacco
0133 Sugar crops, Irish potatoes, hay, peanuts and other field crops (0133, 0134, 0139)
016 Vegetables and melons
017 Fruits and tree nuts
018 Horticultural specialties
0191 General farms, primarily crop
021 Livestock, except dairy, poultry, and animal specialties
025 Poultry and eggs
024 Dairy

type of workers employed. Fruit and tree nut farms rank fourth or fifth in hiring casual, seasonal, and regular farm workers, while tobacco growers are fourth in the employment of casual workers, seventh in seasonal workers, and tenth in regular hired labor. Cotton farms rank ninth in employment of casual and seasonal workers, but sixth in regular workers.

The number of workers employed per farm varies widely among the different types of operations. Ten percent of vegetable and melon farms reporting and 11% of the horticultural specialties employed over 20 regular workers (Appendix Table 11.7). At the other extreme, less than 1% of the cash grain or livestock farms reported 20 or more regular employees. A similar pattern can be observed among farms employing seasonal workers. Twenty-seven percent of vegetable farms, 19% of fruit and tree nut operations, and 11% of horticultural specialties hired more than 20 seasonal workers. Cash grains, livestock, and dairy accounted for 1% apiece. Finally, 26% of fruit and tree nut farms and 28% of vegetable and melon farms that hired casual workers had over 20 such employees,

Appendix Table 11.7. Percentage of farms hiring workers, by SIC of farm and number and category of workers

Number of workers hired per farm	SIC codes[a]											All farms
	011	0131	0132	0133	016	017	018	0191	021	024	025	
Regular workers												
1	61	39	49	43	25	40	23	51	61	57	43	53
2	21	23	24	23	17	21	17	22	20	23	22	21
3-4	12	17	17	18	20	17	19	15	12	14	15	14
20+	0.3	2	1.2	3	10	5	11	2	0.8	1	5	2
Seasonal workers												
1	51	34	21	24	12	18	19	38	51	47	34	41
2	24	21	16	18	12	13	17	21	24	24	23	22
3-4	16	19	17	18	17	16	20	17	16	19	19	17
20+	1	5	6	7	27	19	11	4	1	1	4	4
Casual workers												
1	36	22	13	24	14	9	17	25	36	31	20	30
2	15	12	9	11	8	6	14	12	15	16	13	14
3-4	19	16	16	16	14	10	18	18	20	22	20	19
20+	4	13	14	12	28	36	16	10	3	9	10	8

Source: U.S. Department of Commerce, Bureau of the Census, 1974 Census of Agriculture.

[a]Key to SIC codes:

011 Cash grains
0131 Cotton
0132 Tobacco
0133 Sugar crops, Irish potatoes, hay, peanuts, and other field crops (0133, 0134 & 0139)
016 Vegetables and melons
017 Fruits and tree nuts
018 Horticultural specialties
0191 General farm, primarily crop
021 Livestock, except dairy, poultry, animal specialties
024 Dairy
025 Poultry and eggs

while less than 5% of reporting livestock and cash grain farms had this many workers.

Ninety-four percent of cash grain or dairy farms, 93% of livestock farms, 90% of tobacco farms, and 88% of general crop farms hired 4 or fewer regular workers. Ninety percent or more of cash grain, livestock, and dairy farms hired 4 or fewer seasonal workers. Only four categories of farms (tobacco, vegetable and melon, fruit and tree nut, and horticulture) employed more than 4 casual workers on the average. Only among contract workers, for whom a breakdown of employers by number of workers and classification of farm is not available, does it appear that the majority of employers hire more than 4 workers (Appendix Table 11.8). It appears that there are substantially different patterns of labor use among farms employing contract workers than in other employment contracts, since one-fifth of the farms utilizing contract labor reported 20 or more workers. A much smaller percentage of other employers reported hiring such large numbers of workers.

Of the SIC farms, some produce crops for which labor demands are more likely to be concentrated, due to seasonal production activity. Other types of farms, such as dairy farms, may require a high level

Appendix Table 11.8. Farms by number of hired workers in four categories of employment

Number of workers	Casual	Seasonal	Regular	Contract
1	133,279	95,796	119,163	4,149
2	61,103	50,025	47,275	5,434
3-4	84,624	38,932	31,629	9,641
5-9	84,150	24,618	14,485[a]	9,932
10-14	36,636	9,209	4,960[b]	5,115
15-19	15,739	3,771	1,668	2,411
20-29	16,121	3,830	3,913[c]	4,028
30-39	6,831	1,609	...	1,785
40-49	3,319	887	...	996
50 or more	7,881	2,474	...	2,590

Source: U.S. Department of Commerce, Bureau of the Census, 1974 Census of Agriculture.

[a]5-6 and 7-8 workers.

[b]9-10 and 11-14 workers.

[c]20 or more hired workers.

of short-term labor input during the year, but the incidence of this activity is less predictable and more likely to be distributed throughout the year.

Crops with high seasonal employment peaks are more prominent in some states than in others. Three of the five highest seasonal- and casual- worker-employing crop categories in California are fruit and tree nuts, vegetables and melons, and the category which includes sugar beets, potatoes, hay and field crops. The largest group of employers in North Carolina and Kentucky is in the tobacco industry. Texas, Arizona, and Mississippi have high cotton labor use. Florida and New York have extensive employment in vegetables and melons, fruits and tree nuts, and horticulture. The three northwestern states (Oregon, Washington, and Idaho) have tree fruit, sugar beet, potato, hay and field crops, and some vegetable production. By contrast, other states with relatively high farm labor utilization, such as Iowa, Arkansas, and Missouri, have primarily crops that are not as highly seasonal in labor demand and/or in which the number of workers per farm is generally very small.

Discussion

JOSEPH D. COFFEY

As a discussant of Sue Eileen Hayes's evaluation of the 1975 CALRA I propose to highlight her main points and to elaborate on some issues concerning the performance and impact of CALRA. A landmark bill, CALRA extends to farm workers the rights to organize, bargain collectively, and strike. These rights are the counterpart to the rights afforded nonagricultural workers in the NLRA passed 40 years earlier. The NLRA specifically denied such rights to farm workers.

Hayes's major points can be briefly summarized as follows:

1. Although not the first of its type, the CALRA is nevertheless very important due to the large size of California agriculture and the notoriety of its farm labor conflicts.

2. The CALRA, although modeled after the NLRA, contains three crucial differences that enhance its applicability to agriculture's highly seasonal employment and perishable products:

(a) The "show of interest" in unionizing must involve 50% of those currently employed when employment is not less than 50% of the seasonal peak, versus NLRA's 30% of current but not necessarily peak employment.

(b) Elections must be held within 7 days of filing unless a strike is in progress, in which case it is 48 hours, whereas the NLRA does not specify a period.

(c) Workers are required to join the union after the fifth rather than the NLRA's thirtieth day of employment.

3. Relative to the NLRA, the CALRA strengthens labor's bargaining position and organizing effectiveness by: permitting secondary boycotts; requiring employers to "make whole" employees' earnings, that is, to retroactively pay workers at a higher wage during the period in which the employer was not bargaining in good faith; and allowing through regulation "access privileges" of labor organizers to the farm.

4. There is some merit to using the NLRA's approach rather than the CALRA's or separate legislation on a state-by-state basis, in that national legislation would draw upon a broader base of case law and would be more uniform from state to state.

5. However, the California approach is on balance preferable because it does not disenfranchise the large number of short-term workers and it permits a more speedy settlement of disputes.

6. Larger employers in areas where farm labor employment is concentrated are the most likely to be organized.

7. The increase in wages and fringe benefits received by California farm workers has not directly

resulted from union contracts but can be attributed in part to employer reaction to unions.

8. The economic impact upon producer returns and product prices depends upon the price elasticity of demand and monopoly power of producers.

9. Less than a third of hired farm workers will ever be organized.

Although her arguments are plausible, they are not well-substantiated. Hayes does not provide evidence concerning the extent to which the CALRA has been used nor how it has performed. She does not provide estimates of the CALRA's actual or potential economic impact on wage rates, employment, farm structure, etc. She does not report any comments of organizers, workers, growers, or government officials who are directly involved, nor findings of any researchers or observers. Her discussion of the impacts of higher wages on producers and consumers focuses upon the demand elasticity and neglects the elasticity of substitution between capital and labor, the share of labor expenses to total expenses, and the elasticity of supply of capital, which are the other key elements in the theory of derived demand. In short, Hayes does a good job of describing the CALRA and comparing it to the NLRA, but she does not give much insight into the CALRA's performance, applicability, and impact. It is hoped that Hayes and others will provide additional analysis of the CALRA's performance and applicability. In the meantime, based on a hurried literature review, I have formed the following impressions concerning the experience with the CALRA.

1. There was a pent-up demand for union representation by farm workers in California. According to Rochin (1977), almost 25,000 farm workers voted in 173 elections during the first 30 days of the CALRA. During the first 5 months, 429 elections were conducted with over 84% of the workers voting for unionization.

2. There is less conflict among unions. The

rivalry between Cesar Chavez's UFW and the Teamsters has been settled by an agreement in which the UFW agreed to organize agricultural workers and the Teamsters agreed to organize nonagricultural workers.

3. There are continuing legal disputes among the workers, unions, and agricultural employers. Numerous suits have been filed in court and several complaints have been placed before the ALRB. The "access rules" and the "make whole" provisions have been of particular dispute. Although conflict persists, the CALRA has remained intact with only minor amendments.

4. From the perspective of the workers, especially the seasonal workers, as Hayes (1979), Yates, and Rochin (1977) indicate, the provisions of the CALRA appear to be more favorable than those of the NLRA.

5. From the perspective of the employers, the CALRA formalizes the labor negotiating process and provides a mechanism (ALRB) for settling disagreements (California Labor Code).

In terms of the future direction and impact of the CALRA or similar legislation elsewhere, I offer the following hypotheses:

1. Although the economic impact for some specific regions and commodities may be significant, nationally the proportion of farm workers unionized will remain small and the direct impact on total agricultural production costs will be small. Hired labor represents 8% of agricultural production expenses. Even under the extreme assumptions of one-half of the hired workers being unionized, wages doubling, and employment constant, production expenses would increase by only 4%.

2. The CALRA and similar legislation may strengthen somewhat worker bargaining power and result in greater increases in the wages and benefits of unionized workers, but it is not likely to have a significant effect on hired farm wages or employment. Yates (p. 672) reports ". . . that during the first year of these UFW contracts, workers had gained an average wage increment of over 11%, in addition to a

host of strikingly similar fringe benefits, which practically none of them had ever enjoyed." Yates does not provide any benchmarks with California farm wage rates of all hired field and livestock workers during the CALRA's first year increased from $2.82 per hour in October 1975 to $3.15 per hour in October 1976, or 11.7% (USDA's *Farm Labor*).

Comparisons of California and U.S. aggregate hired farm employment and wage data for 1976 to 1979 do not reveal any perceptible influence of the CALRA. The ratio of July hourly wages of California workers to those of the United States have tended to decrease rather than to increase. The comparable ratio of employment exhibits no trend.

3. Unionization of farm workers will not result in a significant reduction in the poverty of the agricultural work force. The poverty of farm workers is not primarily due to their lack of bargaining power nor due to unfair labor practices. This is not to say that discrimination and monopsonistic hiring of farm workers do not exist. They are more a symptom than the cause of low wages in agriculture. Nor is it to imply that unions may not achieve greater wage or benefit increases than otherwise. Rather, poverty among farm workers is due to the low marginal value productivity of the tasks they perform and to the short duration of their employment.

4. The labor problems associated with seasonal and casual farm workers appear to be different from those of regular workers. The fact that only a small proportion of regular farm workers are likely to be unionized is not due to the unique characteristics of agriculture. Rather, the reasons are similar to those behind the lack of unionization among employees of small employers in general. The casual and seasonal farm workers, on the other hand, present different problems due to the low level of their skills, the temporary and onerous nature of their work, the constant threat of mechanization, and their low degree of career commitment to agriculture. In the long run, I expect the number of seasonal workers to decline as mechanization increases and agriculture shifts away

from commodities requiring extensive seasonal labor.

5. Curtailing public support of farm mechanization research in order to preserve seasonal agricultural employment is not a desirable policy. Policies should be focused on enhancing employer-employee mutual interests and harmony, thereby reducing premature mechanization and shifts in cropping patterns. Policies should be implemented to facilitate the adjustment of seasonal farm workers to more continuous and productive employment, either in agriculture or elsewhere.

6. Farm workers and their unions will become less crusading and more calculating. From the union's perspective, the costs of obtaining additional members are likely to be lower on large farms, in regions where large farms predominate, and for regular workers. The highest costs will be for obtaining members on widely scattered small farms and for casual workers. From the worker's perspective, the benefit/cost ratio of unionization will be more favorable the longer the duration of employment and the larger the employer.

7. The farmers also will need to consider the calculus of unionization. From the farmers' perspective, the costs of unionization will likely be lower and the benefits greater on large farms. The unions may provide services such as recruitment, training, discipline, dependability, scheduling, fringe benefit programs, etc., which would reduce the services the farmer must provide or acquire through a labor contractor. Importantly, the unions may reduce labor uncertainties.

8. Finally, a word about farm structure--a current Washington "buzzword." Despite the greater feasibility and likelihood of unionization of larger farms, I do not see unionization as being a major factor either encouraging or discouraging larger farms. I basically agree with Holt (1979) that the structure of farming will have more of an effect on labor than labor will have on the structure of farming.

12

Impact of Labor Laws and Regulations on Agricultural Labor Markets

BERNARD L. ERVEN

Federal and state labor laws and regulations exert an impact on agricultural employers and employees in several ways. They affect the productivity and cost of hired labor, which in turn influence the agricultural producers' demand for labor. They affect the supply of labor through explicit impacts on the monetary and nonmonetary compensation received by workers. There are also implicit supply impacts because the characteristics of farm work as perceived by potential farm workers are influenced by labor law coverage. Exclusions of agricultural workers that result in their receiving fewer benefits than nonfarm workers are particularly important in this regard.

Labor laws and regulations also have an impact on the employer-employee contractual relationship. A contract of employment between an employer and employee commonly specifies such items as job description, compensation, grievance procedures, disciplinary practices, and benefits to follow termination of the contractual relationship by either employer or employee. Labor laws and regulations affect these specifics of the contract. A final impact is on the labor management practices of employers. Recruiting, hiring, firing, record keeping, training, wage compensation, perquisites, and disciplinary procedures are examples of labor management practices potentially influenced by labor laws and regulations.

Concern about the impact of government intervention in markets extends from the popular press to the most sophisticated and complex economic analyses of the day. Some see government intervention as a factor in the fate of small businesses, our capacity to provide employment for minorities and underprivileged workers, the future of the family farm, and the survival of the industrial base of some communities. No analysis of the structure of labor markets is complete without consideration of government intervention.

This chapter does not address the question of whether or not government, through labor laws and regulations, should intervene in agricultural labor markets. That decision has been made. During the last 20 years, the differences in coverage between farm and nonfarm workers have decreased substantially. The trend is clearly toward expanded coverage. The fundamental questions that remain relate to the advantages and disadvantages to various interest groups of increased coverage, and to the effective implementation, administration, and enforcement of current and proposed coverage provisions.

Other sections of this volume identify objectives for farm labor and rural manpower public policies. There are some general objectives specifically related to labor laws and regulations that pervade and provide the base for analysis of the impact of labor laws and regulations on agricultural labor markets. The most easily understood and most widely recognized objective is the elimination of worker abuse and unscrupulous labor practices on the part of some employers. Although these abuses are common to only a small portion of employers, their visibility provides the incentive for government intervention in the market, which influences all employers. These abuses by employers are often counterproductive in the long run, inconsistent with good labor practices, and detrimental to the progress and growth of the farm firm. Therefore, labor laws and regulations may upgrade the quality of labor management and the sensitivity of employers to good labor management, even though this is rarely their explicit objective.

A closely related farm policy objective is the protection of the economic and social interests of workers. The social insurance programs for workers--for example, unemployment insurance, social security, and workers' compensation--are the best examples of the implementation of this policy objective.

A third objective is to have a supply of labor such that farmers are able to produce high quality agricultural products and operate sufficiently profitable businesses to keep them in operation year after year. The struggles with policies concerning certification of foreign workers demonstrate that this policy objective is taken seriously.

Equity is also a policy objective. This objective is less easily identified, demonstrated, and analyzed than the three previous objectives. But it can be easily seen that there are equity questions related to coverage of farm workers vs. nonfarm workers, workers on small farms vs. workers on large farms, seasonal workers vs. year around workers, employers in one state vs. employers in another state, and large employers vs. small employers.

Both federal and state labor laws and regulations affect agricultural labor markets. The decision to concentrate on federal laws in this chapter is not intended to imply that state laws are inconsequential. State laws may go beyond federal laws in their coverage, provisions, and enforcement implications. State laws may also affect some labor practices left untouched by federal laws. However, a comprehensive review and analysis of state laws, and particularly the variation among state laws, is beyond the scope of this chapter.

OBJECTIVES

The objectives of this paper are (1) to provide an historical perspective for addressing farm labor policy issues, (2) to review the stated objectives and major provisions of current labor laws and regulations, (3) to identify general policy issues emerging from current laws and regulations, and (4) to analyze four laws presently of major concern to employers, employees and policy makers: the Fair Labor Standards Act, the Farm Labor Contractor Registration Act, unemployment insurance, and the Occupational Safety and Health Act.

HISTORICAL PERSPECTIVE

An understanding of the present status of labor laws and regulations will be aided by knowledge of the evolutionary process that produced it. First, one must realize that U.S. farm labor policy has lacked a central thrust, particularly in the legislative area of intervention in the market through employment laws and regulations. Rather, there has been piecemeal legislation. Definitions, coverage, research preceding implementation, and educational programs following implementation have varied substantially. The net result is that today neither employers nor employees have a good understanding of their realized and unrealized benefits, costs, rights, and reporting requirements under current law.

Farm organizations and agricultural employers have systematically opposed the inclusion of agricultural employment under labor laws and regulations. The position of these organizations and employers has generally been that agricultural employment warranted different coverage from nonagricultural employment, due to its unique characteristics. Efforts to exclude agriculture have been successful in slowing but not in stopping the trend toward expanded coverage. It now appears that these organizations are putting much less emphasis on opposition to coverage and more emphasis on: (1) careful analysis of additional coverage, (2) fairness and consistency in enforcement, (3) understanding the potential advantages to both employers and employees that may accrue from the expanded coverage, and (4) assistance to members in meeting record keeping and reporting requirements.

Farm organizations were effectively representing the interests of their members by taking the position they did. There were historically important differences between the agricultural and nonagricultural sectors with regard to the nature of employers and employees, the work, and the production processes. However, the industrialization of agriculture, increasing farm size, increased sophistication and complexity of farm businesses, and the mechanization of many production processes have substantially altered the characteristics of agricultural employment. The old arguments for exclusion are unlikely to gain new strength, relevance, or significance in the coming policy debates.

Uneven enforcement of laws and regulations has been a major complication. Several different federal and state agencies have farm labor law enforcement responsibilities. There has been little effort to coordinate enforcement activities in order to facilitate employer compliance and assure workers their rightful benefits. The large number of employers with few employees, by nonfarm employer standards, has caused enforcement costs to be very high on a per employer basis. Enforcement budgets have often been severely limited relative to an agency's enforcement responsibilities.

Farm labor policy questions, and in particular questions concerning labor laws and regulations, have been dominated by interstate migrant farm worker issues. Although migrant farm workers constitute less than 7% of the total hired farm labor force, although their earnings are higher than the average earnings of nonmigrants, and although agriculture is often the employer of last resort for these people, many have argued that migrant worker issues are paramount in the farm labor policy arena. The problems of migrants have been apparent, often extreme in nature, highly visible in some communities, and subject to oversimplification. Much has been accomplished with regard to migrant farm workers, but as other analyses in this volume suggest, much remains to be accomplished.

Lack of published resource materials written in

language understandable to employers and employees has been a major problem. Enforcement agencies generally assume that it is the responsibility of employers and employees to inform themselves of the applicable provisions, record keeping requirements, enforcement procedures, and a host of related matters. This lack of systematic organization and presentation of information, in combination with the piecemeal nature of the legislation, has left many agricultural employers believing that the enforcement agencies "were out to get them." Good working relationships between employers and enforcement agencies, resulting in a high level of compliance with the law, are the exception rather than the rule. It is common for employees to believe that they have few, if any, rights and that they are not getting all the benefits to which they are entitled. Also, there is a common feeling among enforcement agency personnel that agricultural employers are generally conniving in innumerable innovative ways to frustrate the realization of the objectives of farm labor laws.

OVERVIEW OF CURRENT LAWS AND REGULATIONS

The identification and analysis of problems and issues should be based on an understanding of the coverage and provisions of current laws and regulations. There follows a brief discussion of the objectives, coverage provisions, and agencies responsible for the major farm laws and regulations.

Fair Labor Standards Act

The act is specifically concerned with the maintenance of the minimum standard of living necessary for the health, efficiency, and general well-being of workers. It contains provisions and standards concerning minimum wages, equal pay, overtime pay, record keeping, and child labor. The act applies generally to all workers who are engaged in or are producing goods for interstate commerce. However, there are some specific exemptions from requirements. Only agricultural employers with more than 500 man-days of hired labor in any calendar quarter of the preceding year are required to pay the minimum wage. The act exempts all agricultural employment from overtime pay. There are also provisions for employing a limited number of students at hourly rates lower than the minimum required for other farm workers.

There are explicit provisions affecting employment of minors. The objective is to provide for the health, safety, and welfare of employed youth and to prevent their exposure to certain hazardous jobs. Minors 16 years of age or over are not covered. Children 14 and 15 years old can be employed in any nonhazardous agricultural occupation outside school hours. A child 12 or 13 years of age can be employed outside school hours if he/she has the written consent of parents or if employment is on the same farm where his/her parents are employed. If a child is less than 12 years of age, employment by the parents is permitted on a farm owned and/or operated by the parents. A child less than 12 years of age can also be employed with the parents' written consent on a farm that is exempt from minimum wage and equal pay provisions under the 500 man-day test.

The 1977 amendments to the Fair Labor Standards Act established a schedule of increases in the minimum wage for farm workers. The minimum wage for farm and nonfarm workers is now the same. The minimum has increased from $2.65 an hour for calendar year 1978 to $3.10 an hour beginning January 1, 1980. The minimum wage for calendar year 1981 will be $3.35 an hour.

The Wage and Hour Division of the USDL is the responsible agency for the Fair Labor Standards Act.

The Occupational Safety and Health Act of 1970: OSHA

The purpose of this act is to assure, as far as possible, every working man and woman in the nation safe and healthful working conditions and to preserve human resources. The law covers every employer in the United States engaged in any business that affects interstate commerce. Most farmers hiring 10 or fewer employees at any one time during the year are exempt from OSHA inspection and all subsequent rules and penalties. However, serious, willful, or repeated violations by any farm employer are subject to citation.

For covered agricultural employers, there are standards for slow moving vehicle emblems, anhydrous ammonia equipment, temporary labor camps, pulpwood and logging, rollover protection structures for farm tractors, and machinery guarding and shielding. There are also employee training, record keeping, and reporting requirements.

Employees must comply with safety and health standards. All rules, regulations, and orders issued under the terms of the act that pertain to conduct in the workplace must be obeyed. Employees are required to participate in training and instruction as it relates to specific job assignments and to use and maintain personal protective equipment provided by the employer. However, employees are not subject to fines for noncompliance as are employers.

The law is administered by the Occupational Safety and Health Administration of the USDL.

Unemployment Insurance

The objective of unemployment insurance is to replace part (usually about 50%) of a person's income loss due to unemployment. These benefits are limited to persons temporarily out of work through no fault of their own. Effective January 1, 1978, some agricultural employment was covered by unemployment insurance. Coverage includes those farm employers who, during the current or previous calendar year, (1) employed 10 or more workers in each of 20 or more weeks, or (2) paid $20,000 or more cash wages in any calendar quarter of the current or preceding calendar year. Most states have adopted this federal standard, but some have exceeded it by including a higher proportion of agricultural employment. It is possible for a crew leader, rather than the farm operator, to be the employer liable for paying the unemployment tax, maintaining the required records, and submitting the required reports.

To receive unemployment insurance benefits, an

unemployed farm worker has to meet certain requirements. These requirements are typically based on employment with a covered employer for some minimum period of time and/or minimum compensation level. Employee provisions are determined by state law since there is no federal law specifying minimum benefit requirements and levels. Unemployed migrant farm workers having returned to their home states may file claims at their local employment services office. The responsible agency is the state employment agency operating the unemployment insurance program under the Federal Unemployment Tax Act. The secretary of labor must approve all state laws and their operation.

Workers' Compensation

Workers' compensation is an insurance system that provides protection for workers having job-related injuries or diseases. It frees the employer from liability for these injuries and illnesses. Workers' compensation programs in the United States operate under state law. There are neither federal programs nor federal guidelines for individual state programs. Consequently, the coverage provisions and employee benefits vary substantially.

The variation in coverage and provisions among states has led to several studies that conclude coverage is "inadequate and inequitable." Changes often mentioned as desirable include compulsory coverage of all employment, full coverage of all work-related diseases, improved rehabilitation services without arbitrary limits, and elimination of arbitrary limits on duration of some benefits. However, to date the states' rights approach has prevailed and workers' compensation provisions have been left to individual states.

Farm Labor Contractor Registration Act

The objective of the act is to restrict the irresponsible activities of farm labor contractors that result in exploitation of farm workers, farm operators, and the general public. This objective is accomplished by requiring farm labor contractors, their full-time or regular employees, and farmers using the services of farm labor contractors to observe certain rules set forth in the act.

This act, as amended, is concerned primarily with farm labor contractors (crew leaders). A farm labor contractor (crew leader) is any person who, for a fee, for himself or on behalf of another person, recruits, solicits, hires, furnishes or transports any number of workers (excluding members of the contractor's immediate family) for agricultural employment, whether within a state or across state lines.

There have been unusual and perhaps unique definitions of key words from the act by the USDL. "Person" includes any individual, partnership, association, joint stock company, trust, or corporation. "Agricultural employment" is defined very broadly to include virtually all aspects of employment in agriculture. In addition to on-farm employment, the definition includes handling, planting, drying, packing, packaging, processing, freezing, or grading prior to delivery for storage of any agricultural or horticultural commodity in its unmanufactured state. The term "migrant worker" is defined for the purposes of this act to include any individual whose primary employment is in agriculture, or who performs agricultural labor on a seasonal basis or other temporary basis. Any individual performing agricultural work is a migrant worker. Whether or not the worker migrates is irrelevant.

Farm labor contractors covered by this act must register with the USDL. They must also, at the time of recruitment, inform each worker in writing, in a language in which the worker is fluent, about the conditions of employment. Contractors must clearly post, in a language in which the worker is fluent, the terms and conditions of occupancy for housing owned or controlled by the contractor. Contractors must, upon arrival at a place of employment, post the conditions of employment. Finally, the farm labor contractor, if responsible for paying the wages, must keep payroll records and provide each worker with a statement of earnings, withholdings, and reasons for withholding.

The agency responsible for the implementation and enforcement of the Act is the USDL, Wage and Hour Division.

Civil Rights Regulations

The objective is to prevent discriminatory employment practices on the basis of race, color, religion, sex, national origin, handicap, or ancestry. The Federal Civil Rights Act of 1964 applies to farm employers with 15 or more employees. The responsible agency is the USDL, Wage and Hour Division.

Alien Worker Employment

An alien is a foreign-born citizen in the United States who has not become naturalized. Alien farm workers may be legal or illegal aliens. A certified alien farm worker is one who is legally in the country through a certification program administered by the USDL. An illegal alien (undocumented alien) is not certified by the USDL and his presence in the United States is in violation of the Immigration and Nationality Act. With the exception of registered farm labor contractors, farm employers are not prohibited by any federal law from employing illegal aliens. However, actual involvement in securing such employees or shielding them from detection can lead to a severe penalty for criminal violations.

The responsible agencies for alien worker matters are the Division of Labor Certification of the USDL, and the Immigration and Naturalization Service of the Department of Justice.

Federal Motor Carrier Safety Regulations

The objective of these regulations is to assure the reasonably safe condition and operation of vehicles in which migrant farm workers are transported. These regulations apply to the transport of migrant farm workers if the total distance is more than 75 miles, but only if such transportation is across a state line. The regulations do not apply if fewer than three workers are transported at any one time, or if a passenger automobile or station wagon is used. A migrant worker transporting himself or his immediate family is not affected. Compliance is required of the person or business responsible for the transportation of the workers. The responsible agency is the U.S. Department of Transportation, Federal Highway Administration, Bureau of Motor Carrier Safety.

Social Security

The objective of the social security coverage of hired farm workers is to provide monthly cash benefits to replace a part of the earnings lost through an employee's retirement, death, disability, or hospitalization.

Farm employers and employees are covered if there are one or more agricultural employees on the farm who meet either of the following tests: (1) employee was paid $150 or more in cash wages in the year or (2) employee performed agricultural labor on the farm for 20 or more days during the year for cash wages computed on a time basis (e.g., hourly, daily, weekly, or monthly). Some types of family employment are not covered by social security.

Covered farm employers must withhold tax from their employees' cash wages and match the employee tax with an equal amount. The wage base for 1980 is $25,900 and the tax rate 6.13%. In 1981, the wage base will increase to $29,700 and the tax rate will be 6.65%. The wage base is an individual employee's maximum total earnings in a calendar year on which an employer and employee pay social security tax. The Internal Revenue Service collects the taxes for the Social Security Administration.

Targeted Jobs Tax Credit and Work Incentive Credit

These tax credit programs are established to provide economic incentive for the employment of certain groups of workers. Included are welfare recipients, handicapped persons undergoing vocational rehabilitation, certain members of economically disadvantaged families, certain ex-convicts, and certain other groups receiving general assistance or undergoing qualified cooperative education training. A percentage of the wages paid new employees may qualify as a direct credit against the tax liability of the employer.

GENERAL FARM LABOR LAW POLICY ISSUES AND PROBLEMS

There are two kinds of policy issues associated with current farm labor laws and regulations. First are general issues that stem from more than one law or regulation. Second are issues related to a specific law or regulation. Resolution of these policy issues and problems would involve in almost all cases a trade-off between employers and employee economic interests. The purpose of the following discussion is to identify the issues and problems and to suggest some alternatives for the resolution of the problems.

Five general policy issues and problems are discussed: (1) coverage of agricultural employers and employees, (2) record keeping and reporting requirements, (3) impacts on cost of production, (4) unique problems of interstate migrant farm workers, and (5) information for employers and employees about coverage and provisions of laws and regulations.

Coverage of Agricultural Employers and Employees

Coverage refers to the specific groups of employers and employees coming under the provisions of a law or regulation. As has been illustrated, coverage varies from law to law. It is common for medium-size agricultural employers to be covered by some, but not all, agricultural labor laws. A further complication is the variation in the criteria on which coverage is based. Coverage may be determined by number of employees, size of payroll, duration of employment, man-days of labor, or some combination of these factors.

The coverage problem and its resulting confusion can be illustrated by a comparison of some of the actual coverage criteria used in federal laws. The number of employees criterion is used for civil rights regulations. The Federal Civil Rights Act of 1964 applies only to employers with 15 or more employees.

The payroll criterion is used for social security employee taxes. Farm employers are included if there are one or more employees paid $150 or more in cash wages in the year. Also, farm employers are included if one or more employees performed agricultural labor on the farm for 20 or more days during the year for cash wages. This illustrates the duration of employment criterion. The man-days of labor criterion is used for coverage under the minimum wage provisions of the Fair Labor Standards Act. Agricultural employers who use more than 500 man-days of labor in any calendar quarter of the preceding year must pay at least the minimum wage.

Unemployment insurance illustrates the use of a combination of these criteria. Coverage includes those farm employers who during the current or previous calendar year (1) employed 10 or more workers in each of 20 weeks or (2) paid $20,000 or more in cash wages in any calendar quarter of the preceding calendar year. For many agricultural employers, coverage questions can be answered only by a careful review of the coverage criteria for each law or regulation. Furthermore, exclusion or inclusion may change from year to year for a particular employer as his use of hired labor varies.

Exclusions from coverage may limit the ability of noncovered employers to compete with nonagricultural and covered agricultural employers for new employees. Potential employees would be expected to favor covered employers because of the greater number of fringe benefits. Coverage of employers is generally at little or no cost to employees.

Employees also have coverage problems and suffer from confusion. A change in employers with no perceptible change in job description or employment conditions can result in gaining or losing certain fringe benefits. Coverage often differs between farm and nonfarm employment. Employers may not dispense or may not even have information about fringe benefits required under the law. Employees may hesitate to seek information about coverage for fear of jeopardizing their employment.

The simple solution to coverage problems would be

uniform coverage provisions for all agricultural and nonagricultural employment under all laws and regulations. This resolution is unlikely. The piecemeal approach to legislation, the precedent of defining coverage on a law-by-law basis, and the continued efforts of employer interest groups to limit coverage make the logical policy of uniform coverage a very distant possibility. However, as a minimum, the elimination of differences in criteria for defining coverage would be helpful. For example, the concept of number of employees in combination with length of employment or quarterly payroll, as used in defining unemployment insurance coverage, could be applied to minimum wage, workers' compensation, farm labor contractor registration, OSHA, civil rights regulations, transportation of migrant workers, and social security. This would facilitate both employer and employee understanding of coverage and fringe benefits.

Record Keeping and Reporting Requirements

Most labor laws and regulations specify data and reports that employers are required to submit regularly to enforcement and administrative agencies. Ideally, the data necessary for answering questions from enforcement agencies would be the same as that necessary for good employment practices. However, employers often see record keeping and reporting requirements as burdensome because of demands for data beyond that routinely needed for their own management decisions. The profusion of paperwork requires a significant amount of time from most agricultural employers.

An important problem is the variation in record keeping and reporting requirements among government agencies. Reports may be monthly, quarterly, and/or annual. They may require data about payroll, number of employees, wage rates, perquisites, hours of work, job descriptions, training, and injuries.

Some current record keeping and reporting requirements illustrate the problem of variation in timing and content. The Fair Labor Standards Act requires a farm employer to maintain payroll records containing the following information with respect to each worker subject to the minimum wage: name, address, sex, occupation, birth date, number of man-days worked each week or each month, time of day and day of week when work week begins, basis on which wages are paid, hours worked each workday, total hours worked each work week, total daily or weekly earnings, total additions to or deductions from wages paid each pay period, total wages paid each pay period, date of payment, and period covered by payment. No reports are required but employers must have these data routinely available to personnel of the Wage and Hour Division of the USDL. Also, an employer not employing workers subject to the minimum wage is required to have data routinely available to substantiate the exclusion from coverage.

The OSHA of 1970 has detailed record keeping and reporting requirements for employers with 11 or more employees. Requirements include a log of occupational injuries and illnesses, a supplementary record of each occupational injury and illness, and an annual summary of occupational injuries and illnesses. The summary must be posted during the month of February each year. In addition, employers must report to the secretary of labor within 48 hours each accident or health hazard that results in one or more fatalities or the hospitalization of five or more employees.

Although workers' compensation and OSHA are both related to accidents and illness in the workplace, the reporting requirements are quite different. This can be illustrated with the requirements for employers in Ohio. The Ohio requirements are similar to those in most other states. There is no 10-workers-or-less exemption for workers' compensation. All Ohio employers are required to report regularly to the Bureau of Workers' Compensation. Payroll reports and premium payments must be made every six months. Even if there are no employees, a previously covered employer must file a biannual payroll report and indicate "no payroll this period."

Social security employee tax requirements may result in monthly or annual reports to the Internal

Revenue Service. An annual report must be submitted by January 31 each year. However, if the total social security tax due reaches $200 or more for part of the year, payment and reports must be submitted by the fifteenth of the month following the month in which a total of $200 or more has been withheld. Each employee from whom social security taxes have been withheld must be provided a statement showing total wages and social security taxes withheld.

Each state specifies record keeping requirements for employers subject to unemployment insurance contributions. For example, in Ohio covered employers are required to keep employees informed as to their "covered" status, to furnish identification notices to employees upon separation, to submit quarterly payroll reports to the state employment service, maintain a 5-year record of employment, and upon request, to supply wage, separation, and other pertinent information to the state employment service.

Farm operators using the services of registered labor contractors are required to maintain payroll records of workers recruited for their benefit. The farmer must have these records even if the workers are paid directly by the contractor.

The record keeping and reporting problems center on the quantity of reporting, variation in information required, and variation in forms. The problem stems from the piecemeal nature of legislation and the lack of coordination among responsible agencies to eliminate duplicate reporting requirements. As long as the record keeping and reporting requirements are specified in each law, without regard to other laws and regulations, the problem will not be resolved. Reducing variation in coverage criteria, coordinating reporting requirements so that the same report could be submitted to several agencies, and adopting standard definitions of key words and concepts would be major steps toward decreasing the time and frustration of record keeping and reporting by employers. These changes would also increase the quality of data available for the conduct of enforcement programs and the provision of services and benefits to employees.

Impacts on Cost of Production

Most farm labor laws and regulations increase the costs of production for employers. Employers tend to evaluate the impacts of these additional costs without considering the benefits conferred on employees. There is a trade-off between the higher cost of production for employers, and thus higher food costs for consumers, and the increased wage and fringe benefit package for employees.

The cost impacts vary among employers because of variations in coverage provisions, in capacity to pass the increased costs on to consumers, and in the availability of opportunities for the substitution of capital for labor through mechanization. However, a review of cost of production budgets will demonstrate that for most agricultural products the proportion of total cost accounted for by fringe benefits required through farm labor laws and regulations is minimal. One also finds that in most cases other costs of production have increased more rapidly than the cost of required fringe benefits. Employer opposition to farm labor laws probably centers more on record keeping and reporting requirements, perceived harassment by enforcement agencies, and loss of flexibility in employment practices than on increased cost of production. However, cost of production impacts will continue to be at issue as long as they vary among employers because of coverage criteria and employers fail to capitalize on the benefits of increased and improved fringe benefit packages.

Unique Problems of Interstate Migrant Farm Workers

In the historical perspective section of this chapter, reasons for the special attention paid migrant farm workers in farm labor laws were discussed. The consequence of this attention is that a much higher percentage of migrants than nonmigrants are covered by the federal minimum wage, OSHA, unemployment insurance, and workers' compensation. This is directly due to the characteristics of the farms on which migrants tend to be employed. These farms are relatively large and consequently the exclusions granted by many of the laws do not apply. It appears that there is widespread agreement that migrant farm workers should be covered by all or virtually all labor laws and regulations.

A policy question is whether or not migrant and nonmigrant farm workers should be treated differently. A recent example from Ohio illustrates the kind of explicit distinction sometimes drawn between migrant and nonmigrant employees. Practically all employed minors in Ohio are required to have age and schooling certificates (work permits). However, the state code was recently revised to exclude all minors in agricultural employment from the work permit requirement except those living in temporary agricultural labor camps, that is, children of migrant farm workers. It is more difficult for migrant than nonmigrant children to get work permits because the migrant children must provide proof of birth from their home state to the Ohio school district, while the local children need not provide the proof of age since the school district already has it on file. An additional consequence is the exclusion of 12 and 13 year-old migrant children from employment through the work permit regulation, even though such employment is permitted under federal law.

The net result in Ohio is that migrant children will find it harder to qualify for agricultural employment than nonmigrant children will and a smaller proportion are able to qualify because of the state age restriction. The irony of this situation is that many of the minor migrant children in Ohio come to the state with their parents for the express purpose of finding agricultural employment. Yet the state law makes it more difficult for migrant than for nonmigrant children to obtain employment.

Information for Employers and Employees

Several references have been made to the variation in the coverage and the provisions of farm labor laws and regulations affecting agricultural employment. The number of different agencies with which employers and employees must deal has also been emphasized. This is the kind of compliance and enforcement maze in which systematic dissemination of information by government agencies would be very helpful. However, in most cases there is little effort by these agencies to assist employers and employees with reference material. In some cases, the only source of information is the official publication of laws and regulations. These official publications are not readily available to employers and employees and more importantly, are rarely understandable to persons not having legal training. Reference materials from government agencies written for employers and employees have little impact. They are spotty in their coverage, oriented to a summary of provisions rather than to current questions facing employers and employees, difficult to keep current through reorder, and generally unknown to local enforcement personnel.

The myriad of farm labor laws and regulations, in combination with the dearth of information from government agencies, has caused the extension services in some states to publish farm labor law handbooks. (Some examples are Erven et al., *Ohio Farm Labor Handbook*; Covey, *Handbook of Regulations Affecting Florida Farm Employers and Employees*; Shapley, *The Law and Michigan Agricultural Labor*; and Fisher, *Farm Labor Regulations*.) Employers and employees in these states can develop a reasonably good understanding of the laws and regulations affecting them. However, employers and employees in other states have little, or more usually no, reference material available to them. It appears that the government agencies at both the federal and state levels responsible for enforcement of farm labor laws could improve compliance, reduce employer and employee frustration, and improve their working relationships with employers and employees by assuming the responsibility for systematic dissemination of farm labor law information.

POLICY ISSUES AND PROBLEMS FOR SELECTED LAWS AND REGULATIONS

In addition to the general policy issues and problems discussed in the previous section, there are specific issues related to individual laws and regulations. In this section, issues and problems relative to the Fair Labor Standards Act, Farm Labor Contractor Registration Act, unemployment insurance, and OSHA will be discussed. These four were selected because employer or employee groups have identified specific problems with them, because the current laws are ineffective in accomplishing their stated objectives, and/or because Congress and the USDL are now or soon will be considering changes in them.

Fair Labor Standards Act

This act has many provisions and affects agricultural employment in more ways than any other single act. Systematic review of all of its impacts on agricultural labor markets is beyond the scope of this chapter. The following discussion is limited to child labor and minimum wage issues.

The child labor provisions have major impacts on agricultural employment practices. The seasonal demand for labor, minimum skill levels required, minimum emphasis on training programs, unimportance of worker turnover, willingness of children to work at lower wage rates than adults, and the availability of children in most rural communities combine to make youth an important source of labor in agriculture. Youth would constitute a much higher percentage of the agricultural labor force in the absence of the child labor provisions of the Fair Labor Standards Act. There are persuasive arguments for the current limitations on employment of youth in agriculture. However, prior to adoption of more restrictive child labor laws careful consideration should be given to the benefits derived by youth from the employment opportunities provided by agriculture.

Two issues related to child labor are of immediate concern: reentry to fields following pesticide application and employment of children less than 12 years of age. "There is no issue" is probably the intuitive reaction of most people. The children's welfare overrides any employer interest. More careful examination reveals that there are some unique aspects of the issues. The reentry problem hinges on standards. No one could reasonably argue that children should be exposed to pesticide injury through employment that requires premature reentry to a field. However, the establishment of standards acceptable to the USDL, the Environmental Protection Agency (EPA), the courts, and employers has not been accomplished. Many studies are currently under way that are designed to provide the data base for development of defensible reentry standards. Resolution of the problem evidently awaits completion of these studies.

Exclusion of most agricultural employment for children less than 12 years of age causes little problem for agriculture as a whole. The exceptions are the strawberry harvest in Washington and Oregon and the potato harvest in Maine. In these situations, children less than 12 years of age have been an important part of the harvest work force. This has led to specific minimum wage exemptions and authorization for the secretary of labor to grant a waiver from Fair Labor Standards Act restrictions for children aged 10 and 11. The necessity of a harvest work force and the difficulty--perhaps the impossibility--of accomplishing the harvest without the employment of children less than 12 years of age has been effectively argued by employers. The tendency for the wages prevailing in such circumstances to be considerably less than the minimum wage, and less than a wage necessary to attract older youth and adults to harvest employment, has been an effective argument by those opposed to the position of the employers. A long term resolution of the problem acceptable to all interested parties is not apparent.

From May 1, 1974, to January 1, 1980, the federal minimum wage increased from $1.30 to $3.10 per hour, a 138% increase. According to unpublished USDL data, only 4.4% of 1978 U.S. agricultural employers had more than 500 man-days of labor in any calendar quarter and were thus required to pay at least the minimum wage. However, these employers accounted for about 43% of all agricultural employees. Historically, there has been a close relationship between the wage rate paid uncovered workers and the required minimum for covered workers. The unpublished USDL data show that this is no longer the case.

Assuring a wage floor for those least likely to compete effectively for high paying jobs has social appeal. This is particularly true in agriculture, where wage rates have historically been low compared to nonfarm rates. The importance of youth, elderly, and unskilled workers to the farm labor force also suggests the desirability of having a wage floor. However, there are important employment implications of the minimum wage. The jobs in agriculture most likely to be affected by the major increases in minimum wage are those held by youth, the elderly, and part-time workers not paid on a piece-rate basis.

The impacts of minimum wages on labor markets have been studied extensively by economists, but the results are inconclusive. Of particular importance to agricultural labor markets are the impacts of the minimum wage increases on employment opportunities for youth and the elderly, on total employment, and on the rate at which jobs in agriculture are being lost to mechanization. The Minimum Wage Study Commission is currently investigating these and many other issues. One hopes their comprehensive reports will provide new insights and policy guidelines.

There are some important relationships between the minimum wage levels and child labor issues. There is an exemption from minimum wage coverage for hand harvest workers who commute daily from their permanent residence, are paid on a piece-rate basis for work generally recognized as piece-rate work, and were employed in agriculture less than 13 weeks during the preceding calendar year. Also exempted are children of migrant farm workers less than 16 years of age employed in piece-rate harvest work on the same farm where their parents are employed. If these two exemptions were removed, it is likely that employment of children less than 12 years of age would no longer be at issue. There is a high probability that these children would not be employed if the wage rate had to be as high as the minimum wage. However, this would not resolve the basic problem of a labor supply for those agricultural employers to whom 10- and 11-year-olds are now important.

Farm Labor Contractor Registration Act: FLCRA

Irresponsible and unscrupulous activities of farm labor contractors (crew leaders) caused Congress to take action through the FLCRA. Although enacted in 1965, it had little impact until amended in 1974. There are currently two important problem areas related to the FLCRA. The first concerns the guidelines and activities of the Employment Standards Administration of the Department of Labor. The second is lack of enforcement.

Although these problems are of major concern to employer and/or employee interest groups, few would argue that the original objectives of the FLCRA are any less relevant today than at the time serious problems with labor contractors were first identified. The unscrupulous activities of some labor contractors continue. Farm operators and the general public suffer, but migrant farm workers are the big losers. The contractors exercise extensive control over workers. The workers may depend on contractors for job information, transportation, housing, and even choice of retailer for basic purchases. Historically, farm workers claiming to be aggrieved by contractors had little recourse.

Several agricultural employer groups are on record protesting the USDL's implementation of the FLCRA in ways that go beyond the intent of Congress. The implementation has caused many compliance and reporting problems for employers without providing significant benefits for migrant farm workers. Polopolus (1979) has identified the fundamental question: has congressional intent been usurped by administrative prerogatives? The answer appears to be yes. The major problem areas are the definitions of a farm labor contractor and of a migrant worker, the concept of acting "personally," and the exemption based on the concept of "on no more than an incidental basis."

Prior to the FLCRA, the description of a crew

leader and his role with regard to migrant farm workers were widely understood and not controversial. Crew leaders provided migrant workers for agricultural employment in receiving states by assembling groups in a supply state, transporting them to one or more states of employment, and providing some personnel services for both migrant workers and farmers during the period of employment. However, under the FLCRA the definition of farm labor contractor may include personnel officers of corporate packing houses, farm employees who drive trucks in the field while other employees ride along, growers who pick up local workers at their homes and take them to their own fields, farm supervisors using their personal automobiles to show crew leaders the next day's work location, and foremen and officers of corporate farms (Polopolus 1979).

The original focus of the FLCRA was on migrant farm workers because there has been a traditional relationship between migrants and crew leaders. The typical definition of a migrant farm worker incorporates the idea of crossing a state line for temporary employment. However, in the FLCRA's definition of migrant farm worker, actual migrancy is inconsequential. For purposes of the FLCRA, practically all agricultural employees are migrant farm workers.

The FLCRA defines "person" very broadly to include legal entities such as trusts and corporations. However, in the implementation of the act, corporations have been ruled incapable of acting personally. Therefore, the exemption in the act for corporations supplying only their own migrant workers is void.

The act also exempts an employer's regular or full-time employee who engages in farm labor contractor activities only on an incidental basis and only for the employer. The problem is that virtually any level of farm labor contracting activity engaged in on a regular basis has been determined to be on more than an "incidental basis." This effectively voids the "incidental basis" exemption provided in the act.

The second general problem with the FLCRA is

enforcement. The enforcement emphasis appears to have been on registration of labor contractors rather than on finding and charging the irresponsible and unscrupulous activities of contractors (Waterfield). This kind of enforcement activity is difficult and sometimes even dangerous to USDL personnel. Crew leaders are generally difficult people to deal with and they are understandably unenthusiastic about the objectives of the FLCRA. But given the continuing problems with crew leaders and the enforcement responsibilities of the USDL, it seems that more emphasis on enforcement would be in order. In a recent hearing by the Manpower Subcommittee of the House Government Operations Committee, USDL spokesperson Craig Berrington reported that more resources would be devoted to enforcement work (Waterfield).

It appears that the original legislative intent and stated objectives for the FLCRA will not be accomplished until Congress takes corrective and clarifying action. It would be helpful if the authors of such action took cognizance of the stated objectives for the FLCRA, the USDL interpretations and enforcement activities to date, the concerns of employers and migrant workers and, most importantly, of the continued exploitative activities of crew leaders.

Unemployment Insurance

The extension of unemployment insurance coverage to some agricultural employment on January 1, 1978 followed careful study of the likely impacts of coverage (Bauder et al.). With the current coverage provision, relatively few employers are affected, but given the characteristics of these employers, a relatively high percentage of farm workers are covered. There is almost universal coverage of nonfarm employment. Therefore, an important policy issue is extension of coverage to a higher proportion of agricultural employment.

Many arguments have been used by agricultural employers and farm organizations in opposition to more inclusive coverage of agricultural employment. The most important have concerned the cost to employers, disincentives for employment in agriculture, administrative problems and fraudulent claims, and the unsuitability of unemployment insurance for temporary employees (Sosnick). However, on the basis of nonfarm experience with unemployment insurance, experience with temporary coverage through Supplemental Unemployment Assistance (SUA), and experience to date with partial coverage of agricultural employment, one can conclude that there are no convincing arguments against extending coverage to more agricultural employers. It appears that extending coverage is now a political rather than an economic or social question.

There are some important problems associated with the current coverage criteria. Some unemployed farm workers are denied benefits simply because of the characteristics of their former employer(s). Their own attachment to the labor force, inability to find employment, and desire to return to agricultural employment the following season do not influence whether or not they receive benefits. Two farm workers with the same job description, length of employment, earnings, and reason for unemployment may be treated differently for benefit purposes simply because of differences in the characteristics of their employers. In addition, employers not covered may face recruitment problems due to their inability to provide the same fringe benefit package available through a competing, covered employer.

Another issue is administration of the program so that all of those, but only those, entitled to benefits actually receive them. This is by no means a new issue or one unique to agriculture. But there are some characteristics of agricultural employment which make administration of the program difficult. Some workers may have several employers during the year. This complicates construction of an accurate employment history. There may be problems with language, interstate claims, employers not responding to requests for information, and reluctance by government agencies to struggle with the complexities of benefit claims for farm workers. Consequently, some workers are probably denied their rightful benefits and some employers probably overpay their unemployment insurance taxes. The overpayment stems from inadequate data on which to base reports and lack of understanding of the consequences of untimely and inaccurate reporting.

OSHA

The uniformity of OSHA coverage between farm and nonfarm employment means that almost all policy issues and problems related to it are general rather than specifically related to agriculture. The agricultural standard for temporary labor camps is an exception.

In addition to the OSHA standards for temporary housing, there are other USDL standards for housing. These other standards have been in effect for several years. The older standards, referred to as "620 standards" after the part of the Code of Federal Regulations where they are officially published, have been used as a basis for determining which farm employers could receive farm placement and other services from the USDL. Only those employers with housing approved under 620 standards could receive USDL services. Because the 620 standards and OSHA housing standards are different in some details, an employer may have more than one USDL inspection of his temporary housing. It has been possible to have housing acceptable under one standard but not necessarily under the other.

The solution to this problem is straightforward. The USDL could decide to use one or the other set of housing standards in all of its inspections. The other standard could be "grandfathered" so that an employer would not face a changing standard for his already constructed housing. Informal reports from the USDL indicate that this elimination of duplicate housing standards will be accomplished in the very near future.

SUMMARY

Government intervenes in agricultural labor markets through labor laws and regulations. The objectives of this intervention are to eliminate worker abuse and unscrupulous labor practices, to protect the economic and social interests of workers, to guarantee a supply of labor for producers, and to provide equitable treatment of workers and employers. The specific objectives for this analysis are: (1) to provide an historical perspective for addressing farm labor policy issues, (2) to review the stated objectives and major provisions of current labor laws and regulations, (3) to identify general policy issues emerging from current laws and regulations, and (4) to analyze four laws presently of major concern to employers, employees, and policymakers.

Current farm labor laws and regulations are the result of piecemeal legislation. Farm organizations and agricultural employers have systematically opposed the inclusion of agricultural employment under labor laws and regulations. There have been important differences between farm and nonfarm employment, but the industrialization of agriculture has eliminated most of them. Laws and regulations have been enforced unevenly. Issues concerning interstate migrant farm workers have dominated the farm labor policy arena. Lack of published resource materials understandable to employers and employees has been a major problem.

The most important federal farm labor laws and regulations currently affecting employers and employees are the Fair Labor Standards Act, OSHA, unemployment insurance, workers' compensation, the FLCRA, civil rights regulations, alien worker employment regulations, federal motor carrier safety regulations, social security, and the targeted jobs tax credit and work incentive credit.

Five general policy issues and problems were discussed: (1) coverage of agricultural employers and employees, (2) record keeping and reporting requirements, (3) impacts on cost of production, (4) unique problems of interstate migrant farm workers, and (5) information for employers and employees about coverage and provisions of laws and regulations.

The final section of this chapter is a discussion of specific issues and problems concerning the Fair Labor Standards Act, FLCRA, unemployment insurance, and OSHA. Reentry to fields following pesticide application and employment of children less than 12 years of age are the most important issues relative to child labor provisions. Although the impacts of minimum wages have been studied extensively, the results are inconclusive. There remain questions about their impact on agricultural employment opportunities for youth and the elderly, on total employment, and on the rate at which jobs in agriculture are being lost to mechanization.

Irresponsible and unscrupulous activities of crew leaders continue to harm migrant workers and their employers. The FLCRA is intended to eliminate these activities. However, problems with the implementation and enforcement of the act have limited its impact. Specific issues include the definition of a farm labor contractor, definition of migrant worker, the concept of acting "personally," and the exemption based on the concept of "on no more than an incidental basis." The enforcement emphasis has been on registration of labor contractors rather than on finding illegal activities and charging crew leaders.

More extensive coverage of agricultural employment is a major question relative to unemployment insurance programs. Historically there have been persuasive arguments against more extensive coverage of agricultural employment. The experiences with nonfarm coverage, the temporary SUA program, and partial agricultural coverage suggest that there are no longer sufficient reasons for limiting coverage.

The OSHA agricultural standards for temporary labor camp housing are not entirely consistent with the older "620 standards" of the USDL. The dual standards and resulting multiple inspections of the same labor camp by the USDL cause compliance problems for agricultural employers. The problem could be resolved through adoption of a single set of housing standards.

Discussion

LEO POLOPOLUS

Professor Erven has provided a thoughtful overview of the major federal programs that affect agricultural labor markets. He has adequately fulfilled his stated objectives of sketching the historical perspectives, reviewing the major provisions of labor laws, identifying general policy issues, and analyzing in more detail agricultural labor laws. Since Erven's analysis did not systematically evaluate the impact of labor laws and regulations upon agricultural labor markets, my remarks will focus upon the relationships between market behavior and laws.

IMPACT UPON LABOR MARKET STRUCTURE

An agricultural labor market involves a common group of employers and employees of a particular agricultural labor service for a specific time frame. Thus a labor market is quite specific with respect to location, type of service, time, and duration. Because of unique differences among many agricultural production processes, the market is often also specific to particular farm products.

Whether collectively or independently determined, the ultimate result of the market process is the determination of wages, hours, and working conditions. At issue is the effect that agricultural labor laws and regulations have upon wage rates and the agricultural labor market structure and environment.

NUMBER OF EMPLOYEES AND EMPLOYERS

Since the farm labor market employs many persons who have no alternative employment opportunities, labor laws and regulations that increase the farm wage rate or production costs usually lead to decreases in the number of workers employed. Workers who continue their employment are obviously better off. But unfortunately those farm workers no longer employed are not only not helped--they have lost what livelihood they once had, as meager as it might have been. For the disadvantaged and the unemployed workers, the problem is shifted from farm labor policy to a problem for our society in general (Polopolus 1977, p. 3).

Several econometric studies on the impact of the minimum wage law (Fair Labor Standards Act) upon wage rates and employment have consistently concluded that the extension of the minimum wage law to hired farm workers has increased the average farm wage rate and decreased hired farm employment (Gardner 1981, Gardner 1972, Lianos).

Agricultural labor laws and regulations have also contributed to the decrease in the number of employers over time. Increased costs of production through minimum wages, unemployment insurance, workman's compensation, and occupational safety/health standards have at the margin led to the demise of many agricultural firms. The impact of labor laws upon the number and size distribution of agricultural employers is not well documented in the scientific literature.

CONDITION OF ENTRY AND EXIT

Because of the somewhat "structureless" nature of the farm labor market and the low level of unionization in most labor market areas of the United States, the farm labor market is characterized by relatively free entry for prospective employees. While the skill requirements are increasing over time because of technological and scientific developments, the bulk of the hired farm labor performed in U.S. agriculture is commonly described as unskilled work. And while farm workers are extremely heterogeneous in terms of their socioeconomic composition, the employer-employee relationship is often quite casual. This permits both relatively free entry to and exit from the farm labor market. Passage of laws such as the CALRA has the effect of "structuring" the farm labor market and affecting the conditions of worker entry to and exit from the market.

SPATIAL/GEOGRAPHIC MARKET IMPACT

Because of the geographic dispersion of agricultural production in the United States, labor supplies are not often available in adequate quantity, quality, and duration to fulfill local market requirements. These market demands have historically been met by intrastate and interstate migrant workers, particularly for harvesting perishable crops. There are numerous state and federal laws that have been enacted to improve the economic and noneconomic well-being of migrant workers and their families. Of concern here is the impact of federal and state labor laws upon the migration of farm workers. It has been clearly established, for example, that the unemployment insurance program reduces a farm worker's incentive to migrate for additional employment (Emerson and Arcia).

MARKET INFORMATION AND KNOWLEDGE

As noted in Erven's analysis, providing adequate information to both farm employers and employees regarding labor laws and regulations is a major problem area. In addition to information concerning labor laws and regulations, there is a critical need for some agency to provide labor market information on a regular basis concerning the available jobs, their location, duration, rate of pay, and skill or experience requirements. While the state and federal labor agencies provided these types of services in the past, farm labor market services are presently not available on a regular basis. The serious economic question relates to the competitiveness of wage rate determination in farm labor markets. Is there adequate market information on both the demand and supply sides of farm labor markets to permit rational and competitively determined wage rates? Would the reimposition of federal-state farm labor market services provide economic and social benefits in excess of the cost of providing the services? Is the present labor market information system (which relies heavily upon private communications) sufficiently effective?

DEMAND FOR AGRICULTURAL LABOR

The demand for farm labor is derived directly from the demand for agricultural products, assuming constant technology and foreign competition. However, laws and regulations that adversely affect the competitive position of domestic agricultural production have an obvious and negative impact on the demand for farm labor. For example, reductions in tariffs or a presidential embargo on agricultural exports can have serious economic consequences including a dramatic impact upon the farm firm's demand for labor.

Throughout his discussion, Erven properly stresses the adverse impact of increased production costs upon the demand for labor. Production costs have increased due to compliance with rising minimum wages, broadened farm coverage of various labor laws, and increased bureaucratic paperwork and red tape, along with other factors. While these "costs" may not be reflected in cost and return budgets for individual enterprises as developed by farm management specialists, their costs are determinable within the context of the overall management structure of the farm firm. The main point here is that product-cost increases for firms in atomistically competitive industries cannot be individually passed on to buyers of farm products. Instead this phenomenon usually leads to cost-minimizing activities and quite often the substitution of capital for labor in the agricultural production process.

With the dramatic rise in the price of energy in recent years, the human factor in agricultural production may become "cheap" in relation to alternative capital-intensive technologies. Formulators of government laws and regulations should attempt to anticipate future and expected changes in the farm capital and labor market.

SUPPLY OF AGRICULTURAL LABOR

While several federal laws directly affect the supply of agricultural labor through their monetary and nonmonetary incentives and disincentives, the supply of alien workers under the Immigration and Nationality Act is a timely issue.

The number of legal aliens admitted for agricultural employment in the United States has decreased from approximately 430,000 in 1958 to 22,000 in 1976. Over the same period the number of deportable aliens apprehended in U.S. agriculture has increased from approximately 6,000 in 1958 to 116,000 in 1976 (Sikes and Sorn). While the illegal and legal alien issues are complex and somewhat contradictory, aliens affect the farm labor market in terms of the supply of workers. In one empirical study it was demonstrated that the presence of foreign (H-2) workers in the Florida citrus industry reduced the wage rate for domestic workers below what it would have been in the absence of offshore labor (Emerson et al.). On the other hand, Sikes and Sorn argue that the H-2 program in the Florida sugarcane market has not depressed wage rates (Sikes and Sorn, p. 22). It appears obvious, however, that the dramatic increase in illegal or undocumented alien workers in U.S. agriculture has had a negative impact upon wage levels (Chap. 4). Because of the importance and complexity of the issue of alien workers in U.S. agriculture, and the relative dearth of scientific inquiry, high priority should be given to this area in future allocations of research study grants.

CONCLUDING REMARKS

Rather than conduct an extensive critique of Erven's analysis, my remarks are intended to broaden the scope of the discussion of the impact of labor laws and regulations upon agricultural labor markets. Included in this discussion has been the impact of labor laws upon labor market structure, demand for labor, and supply of labor. Emphasis was upon federal laws, with only minor reference to the impact of administrative and bureaucratic dealings. Erven did cite my recent interpretation of the FLCRA, which characterizes the administration of this law as a classic example of regulations not compatible with legislative intent (Polopolus 1979).

Overall, labor laws and regulations do have an impact upon wages, hours, and working conditions. Unfortunately, there is insufficient research that authoritatively demonstrates the direction and magnitude of the forces affecting the agricultural labor market as the result of government actions.

13

Farm Worker Service and Employment Programs

REFUGIO I. ROCHIN

Labor economists generally agree that employment and training programs are indispensable to a strategy for improving conditions for farm workers. Such programs should provide farm workers with the following (Marshall, p. 89):

1. Education and training, whether on the job, in classrooms, or some combination of the two, to upgrade skills in agriculture and to expand employment opportunities in nonfarm occupations
2. Preemployment supportive activities to help workers prepare for training or for alternative employment
3. Public employment programs for farm workers who cannot either find year-round jobs or become self-employed in some capacity
4. Measures to improve the operation of the labor market through better information about farm and nonfarm job opportunities
5. Relocation assistance, financial and informational, to move workers from labor surplus to labor shortage areas

---

Editorial assistance with this chapter by Carole F. Nuckton is gratefully acknowledged as are helpful comments and materials from Roger Granados, Hermelinda Rendon, Ann C. Hartfiel, Mike Egan, Aldo Sordi, Tom Haller, and Ron Jones.

It is recognized that employment and training programs alone cannot meet all the needs of farm workers. However, when supplemented with other services (especially health, housing, and income maintenance) such programs can do much to promote their general welfare.

Programs designed to address the problems of the disadvantaged, particularly poverty groups, are dispersed among a wide variety of public agencies, both state and federal, and among private nonprofit groups as well (U.S., Congress, House, *Federal and State Statutes Relating to Farm Workers. . .* , 1976). Farm workers and their families, as part of the disadvantaged population, can benefit from many of these general service and employment programs (Levin; Levitan). Only a few, however, are directed specifically at the farm worker population. Several that are so directed include:

1. Title I of the Elementary and Secondary Education Act of 1965 (P.L. 89-750, 20 U.S.C., 241), administered through the Office of Housing, Department of Health, Education, and Welfare (DHEW), to meet the special educational needs of children of migratory agricultural workers
2. Section 319 of the Public Health Service Act of 1975 (42 U.S.C., 247a), administered by Health, Education, and Welfare (HEW) to provide migrant farm workers with health care
3. Title III, Section 304 of the Rehabilitation Act of 1973 (P.L. 93-112, 29 U.S.C., 770, 774), also administered by HEW, to partially support the vocational rehabilitation of handicapped migratory agricultural workers
4. Section III on farm housing of the Housing Act of 1949 [42 U.S.C., K 1814 (f) (4)], administered by the Department of Housing and Urban Development, to give financial assistance for low-rent housing to groups of farm workers
5. Community Development Corporations funded under Title VII of the Community Services Act of 1974, to provide assistance to small groups of farm workers to establish producer cooperatives

6. Title III, Section 303 of CETA, administered by the USDL to provide training and job placement assistance and services to farm workers (Provisions of Section 303 will be studied in detail later.)

In addition, some seasonal and migratory farm workers are served by the following programs created to serve broad categories of individuals: (1) CETA, Titles I, II, and VI; (2) Cooperative Extension Service, USDA; (3) Rural Development Act of 1972, Title V under USDA; and (4) Farmers Home Administration (FmHA), USDA, under programs for "community development."

The oldest employment and training program that aids both farm workers and others, USES, is administered at the state level and is federally supported by USDL under the regulations of the Wagner-Peyser Act of 1933. Farm labor placement offices administered under USES have played an important role in the history of the nation's agriculture. This aspect of USES will be explored later.

An attempt will now be made to sort out from the myriad of welfare programs those directly aiding in the education, training, and job placement of migrant and seasonal farm workers. Particular emphasis will be given to the USDL farm worker employment and training program (CETA, Title III, Section 303, mentioned above) and to the job placement services under USES, also mentioned above. Services other than these job-related ones provided to seasonal and migrant workers will be given only cursory treatment.

In this paper the following questions are addressed: (1) What target groups of farm workers are covered by employment and service programs? (2) How successful have these programs been in serving their target groups? (3) How well do administrative structures for the delivery of services function? (4) What are the policy recommendations for the improvement of services? (5) What are the urgent research needs in the whole area of farm worker employment and service programs?

THE COMPREHENSIVE EMPLOYMENT AND TRAINING ACT

The purpose of CETA is "to provide training, public service jobs, and other services leading to unsubsidized employment for economically disadvantaged, unemployed, and underemployed persons" (*Employment and Training Report of the President* 1978, p. 39). CETA was signed into law December 28, 1973, to be effective for a period of four years (P.L. 93-203). Since then it has been amended and extended several times: by the Emergency Jobs and Unemployment Assistance Act of 1974, the Emergency Jobs Extension Act of 1976, the Youth Employment and Demonstration Projects Act of 1977, an extension for an additional year in 1977, and reauthorization on October 27, 1978, for another four years (P.L. 95-524).

When enacted in 1973, CETA authorized four major program efforts under four corresponding titles (these were soon expanded to seven titles and the 1978 version of CETA has eight):

1. Title I set up a nationwide program of comprehensive local services including training, employment counseling, and testing.

2. Title II provided a program of transitional public service employment and other services in areas where there was 6.5% or more unemployment for three consecutive months.

3. Title III maintained supervised training, employment, and job placement services for special groups: native Americans, migrant workers, youth offenders, persons of limited English-speaking ability, older workers, and others determined by USDL to have particular disadvantage in the labor market. (Title III was expanded in the 1978 law to include other persons seen as disadvantaged in the labor market: women, single parents, displaced homemakers, individuals lacking educational credentials, and public assistance recipients.)

4. Title IV established the Job Corps for disadvantaged youths.

Thus CETA provides, as a special federal responsibility, funds to operate a broad range of manpower programs. Its funds are distributed to states and local jurisdictions by the USDL through a decentralization process that began in 1973 as part of the Nixon administration's "New Federalism." Part of the government's aim with CETA was to end the fragmentation that had resulted from the centralized categorical programs of the 1960s. It hoped to accomplish this by moving the decision-making power closer to the people. Under the decentralization scheme, state and local "prime sponsors," designated under Title I of the Act, are responsible for assessing local needs and developing program activities to meet these needs through a mix of services. Prime sponsors can arrange to provide services directly or through contracts or subgrants with organizations such as state employment services, vocational education agencies, community groups, and private firms.

Section 303 of Title III, CETA

Migrant and seasonal farm workers are covered exclusively under Section 303 of CETA Title III. Funds for Section 303 were set at 5% of the total amount allocated to state and local prime sponsors under Title I. This part of CETA amounted to a transfer of funding power from the Office of Economic Opportunity (OEO) under the Community Services Administration to USDL. The funding shift reflected a change in policy emphasis as well, from OEO's full range of service offerings--social and manpower--for the entire migrant community, to the USDL's focus on manpower services for a somewhat narrowed target group. Although authorized to provide other services such as health and medical, child care, transportation, emergency, residential support, nutritional, family counseling and planning, and legal assistance, grantees under Section 303 have concentrated on training and employment services. The National Association of Farmworker Organizations (NAFO) has regarded the shift in funding from OEO to USDL and the corresponding shift in policy emphasis as unfortunate indeed (NAFO 1978).

There are two objectives to USDL's efforts under Section 303: (1) the betterment of agricultural employment conditions, by providing the supportive services to improve the well-being of migrants and other seasonal farm workers and their families remaining in agriculture, and (2) the development of alternatives to seasonal agricultural labor, by equipping those who seek alternative employment to compete in other labor markets and to obtain year-round employment providing an income above the poverty level (44 *Federal Register* 30596). Thus there are two distinct groups of people affected--those who want to stay in agriculture and those who seek to move out of it.

Eligibility: Who Is the Target Group of Section 303?

Section 303 is aimed at seasonal or migrant farm workers and their dependents who are identified as disadvantaged with respect to the poverty line defined by the Office of Management and Budget. Only U.S. nationals and aliens legally residing in the United States are included. Illegal aliens are excluded. "Seasonal" by the USDL definition means a person who was employed during the last 24 months for at least 25 days in farm work, in either crops (excluding landscape and horticulture) or livestock (excluding veterinary and animal specialty services), or who earned at least $400 in such farm work and who is employed on a seasonal basis, not having a year-round salary. "Migrant" is a seasonal farm worker who performed farm work during the preceding 24 months such that he/she was unable to return to his/her domicile within the same day (44 *Federal Register* 1665). Thus those doing farm work on a year-round basis are excluded from Section 303 coverage, as are those whose incomes during the 12-month period prior to application exceeded the poverty threshold.

According to an estimate by Rowe and Smith, there were about 169,000 farm workers eligible for Section 303 in 1973, or about 6% of the 2.7 million in the hired farm work force that year.[1]

These workers resided in 122,000 households (1.4 farm workers per household) and had 191,000 persons under 18 years of age in their households (1.6 per household) who were also eligible for the program. According to Rowe and Smith, approximately 14,000 (8%) of the eligible farm workers lived in migratory households that contained, in aggregate, about an equal number of dependents (14,000) under 18 years of age. Forty-seven percent of the eligible farm workers were white, 17% Spanish-American, and 36% black and other.

Another idea of the composition of program recipients can be formed from data provided to the author in 1976 by Pierce A. Quinlan, former USDL administrator of CETA. In 1975, all USDL farm worker programs served 272,900 participants, 57% of whom were male (43% female). Over 50% were under 22 years of age, 36% between 22 and 44, 14% over 45. Sixty-seven percent had 8 or fewer years of schooling, 20.5% had 9-11 years, 10.5% had completed 12 years, and 2.1% had more than 12 years of schooling. About one-third were blacks; another third, Spanish-Americans. These data, however, are describing a population broader than that covered by Section 303; neither more recent data nor data fitting Section 303 participants more precisely are available.

Funding and Service Deliverers under Section 303

Federal funds under Section 303 amount to about $70 million a year, with a high of $75.9 million in 1978 (see Table 13.1). The number of grantees ranges from 34 to 62, with the actual number of grants averaging about 90 a year. California is the top recipient, being allocated $14.9 million in fiscal year 1980; Florida and Texas rank second and third, respectively (see Table 13.2). Together these three states capture 36% of the funds, but these are the states with the greatest numbers of seasonal and migrant workers.

Grants to operate programs for seasonal and migrant farm workers are awarded by USDL on a competitive bidding basis to public and private organizations. Public organizations (Title I prime sponsors) are eligible to compete if there is a significant number of seasonal or migrant workers in their jurisdictions; private nonprofit groups must have charters or acts of incorporation authorizing them to operate

Table 13.1. Number of sponsors and funding levels for Title III programs for migrant and seasonal farm workers, CETA, fiscal years 1974-1980

Fiscal year ending in	Number of sponsors[a]	Funding level (millions of dollars)
1974	b	42.5[c]
1975	50[d]	63.2[d]
1976	62	63.2[e]
1977	54	65.8
1978	34	75.9
1979	60	65.0
1980	53	69.8

Source: USDL, Annual Reports, 1974, 1975, 1976 and Table 13.2.

[a]Sponsors or grantees selected through a competitive bidding process. The program year established for migrant and seasonal farm worker programs begins on January 1 and ends on December 31. The actual number of grants awarded under Section 303 is about 90 in each year, going to Title I sponsors, nonprofit farm worker organizations, and universities.

[b]Information not available.

[c]Fiscal Year 1974 represented the first year that the USDL assumed responsibility for OEO farm worker programs. This figure represents the OEO allocation handled by the USDL.

[d]In September 1974, 174 Title I prime sponsors and private groups had submitted qualification statements for programs in 49 jurisdictions. Of these some 90 applicants were identified as qualified to submit funding reports, and more than 50 were designated as grantees by the end of the calendar year.

[e]According to the 1975 USDL Annual Report, 20% of the total $63.2 million was "set aside for discretionary use by the Secretary of Labor for national programs, including the High School Equivalency and College Assistance Migrant Programs, for permanent farm worker housing projects, for experimental projects, and for efforts to meet emergency situations or special needs arising from changing farm technology." The remaining $50.6 million has been allocated for programs in states according to a formula based on each state's proportion of the nation's total man months of farm labor.

manpower programs for the Section 303 target population. Funding requests are evaluated by a panel of USDL officials who rate the bids by assigning a range of possible points in the following six different categories:

1. Program development: training, services and program impact	0-20
2. Delivery system	0-20
3. Administrative capability	0-15
4. Responsiveness to farm workers (including involvement of farm-worker boards and advisory councils)	0-15

Table 13.2. CETA, Title III-Section 303 funding levels in dollars by states, fiscal years, 1977-1980

Region Major states	(1) FY[a] 1977	(2) FY 1978	(3) FY 1979	(4) FY 1980
Region I	1,267,900	1,445,200	1,651,300	1,825,000
Connecticut	261,900	235,700	429,900	550,000[b]
Maine	255,600	301,500	552,800	536,700[b]
Massachusetts	364,300	408,700	355,900	364,400[b]
New Hampshire	62,800	83,200	0	106,000[c]
Rhode Island	45,000	40,500	51,500	32,900[b]
Vermont	278,300	375,600	261,200	235,000[c]
Region II	4,081,500	4,521,000	2,047,100	3,605,400
New Jersey	469,800	450,800	700,200	630,200[b]
New York	1,483,200	1,981,700	1,373,900	1,351,800
Puerto Rico	2,128,500	2,088,500	1,699,100	1,623,400[b]
Region III	3,557,100	4,871,400	3,810,200	3,478,100
Delaware	90,000	81,000	72,900	132,500
Maryland	526,700	678,800	465,400	418,900
Pennsylvania	1,626,400	2,027,000	1,634,500	1,471,100
Virginia	1,132,500	1,571,600	1,167,800	1,051,000
West Virginia	181,500	513,000	469,600	404,600
Region IV	14,179,100	14,409,800	13,442,040	13,947,700
Alabama	972,900	1,213,800	870,040	861,400
Florida	3,459,600	3,113,600	4,014,600	5,208,300
Georgia	1,409,500	1,833,700	1,324,400	1,192,000
Kentucky	982,400	1,174,700	999,200	899,300
Mississippi	1,017,900	916,100	1,085,200	1,153,000
North Carolina	4,311,900	3,880,700	3,492,600	3,143,300
South Carolina	1,256,700	1,445,400	926,300	833,700
Tennessee	786,200	813,800	729,700	656,700
Region V	9,289,100	11,991,700	8,872,400	8,712,400
Illinois	1,477,700	1,985,500	1,876,200	1,688,600
Indiana	1,188,400	1,572,800	1,087,300	978,600[c]
Michigan	1,200,700	1,544,600	1,191,800	1,444,500
Minnesota	1,799,700	2,321,500	1,592,000	1,451,200
Ohio	1,424,500	1,726,200	1,175,500	1,384,900
Wisconsin	2,198,100	2,841,100	1,949,600	1,764,600[b]
Region VI	8,560,200	7,965,800	7,879,392	8,129,500
Arkansas	1,017,900	916,100	1,126,600	1,153,000
Louisiana	761,400	685,300	1,028,100	925,300
New Mexico	729,000	656,100	590,492	531,500[b]
Oklahoma	537,600	745,400	667,600	649,400
Texas	5,514,300	4,962,900	4,466,600	4,870,300
Region VII	4,603,700	6,187,500	4,931,500	4,600,300
Iowa	1,765,600	2,475,600	1,741,000	1,566,900
Kansas	810,500	1,103,800	1,130,600	1,179,500
Missouri	1,219,800	1,548,200	1,056,200	950,600
Nebraska	807,800	1,059,900	1,003,700	903,300
Region VIII	2,789,200	2,859,200	3,001,500	3,289,900
Colorado	767,700	690,900	732,800	947,600[b]
Montana	436,300	453,300	659,400	636,100
North Dakota	294,300	264,900	503,900	609,600[b]
South Dakota	660,400	800,300	499,600	449,600
Utah	372,600	335,300	331,400	351,200
Wyoming	257,900	314,500	274,400	304,800

Table 13.2. (Continued)

Region Major states	(1) FY[a] 1977	(2) FY 1978	(3) FY 1979	(4) FY 1980
Region IX	13,811,500	17,056,300	13,215,400	16,841,500
Arizona	1,035,000	913,500	909,300	1,570,400
California	12,325,100	15,697,200	11,908,500	14,896,000
Hawaii	360,000	324,000	291,600	262,400
Nevada	91,400	121,600	106,000	112,700
Region X	3,580,300	4,558,100	4,452,100	5,393,800
Idaho	708,100	967,200	1,052,600	1,186,100[b]
Oregon	1,114,800	1,375,800	1,081,100	1,517,400
Washington	1,757,400	2,215,100	2,318,400	2,690,300[b]
Total	65,719,900	75,920,000[d]	65,029,492	69,836,000

Source: USDL news reports issued by the Office of Information: Apr. 11, 1978; Feb. 6, 1979; Mar. 7, 1979; Sept. 14, 1979.

[a]FY refers to Fiscal Year ending in the year indicated.

[b]Approximate allocation on a "conditional basis" as of Sept. 14, 1979.

[c]Approximate allocation pending clarification of application from that state, Sept. 9, 1979.

[d]The FY 1978 allocation was $63,920,000 plus $12 million from FY 1977 made available to FY 1978 program operators as the result of a court decision.

5. Linkages and coordination--that is, demonstrated and documented ties with appropriate state and local entities 0-5

6. Review of program experience, including effectiveness and degree to which the organization has operated a comprehensive and multiactivity program for farm workers 0-25

The rating procedure gives considerable weight to the organization's previous experience in employment training and has been criticized by the NAFO as being inhibitive in the supportive services area (NAFO 1978).

In addition to being judged by the USDL rating procedure, grantees must be cleared by the USDL's Office of Inspector General of possible fraud and abuse. The rules and regulations pertaining to Section 303 also state that:

> In the event that no Funding Requests are received for a specific state or area or that

> those received are deemed to be unacceptable, or where a grant agreement is not successfully negotiated, the Department reserves the right to invite one or more organizations to submit a proposal for that state or area. In the event of a second invitation, funds may be awarded at the discretion of the Department. (44 *Federal Register* 30601)

Thus the USDL has considerable authority in determining the allocation of grants, the qualifications of potential grantees, and the ultimate content of CETA, Title III, Section 303 programs. Furthermore, it is possible for grantees to assume responsibility for Section 303 programs in more than one area of a state and even in more than one state of the nation (see Table 13.3).

Overall, it is not known whether competitive bidding results in better service to the target population--more people trained and placed--but it is thought that the year-to-year bidding process makes the programs somewhat tentative. Grantees are required to devote considerable time and expense to preparing proposals just to preserve their territory; attention is diverted from program content and the dependability of the services offered is reduced. No solid network of farm worker training and employment centers lasting from one year to the next can possibly be developed under the present system.

Another problem with the competitive bidding system is that it has resulted in increased concentration of funds--that is, fewer grantees. In California such consolidation of funds has reduced the number of programs from eight in fiscal year 1979 to only four in 1980.[2] The largest program in the state is the California (formerly North Bay) Human Development Corporation, which covers all of Northern California, including Center for Employment Training, San Jose (CET), and Oregon. Similar consolidation has occurred in the case of Migrant and Seasonal Farmworkers in North Carolina (see Table 13.3).

Table 13.3. CETA, Title III-Section 303 grantees selected on a competitive basis to cover farm workers in more than one state, fiscal years 1979 and 1980 (in dollars)

		FY 1979	FY 1980
1. New England Farmworkers' Council, Springfield, MA			
Massachusetts		355,900	364,400
Connecticut		429,900	550,000
Rhode Island		51,500	32,900
Vermont		261,200	Decision Deferred (Possible[a])
	Total	1,098,500	947,300
2. Migrant and Seasonal Farmworkers, Raleigh, NC			
North Carolina		3,492,600	3,143,300
Delaware		72,900	132,500
Georgia		1,324,400	1,192,000
Maryland		465,400	418,900
Virginia		1,167,800	1,051,000
West Virginia		0	404,600[b]
South Carolina		0	833,700[b]
	Total	6,523,100	7,176,000
3. ORO Development Corporation, Oklahoma City, OK			
Oklahoma		667,600	649,400
Kansas		1,130,600	0[a]
	Total	1,798,200	649,400
4. Tennessee Opportunity Program for Seasonal Farmworkers, Nashville, TN			
Tennessee		729,700	656,700
Kentucky		999,200	899,300
	Total	1,728,900	1,556,000
5. CET-Center for Employment Training, San Jose, CA			
California		1,543,388	c
Nevada		106,000	112,700
	Total	1,649,388	c
6. California Human Development Corporation, Windsor, CA			
California		2,475,100	c
Oregon		1,081,100	1,517,400
	Total	3,556,200	c
7. Migrant Action Program, Des Moines, IA			
Iowa		1,741,000	(Allocation to Proteus, CA)
Nebraska		1,003,700	0[a]
	Total	2,744,700	0

Table 13.3. (Continued)

		FY 1979	FY 1980
8. Rural New York Opportunities, Rochester, NY			
New York		1,373,900	1,351,800
Pennsylvania		1,634,500	1,471,100
	Total	3,008,400	2,822,900
9. Minnesota Migrant Council, St. Cloud, MN			
Minnesota		1,592,000	1,451,200
South Dakota		499,600	449,600
	Total	2,091,600	1,900,800
10. Proteus Adult Training, Visalia, CA			
California		4,430,600	c
Iowa		0	1,566,900[b]
	Total	4,430,600	c

Source: USDL news releases.
[a]Funding allocated to organization within own state.
[b]New addition.
[c]Exact amount unknown by authors. The amount includes part of the $14,896,000 that went to four California grantees in FY 1980, including: Central Coast Counties Development Corporation (which received $1,316,800 in FY 1979), California Human Development Corporation ($2,475,100 in FY 1979), Center for Employment Training of the Central Coast Counties ($1,543,388 in FY 1979), and Proteus Adult Training ($4,430,600 in FY 1979).

Program Content and Outcome: The Results So Far

Section 303 program regulations have been written with the recognition that seasonal and migratory farm workers and families are a heterogeneous group and therefore face a broad range of problems. Accordingly, Section 303 programs are usually designed to provide clients with job training.[3] But it also provides some of the following types of services: outreach; intake (i.e., screening and assessment of individuals); orientation, counseling, and employment-related testing; placement and supportive services related to non-303 funded training; job development; job placement; follow-up; health and medical services; child care; transportation; emergency assistance; relocation assistance; residential support; nutritional services; assistance in securing bonds; family counseling; family planning services on a voluntary basis; legal and paralegal services; postplacement service.

How well have CETA, Title III, Section 303 programs performed? Who are the beneficiaries in terms of both grantees and program participants? What is the impact of CETA participation on postprogram earnings and employment?

It should be noted at the outset that evaluations of USDL program outcomes are limited to information published in a few references, including: the USDL's *Employment and Training Report of the President*, issued annually; ad hoc evaluative studies sponsored by the USDL and conducted by traditional USDL consultant firms, a few private reports by groups like NAFO; and the annual reports from USDL sponsors or grantees.[4] Most of these sources merely report on the general nature of services offered and the number and socioeconomic characteristics of participants who terminate (leave the program for any reason), including those placed (leave the program for unsubsidized jobs). There are no uniform standards for grantees to follow in their annual reports. Since programs vary considerably from one another in the level and mix of services offered, it has been hard to come up with an overall evaluation of Section 303. Further, there are no nonparticipant "control" groups with which to compare program participants. Follow-up checks on worker success have been lacking and there has been little feedback from placed workers. It is difficult, therefore, to relate program content to actual changes in the welfare of farm workers and their families.

Notwithstanding the data limitations, the effectiveness of Section 303 programs has been assessed from two different approaches. One is a comparison of preprogram and postprogram employment, earnings, and other socioeconomic and labor market trends over time. The other is an assessment of the magnitude and dimensions of Section 303 support relative to the needs of all farm workers, not just those participating in CETA programs.

Preprogram and Postprogram Comparison

A recent attempt to assess Section 303 by comparing preprogram and postprogram indicators has been made by Kirschner Associates (1979) in their study of a group of participants over time. An initial assessment was made in 1975 by personal interviews with 2078 persons being served under Section 303, a sample selected from among 15 of the 36 projects previously administered by OEO. Socioeconomic characteristics of the group are given in Table 13.4. Over 92% of the trainees interviewed were either black or of Spanish origin; placement percentages were considerably better for blacks (nearly 70% of placements interviewed).

Two and one-half years later an attempt was made to reinterview the group, and 941 of them were successfully traced. Changes that had occurred in labor force variables over the period are shown in Table 13.5. The unemployment rate was down; real earnings were up. The proportion of time spent in farm work was down, as was the proportion of persons employed in farm work. Job stability increased substantially as shown by the 55-week increase in the average length of time a job is held.

Three-fourths of the people interviewed expressed positive reactions to the program, particularly those who received a combination of education, training, placement, and support services. Least favorable

Table 13.4. CETA-Section 303, migrant and seasonal farm worker participant characteristics, selected by stratum, 1975

	Stratum			
Characteristic	Trainees	Placements	EFMS[a]	Misc.
Number interviewed	1328	354	140	256
25 years of age or under, %	68.0	62.1	23.5	39.6
Male, %	45.9	47.5	60.7	46.9
Head of household, %	47.7	38.2	73.6	57.4
No children, %	49.0	47.3	25.9	21.2
Mean years of education	9.9	10.1	5.3	8.4
Buying or owning present home, %	38.5	41.1	25.0	33.9
Single family dwelling for present home, %	71.7	84.7	54.7	76.5
Mean number of facilities (out of 7)	6.0	5.4	4.9	6.2
Mean rooms per capita	1.25	1.16	0.84	1.08
Spanish origin, %	48.3	22.0	78.2	78.7
Black, %	43.9	69.9	12.8	13.3

Source: Kirschner Associates, 1979.
[a]Emergency Food and Medical Services.

Table 13.5. Pre-program/post-program changes in labor force variables of persons who received USDL employment and training services, 1975 to 1977/78

Labor force variables	1975	1977/78	Change
	n=2,078	n=941	
1. Average unemployment rate, %	30.2	19.6	-10.6
2. Proportion of working time spent in farm work, %	42.3	10.5	-31.8
3. Proportion of participants who held farm work jobs, %	39.9	14.0	-25.9
4. Average length of jobs held, weeks	17	72	+55
5. Average weekly job earnings, 1975 dollars	87.00	122.00	+35.00
A. Nonfarm work only	88.96	118.60	+29.64
B. Some farm work, some nonfarm work	84.84	116.26	+31.42
C. Farm work only	84.15	113.31	+47.16

Source: Kirschner Associates, 1979.

reactions were from those who had been only in adult basic education courses. Many of these would be functionally illiterate, of limited English-speaking ability, and in need of intensive prevocational and vocational training to succeed in the labor market.

The study indicated that Section 303 programs had been successful in facilitating job mobility and that a significant proportion of participants were making a shift from farm to nonfarm work, as is shown in the following summary statistics: 63% of persons who had only farm work jobs in 1975 had nonfarm jobs in 1977/78; 76% who did both farm and nonfarm work in 1975 did nonfarm work exclusively in 1977/78; 89% of those who were unemployed in 1975 were employed in nonfarm work in 1977/78; only about 10% of the persons interviewed in 1977/78 were employed in agriculture, another 10% did both farm and nonfarm work.

Substantial changes, then, had occurred in this group over the two and one-half year period, but it is not possible to determine to what extent these changes were wrought by Section 303 participation. Furthermore, there is considerable bias built into the statistics, since the 941 who were located to be reinterviewed were presumably the most successful program participants. The Kirschner Associates report (1979) notes that the recovery rate of respondents (from 2078 in 1975 to 941 in 1977) was lower than anticipated due to the time lag and high mobility of the farm workers. The authors note that highly mobile migrant farm workers are probably underrepresented in the second survey. To quote: "To the extent that these persons were not located because they have retained those characteristics, the findings of the study are biased, to an unknown degree, toward showing favorable program results in terms of participants moving from agriculture to nonagriculture jobs." (p. 120)

CETA and Farm Workers in General

The second approach to assessing CETA has been to compare CETA coverage with the set of employment and training problems facing all farm workers in general. In short, is CETA meeting the needs of farm workers in the United States? To answer this question analytically, an acceptable definition of farm workers is needed. Unfortunately, none exists. Without an acceptable definition denoting precisely who is meant by "farm workers," any program serving farm workers is bound to be criticized as being either too narrow and concentrated or too broad and thin in coverage.

In this regard, Rural America and the NAFO have asserted that Section 303 excludes five-sixths of the target population formerly covered by OEO. Rural America asks, in the title of Research Report No. 1 (1977), *Where Have All the Farm Workers Gone?* The rest of the title continues: *The statistical annihilation of migrant and seasonal farm workers by Federal Agencies*. Those who work for farmers raising fur-bearing animals and rabbits and those employed in landscaping and horticultural crops are defined out of coverage, as are full-time students, who represent about 26% of the seasonal workforce. Much more important than these eliminations is the fact that those employed by labor crew leaders are not counted. The narrowed coverage may be a legitimate concern, but a more pertinent point is that only a small proportion of the *existing* Section 303 target population is actually being served. Opening the doors to many more people may not solve this problem.

Besides voicing their complaint about the shift of emphasis from general services (under the OEO) to a focus on manpower, NAFO pointed out a serious limitation of CETA, Title III, Section 303. Former programs under OEO allowed an 18-month settle-out period between the last agricultural job and the application date for the program. The USDL reduced the maximum settle-out period to only six months. Now a worker who takes a nonfarm job, perhaps on a temporary basis, will lose his program eligibility in only six months rather than the previous longer period.

Other Services under CETA, Title III, Section 303: Legal Assistance, High School Equivalency, and College Training Programs

It is reported in the USDL 1978 and 1979 annual reports that $36 million was awarded to sponsoring organizations under the Farmworker Economic Stimulus Program. The mandate and evolution of this program are unknown to the author, but the 1978 USDL annual report listed the following activities: "Residential skill training, employment and training coordinated with rural economic development, rehabilitation and weatherization of farm worker-owned housing. These activities were expected to generate about 8,000 jobs for farm workers." Certainly a clearer statement and assessment of this aspect of Section 303 is warranted, especially considering that the $36 million represents over half of the total 303 funding.

As protective labor laws and regulations for farm workers have increased, so has their need for legal assistance to rectify violations of the new coverage. Some legal services have been provided for seasonal and migrant farm workers through general rural legal assistance to disadvantaged groups under the former Economic Opportunity Act of 1964 and later the Headstart, Economic Opportunity, and Community Partnership Act of 1974. The funding, however, has been meager. A report to the Legal Services Corporation (Lillesand et al.) revealed that the $1.2 million designated in 1977 for legal assistance to migrants amounted to less than $1.50 per person for a target population of some 830,000. In addition to appealing for more adequate funding, the authors of the report recommended that there be a legal staff experienced in farm worker problems. Such a staff should be somewhat mobile to better serve transient workers. Ex-migrants might be hired as part of the staff, or farm worker advisory committees established. Better coordination with the migrants' home-base states is needed. It is particularly important that legal information be made accessible to farm workers and that they be educated in how to use available legal services.

Some of the gap between farm workers' need for legal assistance and the actual services offered may be (is being) closed by Section 303 funds. The extent of CETA efforts in this area, however, is not known to the author at this time.

Since 1975, Section 303 funds have been set aside for use by the secretary of labor for other national farm worker programs including the High School Equivalency Program (HEP), College Assistance Migrant Programs (CAMP), permanent farm worker housing, certain experimental projects, and efforts to meet emergency situations or special needs arising from changing technology in agriculture.

In 1977, 18 colleges and universities were awarded grants totalling $5.7 million to educate Section 303 eligibles through HEP and CAMP. In 1980 (September 1979-August 1980), 16 colleges received grants totalling $6.8 million. Participants in HEP reside on campus where they are helped to pass the General Educational Development Test. The high school equivalency diploma enables the recipient to compete more favorably in the nonfarm job market and qualifies the person for further education. Higher education is made more available to migrant and seasonal farm workers and their families through CAMP, which offers tuition assistance, tutoring, and counseling. These innovative programs enroll about 2,500 to 3,000 persons a year.

The Question of Federal Decentralization

While most CETA programs are decentralized to state and local jurisdictions, the Employment and Training Administration of the USDL is authorized to administer programs of Title III at the national level. (For an early review of the CETA decentralization issue, see Snedeker and Snedeker.) National level administration was thought necessary because the work and travel patterns of migrants are not limited to government-designated local boundaries, and local agencies may not recognize migratory workers as part of their constituency. However, USDL has expressed an interest in decentralizing the control of Title III programs since the enactment of CETA. The 1978 amendment, however, continued the national emphasis: "Because of the special nature of the problem faced by migrant and seasonal farm workers, the program developed and implemented under this section [303] of the Act shall be administered by the Employment and Training Administration at the national level" (*Federal Register* May 25, 1979, p. 30595). Pierce Quinlan, then Director of CETA programs, said: "Within three years, all 303 programs will be in the hands of state government" (NAFO 1978, p. 108). Further, deletion of Section 303 (a) (2), which addresses the special need for national administration of farm worker programs, was seriously considered in the discussion of the administration's 1978 bill.

Standard arguments against maintaining centralized support programs for migrant and seasonal farm workers include the charge that centralization results in serious deficiencies in the following areas (National Academy of Sciences):

1. Local input for the development of priorities and goals
2. Flexibility for tailoring programs to meet local needs and conditions
3. Coordination of program operation; poor coordination results in inefficient management, fragmented delivery systems, overlapping services, and conflicting policies and regulations

4. Adequacy of the assessment of the overall effectiveness or impact of federally funded manpower efforts

While there is some agreement that decentralized CETA systems other than Title III are to a large degree working effectively (National Academy of Sciences), there are several arguments against decentralizing migrant and farm worker programs (NAFO):

1. Since farm worker problems transcend local boundaries, a broader focal point is needed for identifying general needs, defining goals, and coordinating programs.
2. If politicization of local boards takes place, locally based programs may face a reduction in their role of farm worker advocates, since the staff may find itself caught between the political persuasion of local public bodies and the continuing needs of farm workers.
3. When the characteristics and needs of the farm worker population are substantially different from those of the populations certain local prime sponsors are accustomed to serving, a widespread shift to local sponsorship could mean a decreased capability for serving farm workers.

The heart of the centralization-decentralization issue is differing accountability for decision making among alternative plans, programs, and places. Can congruence between national policies and local prime sponsor practices be achieved? Can institutional networks traditionally providing farm worker training and employment programs nationally be maintained under decentralization? Would CETA programs accommodate local political purposes rather than improve the employability of farm workers? Most importantly, would the interests of farm workers be better served by centralized or decentralized CETA, Title III, Section 303 programs?

Further Comments on CETA, Title III, Section 303

In conclusion, it can be said that while some migrant and seasonal workers have been assisted significantly by Section 303 provisions, allocations have in general been spread too thinly across the nation. There has been a high turnover of program offerings and a lack of depth. By the time a program is set up and implemented, there are often insufficient operating funds left with which to provide the needed services. A firmer participation in training programs by private employers would be of considerable help in promoting the success of Section 303.

In response to the criticism that Section 303 is short on social services while emphasizing manpower services, it can be asked: Should Section 303 take on the welfare role in addition to its training and employment functions? Were such additional services offered, farm workers might be given the wrong incentive to join what is now basically an employment program.

While the intent has been to prepare workers for unsubsidized positions, only a small portion of participants have been so placed. Rather, Section 303 has something of a reputation for buying jobs for workers, thereby providing cheap labor for certain employers. Such placements do not merit the respect of either worker or employer.

Section 303 has had a pronounced emphasis on nonfarm work. The reason for this may be that more or better opportunities are recognized off the farm, Grantees might do well to establish better relations with farm employers and to give more attention to developing careers in farming for Section 303 participants.

Another direction Section 303 training efforts might take would be to explore the possibilities for converting farm workers into farmers. Such a transition has been taking place in California with remarkable success (Hartfiel). In particular, a production cooperative movement which started in about 1971 has enabled more than 300 former farm workers and their families, mostly of Mexican descent, to enter farming as self-employed entrepreneurs. As cooperative members, these former migrant and seasonal workers have been able to pool their resources, secure bank loans, acquire land, and jointly cultivate labor-intensive crops (mainly strawberries and vegetables) that utilize the labor of the entire family. During the 1970s the OEO, USDA, and the state CETA office supported production cooperatives with technical assistance. Today in California there is a confederation of 12 member cooperatives, all legally incorporated.

From July 1976 through August 1977, a peer training project, *Tecnica*, was supported by a CETA grant from the California governor's discretionary fund. This project illustrates that successful production cooperative members (former farm workers) can transmit information on farm management, production techniques, and cooperative organization to their peers so that the peer group can subsequently achieve success in an independent cooperative farming venture. It could be that Section 303 funds would benefit more farm workers if greater emphasis were placed on the farm production cooperative possibility.

THE USES

The largest and oldest delivery system for labor market services is USDL's USES, with origins dating back to World War I. It was formally established in 1933 by the Wagner-Peyser Act (for details see USDL 1977 annual report, pp. 1-87). The mission of the USES as set forth in the act was the establishment of a national system of employment offices for men, women, and juniors. Singled out for special services were the handicapped and veterans; also specifically mentioned was "the maintenance of a farm placement service." Since 1933, the role of the USES has been modified and expanded several times, until today it is a $2 billion operation. In addition to its Wagner-Peyser Commission, USES administers 22 other laws, 17 executive orders, and 14 agreements. Special duties to target groups have been spelled out, and among them are services to seasonal and migrant farm workers. Under the USES's unique federal-state structure--federal funds, state administration--services to such target groups vary from state to state. The USES also has a role in the admission of temporary alien workers. The USDL is required by the Immigration and Naturalization Service to give advisory opinions on the availability of resident workers for jobs being offered to aliens and on the adequacy of wages and working conditions. The employment of aliens in agriculture (such as braceros) is noteworthy but is discussed elsewhere in this volume.

The USES farm labor offices have not been widely used by either employers or by workers, at least in California. In 1966 only 9% of seasonal workers interviewed in the Sacramento Valley had obtained their jobs through such an office (Sosnick). A 1978 survey revealed that only 15% of 584 California farm worker respondents ever obtained jobs through California's USES office, the Employment Development Department (California Commission on the Status of Women 1978). While another survey, conducted in the summer of 1979 by the Rural Economics Institute, found that 109 farm workers out of 250 reported receiving services from the USES, 95% of these respondents indicated that their connection was only in the receipt of unemployment insurance payments (Haller).

In his recent book, Sosnick explores the reasons for such limited use of the state's USES by both growers and farm workers. Growers do not list jobs because they generally expect unsatisfactory referrals; they worry about whether referred workers would fulfill their midseason commitments. Many growers, partly because they are unsure about the timing of their production, prefer to recruit on their own.

Many workers too fail to use the service, preferring to locate jobs by themselves. Applying at a farm placement office is somewhat burdensome, and many offices do not have a Spanish-speaking staff person for their non-English-speaking potential clientele. Farm placement offices do not have information on nonfarm jobs and have only incomplete information on farm jobs (since so many farm employers do not use the service), so workers realize that office listings may not include the most desirable openings in the area. Most serious of all is the general distrust of farm placement offices among the workers. Rightly or wrongly, they are regarded as handmaidens to the growers.

Some of these same points were made in testimony in 1971 before the Senate Subcommittee Hearings on Migrant and Seasonal Farm Worker Powerlessness and in the public complaint against USDL filed in 1972 in the U.S. District Court by California Rural Legal Assistance, Migrant Legal Action Program, the NAACP, Western Region et al.--a total of 16 organizations and 398 individuals. The USES, intending to provide equity of access to manpower services to both farm and nonfarm groups in rural areas, created the Rural Manpower Service in 1971. At that time many state USES agencies changed titles from Farm Placement or Farm Labor Office to Rural Manpower or Employment Development Office, but this has been regarded by many as a change in name only. The suit charged the USDL with "bureaucratic malfeasance" and the USES state offices of being "grower staffed and oriented," serving farmers' seasonal needs and failing to provide equal treatment to migrants (NAACP, *Western Region et al.* v. *Brennan et al.* 1972).

In response, Assistant Secretary of Labor Hodgson ordered a special review of the Rural Manpower Service (USDL, Manpower Administration, 1972). The review committee found that the USES was indeed primarily responsive to employer needs, partly because farm workers lack the organized economic and political power needed for self-assertion. The charge was that even when the employment agency performed perfectly according to its own procedures, it erred in favor of the employer and to the detriment of the worker. Further, field offices were said to practice race and sex discrimination in making referrals, especially those made to crew leaders, and to help employers discriminate against domestics in favor of aliens

(Marshall, p. 103). Foreign workers were said to be preferred because they would work for less and could be "kept in line" by threats of repatriation. It was found that farm workers were reluctant to press charges of discrimination, out of fear of eviction from housing or even the loss of their jobs. Language barriers were seen to add to farm workers' problems, for few agency staff members are bilingual; many were considered insensitive to farm worker complaints.

The secretary's review committee also found that very few referrals were to permanent or off-farm positions--of 266 jobs orders, only 9% were to permanent jobs; 38% were for jobs lasting only a few hours or a few days. The lack of cooperation between farm and nonfarm placement offices created an impediment to farm workers' finding out about nonfarm job opportunities.

According to the committee's review, many well-documented violations of laws and regulations covering farm workers went uncorrected: abuses in social security payments, minimum wage and child labor laws, and regulations under the FLCRA of 1963. Many workers were referred to farms that provided substandard housing, contrary to USDL's housing regulations of 1967.

In response to the review, Assistant Secretary of Labor Hodgson set up a 13-point program of reform, sending guidelines and a mandate to each state and requesting signatures of compliance. In May 1973, U.S. District Court Judge Richey issued a declaratory judgment regarding the alleged discrimination and unlawful practices against migrant and seasonal workers by the USDL and state USES services. The USDL was directed to implement the 13 point program and to establish an effective complaint and monitoring system as well as sanctions and remedial measures to ensure the USES agencies' compliance with the 13 point program. Then in August 1974, having denied the USDL's request to dismiss the 1972 public complaint, Judge Richey signed a consent order, negotiated by the parties of the suit, requiring the USDL officials to take a number of specific actions to provide equitable services, benefits, and protections to migrant and seasonal farm workers. The court order, named after Judge Richey, took precedence over the original 13 points and remained in effect until 1980.

The Judge Richey Order

The court order, first of all, spelled out the provision of services to migrant and seasonal farm workers that are to be qualitatively equivalent and quantitatively proportionate to those provided to nonfarm workers. Job order information is to be extended to both urban and rural areas on a nondiscriminatory basis, and on each job order sufficient information must be given to ensure compliance with minimum wage, child labor, social security, health and safety, and farm labor contractor registration laws. Services must be tailored to the special needs of migrant and seasonal farm workers, including communication assistance for non-English-speaking clients. Uniform application forms must be completed by each job applicant utilizing any USES office; assistance must be provided to those with language difficulties. Employers and crew leaders must comply with all federal and state labor laws; any violations must be referred to appropriate enforcement officials for expedient action.

The court order established an information system to ensure that urban and rural USES offices in the same service area have access to all work orders in the area. Also, information on the availability and operation of the complaint system must be provided to migrant and seasonal farm workers. Complaints must be followed up and unresolved complaints reviewed by a federal monitor/advocate designee. The monitoring system setup also provided assurance of the compliance of state USES officials with all applicable laws, regulations, and directives by means of on-site reviews on a regular basis. Actions necessary to correct instances of noncompliance were to be taken: decertification proceedings under the Wagner-Peyser Act could be initiated or fiscal restraints imposed.

Finally, the court order set up a special review

committee composed of three members representing migrant and seasonal farm workers, selected by the plaintiffs, three members selected by the defendants, and a seventh member selected by the foregoing six, to serve as chair. The committee was given the responsibility to review the USDL's implementation of and compliance with the court order.

Evaluation of the USES under the Judge Richey Court Order

Very few evaluative studies have been done to determine the effectiveness of the court order in ameliorating the conditions that gave rise to the original complaint. The limited evaluative information that is available reveals a mixed assessment--that is, there are some positive and some negative findings.

Marshall noted that some corrective action must have been taken, for on-site reviews of 53 offices in 15 states, conducted between July and September 1973, revealed no "substantial" difference between "the level of service provided to rural and urban workers or between farm workers and other workers." Further, the reviews did not "surface any pattern of discrimination in service given minority applicants" (p. 106).

Recent reports from the Employment and Training Administration indicate that more migrant and seasonal farm workers are being served than ever before. According to the 1979 USDL annual report, nearly 82,000 migrant and seasonal farm workers were placed during the fiscal year ending in 1978, or about 47% of the 173,000 registered with the job service that year. In addition, 12,000 were counseled, 3,000 were tested, and 36,000 were referred to other agencies for supportive services (*Employment and Training Report of the President* 1979). These figures indicate that migrant and seasonal farm workers received a proportionately greater share of these services than did other applicants. Similarly, five USDL job-service indicators showed that, statistically, service to this group significantly exceeded equity with other applicants.

A follow-up study on the Judge Richey Order with respect to one aspect of the USES--the effectiveness of the USES's comprehensive employment scheduling plan in serving migrant workers--was contracted by the USDL to Kirschner Associates in 1975. The service under review was the Annual Worker Plan (AWP), begun in 1954, now known as the Rural Manpower Mobility Plan (RMMP). (For a good summary of problems with the plan, see Abt and Associates, 1971.) AWP was designed to coordinate the supply of and demand for migrant labor. The USES agencies in the supply states determine the number of workers available; agencies in the demand states, the number and location of jobs. From this information, itineraries are prepared for migrating crews and families (Marshall, p. 54).

The Kirschner report (1976) was based primarily on interview data collected in the spring of 1976 by a subcontractor, Management Consultants Unlimited, among 839 migrant farm workers covered by itineraries filed in 1975 as AWPs (using USES form MA7-85). All respondents were members of migrant families or home-based crews in Texas or Florida. Nearly all Texas-based respondents were Chicanos (99% of 435). Thirty-seven percent of Florida-based respondents were Chicanos; most were blacks. On the average, the farm workers were 36 years old, had worked on farms for about 18 years, and had completed about 6 years of schooling. In addition, 69 interviews were conducted with migrant crew leaders (farm labor contractors), and other information was obtained informally through discussion with USES state officials in Texas and Florida.

Based on these data, it was concluded that AWP (now RMMP) had been ineffectual in serving its target population. Ninety percent of the 839 respondents reported that they had never heard of the program (in spite of their being listed on USES forms MA7-85). Only 5 of the surveyed farm workers and 7 of the 69 crew leaders were aware that they were covered by AWP in 1975. However, those who knew their coverage did credit AWP with finding farm jobs faster and with finding jobs with better wages, housing, and working conditions than might have been the case without the plan. It was also true that about one-fifth followed an itinerary that did not differ substantially from the one listed on their MA7-85.

One of the biggest problems with AWP (or RMMP) is that farm workers spend most of their time in their home state, where they experience the greatest employment difficulties. Many seem to be able to prepare out-of-state employment schedules outside the auspices of state USES agencies but need more help with employment in their home areas.

In addition to specific questions about AWP, workers were queried about other services received from the USES. Those who had the closest contact with the USES tended to have higher employment rates--which explains in part their frequent contact with the USES. Although evidence about the relationship is somewhat circumstantial, higher levels of USES services were found in areas where workers earn higher wages, have fewer farm jobs (more nonfarm jobs), work longer hours, and receive more support services.

Although AWP had received many negative assessments even prior to the court order, and the numbers of migrants and migrant groups using the plan has been on the decline since the 1960s, AWP was never abandoned. In fact, it is incorporated into the Farm Labor Contractor Act in both Texas and Florida, so that whenever a crew leader registers through a USES agency he must also file form MA7-85 of RMMP.

A non-USDL-sponsored assessment (Sulton and Enos) found the USES and the Rural Manpower Service (RMS) to be of only limited help to farm workers. It was felt that the capacity of the USES to provide jobs had been greatly diminished and that RMS operated almost exclusively as a job exchange--placing individuals on farms without regard to the conditions, duration, or wage levels of the work or the skills of the applicant.

Follow-Up Action to the Judge Richey Court Order

On October 13, 1975, a directive was issued by the USDL to all state USES agencies regarding implementation of the Judge Richey Court Order, and on January 25, 1977, rules and regulations on "Migrant and Seasonal Farmworkers: Employment Service Complaint System, Monitoring and Enforcement" were published in the *Federal Register*. (The most current version of these regulations may be found in Title 20, C.F.R. Part 653, Subpart B, Section 53.100-653.115, "Services for Migrant and Seasonal Farmworkers.") A submission to Judge Richey stating that the USDL had implemented all the terms of the court order was filed on February 8, 1979. To avoid prolonged adjudication over the USDL's compliance, a settlement was agreed upon in which the requirements of the original consent order were clarified and amplified. (In particular, in the fall of 1977 the plaintiffs alleged that the defendants [the USDL employment service] were "continuing to violate" the conditions of the 1974 consent order and other orders of the court.) The settlement agreement was approved by Judge Richey on January 4, 1980.

Then, on January 11, 1980, the USDL published in the *Federal Register* regulations for coordinating enforcement activities relating to migrant farm workers among its several agencies and offices that deal with these workers: the Employment Standards Administration (ESA), the OSHA, the Employment and Training Administration, the Office of the Under Secretary, and the Office of the Solicitor. The ESA farm worker specialists and OSHA farm labor contact persons were to be placed in area offices. The general idea was to make the whole system more responsive to migrant and seasonal farm workers' needs. In particular, this was to be done by facilitating speedy referral and follow-up of complaints and other enforcement matters through the better coordination of all involved.

On the same day, January 11, 1980, the USDL spelled out in detail in the *Federal Register* regulations to be followed by state USES offices in offering services to the public. New responsibilities relating to migrant and seasonal farm workers were established, old ones were updated and clarified. In response to advocacy groups working on behalf of farm workers, provisions supplementing the regulations laid out in 1977 were added.

A 150-day period was granted the USDL to implement, the terms of the agreement of January 4th. If at the end of this period the agreement is determined to have been fully implemented, Judge Richey has agreed to dismiss the litigation.

CONCLUSION

Challenges Facing the USES

The general issues facing the USES, as outlined in the USDL 1977 annual report (see *Employment and Training Report of the President*), have to do with adjusting the focus of its programs and activities so that it serves the interests of both employers and job seekers. As with any government agency, funding the programs to the desired level system-wide while at the same time controlling expenditures is a perpetual problem. In addition to its basic role as a labor exchange, the post-Judge Richey USES has an additional role in the enforcement of and compliance with the established mandates. The appropriate relationship of the USES to other government-funded programs must be clarified, as in the administration of work tests prescribed for persons applying for and receiving benefits under unemployment insurance, for example. Further, the optimal relationship between federal and state USES agencies must be sought.

There are, as we have seen, many problems specific to the farm worker aspect of the USES program. In particular, the participation of both farmers and farm workers in the job referral system and in RMMP should be augmented. The employer-oriented image of USES farm labor offices lingers on and needs to be corrected. One of the stickiest problems facing the USES with regard to farm workers can be posed as a dilemma: how to get employers to meet health, housing, wage, and working standards without losing their USES participation. Seizing one horn of the dilemma would mean strict enforcement--imposing sanctions on employers and possibly thereby losing their job listings. Employees would then take these jobs without USES benefits and protection. The other alternative would be to place no requirements on employers, removing all pressure for improvement of working conditions. In any case, as long as there are labor surpluses or an alternative source of supply (illegal alien crews), the denial of USES services to employers is a particularly weak remedy.

It remains to be seen whether deficiencies in the USES services to migrant and seasonal farm workers have been rectified in the postsettlement-agreement era. Surely, the legal apparatus has been set up, an effort toward better coordination has been made, regulations have multiplied as new ones have been created and old ones revamped, grievances have been heard, and complaints responded to. The stage is set: the play (that is, implementation of all this) begins. Surely an evaluation of the Judge Richey Court Order at this time is premature. However, attempts might be made now to collect valuable benchmark data pertaining to the USES for comparisons at a later date.

CETA, Title III, Section 303

As the USES enters a new phase in its relationship to farm workers, Section 303 remains in need of revitalization. Recall some of the problems that have already been mentioned. Apparently, migrant and seasonal farm workers are not being served in proportion to their need. Funds are spread thinly to begin with, and after programs are set up there is little money per worker-participant left for implementation and follow-through. Consequently, the participant turnover rate has been high, and services provided have lacked the depth necessary to enhance participant well-being.

Partly because of the annual bidding process required of grantees, programs remain tentative and workers treat them as such. Who can blame grantees under the present system for their concentration of effort and expense on preparing program proposals rather than on program content and delivery? At the least, centers of excellence should be recognized as such and longer-term plans should be arranged for them, perhaps in five-year stretches. At best, a permanent network of training and employment centers could be established. With the assurance of continuing federal support, they would be able to set up programs lasting from one year to the next. Wider and stronger participation of private employers in training programs might then be secured.

Posttrainee placement service should certainly be coordinated with USES offices already established in each state, so that duplication of effort between the two big federally funded systems--CETA grantees and USES--is scrupulously avoided.

Duplication of offerings must also be guarded against as demand increases for the expansion of CETA farm worker services into general welfare and education areas. In 1977 a pilot project was undertaken in California, Florida, New York, and Texas to coordinate and improve the delivery of farm worker services by Title III, Section 303 sponsors, state employment security agencies, and CETA Title I sponsors serving rural areas (*Employment and Training Report of the President*, 1977). Although plans for a 1978 evaluation of the project were made, the results are as yet unknown to the author.

The CETA program grantees must respond with positive steps to the allegation that they are, on the one hand, only buying jobs for participant workers and, on the other, subsidizing employers with cheap labor. Such placements deserve the respect of neither worker nor employer. Further, to the charge that too much emphasis is placed on nonfarm work, on-farm employment opportunities might be better exploited. In particular, grantees should establish positive working relationships with potential farmer-employers. Another avenue to explore further and perhaps expand upon is the cooperative effort to convert farm workers into farmers, as described earlier in the text.

Finally, ongoing evaluative research needs to be

undertaken for national policy purposes. One of the best evaluation methods would be to implement better posttraining worker follow-up. Also, eliciting participant feedback would be invaluable in learning which program elements are most effective and exactly which program participants have been best served.

Overall, in the author's assessment, the farm workers of America deserve continued recognition as a group in need of improved employment opportunities. Serious attempts at rendering better services, especially to migrant and seasonal workers, are being made. Two such federally funded efforts, the USES and CETA, have been described in this chapter and their shortcomings have been exposed. Especially in this age of advanced technology, it is imperative that programs be implemented that will facilitate the adjustments necessitated by change for this group that typically lives and works outside the mainstream of American life. Surely, programs facilitating adjustment through services such as job training and job placement are greatly to be preferred to those that are merely compensatory in nature.

Discussion

ALLEN E. SHAPLEY

Rochin does an excellent job of discussing the CETA Title III program. However, discussion of other service programs is extremely limited. About half of the discussion is devoted to CETA while Legal Services, HEP, CAMP, and so on are mentioned briefly and food stamps and health clinics are entirely overlooked. The USES is given as much or more consideration than it deserves, and the author is very kind.

All through the analysis I sensed a strong feeling of frustration and aggravation concerning the lack of reliable data--not only data relevant to program evaluation, but even basic data on program operation. This is a very familiar problem.

Concerning Rochin's discussion of CETA, Title III, Sec. 303, I would like to make the following observations:

1. Section 2F of CETA excludes five-sixths of the farm work force. The author believes it is too narrow. He suggests, however, that broader coverage might *not* produce more effective programs. I agree, but would go further and suggest that the target population should be narrowed, not broadened.

The aim of the overall CETA Title III program is to provide training, public service jobs, and other services designed to lead to unsubsidized employment. One of the aims of CETA, Title III, Sec. 303, is to provide supportive services to improve the well-being of migrants and seasonal workers who remain in the agricultural labor market. These two aims may be complementary in some areas of the country, but in the Midwest they are in conflict. Providing supportive services to a disadvantaged migrant without settling him or her out is doing nothing more than subsidizing that person and thereby perpetuating the undesirable situation. Rochin raises this as a question. I want to stress that it is a commonly observed reality.

2. This concerns distribution of funds under Title III, Sec. 303. In the first place, how can we determine if funds are fairly distributed on the basis of number of workers in the state, when we all agree we really do not *know* how many eligible seasonal and migrant farm workers are in the state? In the second place, is the number of workers the best criterion?

A Michigan experience went something like this. United Migrant Opportunity (UMOI) misused their funds. They were to spend the majority of their funds to settle migrants out. However, there were few job opportunities but great demand for supportive services, so they responded to the demand. The Michigan Agricultural Labor Commission was asked if it wished to administer the Title III funds. Since the Commission is advisory, not administrative, it turned down the offer. As chairman, I suggested that since Michigan had the highest unemployment rate in the country at the time, and since very few migrants *wanted* to settle out in Michigan, we give our $1 million allocation to Texas. The Michigan Department of Labor would not accept my suggestion. Instead, it fired the director of UMOI, then funded it under a new director.

Our UMOI (now MEHD [Michigan Economic and Human Development]) employees are dedicated and work hard, but I contend that the primary effect of the program in Michigan is to provide jobs for those employees--a few middle-class minority people.

3. The author notes that farm workers have little say regarding Sec. 303 programs. This is true. Farmers also have no input. There seems to be a fear that farmers will somehow kill or subvert a program if allowed to have input. I personally feel that if farmers were asked to *advise*, these programs would be more effective. It is not necessary to give them voting power, just an opportunity to advise.

4. The author questions why Sec. 303 programs place so much emphasis on off-farm work and suggests two reasons. I suggest a third. Many government employees having responsibility for Sec. 303 have very antifarm, antiagriculture attitudes and regard farm work as low-prestige employment.

5. I was intrigued with the work in California involving conversion of farm workers to farmers. I would like to learn more about this project to evaluate its potential for success elsewhere.

The author does an excellent job of discussing the USES given its size and complexity. I would like to make the following comments:

1. It is touched on in the paper, but I must stress that a service agency cannot be an enforcement agency as well and still attract users. It has been suggested that if a farmer does not use the service because of enforcement rules, he must be hiding something. That is not the case. Employers must comply with many laws, and they seldom feel comfortably

certain of complete compliance. It is like being followed through town by a policeman. I would rather not be followed by a policeman and I would rather not have a compliance officer snooping around. If I can avoid it by not using the USES, I'll not use the USES even though I think I am complying with the laws.

2. Most migrants who came to Michigan ten years ago used the USES. Now less than 5% do. Some of that drop is due to the Judge Richey Court Order, but most of it is due to a decision concerning interstate job orders. Michigan job orders used to go to Texas in January and February. On each order, the farmer agreed to provide housing. Migrant agencies charged, and it was ruled, that housing must be *licensed* prior to submitting job orders. It is impossible to license housing in January with six feet of snow on the ground, so no more job orders were sent. The attitude at Michigan Employment Security Commission seemed to be "if you don't like the way we do things we won't do anything." I never saw any effort to develop a workable alternative system.

The handling of these two issues was largely responsible for effectively eliminating the USES for migrant labor in Michigan.

14

Seasonal Farm Labor and U.S. Farm Policy

BRUCE GARDNER

During the past fifty years the focal point of U.S. farm policy has been intervention in the agricultural commodity markets. While the goals of this intervention have been described in many ways, the apparent chief goal--the source of the political push that keeps the federal government actively involved--is the desire to increase farmers' returns from commodity production. There is no comparable intention to improve the economic well-being of hired farm workers through commodity programs. Nonetheless, employment and wage rates of farm workers are inevitably influenced by these programs. The purpose of this analysis is to assess these influences and their relationship to the goals and effects of other federal policies directed specifically at farm labor. This chapter considers first the place of hired farm labor in the context of the farm sector as a whole and then examines the consequences of particular types of farm programs for hired farm employment and wage rates.

CONCEPTIONS OF THE "FARM PROBLEM" AND THEIR RELATION TO FARM LABOR

Policies to improve the economic status of farmers have gained the adherence of a wider public than those who benefit most directly from them, support that indeed would seem politically indispensable given the numerical weakness of farmers in the polity. This support, certainly among academics and probably among the general public, has been based on a perception of farmers as caught in an economic situation outside their own control, which may be broadly characterized as the "farm problem." The essential nature of the situation has been seen in many alternative and sometimes incompatible ways. The consensus view, insofar as one exists, contains two strands of thought. One idea concentrates on the interaction of the farm and nonfarm sectors and emphasizes product demand. It is well summarized by Houthakker (p. 5):

> To put it briefly: the demand for farm products grows more slowly than the demand for nonfarm products; consequently economic growth requires a steady shift of labor and other resources from agriculture to other sectors. Since there is resistance to this shift, there are usually too many people in farming, and as a result per capita income is depressed.

The other basic strand concentrates internally on the farm sector, and stresses the supply side, especially shifts in supply due to technical progress, in the context of inelastic demand. O'Rourke (p. 83) summarizes the situation as follows:

1. U.S. agriculture faces a highly inelastic demand for its products.
2. Its products have a low income elasticity.
3. It experiences rapid rates of technological change which lead to output increases.
4. Its competitive structure leaves it vulnerable to price and income slumps.
5. Asset fixity tends to prolong these slumps because resources do not move out of the industry rapidly.

What is the place of hired farm labor in this scheme of events? In the broadest interpretation, the reduction in demand for agricultural resources resulting from technical progress, and the problems created by price- and income-inelastic product demand, could be taken to affect all inputs in the same way, at least in qualitative terms. However, students of the farm problem have generally recognized that particular conditions in particular factor markets were crucial in analysis of the farm problem, whether its exogenous source is technical progress or general economic growth with low income elasticity of demand for food. On the factor-demand side, technical progress in agriculture is unlikely to be exactly factor neutral. Some innovations, like improved varieties of crops or improved livestock, are likely to be capital or land saving, while others, such as mechanical harvesting equipment, are laborsaving. On the factor-supply side, the price and factor-income effects depend on the mobility of the resource in question--on short-run and long-run factor supply elasticities.

During the whole period of reliable historical data, the ratio of labor to nonlabor inputs in agriculture has exhibited a downward trend. In 1978, the labor input into U.S. agriculture was one-fourth its 1920 level, an annual rate of decline of 2 1/2 %. During the same period, USDA's land input index remained about constant, while the power and machinery input index tripled and agricultural chemicals increased 20-fold (USDA, Economic Research Service 1978).

While much attention has been given to the analysis of such input categories in production function and resource-price studies, the distinctions among operator, family, and hired labor have not been fully treated. The assumption, sometimes explicit but more often implicit, is that hired and self-employed labor are perfect substitutes. It then follows that they can be aggregated by simple addition and that the same wage rate, or a proportionally adjusted wage rate, applies to all farm labor. The most important empirical research that treats hired farm labor as an analytically distinct market is the work stemming from Schuh (1962). Regional and demographic submarkets have been analyzed econometrically in Tyrchniewicz and Schuh (1966, 1969).

These studies, as well as the raw data and papers such as Wallace and Hoover and Gisser indicate substantial downward shifts over time in the demand for hired farm labor, but also relatively elastic supply, particularly in the long run. Consequently, one might expect that following short-term adjustment problems, hired farm labor may be relatively unaffected in terms of real wages by a steady trend toward less employment in agriculture.

Nonetheless, there appears to have been a general excess supply of farm labor up to 1970. In earlier work (Gardner 1974), I considered the consequences of out-migration from agriculture on permanent income in agriculture, composed of returns to human and nonhuman resources owned by farmers. I found that states and counties with greater out-migration in 1950-1970 experienced larger income increases, *ceteris paribus*. This is consistent with the idea that factor market disequilibrium existed during the period. The same general results occur for wage rates of hired farm labor.

There is evidence that the excess-labor situation may have ended during the 1970s. The wage rates of hired farm workers relative to nonagricultural workers have been rising since 1960, after declining in the immediate post-World War II years. Not only have real farm wage rates been increasing, but in the 1970s the number of hired farm workers has ceased to decline and has risen during the 1973-1979 period. The increase in farm workers has occurred in the face of increases in the minimum wage and other labor-regulatory measures that have continued to exert downward pressure on the demand for hired farm workers. These events suggest not only a strong pull from nonfarm employment that has shifted the supply curve of farm labor to the left even more rapidly than labor demand shifted, but also in recent years an actual rightward shift in the demand for farm labor.

A couple of structural features of the hired farm

labor force are worth recalling in this connection. First, there is a strong trend away from the hired farm worker who lives on the farm that employs him. In 1950, 65% of farm workers had rural-farm residence, while the comparable figure for 1977 is 21%. Second, the importance of the full-time hired farm worker has declined relative to part-time workers. As of 1977, only 14% of hired farm workers were employed 250 days or more in agriculture (USDA, *Hired Farm Working Force of 1977*).

These figures indicate that seasonal farm labor is increasingly relevant to discussion of the farm labor force. However, *migratory* farm labor seems not to be such a large element in part-time farm employment as is sometimes supposed. Recent CPSs find that of those who report some farm work for wages in the preceding year, only 7-8% are migratory workers. (The definition of a migratory worker is one who leaves his place of residence and crosses a county line to work and remains overnight away from his place of residence.)

The preceding discussion suggests that seasonal farm labor has come to occupy a somewhat anomalous position with reference to the general farm problem. This has implications for the justification of federal policy toward farm labor. It makes little sense, for example, to conduct a long-term policy of resettlement of hired farm workers in nonfarm employment if such workers are already mobile, tend already to have part-time off-farm employment, and if the demand for labor in at least some segments of agriculture is increasing. Moreover, there is a question whether the farm problem as classically conceived still exists, and this raises doubts about the broader approach to farm policy that has persisted since the 1930s and remains embodied in current U.S. farm commodity legislation.

I see three alternative conceptions of the farm problem that make a difference in the development of policy with reference to agricultural markets in general and hired farm labor in particular.

1. *The farm problem as a chronic tendency to*

disequilibrium. This is, I believe, the mainstream interpretation of events as modeled in the discussion above and the literature from which it draws. Under this conception of the problem, the low farm incomes and real farm wages of the 1950s and 1960s can be expected to recur as a general rule. Therefore, policies to continue to encourage agricultural labor to seek employment in the nonfarm sector are in order.

2. *The farm problem as a unique phenomenon*. In this conception, the 1930s were unique because of the Great Depression, and the 1950s and 1960s were a unique manifestation of mistaken expectations resulting from the World War II situation coupled with the resource immobility that has become enshrined in our models of the farm problem. However, in the 1970s there was either a permanent shift toward stronger markets for U.S. commodities, or a permanent improvement in the mobility of agricultural resources or in the managerial skills of and information available to farmers, or all of these.

3. *The farm problem as a cyclical adjustment problem*. The idea here is not that the economic well-being of the farm sector as a whole fluctuates in predictable standard-length cycles as some believe that hog and cattle numbers do. It is the less restrictive view that the farm sector experiences serially dependent deviations from trend values of economic variables. They result from lagged response to unanticipated shocks and mistaken expectations coupled with inherent constraints imposed by the life cycle of animals and of durable equipment.

Only time can tell, and even time will probably not do so definitively, which conception is most nearly accurate. It seems to be generally accepted that the farm problem as diagnosed for the 1950s and 1960s does not exist today, and has not since the early 1970s. (See, for example, Tweeten (1980) and accompanying discussion.) Some economists, for example Houthakker, claim that the disequilibria seen as the essence of the farm problem had disappeared by the late 1960s. My own view is that a combination of items 2 and 3 most appropriately depicts what happened in the 1950s and 1960s. The cyclical elements appear strongly evident, but not strong enough to account for the length and severity of the depression in returns to agricultural resources during the period. The unique elements of the period seem by and large well captured by the agricultural economists' models formulated in terms of "chronic" disequilibrium. The mistake is to see the model as describing permanent, inherent tendencies toward disequilibria characterized by long-term lower returns to resources in agriculture compared to what the resources could earn elsewhere. And the key feature left out of the model is long-term expectation formation and labor-market adjustment.

The implication for policy is that the use of long-term production controls or incentives to move resources out of agriculture are misguided. Set-asides or short-term supply management seems a much preferable stabilization tool. Set-asides are too unpredictable in their effects as a policy instrument and must be put in place too far in advance. I venture the hypothesis that their use to date under the Food and Agriculture Act of 1977 has been destabilizing. With respect to resource mobility, particularly in the hired farm labor area, the implication is that flexibility and mobility should be encouraged, but without systematic long-term efforts to push labor either into or out of the farm sector.

FARM LABOR UNDER SPECIFIC PROGRAM APPROACHES

The preceding discussion suggests a general thrust for overall farm policy. But the most important elements of commodity policy have not been and are not now conducted in this context. Instead, programs are established independently for particular commodities. While the 1977 act provides greater integration of commodity programs than previous legislation--particularly with respect to cross-commodity coordination of loan rates, target prices, and set-asides--the disparate nature of programs for different commodities is still more notable than the uniformities. It is not clear that the effects of programs on the demand for and price of labor or other farm inputs will be uniform across commodities. Indeed, different policies can be expected to have quite different effects on the farm labor market. This section considers the effects of the following approaches: deficiency payments, production restraints, price supports, and import restraints.

Deficiency Payments

The trend toward direct payments to farmers as a substitute for market price supports culminated in established or "target" prices as the primary basis for farm income support in the 1977 act. The target prices, which are supposed to be based on the costs of production of the commodities covered, determine the amount of deficiency payments to producers. The payments are roughly the difference between the target price and the market price (or the loan rate if the relevant market price is below the loan rate) times a producer's established yield on harvested acreage.

The effects of the target price/deficiency payment approach on the market for hired farm labor are illustrated in Figure 14.1 (a). The guarantee of price PT to producers induces them to aim at output level Q_1, which clears the market at price P_1. Payments are $(PT - P_1)Q_1$. The effect in the factor markets is to increase the demand for all inputs in order to increase intended production from Q_0 to Q_1. The effect on the labor market is illustrated in the bottom panel of Figure 14.1 (a). Both farm employment and the wage rate are increased.

Recall that the relevant supply function pertains to the supply of labor to production of a particular commodity that receives payments. If the commodity uses only a part of the farm labor force, this supply function is likely to be extremely elastic. For example, the supply of labor to grain sorghum production involves largely shifts from use in other farm enterprises. Since comparably skilled hired farm labor is expected to earn roughly the same wage rate

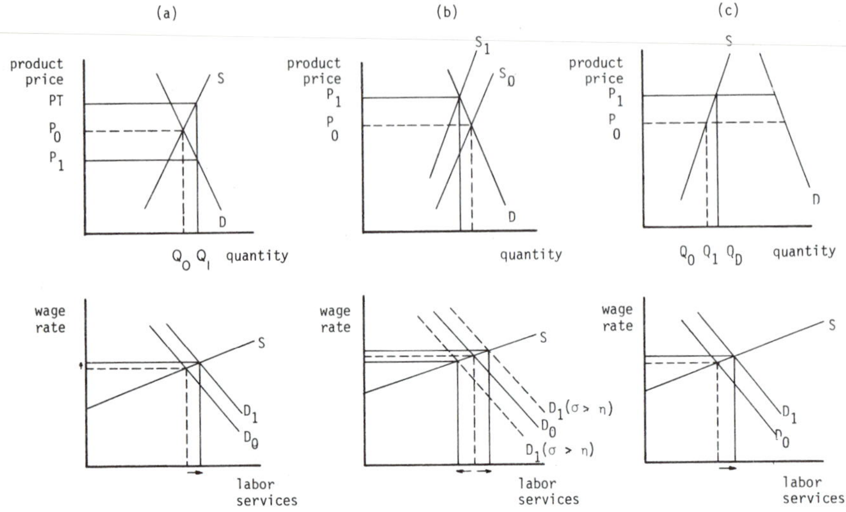

Fig. 14.1. Schematic effects of farm commodity programs on the labor market.

in all uses on farms, the wage rate paid for workers in grain sorghum will increase only to the extent that the wage rate paid in competing commodities is increased by drawing labor into sorghum production.

The only wage effects that are likely to be significant are those induced by target prices applied to several crops simultaneously. Even in this case hired labor must be quite elastic in supply to the supported commodities even in the short run. (The shortest time period relevant is approximately a year, since target price levels are known roughly a year in advance of the main labor-use decisions in production.) In the long run, it is difficult to imagine a supply function of labor that is much less than perfectly elastic. Thus the long-run wage effects of target prices are expected to be essentially zero unless target prices affect a large fraction of farm output.

In 1978 substantial deficiency payments were made for wheat ($1.2 billion) and feed grains ($1.0 billion), with relatively small amounts for cotton ($127 million) and wool ($27 million). If fully anticipated, these payments could have increased expected revenue per unit of output, that is, effective producer prices, by perhaps 10% for the grains. Using the relationship developed by Floyd, the resulting percentage increase in the hired farm wage would be

$$10(\sigma + e')/(\sigma + \bar{e})$$

where σ is the elasticity of substitution in production between hired labor and all other inputs as a group, e' is the elasticity of supply of nonlabor inputs to grain production, and $\bar{e}$ is a weighted average of input supply elasticities. The weights are the relative shares of labor and nonlabor inputs in total costs. Unfortunately, our knowledge of each of these parameters is imprecise. Tyrchniewicz and Schuh (1969) estimate the short-run elasticity of supply of hired labor at 0.65. But this estimate pertains to the entire farm sector. Since the grains use only about one-seventh of U.S. farm labor (USDA, Economic Research Service 1978), and the percentage of hired labor used on grains is even smaller, the price effects of an increase in demand for labor in the grains must imply an effective value of e_1 for present purposes of at least (0.65)(7) = 4.55. In order to be consistent with an estimated short-run elasticity of supply of grains that is much lower, around 0.3, the elasticity of supply of inputs other than hired labor must be much smaller. A value of 0.1 is roughly consistent with the 0.3 product supply elasticity. Thus we have e = 0.95(4.55) + 0.05(0.1) = 4.3, using 5% as the share of hired labor in costs. The value of σ is unknown, but is probably not extremely low, since self-employed labor can substitute for hired labor. Using the value of σ = 0.5, the formula for the farm wage rate effect of a 10% grain price increase is

$$10(0.5 + 0.1)/(0.5 + 4.3) = 1.25\%$$

This figure is too conjectural even to be called an estimate, but it illustrates the likelihood of rather small wage effects even from substantial target price increases. As a matter of fact in 1978 and in 1979 (but not in 1980), deficiency payments for grains have been accompanied by supply management schemes that temper the output response; hence the increased demand for labor, expected to result from a price support program. Production restraints introduce new analytical complications, to which we now turn.

Supply Management

The deficiency payments approach has the disadvantage of involving potentially large budget costs to the federal government. In Figure 14.1 (a) they approach a third of commodity receipts. Governmental budget cutters, taxpaying citizens, and many farmers who receive the payments have conceived a distaste for this approach. Many prefer the alternative illustrated in Figure 14.1 (b), a reduction of supply to S_1, so that market-clearing prices attain the target level. From the point of view of nonfarm consumers and taxpayers, the apparent gains from smaller payments are illusory, there being a shift to paying PT entirely through prices paid for food and fiber products rather than paying PT partly through the subsidized market price P_1 and partly through payments PT - P_1. Nonetheless, because of administrative difficulties with the allocation of rights to produce and enforcement of production-restraint incentives, and because demand for some farm products is becoming more elastic relative to the elasticity of supply functions (notably for the heavily exported products), there has been a shift away from supply-control programs in the past 15 years. Even so, production restrictions still exist, most stringently for tobacco, moderately for peanuts, and in some recent years mildly for grains.

It is worth considering the labor-demand consequences of production control primarily because of the tobacco case. USDA (Economic Research Service 1978) estimates are that tobacco accounts for about the same amount of farm labor use as the food grains, even though the value of the tobacco is only one-third the value of food grains produced. Thus tobacco is roughly three times as labor intensive as measured by factor shares. Moreover, tobacco labor is much more heavily seasonal than the grains or other major crops, and a larger fraction of it is hired.

Production controls tend to reduce the demand for labor and for all other inputs, since less is required to produce smaller amounts. However, an interesting possibility arises in the case where production restraint operates by inducements to hold land out of production, as is the case with set-asides and voluntary diversion for grains and cotton under the Food and Agriculture Act of 1977. Floyd shows that the relative size of the elasticity of product demand and the elasticity of substitution between land and other inputs in production is crucial in determining the effects of acreage control programs. The larger the elasticity of product demand, the more output must be reduced in order to attain a targeted product price increase, therefore the larger the reduction in land, labor, and other input use. But the greater the elasticity of substitution, the greater the increase in labor use per acre, and, generally, in yield per acre.

For the grains, the set-aside programs in recent years have probably not reduced output much more than enough to offset the positive inducement to output provided by target prices and deficiency payments. Therefore, as mentioned above, even apart from labor/land substitution, one cannot argue for a strong effect in reducing the demand for agricultural labor.

This is not the case, however, for the tobacco program. The farm price of tobacco in recent years has averaged perhaps one-third above the price in the absence of the program. This estimate is based on the rental value of the flue-cured tobacco marketing quota. There exists no reliable estimate of the elasticity of demand for U.S. tobacco, including both domestic usage and the 40% or so that has been exported in recent years. The data on 1973-1978 annual fluctuations in the farm price of tobacco as a function of marketed quantities suggests an elasticity of total demand (including demand for exports and carryover stocks) in the range around -1, amazingly high in view of the low elasticity of demand for cigarettes as estimated on a U.S. domestic basis.

The figures of the preceding paragraph suggest that the tobacco program may have reduced tobacco production by perhaps one-third from the quantities that would have been produced at market clearing prices in the absence of the program. As a first approximation, the program may be assumed to reduce the demand for farm labor by the same percentage. Actually, the reduction in labor use would probably be greater than that for other inputs as a group, since labor appears to be more elastic in supply to the tobacco industry than other inputs are.

A 33% increase in tobacco labor would involve on the order of 90 million man-hours or roughly 2% of all (hired and self-employed) U.S. farm labor use. If spread over the entire United States, the impact would be about a 3% increase in real farm wages based on a 0.65 short-run supply elasticity. However, the localized effect in tobacco-growing areas would be much greater. In the longer term, however, the production-restraining impact of the tobacco program must have had a substantially smaller wage impact because of the larger supply elasticity of hired labor. In any case, the direction of the effect seems clear: the tobacco program has had a depressing impact on hired farm worker wages, and the elimination of the program would be expected to cause wage increases, quite sharply in the short run.

Price Support through Product-Demand Increase

An increase in product demand can achieve a target level of product price without either of the drawbacks of the preceding two approaches--large government payments and idle agricultural resources. But this approach has its own difficulties.

Three types of demand management should be distinguished:

1. The introduction of policies to shift demand by promotion of domestic and foreign food-aid programs

are probably most important quantitatively. The most effective of these may be the school milk program. But even here only about 4% of milk moves through subsidized consumption channels, and the net addition to demand for milk must be considerably less than 4% (since some of the purchases of the subsidized milk would have occurred even if the purchases had not been subsidized). The food stamp program is large but is basically an income transfer program as currently administered. With $8 billion transferred and a mean difference in marginal propensity to spend on food of 0.2 between recipients of food stamps and nonrecipient taxpayers, there would be a net addition to demand for food of $1.6 billion, or less than 1% of total food demand. The price effects require still further analytical judgments, which are difficult but have the general effect of diluting the impact further (see Belongia; Schrimper).

2. Purchases by the U.S. government and nonrecourse Commodity Credit Corporation (CCC) loans are among the oldest price-support devices. But these have functioned more as stabilization measures than as longer-term demand-increasing programs. The loans and purchases have resulted in stocks of commodities that were later sold. To the extent that sales from stocks are subsidized, as they often have been, they have effects similar to those of the programs described in (1). To the extent that they stabilize prices, such programs may stabilize short-run labor-use and labor-return movements, but do not affect their average level. Because hired farm labor is elastic in supply relative to other farm inputs in the short run as well as in the long run, the stabilization effects should be greater for quantity used, but less for price, as compared to nonlabor inputs.

3. Restraints of international trade in commodities imported into the United States increase the demand for domestically produced substitutes and hence the demand for U.S. farm labor [Figure 14.1 (c)]. Import restrictions are less important than other policy instruments for U.S. agriculture as a whole, but their relative importance with reference to hired

farm labor is greater. The reason is that imported products are among the more labor intensive of U.S. agricultural commodities. Three of these are dairy, sugar, and winter fruits and vegetables.

Winter fruits and vegetables, particularly tomatoes, have become a bone of contention in the current political arena. If imports are restricted, by means of tariffs, quotas, voluntary restraint agreements, packing requirements, or by any other administrative means, the effect is to move in the direction illustrated by a move from P_0 to P_1 in Figure 14.1 (c). Shrinkage of imports increases the U.S. price, and therefore reduces U.S. consumption. At the same time, however, the higher price encourages U.S. production. The derived demand for labor in the winter vegetable business is thus increased (not only for tomatoes directly, but also for other vegetables that are substitutes for tomatoes in consumption and that therefore experience an increase in demand when the price of tomatoes rises). Quantification of the wage and employment effect depends crucially on the particular seasonal labor-market characteristics of the winter growing areas in Florida and the Southwest, particularly on the elasticity of supply of such labor. Econometric evidence for California (Wise) and Florida (Emerson et al.) indicates quite elastic supply functions, with own-price elasticities from 3 to 6 or more.

LINKAGES OF FARM LABOR SUBMARKETS

The discussion of wages in this chapter, as in much of the literature on the subject, contains a major analytical inconsistency. At times we speak of wage rates or returns to labor in wheat, dairy, tomatoes, or other particular commodity markets. At other times we speak of returns to all farm labor or the market for hired labor in agriculture as though the relevant analytical entity were the agricultural sector as a whole. But if it makes sense to treat, say, the average farm wage rate in the state of California as a price appropriately depicted as representing the intersection of aggregate demand and supply curves for farm labor in California, it does not make sense at the same time to talk about supply and demand curves for labor used in different crops independently determining different wage rates for labor used in the different California crops.

If one were to take an extreme market-segmentation view, it would be concluded that the major commodity programs, with the exception of tobacco, do not impinge directly on the use of seasonal farm labor. The use of seasonal farm labor is concentrated in the fruits, vegetables, and specialty crops that do not have programs. Nonetheless, it seems clear that supply/demand conditions in one sector of agriculture influence the labor market in other sectors. Indeed, the common practice of quoting a single U.S. average farm wage, as in the farm wage rates reported in the *Economic Report of the President* (Council of Economic Advisers, p. 290) or USDA's published statistics, is meaningful only to the extent that wage rates within the various submarkets of agriculture move together.

Two empirical issues are important in judging the relationship between policy-induced wage and employment changes in different parts of agriculture. The first is the degree to which labor submarkets within agriculture can be aggregated to an overall agricultural labor market. The second is whether the extent of the relevant market should stop at agriculture at all. Perhaps it is more useful to consider an overall market for labor of a given skill category, whether the labor is employed in agriculture or nearby nonfarm work.

The concepts of a market and a "submarket" for labor are not clearly and distinctly different. The empirically based distinction turns on comovements of individuals' wage rates. If wage rates are identical and show the same changes under exogenous disturbances, then the individuals whose wage rates move together are said to be part of a single labor market. But because workers in different locations and in different commodities have different skills and tastes, and the production processes involve different kinds of activities, one would never expect exactly the same wage rates for workers in all commodities or in all locations. Therefore, the issue of where to draw the boundary of a market becomes empirical. Wage rates for different commodities that move closely enough together can be considered part of the same market, while those that are especially closely related can be characterized as being in the same submarket. Thus we may wish to characterize the U.S. hired farm work force as belonging to a single labor market, while at the same time seasonal workers in the southeastern states form a submarket.

It is not clear how objectively specifiable measures of "closely related" or "especially closely related" wage rates are attainable. Because it is so crucial to the assessment of farm-policy effects on U.S. hired farm labor, I would like herein to give some consideration to the issue. Lacking data on commodity-specific wage rates, regional wage rates are considered. The question is whether they move closely enough together to be plausibly taken as parts of a single, nationwide farm labor market.

Table 14.1 presents correlation coefficients between regional pairs of farm wage rates, between each region and the U.S. average farm wage rate, and between each region's farm wage rate and national nonfarm wage rate. The correlation coefficients are all highly significant, suggesting at least a close relationship among the regions. (Note that the wage rates are all deflated. Nominal wage rates show even higher correlation coefficients. However, the correlation of nominal wage rates is in part spurious. It indicates only a common denomination in terms of a depreciating dollar, not a relationship among the markets. Real (deflated) wage rates are therefore more suitable for the investigation of this chapter.)

Three regions (3, 4, 6), which consist of the United States south of the Mason-Dixon line and the Ohio River and eastward from Texas and Oklahoma, have correlation coefficients of 0.99 between one another and with the U.S. average farm wage rate. It there-

Table 14.1. Correlation coefficients among regional real farm wage rates, 1950-1978[a]

	2	3	4	5	6	7	8	9	US	US*
1	.04	.80	.80	.87	.79	.74	.82	.83	.85	.90
2		.93	.93	.93	.92	.87	.92	.93	.95	.92
3			.99	.89	.99	.93	.96	.97	.99	.87
4				.92	.99	.95	.97	.98	.99	.87
5					.90	.95	.93	.92	.92	.82
6						.94	.97	.98	.99	.88
7							.96	.93	.94	.76
8								.97	.97	.85
9									.99	.89
US										.92

[a]Key to code for regions:
1 New England
2 New York, New Jersey, Pennsylvania
3 Delaware, Maryland, Virginia, West Virginia, North Carolina, South Carolina, Georgia, Florida
4 Kentucky, Tennessee, Alabama, Mississippi
5 Ohio, Indiana, Illinois, Michigan, Wisconsin
6 Arkansas, Louisiana, Oklahoma, Texas
7 Minnesota, Iowa, Missouri, North Dakota, South Dakota, Nebraska, Kansas
8 Montana, Idaho, Wyoming, Colorado, New Mexico, Arizona, Utah, Nevada
9 Washington, Oregon, California
US The U.S. average farm wage rate.
US* The U.S. average hourly earnings in manufacturing, retail trade, and construction. All wage rates are deflated by the CPI.

fore seems appropriate to say that this large area constitutes a single farm labor market for present purposes. Other regions by and large have correlation coefficients of 0.90 or better with one another and with the U.S. average farm wage rate. Thus they are, if not in the same labor market, at least in closely related submarkets.

The exceptional region is New England. Its correlation coefficient with all other regions, except the Mid-Atlantic states, is somewhat smaller. A second striking fact about New England farm wage rates is that they are more closely correlated with the U.S. average nonfarm wage rate than with the U.S. farm wage rate. The resulting suggestion is that New England farm workers are more closely integrated with the national nonfarm labor market than with the farm labor market. Each region, with the possible exception of the Northern Plains states, appears quite closely attuned to the national nonfarm labor market. It may indeed be reasonable to think of the U.S. farm labor market as a submarket of a broader U.S. labor market. These correlations in general point to widespread mobility and ability to adjust on the labor-supply side in the U.S. farm labor market.

Unfortunately, the correlation coefficients do not provide an objective economic or statistical criterion for judging how closely wage rates must move together in order to be considered part of the same market or submarket. From an economic point of view, we would want to develop a loss function that would show, for any divergence between wage rates in different regions (or between wage rates for work in different types of farming in the same region) induced by a change in product demand or other exogenous influence, the potential net return to be earned by resource adjustments to reestablish equilibrium between the regions. If there are short-term net gains that disappear in the longer term, then perhaps we have an identifiable submarket within a larger overall market. If net gains persist in the long run, i.e., if regionally specific economic rents to labor are generated by product-market changes, then we may say that separate (though perhaps closely related) markets exist.

A comprehensive econometric approach to testing the existence of labor markets and submarkets statistically is far beyond the scope of this analysis. However, some relevant research has been done in the past, and some additional suggestive although not conclusive evidence is available. Tyrchniewicz and Schuh (1966), in their study of regional hired labor supply, conducted a test of a national labor market hypothesis based on response to income opportunities. They report results that are "consistent with the hypothesis that members of the (farm) labor force have historically responded more to national than to regional nonfarm income" (p. 549).

A similar type of test is to compare the response of wage rates in different regions to the national farm wage rate and to national exogenous variables. Tables 14.2 and 14.3 report some results along these

Table 14.2. Regression coefficients explaining regional wage rates as a function of the national wage rate (with t statistics)

Region	National farm wage rate
1	0.45
	(8.3)
2	0.52
	(16.2)
3	1.25
	(30.9)
4	1.46
	(38.9)
5	0.50
	(12.5)
6	1.09
	(30.6)
7	0.52
	(13.8)
8	0.52
	(20.8)
9	0.65
	(30.6)

Table 14.3. Regression coefficents explaining regional wage rates as a function of national exogenous variables

	Independent variable[a]					
Region	Nonfarm wage rate	Product price (lagged)	Land quantity (index)	Nonlabor input prices	Time trend	Minimum wage
1	0.58	0.20	-0.22	-0.23	-0.02	0.09
	(4.5)	(1.8)	(0.2)	(1.1)	(2.7)	(2.9)
2	0.32	0.15	-0.72	-0.03	-0.01	0.11
	(3.4)	(1.9)	(1.2)	(0.2)	(1.6)	(5.1)
3	0.90	0.33	-0.45	0.38	0.03	0.14
	(0.7)	(2.8)	(0.5)	(1.7)	(4.2)	(4.4)
4	0.02	0.90	1.02	0.68	0.03	0.23
	(0.2)	(0.8)	(1.4)	(3.6)	(5.7)	(8.4)
5	0.30	-0.05	2.11	0.40	0.00	0.12
	(2.3)	(0.5)	(2.7)	(2.0)	(0.0)	(4.2)
6	0.10	0.25	0.74	0.33	0.03	0.10
	(0.8)	(2.1)	(0.9)	(1.5)	(4.4)	(3.0)
7	0.24	0.05	2.31	0.58	0.01	0.07
	(2.2)	(0.6)	(3.5)	(3.4)	(2.2)	(2.8)
8	0.34	0.16	1.29	0.38	0.01	0.03
	(4.5)	(2.4)	(2.8)	(3.1)	(2.1)	(1.8)
9	0.07	0.17	1.38	0.08	0.02	0.06
	(0.7)	(2.0)	(2.3)	(0.5)	(4.1)	(2.7)
U.S.	0.26	0.10	0.46	0.40	0.01	0.12
	(3.4)	(1.5)	(1.0)	(3.4)	(4.2)	(6.8)

[a]For details of data sources and economic rationale for these variables see Gardner (1981).

lines. The Table 14.2 regression coefficients would be 1.00 for each region if their wage rates all moved exactly with the national farm wage rate. (Differences in wage levels between regions yield different constant terms for each region's regression.) In fact, the coefficients are all significantly different from unity except for region 6.

The regressions in Table 14.3 show the response of each region's wage rate to some important national wage-determining exogenous variables, as used in Schuh's and subsequent work. All monetary variables are put in 1967-dollar terms by deflating by the consumer price index. The coefficients vary substantially from region to region. An overall F test on the residuals of the regressions, compared to a restricted model in which the regional coefficients are constrained to be the same in each region, allows rejection (at the 1% level) of the hypothesis that the regions have the same coefficients.

While the idea can be rejected that annual adjustments in farm labor markets create a completely unified national market, there are obvious connections among wage responses in the different regions. Of particular significance for the topic of this chapter, national average product price movements yield generally similar responses, although the relationship is weak in the Northern Plains and the Lake states. Therefore, it does not seem totally inappropriate to proceed, as in the earlier discussion herein, to consider national wage effects of major commodity programs, even though the programs are commodity specific and to some extent region specific.

A final empirical finding from the regional wage data that is worthy of note is the dramatic decline in regional wage differences during the post-World War II period. In 1950-1955 the standard deviation over regions averaged $0.32 (in 1967 dollars), with a range in 1950 from $0.86 per hour in region 4 (South Central) to $1.72 per hour in region 9 (Pacific). In 1977-1978, the standard deviation was $0.11, with a range in 1978 from $1.81 (in New England) to $2.22 in the Pacific region. These figures suggest a substantial movement towards a national farm labor market.

POLICY AIMED AT THE INDUSTRIAL STRUCTURE OF AGRICULTURE

"Structure" as the term is used here refers to the size of farms, the economic organization of farms in terms of resource ownership and control of production decisions, and the integration of purchased-input supply or marketing services with farm production activity. The issues for hired farm labor are somewhat different than the issues seen from the broader consumer or producer viewpoint. The broader issues, which receive most emphasis in current policy discussion, have to do with the cost of producing the nation's food supply and the market power that increased concentration could generate. From the point of view of hired farm labor, the narrower question is how alternative industrial and institutional structures will affect the market for agricultural labor.

Recent structural changes have their main influences on the demand side of the labor market. Three such effects may be distinguished: changes in the demand for labor relative to capital, changes in the demand for hired relative to self-employed labor, and changes in the skill mix.

Structural changes, of which the paradigm case is the increasing acreage of field crop operations on the typical family-operated farm, are seen mainly as a matter of substitution of capital for labor. The farm operator, who with his family also supplies most of the labor, is limited in farm size by a desire to avoid labor-management problems. As larger machinery becomes economical, farm size grows. There are fewer farmers but more real capital equipment. However, there is not necessarily less hired labor employed. Thus in Illinois, cropland per farm increased 28% between the mid 1960s and the mid 1970s, while the number of hired workers in the state remained unchanged.

In the cases of dairy or other livestock enterprises, structural change also appears to have been technologically based on labor-saving mechanization. But again it is not clear that demand for *hired* farm labor must be reduced. It is true that one man can handle an increasing number of dairy cows, for example. But it may at the same time be the case that the technical conditions of production are changed so that it is relatively less efficient to limit the dairy farm to the number of cows that one man (with family and perhaps one hired man) can handle. It is not a foregone conclusion that larger versions of the "Wisconsin-model" family dairy farm will prevail over the "California" model, relying on crews of hired workers.

In other sectors of animal culture, notably the chicken business, structural change already seems to have occurred that essentially replaces the owner-manager-operator, with separation of labor from capital ownership and from much of the managerial decision making. This sort of development has been seen as the result of vertical integration of farm production, marketing, and input-supply activities. As such it is a valuable risk-reducing arrangement for corporations such as feed manufacturers or meat packers. However, as some corporations (e.g., Ralston-Purina) are finding the benefits of integration as opposed to specialization impossible to realize, it appears that the real advantages of operations such as "broiler factories" have more to do with efficiency gains at the commodity production level than with the advantages of tied-in marketing channels or feed supplies.

Better understanding of structural changes in the economic organization of agriculture depends on progress in the theory of the firm. For these purposes the relevant theory is not the traditional conjunction of an assumed objective function with specifications of short-run and long-run cost curves, but instead the considerations initiated by Coase and pursued more recently by Alchian and Demsetz and by Klein, Crawford, and Alchian. The issues considered here include those of why some cooperative behavior is organized through markets and prices while other activities are internalized in firms, and why task specialization and teamwork in production are organized in different ways at different times and places. The main factor holding back the empirical development of this branch of the theory of the firm is the lack of testable hypotheses and data to test them on. Recent developments in the structure of agriculture may provide a suitable occasion for both.

The role of farm policy in structural change in agriculture has become a very live issue owing to Secretary Bergland's interest in the subject. Agricultural economists have mentioned governmentally supported research and extension, credit programs, tax policies, and commodity programs as important causes of structural change toward larger, less labor-intensive farming. Actually, the only explicit policy goals and directions aimed at farm size are intended to favor smaller farm operations. These include administrative guidelines in credit programs and payment limitations in commodity programs. These factors do not seem to have been significantly effective. For example, it has been estimated that the 1978 deficiency payments of $22 billion would have been $24 million (1.4%) larger had there been no payment limitations (USDA, Economics, Statistics, and Cooperatives Service 1979a). At the same time, there do not seem to be good scientific grounds for concluding that policy has been the major cause of farm size growth that it has recently been asserted to be (USDA, Economics, Statistics, and Cooperatives Service 1979b). The main countervailing fact is that the commodities in which structural change has gone farthest are not those for which farm programs have been most influential. Fruits and vegetables and livestock feeding have been relatively free of market intervention.

I believe that the policy-induced structural effects most pertinent to hired farm labor have not come from the policy areas just mentioned. Rather, they have been results of relatively recent initiatives in the regulation of agriculture, more precisely in the pattern of exemption from these regulations for smaller farm operators. The minimum wage provisions of the Fair Labor Standards Act, for example, exempt farmers who hire less than 500 worker-days in the peak-use calendar quarter, i.e., about 7 workers.

Similar types of exemptions and enforcement difficulties for unemployment insurance and occupational health and safety regulation have structural implications because of their labor-market effects--they reduce the relative cost (compared to larger farm operations) of producing labor-intensive commodities on small farms.

Thus there are two countervailing forces at work affecting structural aspects of the demand for hired farm labor. Increasing vertical integration in some operations and increasing specialization in others are both changing farming from small or moderate-size family enterprises toward systems of economic organization in which hired labor plays a greater role. On the other hand, regulatory exemptions encourage the use of hired labor in small-scale farming even as they discourage it in large-scale farming. In the context of mechanization, it could conceivably turn out that this apparent advantage to smaller operations is illusory. The regulation of wages and labor use gives encouragement to mechanization on large farms, and as familiarity with new techniques increases and the techniques improve, the advantages that small-scale operations initially had, which enabled them to use hired workers in labor-intensive processes more cheaply than large-scale operators, may disappear. Then small farms could find themselves increasingly in a high-cost, technically backward situation. Whether such developments would have adverse or beneficial effects from the point of view of the seasonal farm workers is not clear.

To date, the net result of the technical, economic policy, and regulatory forces in the late 1970s has been to increase the real wages of hired farm workers as well as their wages relative to nonfarm workers and to hold steady and even increase slightly the agricultural hired labor force. The net effect of agricultural policy in these events has probably been to increase the demand for hired farm labor slightly. While public policy has been important in protecting jobs in the sugar and imported vegetable sectors and in reducing employment opportunities in tobacco, the main forces influencing farm wage rates and employment today are market forces. This state of affairs is likely to continue in the future.

CONCLUSIONS

United States farm policy since the 1930s has consisted primarily of commodity programs. While not aimed at the interests of hired farm labor, these programs have influenced wage rates and employment in agriculture. The major issue in analyzing these influences is the degree of integration of the farm labor market. Does a grain price support program, or restraints on imports of winter vegetables, have predominantly local effects on specific workers in particular areas or are the effects diffused throughout the farm sector?

While the evidence discussed in this chapter is not sufficient to resolve the issue completely, there do seem to be strong connections among farm-labor submarkets, at least at the regional level of disaggregation. And the degree of approximation to a unified national farm labor market has increased substantially in recent years. Therefore it seems appropriate to treat policy issues affecting labor at the aggregate level, although detailed study of particular submarkets is undoubtedly essential in some cases.

At the aggregate level, current farm programs do not appear to be exerting a strong push either aiding or harming the interests of hired farm workers. Import restrictions on fruits and vegetables, sugar, and dairy products have a net positive impact on farm wage rates and employment, especially seasonal employment, which probably outweighs the negative impact of production controls in tobacco. The degree of integration of the farm labor market suggests that the net effects of these relatively long-standing programs are diffused throughout the farm sector and probably do not generate net rents or quasi-rents to labor in the production of these particular commodities.

On the other hand, the overall thrust of farm policy can have a significant impact on farm labor if another episode of seemingly chronic disequilibrium arises as in the "farm problem" of the 1950s and 1960s. It has been argued in this chapter that future recurrences of agricultural depression will be more clearly transitory in nature than past episodes and so are less likely to lead to large-scale or permanent commodity programs. But one's confidence in such predictions cannot be great.

Discussion

G. EDWARD SCHUH

This analysis is competently done, as we have come to expect of Bruce Gardner. It is analytical and analytically sound and reasonably comprehensive.

I have four minor comments to make on the chapter, and then I will touch on four issues that are somewhat more significant. These latter come under the rubric of neglected aspects of the author's analysis and/or the questions he did not ask. Let us take up the lesser comments first.

Gardner has a tendency in the early part of his discussion to neglect the supply side of the labor market. There are two dimensions of this neglect. First, when conceptualizing the nature of the farm problem, he fails to mention that, in the past at least, the farm population had a higher birth rate and a higher "natural" rate of increase than did the nonfarm population. Historically, this differential was an important contributor to the farm problem.

In addition, Gardner does not give sufficient attention to the fact that increases in per capita income in the nonfarm sector, in response to economic growth, shift the supply curve of labor to the left.

This neglect is rather noticeable in the early part of the chapter, where the emphasis is on demand factors such as technical change, but it is corrected a little later.

Second, it seems to me that Gardner conceptualizes both the farm problem and the labor market problem in too narrow a context. In conceptualizing the farm problem he concentrates primarily on factors internal to or directly related to agriculture, neglecting such factors as trade and exchange rate policy. In considering the labor market problem (somewhat ironically in light of the neglect of this issue in the first part of his analysis) he puts perhaps too much emphasis on moving labor--or the supply side of the market.

In both his conceptualization of the farm problem and his discussion of labor markets, he neglects the role of monetary and fiscal policies in keeping labor markets tight or loose and the effects this has on the labor transfer process. There is ample evidence in the literature on this aspect of labor markets.

My third comment is to express puzzlement about Gardner's reticence with respect to set-asides and his preference for reserve stocks as instruments of policy. I really do not see that the effects of one of these are more unpredictable than those of the other, as he implies. They do have different costs and benefits, however, with the result that set-asides tend to be viewed as a second line of defense, with reserve policy used first.

The fourth and final of my minor comments is to concur with Gardner's observation that farm people prefer implicit subsidies. I would extend that notion, however, and note that *most* economic entities prefer to receive their subsidies in implicit forms, and that governments, whenever possible, like to do their taxing by implicit means. As economists, we need to give a great deal more attention to these implicit taxes and subsidies and not neglect them as we have in the past.

Now let me turn to the issues that were neglected or the questions that were not asked. First, the role of trade and exchange rate policy needs to be given more attention in discussions both of agricultural policy and of the farm problem. (For a discussion of the role of the exchange rate in particular, see Schuh [1974].) In the first place, the overvalued dollar of the 1950s and 1960s constituted an implicit export tax on agriculture. Even though price support programs, P.L. 480 shipments, and export subsidies may have eventually offset part or all of the effects of this tax, they obviously were not a perfect offset either in timing or in commodity coverage. More importantly, in the context of this volume, the agricultural labor force was forced to bear a significant share of the burden of this implicit tax.

In the second place, a system of floating exchange rates in the presence of well-integrated international capital markets provides a direct connection between monetary and fiscal policy, on the one hand, and export sectors such as agriculture on the other (Schuh 1979). The result is to impose a great deal more instability on agriculture--a phenomenon that we have already seen during the 1970s. This increased instability has important implications for agricultural labor and agricultural labor markets, but we see little discussion of this problem in Gardner's analysis.

Recognition of the importance of trade and trade policy would have focused on another aspect of labor market policy that is totally neglected in Gardner's discussion. Positive adjustment policies to facilitate changes in trade patterns are essential if pressures for protectionism are to be attenuated and if the nation is to realize the benefits from trade. Yet nothing is said about such policies.

A third neglected issue of the labor markets and labor policy is the lack of attention given to industrialization and to economic development policy as a means of dealing with rural poverty problems. The point not given sufficient attention by Gardner is that the U.S. farm problem and in turn the problem of rural poverty was very much a regional problem--a problem of the South. This was pointed out by Ruttan and others as early as the early 1960s. But to this date the problem is still neglected by both policymakers and analysts.

The generalization, of course, is that poverty in most cases takes on a strong spatial dimension. Those who are taken by the naive neoclassical model of migration and labor markets will argue that the solution to these problems is to promote the geographic mobility of labor. What proponents of this argument fail to recognize is that outmigration imposes rather substantial negative externalities on the supplying region, due in large part to the selective nature of migration (Schuh 1982; Greenwood 1975). Unfortunately for the supplying region, it is the young, the talented, the well-educated, and the entrepreneurial who leave a region, taking with them their own private capital and the public resources invested in them. These resources are then given as a free donation to the recipient region. It is little wonder that labor markets take such a long time to equilibrate when migration alone is relied on.

I have argued elsewhere that the solution to this problem is to take industry and capital to labor rather than to force labor to bear all the costs of the adjustment (Schuh 1982). Contrary to what many are inclined to argue, such a policy is not counter to the dictums of economic efficiency, since it internalizes important externalities and reduces negative externalities in both the supplying and receiving regions. Moreover, it would make labor markets perform more efficiently locally, with the result that sectoral mobility would be substantially improved. Hence, we would have a gain in both efficiency and equity.

It should be noted in passing that such a policy is consistent with the implications of Professor Schultz's urban-industrial impact model and the considerable empirical research which supports that model (Schultz 1951; Schuh 1969). Such a policy would approach this problem from the perspective of human capital and the brain-drain literature, however, rather than from the perspective of efficiency of the factor markets.

To digress somewhat, it may be useful to examine the question of how well the agricultural labor markets have functioned, since Gardner and others call attention to this issue. Despite the fact that these markets have been reasonably efficient, it remains that per capita incomes of farm workers have lagged substantially behind those of nonfarm workers. This differential has persisted for a fairly long period of time.

This discrepancy between the evidence that the markets have worked reasonably well and the persistent lag of per capita incomes in the agricultural sector can be accounted for by at least two factors. First, the tests for labor market efficiency have generally been designed in terms of wage rates. In some sense this is only a "local" test. Second, per capita incomes are determined by both the wage rate and the stock of resources an individual or family possesses. In equilibrating per capita incomes, it is most likely the market for human capital that does not perform very efficiently. Unfortunately, very little attention is given to this market in this volume.

The fourth neglected issue in Gardner's analysis is the effects of farm policies on the distribution of income within agriculture. It seems clear that labor was forced to bear a major share of the burden of adjustment to changing economic conditions, and that such policies as we did have acted to protect the asset values of the physical capital owned by farm owner-operators. This differential effect of farm programs is seen perhaps in its sharpest form in the case of the tobacco program, which according to Gardner had a depressing effect on the wage rates and employment of hired labor. From other studies, however, we know that this program gave large capital gains to landowners, since the benefits of the program were capitalized into land values. Although these effects were strongest in the case of tobacco, they have been relevant and significant in the case of other commodities as well. It is disappointing that this important aspect of our farm policies was neglected in Gardner's paper.

CONCLUDING COMMENTS

In closing I would like to make three brief comments. First, I am struck by how wasteful the process of economic development has been in the United States--wasteful of human resources. An important source of this wastefulness is the fact we have never had anything that really approximated a spatial or locational dimension to our development policies.

Second, in the case of agriculture we have not had anything approximating a sensible labor market policy, despite all the theoretical precepts and the supporting empirical evidence that suggest that the agricultural labor force would have to, and did in fact, bear the major share of the costs of adjusting to economic development--an economic development that benefitted handsomely other members of society. (Johnston has cogently discussed the universal transfer of labor from agriculture to the nonfarm sector as development proceeds.)

Finally, as social scientists we need to give a great deal more attention to the reasons why both agricultural and labor market policies took the particular shape they did. Until we understand why we have certain policies, we really have not finished our task of understanding the social and economic world that surrounds us.

15

Summary

ROBERT D. EMERSON

The chapters and comments included in this volume were presented for discussion in earlier versions at a conference on January 9-11, 1980. Since then, the authors have had an opportunity to incorporate some of this interchange into their analyses. Needless to say, the authors have maintained their prerogative to express their own views. The intention of this chapter is to attempt to synthesize the various contributions and recommendations relative to seasonal farm labor.

The fundamental premise serving as the integrating focus of the contributions is that seasonal farm labor is an identifiable segment of the labor force about which there is a need for useful information and a concern for appropriate policy guidance. Holt draws a parallel between the efforts summarized in this volume and the earlier work edited by C. E. Bishop entitled *Farm Labor in the United States*. Moreover, Fuller notes the lack of change in the farm labor problem since the earlier Bishop work and even in studies preceding it, such as the President's Commission on Migratory Labor in 1950-51. There is no question of similarities. As Fuller notes, many of the problems seasonal and migratory workers face remain today as they were 30-40 years ago.

Yet there is a distinct difference between the problems addressed in the Bishop volume and those that are with us now. The concern in the early 1960s was with all human resources in agriculture. There was a disequilibrium in the labor market in that there was an excess supply of labor to agriculture. The policy concern was how best to get the labor markets back into equilibrium. Although there was concern with hired farm workers per se, the major emphasis was on farm operators and farm families. The massive migration out of agriculture has greatly reduced the significance of this problem.

The link between the problem of the early 1960s and that of the present time is the low return to the human resource--this time, hired farm workers. As noted by Holt, it is extremely important that care be taken in interpreting agricultural labor statistics, due to the vast diversity of this labor force. The largest single group of persons doing hired farm work is students. Another major group primarily classified as out of the labor force is housekeepers. Both of these are groups of individuals who have a low opportunity cost for their labor.

On the other hand, there is very definitely a significant component of the work force that has primary attachment to agricultural work. In many areas there appears to be emerging decasualization of the work done by these workers and an increasing professionalism on their part. Yet so long as there remains a large pool of low opportunity cost labor capable of performing most farm work tasks, one cannot realistically expect economic returns to farm workers to dramatically increase.

A third very significant pool of low opportunity cost labor often working in agriculture consists of undocumented aliens. The economic pressures these workers exert on the labor market are in the same directions as those exerted by students and other part-time workers, further limiting potential increases in returns to farm labor. The most commonly agreed upon solution to the low returns problem in agriculture during the 1950s and 1960s was migration out of agriculture. Although major problems resulted from this to which manpower policy was eventually directed, low returns for self-employed persons are currently much less predominant than in earlier years. The economic incentives for additional persons to enter farming simply were not there.

However, to assume that migration out of agricultural employment will resolve the problem of low returns to labor for hired farm workers, as it did for self-employed and family workers, is unrealistic. The supply of low opportunity cost labor available for work in agriculture is simply too vast to expect outward mobility to have a significant impact on wages (or earnings). It thus appears an appropriate juncture to reexamine the alternatives to this situation.

This volume has identified significant problem areas in seasonal farm labor markets in the United States as we enter the decade of the 1980s. While each of the authors has treated a relatively distinct area, the following section represents an attempt to set forth an integrated statement of the operation of seasonal farm labor markets in the United States, drawing from the contributions of the individual authors. Following this are sections devoted to policy alternatives, data needs, and research needs, respectively.

A SYNTHESIS

Two underlying frameworks for viewing seasonal farm labor markets have been utilized in the various chapters. One of these is the approach of neoclassical labor markets and human capital analysis. The alternative framework is the dual labor markets approach. Huffman (Chap. 2) sets forth the basic premises and frameworks for each of these approaches. The dual labor markets approach places heavy emphasis on institutional arrangements within the labor market and discounts the differences in "potential productivity of workers . . . for hiring, promoting, and wage determining decisions." By contrast, the neoclassical approach to labor markets emphasizes the allocative function of labor markets, giving major emphasis to variations in skills and abilities among workers. More importantly, Huffman adds: "[The dual labor markets approach] ignores the basic warning of macroeconomics; options available to individuals and to individuals collectively are generally very different. . . . Any one individual can obtain a good job, but unless only good jobs are supplied, not all individuals can have good jobs and be employed." The neoclassical approach gives greater emphasis to the tendency toward general equilibrium in labor markets, recognizing that at any given time the market may be in disequilibrium. The disequilibrium, however, plays the crucial role in bringing about reallocation between and within labor markets to the benefit of workers, employers, and consumers. It is this reallocation or adjustment process in which public policy may advisedly play a role in providing assistance or cushioning the hardships of economic reality. Such a stance was suggested by Bishop in recommending "the development of an early warning system to detect changes in technology which are likely substantially to decrease farm manpower needs" (p. 17).

It is not the purpose of this volume to refute one or the other of the approaches to studying labor markets. It is, however, important to recognize that the alternative approaches are utilized by the different authors. This is most clearly portrayed by the distinction between those who have emphasized the importance of institutions as opposed to those who have focused primarily on the market allocation and labor market choice processes. It is hoped that the contributions of each approach can be recognized rather than debating the premises of each.

The most commonly agreed upon issues concerning farm workers, and particularly seasonal farm workers, are low incomes relative to the national norm and a high degree of instability in employment and earnings. This section will focus primarily on the question of what we know at this point that contributes to our understanding of these problems, and secondly on how existing governmental policies and programs relate to the problems. The heart of the seasonal farm worker problem is the fundamental nature of fruit and vegetable production: the location and time of production in localized areas of the country is dictated by climatic conditions. Just as the maturation of crops progresses North or South with the seasons, so do the jobs to harvest the crops. There are basically two alternatives for the person who works in the harvest of a seasonal crop: he can remain unemployed during the off-season or he can attempt to find employment elsewhere, most likely by migrating or "moving with the crops."

In the former case, although the worker may find occasional employment during the off-season, he will surely face an uncertain employment pattern until the following season. By the same token, it is important to note that 36% of the 1977 farm work force was classified as primarily attending school and therefore may only be interested in short term employment (USDA, *The Hired Farm Working Force of 1977*, p. 12). Even in the latter case, where workers migrate to find employment in other crops, there are clearly spells of unemployment in the process of moving from one job to another and due to the timing problem--the mere presence of workers does not assure that the crop is ready for harvest. Again, with inevitable unemployment, it is not surprising that incomes are low.

It is essential to recognize that the problems of seasonal agricultural workers do not exist *because* of agricultural employment. Rather, persons with employment problems often find agricultural employment attractive. Previous employment history is generally not of concern to the agricultural employer, nor are most characteristics of the worker. It is generally possible for a person to find employment as a seasonal agricultural laborer when most other sources of employment may be closed to him. It is quite another question whether or not society determines that this situation is acceptable or desirable.

The employer faces the question of how best to harvest his crop. He receives a price signal through the market system indicating that a particular product is desired. In bringing that product to market, various skill levels of labor are required. The price signals are currently indicating that in certain crops it is still only profitable to utilize hand harvest labor for that process. In some instances employers have found it necessary, and the government has agreed, to import labor for the work since domestic workers were not willing to take the jobs at prevailing wages. Only when the product and labor markets adjust to the point that it is no longer economically feasible to use current harvest methods with unskilled seasonal labor will the employer switch to other methods requiring more skilled labor with correspondingly higher earning power. Of course, it must be recognized that the unskilled worker is in this case out of a job, and unless he can obtain new skills, he will experience difficulty in finding other employment.

The extent of short-term labor in agriculture is succinctly summarized by Fritsch (Chap. 3). He estimates that if employment schedules could be reorganized such that employment by workers who worked for 150 days or less were eliminated, "the 4.5 million seasonal hirings could be replaced by fewer than 350,000 full-time workers." The difficult part to determine is the extent to which this disparity is due to short employment episodes from brief harvest periods by given employers or to sporadic employment behavior on the part of the employer and/or worker.

Seasonal employment in agriculture is most heavily concentrated in fruit and nut farms (Chap. 3). Moreover, it is likewise concentrated around the West Coast, southern Border States, and the East Coast. One change that Fritsch does note is the apparent increase from 1969 to 1974 in seasonal employment in the cash grains and other field crops. This is attributed to the increased production in grains through increased export of agricultural commodities.

Although a number of efforts are under way to smooth out peaks in requirements and stabilize agricultural employment, there are clearly limits to what can be achieved in this direction. A case study by Mamer and Rosedale provides clear evidence of the progress that can be made in stabilizing agricultural employment to the benefit of both workers and employers. It is essential to keep in mind that this was achieved on citrus operations where the harvesting season lasts for several months. This is in contrast to those crops that have a harvesting season of only a few days to a few weeks. The coordination and employment of labor across different vegetable crops from location to location while coping with the vagaries of weather is a very difficult problem.

Historically, one means of coordinating the labor movement was through the annual worker plan maintained by the USES. This recognized two important factors, however. One of these was that farm workers regularly migrated from place to place to work. The importance of migratory labor as a major component of the farm labor force has diminished, accounting in 1977 for fewer than 200,000 persons. Secondly, the plan relied upon the role of the labor contractor to gather workers into crews. Currently the USES is playing a relatively minor role in coordinating the scattered employment of farm workers.

While there are surely numerous reasons for the decline in the role of the USES, one major factor is the government's own regulations. Any employer who utilizes the USES must meet a number of stringent conditions covering the employment arrangement, the workplace, housing, and a number of other conditions. It is not in the least suggested that conditions should not be improved nor that government should not promote such activity. Nevertheless, an agency which attempts to provide a service cannot also serve as an enforcement agency. Any employer utilizing the USES is subject to additional workplace inspections. As Shapley notes, although the employer may think that he is in compliance with the labor regulations, he would rather not have someone continually looking over his shoulder if he can avoid it. The apparent result has been the virtual removal of the USES from the labor market. While the efforts were noble, the result was a loss of clientele, leaving the farm work force to patch together pieces of employment as well as they could without the assistance of the employment service.

Technology

American agriculture has undergone massive technological change throughout this century. One of the earliest major influences on hired labor was the development and adoption of the mechanical cotton picker, which displaced considerable amounts of labor throughout the Old South and Delta regions. Another major mechanical development was the tomato harvester, which again displaced large numbers of workers in California. Often coincident with the mechanical developments are biological changes that permit more uniform maturation of the crop. While the above-cited crops are clearly the large ones to have been mechanized in terms of hired seasonal labor displacement, there are many others such as cherries, sweet corn, and beans, to name a few. Among the larger hand harvested crops utilizing seasonal labor yet to be mechanized is citrus.

While the explanation of technological change is not of primary concern for our purposes, it is helpful to recognize its implications for labor markets. Through the works of Hayami and Ruttan, we know that much of the impetus for the direction of technological developments follows from efforts to economize on the relatively scarce factors of production. The technological efforts in American agriculture have been largely to reduce labor costs. Although this may appear at first sight to be a contradiction to the assumption that there is a considerable pool of low opportunity cost labor available, there are a number of additional economic considerations that suggest it is not.

First and foremost is the recognition that growers (employers) must organize their businesses in the most efficient manner possible to survive competitive pressures. Any single grower faces competitive pressures to transfer his managerial abilities into other enterprises or activities. If he can earn a greater return on his time elsewhere, there is nothing to prevent the entrepreneur from moving into some other enterprise or activity. At the industry level, efficient organization of resources is necessary to compete with other countries and with substitute goods. Consequently, the mere availability of a pool of low opportunity cost labor is not sufficient to assure its employment. Producers may still find that even with relatively low cost labor as compared to returns to highly skilled labor, they are still not able to effectively compete in the marketplace for their product. The result is typically the search for new ways of doing things, i.e., new technology, which will improve their competitive position. The alternative is the eventual decline in production in that activity.

Another consideration that may substantially influence the development and adoption of new technology is the uncertainty of the availability of harvest labor *when it is needed.* This issue has been explored by Zilberman and Just (Chap. 7). In a classic work on farm labor markets, Lloyd Fisher emphasized the tendency of growers to have available considerably more harvest workers than were absolutely necessary. This was in part to assure that the crop could be harvested at its peak condition; the cost to the grower of this practice was essentially zero at the time Fisher was writing (1953).

In today's labor markets, the cost of this practice is far from zero, due in part to many governmental programs and regulations on the farm labor market. As a result, employers have in some instances made efforts to decasualize their employment patterns, attempting to reduce harvest costs. Instances of uncertainty of labor availability, however, can be cited. Among these, Zilberman and Just cite the "threats of strikes by farm labor unions and inconsistent enforcement of immigration laws. . . ." They also note the role uncertainty may have played in the adoption of the tomato harvester "by the unstable supply of workers for harvesting that resulted from the end of the bracero program in 1964 and the pursuit of strict control policies with regard to illegal migrants from Mexico in the 1950s and 1960s." The presumption is that increased uncertainty of labor supply might induce further shifts away from dependence on seasonal labor and toward increased mechanization or capital intensity.

The potential impact of uncertainty of labor supply on technology choices is not straightforward. In an effort to clarify this dependence, Zilberman and Just work through a very technical analysis of this relationship. In an analysis of this sort one can always quibble over the necessarily rigid assumptions that must be made. However, their analysis produces some very interesting results, particularly in identifying questions that need to be resolved in order to clarify the relationship between uncertainty of labor supply and technology choices. Although they find that instability of labor supply has implications for technology choices, the direction of the effect is not uniformly towards laborsaving technology.

Among the factors that are pertinent in determining this impact is the extent to which farmers are risk averse. Our information on whether or not farmers are risk averse or risk neutral is indeed limited. Zilberman and Just also demonstrate that the impact of labor supply uncertainty will also depend on the nature of product demand markets. They demonstrate that the stabilization of labor supply may benefit the consumer through a lower product price, but farmers will unambiguously benefit only if product demand is elastic. With inelastic product demand, "stabilization of labor supply can make the farmer worse off" (Chap. 7). Although we do not know the elasticity of demand for each and every agricultural product, most agricultural products have inelastic product demand (George and King). It is noteworthy that in the Zilberman and Just framework, only with highly elastic product markets is mechanization unambiguously encouraged by labor supply uncertainty.

The one common theme that carries through treatments of technology and its impact on labor markets is the extreme dependence on product markets. Basically the message is that the technology in a given market cannot remain static. So long as there are variations in either markets for substitute products or in international markets, technological adjustments in the production process will typically have to evolve for an industry to remain competitive. The important issue is how persons suffering losses from the developments are to be compensated. This concern has never been effectively implemented in American agriculture, nor would it be particularly easy to do so.

Personnel Management

One of the major impacts of technological developments recognized above is the increased level of skills typically needed for the harvesting process. Although adoption of new technology has been a steady process, Mamer (Chap. 10) notes that comparatively little attention has been given to developing a compatible job structure in agriculture. He notes that little is known about the types of agricultural jobs and the magnitudes of employment required at alternative skill levels. Moreover, firms that have instituted any systematic occupational structure are the exceptions rather than the norm. The argument in favor of such a structure is to provide a more formalized means for the worker to progress to jobs with increased responsibility and typically requiring increased levels of skill.

Coincident with an increase in structure often follows greater stability of the work force for the individual employer. While the examples in agriculture are not plentiful, specific case studies suggest the feasibility of more attention to employment practices (Mamer and Rosedale). Glover cites other potential ways in which decasualization might take place. For example, he draws a very interesting comparison between present-day agriculture and the dock workers prior to the decasualization of that industry. The apparent result has been a dramatic reduction in turnover and increase in incomes to those workers remaining in the industry. The opposite side of the coin, however, is the loss of short-term employment opportunities.

From a strictly economic point of view there is a great deal of similarity between the adoption of more systematic employment practices in agriculture and the adoption of new technology. It was observed above that new technology either in mechanical, genetic, or chemical forms typically followed from a demand for techniques or methods to reduce unit production costs. There is no reason to believe that similar mechanisms are not at work with regard to personnel management.

The adoption of more systematic employment practices typically requires an initial investment of resources--both in time and dollars. Moreover, it requires a different way of viewing the world; employees must be considered as individuals with whom a continuing employment relationship is being established. In contrast to the prevailing practice, both the employer and employee would have prescribed responsibilities to each other. As noted by both Mamer and Glover (Chap. 9), the end result is often an increase in labor productivity and a more stable, professional labor force.

Although one may argue that the adoption of modern personnel practices in agriculture has been slow due to a lack of information about the benefits of such practices, a more likely explanation is that it has simply not been profitable to do so under the existing labor market situation. If an employer can profitably operate under existing practices without undue risk, there is little incentive for him to change his practices. When profits become squeezed and/or the risk of not having timely labor becomes sufficiently great, employers are likely to search for new ways of doing things. The adoption of new technology is one such way employers have adjusted; the adoption of improved personnel practices is an additional means by which adjustment could be achieved.

Interactions in the Seasonal Labor Market

There are basically three groups of workers (in addition to those not in the labor force most of the year, e.g. students and housekeepers) who fill temporary labor needs and about whom there has been policy concern: domestic migrant workers, alien workers, and workers from nonfarm labor markets. An adjustment in any one of these groups is likely to bring about a compensating change from the other two groups. However, as suggested by the respective authors, our knowledge about how well they substitute for one another is not extensive at this point. On the other hand, Spreen (Chap. 8) sets forth a rather comprehensive framework for systematically analyzing these interactions. As he suggests, we need a great deal more data on the characteristics of each of the markets before such a system could be empirically implemented.

Matta (Chap. 5) has provided an updated account of our information regarding the interaction of farm and nonfarm labor markets. The data he set forth continue to show the propensity toward higher earnings by nonfarm workers. He also notes the continuation of the substantially larger participation of predominantly nonfarm workers in farm labor markets than of predominantly farm workers in nonfarm labor markets.

Since average earnings of persons having both farm and nonfarm work are higher in nonfarm work than in farm work, a question often raised is what factors are important in influencing the participation or amount of nonfarm work by farm workers. Matta approaches this question with the USDA hired farm work force data by examining the factors influencing the probability of having nonfarm work. The results reconfirm the positive influence of human capital variables such as education and the negative effect of being a member of a minority group. A remaining troublesome question, and one which cannot be answered with a hired farm-worker data set, is the reverse approach: what are the factors that influence the probability of having farm work? To answer this question requires farm workers to be represented as a subpart of a larger sample of the labor force. The difficulty is that farm workers are such a minor portion of the total labor force that existing data sets are unlikely to be very informative.

The importance of the interaction of farm labor markets with nonfarm markets is emphasized by the notion of the farm labor market as a salvage market for low opportunity cost time by nonfarm workers. The supply of labor by nonfarm workers to farm labor markets is expected to vary with unemployment rates; the higher is unemployment, the greater is the supply of nonfarm labor to agriculture. By contrast, in periods of relatively low unemployment, one would expect increased migration within farm labor markets to compensate for this unavailability as well as potentially more efforts to introduce temporary alien labor.

Domestic migration by hired farm workers was examined by Emerson (Chap. 4), finding support for traditional economic variables in the decision to migrate for farm work. The implication of the result is that the economic motivation to migration provides an equilibrating factor to spatially and temporally separated farm labor markets. To the extent that severe local labor shortages are reflected by dramatic increases in wage rates, one would expect workers to migrate from other areas to avail themselves of the increased opportunity. The obvious necessity, however, is that the increased wages and employment must be preferable to what workers in other locations have at that time. For example, if the employment is for only two or three weeks and involves extensive travel to get there and back, it is unlikely that simple adjustments in wages are likely to motivate migration. On the other hand, the results would suggest that the domestic migrant population would probably be considerably larger in the absence of undocumented alien workers. Alternatively, efforts to reduce the domestic migratory labor force might be viewed as providing employment opportunities for alien workers, among others.

Martin and North (Chap. 6) understandably devote most of their attention to the authorized temporary alien workers given the dearth of information on undocumented workers. Questions of alien labor in agriculture have been some of the more controversial ones throughout our history. The views set forth by Martin and North versus those of the discussant are no exception. Martin and North basically set forth the arguments against the use of alien labor in terms of the impact on domestic labor markets, the primary issue debated in hearings on alien labor. While this is unquestionably an important issue, Welch, as the discussant, suggests that given the current magnitude of the H-2 program, the impact is probably quite small.

More importantly, however, Welch expands the discussion in two important ways: the impact on consumers and our responsibility to persons in other countries. Welch argues that due to the gain to consumers through the current level of H-2 alien labor in U.S. agriculture, the gains undoubtedly exceed any losses. Moreover, he argues that in the case of Florida sugarcane there is probably a domestic employment *gain* due to the ancillary activities. The role of international markets for agricultural products is equally important here as it is for questions of mechanization and technology. Increased costs of production for whatever reason are likely to result in increased imports (decreased exports) of the product.

Jobs in which aliens and domestic migrants are employed in agriculture are seasonal. To some extent, this is undoubtedly the case for nonfarm workers taking employment in agriculture as well. All three of these groups are in the same labor market drawing upon the same pool of jobs; adjustment in any one of the groups will affect the other two. For example, efforts to curtail domestic migration are likely to exacerbate the alien situation. Reductions in unemployment in the economy as a whole are likely to "tighten" seasonal labor markets, i.e. shift the supply curve to the left, leading perhaps to increased migration, and/or additional efforts to bring in more alien workers. By the same token, sharp reductions in alien workers would be likely to increase domestic migration.

Organization

One of the predominant features of farm labor markets is that they are largely unstructured much as Fisher described the situation nearly 30 years ago.

Particularly in seasonal labor markets, there are few if any barriers to entry. Virtually anyone can be a harvest worker. Since the piece rate is the characteristic pay method, the burden of productivity is placed on the worker (so long as he meets the minimum wage). Consequently, in the majority of cases there is little selectivity in hiring.

Increased governmental regulation and programs such as unemployment insurance are fostering changes in these practices through increased record keeping and possibly ancillary costs associated with the programs. The incentives are in the direction of employing fewer persons for longer periods of time. However, the extent to which this has occurred is not easily documented with available data. It is interesting to observe, however, that as efforts are being pursued to add more structure to the farm labor market, efforts are underway to provide more flexible employment opportunities such as job sharing for persons in the labor force who so desire them.

Much of what Mamer discusses can be considered as providing additional structure to the labor market. Similarly, Glover considers alternative labor market institutions which provide additional structure. Examples are labor cooperatives and hiring halls, both of which provide organized means of allocating work between a smaller group of individuals over longer time periods. The prototype labor cooperative is Coastal Growers in California, which resulted in a reduction from 8,517 crew members in 1965 to 1,292 in 1978, while over the same period production *increased* by 50% (Chap. 10).

Hiring halls, as discussed by Glover, provide a similar function of providing continuity of employment to a worker if he so desires. However, their experience in seasonal agricultural labor markets has been rather limited. Moveover, there appears to be some question of the viability of the mechanism, since some recent collective bargaining agreements have apparently not included the hiring hall. The hiring hall concept is a clearing house between employers of labor. In contrast, the labor cooperative acts as a single employer, distributing its labor force over several participating growers.

Closely linked with the hiring hall concept is the labor union. Primary experience in agriculture with organized labor and collective bargaining is in California, as discussed by Hayes (Chap. 11). The California experience is particularly valuable as a case study for the viability of labor unions in agriculture. Hayes carefully examines the potential for similar activity in other states and compares the NLRA with the special California legislation. She concludes, as have most other observers, that there is potential in other areas, but it is most likely restricted to those other states that have a significant industrialized agriculture, such as Texas or Florida.

The question of the impact of unionization on wages is not resolved. Nevertheless, Coffey (Chap. 11) notes that we should not expect labor unions to significantly reduce poverty in the agricultural work force. This is a particularly important observation, and one which can also be applied to the increased structure argument.

The argument for a more structured organization to labor markets is often cast as having benefits to both workers, through more stable employment and consequently higher earnings, and to employers, through a more stable, experienced work force. However, if increased structure were to become widespread, there would be significantly fewer persons employed in agriculture, although those remaining would have more stable employment. The trade-offs posed by reducing short term employment in favor of increased structure are in principle no different than are the trade-offs faced in the mechanization issue, where harvest workers are displaced in favor of fewer, more highly skilled workers. Interpersonal comparisons are being made (or ignored) for which we have little basis in resolving. At the very minimum, the question must be addressed if policy is to deliberately pursue these objectives. The issue is the same regardless of the form that increased structure takes.

Governmental Programs and Policy

One of the more significant occurrences in agricultural labor markets through the 1970s has been the dramatic increase in protective legislation. Much of the early legislation that covered other workers in the economy specifically excluded farm workers. As Erven (Chap. 12) notes, farm workers are now covered with the same minimum wage rate as nonfarm workers, albeit with somewhat different inclusion criteria. Similarly, unemployment insurance, social security, and workmen's compensation are now the norm in agriculture rather than the exception. In addition, agriculture has been singled out for additional legislation such as the FLCRA.

One consequence of this recent development is a massive increase in record keeping for employers. Each program has its own inclusion criteria and record requirements. Moreover, the situation is further compounded for those operations that have nonagricultural components as well, since they come under two sets of rules and regulations. This often results in an increase in the cost of doing business. Given the competitive behavior of agriculture and the role of international markets, a predictable result is a decline in employment. The only question is the magnitude of the decrease and we have no information on that.

One way of viewing governmental regulations on the labor market is through their relation with the market process in the determination of wages, hours, and working conditions. There are governmental regulations on agricultural employment now that impact on each of the above three results of the market process. To what extent have they been altered by the regulations from what they would have been in their absence? We simply do not know at this stage of our knowledge.

It is difficult to deny, however, that as wages and working conditions improve, less productive workers will find more and more difficulty obtaining employment. Agriculture is in a somewhat unique case in that it has commonly been referred to as the employer of last resort. One can argue that coincident with low wages for the least productive workers in an economy are the least desirable working conditions. As employers increase wages and improve working conditions (both at a cost), it is inevitable that persons who are not sufficiently productive to warrant this level of compensation will face increased difficulty in obtaining employment. A rational employer will not continue to employ a person at a cost of, say, \$3.50 per hour if the value of this work is only \$2.50 per hour. The result is a continually narrowing set of employment opportunities for the minimally productive worker. He eventually becomes priced out of the market. Although we may find working conditions and wages deplorable relative to a national norm, the alternatives while better for some are likely to be worse for others.

Distinct from regulatory programs is the major service program for farm workers: CETA, Title III, Section 303, which is devoted exclusively to migrant and seasonal farm workers. Rochin (Chap. 13) does an exemplary job of tracing through the programs. Two features seem to stand out. One is that there is very little available data on the programs, and the other is that there has been minimal evaluation of the effectiveness of the programs. To a large extent the first precludes the latter. There appears to be a debate on who should be eligible for the programs; correspondingly, the author and discussant disagree as to whether eligibility should be broadened or more limited. The effectiveness of the program in meeting their goals would appear to be a crucial factor in resolving this question.

A particularly important point raised is that there are two objectives of Section 303 programs. One is to improve agricultural employment conditions for those remaining in agriculture, and the other is to assist those desiring to leave agriculture in obtaining employment and training. Virtually all of the efforts have been directed toward the latter objective to the exclusion of the former. It is noteworthy that many of the issues raised by Glover and Mamer would fall under the purview of the first of these objectives were they to be implemented. While the existing approach would be highly appropriate were agricultural employment declining, it is not so clear in the present case, where employment has been relatively stable. This places an extremely heavy burden on the program to be successful.

A second service program is the USES, also considered by Rochin. As noted above and in a number of the preceding papers, the USES plays only a minor role at this point in time in farm labor markets. The most commonly agreed upon cause for this is the dual role of enforcement and service that it now plays. A service that brings with it additional inspections cannot be expected to gain a great deal of acceptance. The important question is whether or not employers and workers are effectively matching jobs with workers in the absence of significant input from the USES.

Clearly, workers and employers are making contact with one another by the very fact that workers are employed. Presumably, the question is whether or not the operation of the market would improve with a more active role played by the USES. At present no one knows the answer to this; Rochin argues for a larger role, while other participants at the conference argued that this function ought to be left to different means.

The job matching role is often played by a labor contractor in seasonal agricultural labor markets. His primary function is to assemble a group of workers and to piece together spells of employment with various growers. Although the labor contractor is often perceived by interested observers with a great deal of suspicion and even notoriety due to some unscrupulous operators, the labor contractor fulfills an important economic function. It is somewhat of an irony that when a number of policies are directed toward reducing the role of the labor contractor, the demise of the USES has probably had a far greater impact in the opposite direction. It should also be noted that other ways in which this function has been fulfilled are through labor cooperatives and hiring halls. Each provides a means for coordinating workers with jobs. A final consideration is that a lack of a coordinated employment service may have been one factor that has led some operations to move toward improved personnel practices, as noted earlier. If turnover can be substantially reduced and the same workers rehired year after year, there is little need by these employers and their employees for employment services much different than any other nonagricultural employer or employee.

Governmental policies and programs impacting directly on labor are not the only ones of interest in considering farm labor markets. As has been repeatedly observed throughout this volume, the farm labor market is integrally related to the markets for agricultural products. Thus policies that impact on agricultural product markets in which there is a great deal of seasonal farm employment are also of interest.

Gardner (Chap. 14) presents a systematic treatment of traditional farm programs and their relation to farm labor markets, basically concluding that the tobacco program is one of the few that has impacted on the hired labor market. The main commodity programs are concentrated in the grains and fibers, in which seasonal labor does not at this point in our history play a major role. Despite the argument that tobacco is the only major commodity program in which there is likely to have been an impact on hired labor, it is particularly instructive and probably merits further study.

Other programs related to farm products impacting on farm labor are international trade policies, as Schuh (Chap. 14) has emphasized. The particular products of interest are predominantly fresh fruits and vegetables where the major portion of seasonal labor is employed. The common forms of trade policy in force are tariffs on the importation of products, and secondly, restrictions on size and grade of products through the use of market orders. Tariffs on products such as tomatoes during the Florida marketing season remain at a rate that appears to give Florida a modest competitive advantage over Mexico as estimated by USDA (Zepp and Simmons). However, they are unlikely to remain so for long since the tariff is at a fixed level rather than a percentage of value. Increasing production costs in both countries are rapidly eroding the significance of the tariff level. Assuming the tariffs are not increased, domestic producers will continually face a less protected market.

One result of a protected product market on labor is to support wages and employment in that industry over what they would be in the absence of protection. The result is the same whether it is in the form of a tariff or a set of size and grade restrictions serving to restrict imports. The persons paying for the protection are consumers in the form of a higher price for the product in question. A second consideration is that although employment and wages are supported in a protected product market, there is reason to believe that this may have some additional associated costs. In particular, the employment that is subsidized is primarily seasonal in nature. Yet a major concern is the attempt to reduce seasonality. To the extent that seasonal employment is exacerbated beyond what it would be in the absence of market protection, such a policy is counter to a goal of more stable employment. Schuh argues that as we move more and more toward open international markets for products (in this case fresh fruits and vegetables) more attention needs to be given to adjustment policies for displaced labor. This is surely of equal importance to labor displaced by other means.

POLICY ALTERNATIVES

The focus of this volume has been strictly on farm workers and their employers. As has been ably demonstrated by the contributors, there is little question that this is a group of workers at the lower end of the income and wealth scale. They face the problems common to persons in poverty however they may be employed. There are also undeniably unique features associated with agriculture and persons employed in agriculture, yet it is still noteworthy that farm workers are regularly singled out as an occupational group to be studied and have policy prescriptions distinct from other labor force participants.

There are clearly issues within the farm labor market which are relevant for policy; most have been addressed in one way or another in the preceding chapters and will be taken up in this section. However, it is extremely important to consider farm worker policy within the broader spectrum of poverty, regardless of the occupation. The fundamental purpose for this view is that labor markets are dynamic; workers shift from farm to nonfarm markets or out of the labor force and vice versa. Similarly, workers are displaced from various markets as changes occur within markets. A strictly occupational focus tends to ignore workers who silently disappear through various labor market changes--whether induced by either the private or public sector. Moreover, a focus solely in the context of the existing farm labor market tends to point one in the direction of maintaining current participants within the market rather than considering overall welfare within the economy. For example, much of the progress made in our economy over the past two centuries of history can be attributed to the ability of resources to be reallocated among productive activities as opportunities and knowledge have progressed. The initial focus will be on general policies relevant for persons in poverty, of which farm workers are a part; consideration will then be given to those more specific to farm labor markets.

Occupational choice by participants in the economy is a fundamental principle in the United States. (Clearly, occupational choice is limited by a person's abilities and access to capital for training. These limitations are noted throughout this volume.) The system is far from perfect; people make mistakes in a number of ways. Their expectations of the occupation may be in error; their abilities may be better suited to some other occupation; or the occupation may become obsolete over the individual's lifetime. Yet this is a principle that is widely shared, not only in this country but also in most others. In conjunction with this principle and in a market economy in contrast to a planned economy, labor market policy is likely to be more successful the less it impedes mobility between occupations.

Economic Growth

A most innocuous policy for the benefit of farm workers, and everyone else, is a prosperous economy. The pursuit of responsible monetary and fiscal policy to maintain economic growth is vital to the maintenance of employment opportunities. A growing economy is continually developing new employment opportunities into which low income persons can often move. Employment opportunities for farm workers outside of agriculture are unquestionably greater; less pressure is exerted on the farm labor market by fewer unemployed nonfarm workers. Moreover, there is evidence that minorities in particular suffer far fewer economic and employment problems in a growing economy.

Negative Income Tax

A second type of program that is blind to occupational choice but of assistance to persons in poverty is a universal income maintenance program. Income maintenance programs take on many different forms. We currently have a limited type of program through food stamps. There are arguments that the program draws potential labor away from agriculture (as well as other industries), but so far our empirical evidence is not well documented on this issue.

A proposed form of income maintenance program is the negative income tax which has been set forth in several different ways. Basically the program gives a subsidy to families below a predetermined income level; the size of payment depends on the family income level. Viewed from the opposite perspective, the more a family earns, the smaller the subsidy, or income maintenance payment. The two key parameters in the program are the basic guarantee level (assuming no earnings by the family) and the tax rate (the rate at which additional earnings are effectively taxed by the reduction in income maintenance payment).

As with any program, a major issue is its cost. The costs are of two types: 1) the direct costs of the payments and 2) the indirect costs of reduced output resulting from a potential reduction in labor supply. Extensive research has addressed these questions throughout the 1970s. One approach taken has been to make predictions on the basis of projected behavior under the program given our knowledge of how persons respond to changes in wage rates and other forms of unearned income. A summary of some of this work can be found in Cain and Watts. A second approach has been to implement pilot income maintenance programs and observe participants' behavior. A summary of work for rural areas is provided in Palmer and Pechman. The interested reader is referred to these volumes for a discussion of the research; justice cannot be done to it here. Despite the extensive research, we do not at this point have very precise knowledge of the magnitudes of either set of costs.

Clearly an income maintenance program would not be pursued solely for farm workers. If such a program were instituted, it is hoped that occupation would not in any way enter into eligibility for participation. The potential importance of an income maintenance program to farm workers is that it alleviates low incomes and poverty below what society deems to be acceptable. The choice of occupation is then up to the individual. The person is perfectly free to remain in farm work if he so chooses, to find alternative employment, or to simply not work. But in any case, the basic needs of the family are met by the program and the problems are not forced on the particular industry associated with the worker.

Agriculture has often received the label of being an employer of last resort. Persons who have difficulty finding or keeping employment elsewhere have often been able to obtain jobs in agriculture. The reason is that there remains a great deal of flexibility in employment and there remain jobs for which solely physical dexterity is required. The particular skills held by these persons are not highly valued in the rest of the economy, consequently the rate of return to employment is low. A primary problem is the innately low stock of human capital embodied in many persons in the farm work force. This is a problem of society in general, not of a particular industry where the persons are able to find employment. Correspondingly, policy prescriptions need to be at a broader level than occupation or industry.

Our past policies and economic progress have placed an unduly heavy burden on the labor force (see Schuh, Chap. 14), and I would submit a disproportionate share has been on workers at the lower end of the spectrum of abilities and skills. For example, policies increasing the cost of hiring labor raise the minimal level of productivity required of a person to be hired. If he simply does not meet that productivity requirement, he must seek employment from a sector or employers not affected by the policy, or worse yet, be unable to find employment. A negative income tax program addresses this very issue as do few other policies.

Alien Workers

The United States is currently in a particularly difficult policy dilemma regarding the presence of aliens working in the economy. Only a minority are legal H-2 temporary workers. However, there are believed to be significant numbers of undocumented workers, as Martin and North suggest. Since the majority are believed to be from Mexico with whom we wish to maintain particularly good relations, the option of closing the border is clearly not feasible. Our country's heritage as a melting pot argues in favor of immigration. However, the presence of extensive social programs poses a dilemma to this approach. There is little support for permitting extensive immigration if the effect is to increase the cost of social programs beyond the contributions to those programs from immigrants.

Traditionally immigrants have entered U.S. labor markets having the least formal structure and typically taking jobs with low skill. As employment becomes more and more structured and the minimal productivity level increases, job entry by immigrants becomes more difficult. Consequently, the resultant potential social costs to the host country tend to increase.

In the current situation, however, undocumented workers reportedly draw little in the form of benefits from social programs, and, if anything, are net contributors to the programs through payroll taxes. A second consideration is the incentive for employers to thwart programs in which they would otherwise have to participate if the workers were domestic or legal; the illegal worker has little recourse against an unscrupulous employer.

The significance of the undocumented worker in agricultural labor markets is the large pool of labor made available for many harvest jobs in direct competition with domestic workers. This makes efforts to internally improve conditions within the farm labor market very difficult. A market in which the labor supply schedule reflects considerably more available labor at given wage rates than in the absence of undocumented aliens is unlikely to show much improvement in working conditions. Many would argue that the supply of undocumented workers is nearly perfectly elastic.

In contrast to the undocumented workers are those who enter under the H-2 program (Martin and North, Chap. 6). The H-2 program provides a legal means for bringing in workers, much as the bracero program did. Expansion of the H-2 or a bracero program are alternatives which have been considered to bring the aliens into a legal status. These alternatives are clearly not panaceas, as there is considerable dissatisfaction with the H-2 program even at its currently minimal level.

The pertinent considerations for an H-2 program are treated by Martin and North and in the ensuing discussion by Welch. Basically two scenarios need to be considered: the situation when the program is well-established versus new uses for H-2 workers. In each case the gains and losses of a change from the existing situation need to be considered. Welch argues that in Florida sugarcane, an example of the established case, the gains probably exceed any losses from the program. Moreover, terminating the program is likely to induce considerable losses. The second scenario in which new uses for H-2 workers are considered is more problematic. Among the questions to be considered are windfall gains to owners of specialized resources, the gains to consumers, potential losses to domestic workers, and gains to domestic workers employed in ancillary services. The ultimate question appears to come down to a trade-off of trade between countries in the final product versus the importation of temporary labor services. A potential outcome in the future is that some products may simply not be feasible to produce in the United States at a price consumers are willing to pay. Examples in other industries abound: many types of clothing are made and electronic components are assembled in low cost labor countries for use in the United States. The distinctions between this practice and the importation of workers are not great.

The alien worker situation, as are the previous two policy considerations, is far more pervasive in the economy than just agricultural labor markets. Yet the resolution in each case is probably more significant to farm workers than any single program targeted directly to farm workers. In particular, unconstrained mobility into the United States from Mexico will continue to foster an unstructured farm labor market, extending labor-intensive harvest methods beyond what they might otherwise be.

Human Resource Adjustment

Adjustment to change is a necessity in a dynamic economy. However, we unfortunately have abundant evidence that this adjustment process is not always easy nor does everyone gain as a result of change. The policy dilemma is how to deal with losses to individuals or groups through the adjustment process while not totally impeding changes in which gains to society clearly exceed losses. We might parenthetically note that income maintenance programs discussed above would provide some assistance here in providing minimal support for displaced persons until they find an alternative livelihood. This is not in the least a minor consideration, since persons are not uncommonly impacted in affiliated occupations and industries when we might not a priori expect it. Identification of persons suffering losses in economic adjustment is a very difficult problem.

Adjustment to change in agriculture has typically been discussed within the context of technology, with mechanization being the most common form. Throughout this summary, however, we have noted that other types of changes can potentially bring about equally significant adjustments in labor markets (also see Martin and Hall; Martin and Johnson). The instances cited were the decasualization of employment through more systematic personnel practices, governmental commodity or labor policies, and changes in international trade. Significant reductions in employment from what ever source deserve attention for those displaced. This is where Bishop's early warning system enters. Applications are not only with new technology, but also with abrupt changes in tariffs. The more gradual changes are not as amenable to such an approach. One of the most explicit agendas for dealing with the more abrupt changes has been set forth by Just, Schmitz, and Zilberman. Since their statement is so highly germane to our discussion it is included here.

> Generally, there are potential gains from technological changes but whether or not all are made better off depends on the extent to which the gainers compensate the losers and the latter are stimulated to adjust rapidly so that losses do not continue. The amount and form of compen-

sation needed depend on such factors as the age of the displaced workers and the level of employment in the general economy.

We suggest that the following points are important:

1) In agriculture it is difficult to identify the workers displaced by a particular technological change. Care must be taken in developing appropriate definitions and in providing incentives for those adversely affected to identify themselves.

2) Compensation must be paid in a manner that preserves incentives to adjust to a changing world. For example, a program that paid a displaced worker the equivalent of his wages until he found another job would not be satisfactory. A better approach would be to provide a simple severance payment, to subsidize retraining, and to facilitate movement to other work.

3) Adequate predictions of the impact of technological improvements present a problem. Preparation of a meaningful "impact statement" prior to the development of a technology is virtually impossible. However, once a particular machine has been developed, a meaningful study can be conducted on its potential impact, the best way to introduce it and control its adverse effects, and the means by which adversely affected groups can be compensated.

4) Part of the taxation or other revenue from the gains of technological change has to be used to finance agencies overseeing compensation and control. In the absence of such use, other bureaucratic costs are likely to result because displaced workers may otherwise be added to the adjustment.

5) Incentives to entrepreneurs also play a role in increasing productivity over time. If rigid restrictions are continually placed on technological improvements in labor-intensive industries--for example, in the fruit and vegetable industries--then increasing restrictions will

> entice producers to shift into already mechanized production of other commodities. If handled improperly, such restriction could thus lead to more expensive foods and less dietary variety. Hopefully, incentives will be sufficiently preserved to ensure that new improvements will continue to be made so that both efficiency and income distribution goals are met. Without efficient means of production there is little product to distribute among the members of society. (pp. 1279-80)

Although the argument is within the context of technological change, it is equally applicable to other changes discussed earlier.

Professionalization of Farm Work

A number of the preceding chapters have addressed the need for further professionalization of farm work. In particular, one of the two objectives of the CETA 303 program is to assist farm workers who wish to remain in agriculture. Yet little if anything appears to have been done under this component; attention has been given to moving workers out of farm work. Professionalization has tended to improve labor productivity in many instances, thereby improving incomes as well as stability of employment.

Improvements in personnel management are not something that policy can dictate. Yet there are examples where it has been tried and apparently been successful. One approach is to provide information and education on such practices for employers. The President's Commission on Migratory Labor suggested 30 years ago that this was an activity in which Cooperative Extension might play a role. Although there has been some effort in this direction during the 1970s, it is clear that there remains opportunity for additional effort in this direction.

The proviso noted earlier regarding professionalization must again be raised, however. To the extent that fewer persons remain employed as a result of these practices, attention must also be given to those who have lost employment opportunities, many of which may have been only short term. An interesting consideration would be a careful analysis of the gains through professionalization relative to the losses incurred.

Human Resource Development

Predominant efforts of CETA 303 programs have been toward augmenting the human resource in some way so that alternative employment with higher earning power is feasible. A number of the preceding analyses have explicitly or implicitly suggested that further training as a major program for farm workers remaining in farm work as a major program is not one that would be expected to yield high returns in their present work. (This is not to be confused with the idea of professionalization in which workers might be trained for new specialized skills such as mechanics, etc.) Again, agriculture appears to be one source of employment for persons who for whatever reason have a low earning power. Efforts to improve the earning capacity within the context of an overall policy for augmenting human resources have become a standard part of our educational and training system. Yet to believe that training will significantly alter in a permanent fashion the farm work force is probably not justified.

The reason is that no matter how much training is done, there will always be significant numbers of persons in the economy who are undertrained or unable to attain other than minimal earnings. There is no reason at this juncture to believe that the "successes" of training will not again be replaced by a new generation of persons with low earning power in search of work. Under an alternative scenario in which agricultural jobs were restructured requiring increased skill levels, training would be expected to offer a significant payoff to workers, employers, and society. But as argued elsewhere in this summary, fundamental changes in the supply and demand for farm workers are necessary before extensive restructuring can be expected.

Given the heavy concentration of low incomes

among farm workers, continued emphasis toward the children of farm-worker families appears highly appropriate. Whether or not programs directed toward adults are successful, society has an even greater stake in their children.

Traditional Programs and Policies

Explicit attention has been given to the predominant labor programs and policies in preceding papers of the volume. Unlike the situation even five to ten years ago, there is now a great deal of similarity between farm and nonfarm coverage by programs such as minimum wages and unemployment insurance. Enforcement is a serious problem given the dispersed nature of agriculture. Other problems raised by employers are record keeping requirements, which have dramatically increased with the extension of these programs to agriculture. Worthy of consideration is removing the distinction between agricultural and nonagricultural coverage. The issues surrounding collective bargaining are largely covered by Hayes (Chap. 11) and the ensuing discussion by Coffey. The only point to be made here is that although choices are to be made, e.g. extending NLRA to agriculture, most are peripheral to the fundamental problem in farm labor markets; collective bargaining will not alleviate low incomes associated with low earning power.

DATA NEEDS

Researchers and policy analysts never have adequate data regardless of the program under study; seasonal agricultural employment data are no exception. No attempt is made here for an exhaustive coverage of farm worker and employer data; Chapters 1, 3, and 11 by Holt, Fritsch, and Hayes, respectively, give considerable attention to the existing data base. A recent AAEA-USDA task force critiqued agricultural employment data and offered suggestions for improvement and extension of the data base (Holt et al.). The purpose of this section is to point to data needs as expressed by the various contributors within the context of the problems addressed. The distinction is that these might not be components of a continuing data system, but they are current informational needs within the existing problem situation.

Both Holt and Fritsch caution data users on the two conceptually distinct sources of employment data, urging that extreme care should be exercised in utilizing the correct source for the problem at hand. Household data are the appropriate source for studying workers and their characteristics. Establishment data are the appropriate source for jobs and characteristics of the jobs. Although we would often find it useful to be able to associate jobs with workers, there is simply no logical way of doing so with existing data. A continuation of approaches to establishing a linkage with alternative data collection methods is a high priority item.

Household Data

The primary household data are the USDA hired farm work force series. This is an extremely useful data series from which we learn what we do know about farm workers. The data are reasonably complete; we would be able to say very little about farm workers in the absence of the series.

One feature about which we are able to learn little from the existing household data is the labor force behavior of farm workers over time, as suggested by Matta (Chap. 5). Fritsch describes much of farm work as an entry level occupation. It would be useful to know more about the behavior of these workers after they leave farm work, particularly for training programs directed toward finding alternative employment. This requires a longitudinal data collection system in which information on the same household is collected over a number of years. Although this would provide a vast wealth of information, it would be extremely difficult to collect primarily due to the mobile characteristic of farm workers. The very reason we are interested, however, is that we want to know what happens to them after they move on to something else.

Establishment Data

Mamer (Chap. 10) convincingly argues that little is known about the types of jobs which are available in agriculture. As agriculture becomes more and more industrialized, job specialization will continue to grow. One area in which additional information on the variety of jobs would be particularly useful is in knowing the set of skills required for agricultural employment and orienting vocational training in that direction. The refinement of occupational categories will contribute in the same way.

Nonagricultural establishment data typically include information on employment costs in addition to wages. As farm workers are covered under additional programs such as unemployment insurance and workmen's compensation, data on the associated employment costs will be useful. Further data on fringe benefits and their associated employer costs will likewise be useful. Historically, agriculture has had little to report in either of these areas, but there is considerable evidence that this is changing. From the employer's standpoint, there is little difference whether costs increase due to higher wages or to other employment related costs. Yet if we measure only wages, an important part of employment costs is being ignored.

Particularly problematic is the information regarding undocumented aliens. Domestic farm workers are sufficiently difficult to systematically count as a result of their mobility. But an undocumented worker is not likely to be represented in the household data at all. One reason is the likelihood that the illegal will elude the interviewer due to fear of being discovered and apprehended. A second reason is that the primary household data base (USDA Hired Farm Work Force) is collected as a supplement to the December CPS. December is not a peak seasonal farm labor month; consequently fewer are likely to be in the United States at the time of interview. It is particularly troublesome that although we can address questions with some degree of confidence regarding domestic farm workers, there is a large number of undocumented workers (and no one knows how large) about whom we know little or nothing and who can dramatically influence the seasonal farm labor market.

RESEARCH NEEDS

The emphasis in this volume has been to document our present state of knowledge about seasonal agricultural labor markets rather than conducting original basic research. One purpose in doing so is to provide insights into our research needs. Priority items in need of further research are thus outlined in light of our present stock of knowledge about this labor market.

Labor Displacement

One of the predominant problems continuing to face seasonal farm labor markets is adjusting to new forms of laborsaving technology. Our past experience in handling the distribution of gains and losses has been to largely ignore them. The primary beneficiaries are typically consumers, while the displaced workers bear the adjustment burden. A reasonably complete set of considerations for addressing the compensation issue has been set forth by Just, Schmitz and Zilberman as previously cited. However, much additional work is necessary before such a plan could ever be successfully implemented. As Just, Schmitz and Zilberman note, unemployment insurance, which now includes agriculture, does provide one scheme for compensating workers. However, it has typically been viewed and analyzed in the context of compensation for cyclical changes in employment.

Additional sources of displacement noted above were through increased levels of imports via liberalization of trade agreements and decasualization of seasonal employment. In each case there are workers who lose to the benefit of other persons in the economy. In the case of increased imports, the Trade Act of 1974 provides adjustment assistance to displaced workers. However, the short term nature of employment in seasonal agricultural crops presents a more complicated case than for an industry such as automobiles. Again, the issue is one of properly identifying those who are truly displaced. The difficulties are the same whether the source of displacement is technology, trade, or decasualization. Presumably similar principles could be applied in each case.

Empirical research measuring the economic gains and losses that accrue to labor, producers, consumers, and taxpayers resulting from changes that (may) have displaced labor would greatly enhance available information for policy choice.

Income Maintenance Programs

Income maintenance programs were discussed relative to the important role they could play in alleviating poverty problems often associated with persons who take farm work. The presumption is that this type of program does not impede the allocation of labor between different types of employment as do many programs targeted for a particular occupational group. Although there has been a vast amount of research on income maintenance programs, none of it has focused specifically on farm workers. There are currently no estimates of its impact on the farm labor market. Major questions of interest concern who would benefit and by how much. How would it alter the supply of labor to agriculture? Given experience in examining other sets of data within the perspective of income maintenance programs, one cannot expect precise a priori answers. However, given the potential for benefit to this segment of the labor force and their families, there is every reason to examine the program's potential impact.

International Trade

The United States is increasingly in an open international economy; agricultural products are no exception. In addition, since many fresh fruits and vegetables are produced in low income countries, there is little reason to believe that any action will be taken to impede imports from those countries. Although we have considerable knowledge about trade in commodities, rarely is it traced through to the impact on domestic employment. A better understanding of the linkages between trade and employment would improve our ability to predict changes in agricultural employment resulting from changing international economic conditions in competing product markets. This in conjunction with the ability to deal with losses to particular groups would surely enhance our ability to accept change in the economy for the benefit of a majority of society.

Alien Labor

Research on H-2 alien labor has focused largely on the question of direct substitution of alien workers for domestic workers. While this is highly informative, a number of additional considerations could lead to a different set of conclusions. In particular, additional research needs to address the impact of the programs on consumers, and secondly, the employment impact on ancillary industries. Another consideration, particularly in the context of potential H-2 or similar programs, is a careful analysis of the gains and losses of importing the product in question versus utilizing temporary alien labor to produce it domestically.

Given the assumed magnitude of undocumented workers, research contributing to our ability to deal with the situation is of considerable importance. Yet by the nature of the problem, it is clearly a difficult one with which to deal. Innovative work in this area should definitely be encouraged.

Labor Market Regulations

Farm labor markets have experienced a dramatic increase in protective legislation and other labor market regulations throughout the 1970s. However, the impact of these regulations on wages, level of employment, and working conditions has received little research attention. Since such programs are not uncommonly amended, it would be useful to know what modifications might be most beneficial and assist the programs in meeting their goals.

A second major concern is the issue of enforcement of labor laws and regulations in agriculture. Enforcement of workplace regulations presents a more difficult problem than in factories, due not only to the inherent mobile work environment, but also to the dispersed location of work crews. Not only is excessive enforcement an irritant to those employers who are striving to meet the regulations, but it is also expensive. Consideration should be given to devising alternative forms of incentives to meet the objectives of the programs in lieu of increased enforcement.

Supply and Demand for Farm Labor

A number of authors have pointed to the lack of information on basic supply and demand response in seasonal farm labor markets. These are undoubtedly among the most crucial pieces of information with which to predict the impact of most programs and policies on the labor market. By the same token, the need for additional analysis of migration behavior was recommended. The supply, demand, and migration analysis is crucial to our ability to deal with the interrelations between the temporally and spatially separated labor markets in agriculture. The three components are basic inputs to a framework such as set forth by Spreen, for systematically analyzing such labor markets.

Product Markets

Farm labor is as dependent for jobs on continued production as growers are dependent on labor for the production of their crop. Since the demand for labor is a derived demand, knowledge of the demand conditions for the crop in question is necessary to draw conclusions on the impact of various policies or changes in agriculture on the labor market. Our knowledge of the demand elasticities for many of the crops in which seasonal farm workers are employed is relatively sparse. Additional empirical research estimating product demand elasticities in labor intensive crops would improve our capability of predicting potential changes in labor markets.

Labor Market Organization

There are a number of different potential institutions for coordinating workers and jobs. Within agriculture, labor contractors, the USES, labor cooperatives, and hiring halls all have attempted to fulfill this function. Research on the efficiency of these alternative forms would be useful, for example, in evaluating how extensive a role the USES should attempt to play in farm labor markets.

Labor Management

Various authors have recommended that additional attention be given to upgrading work in agriculture as a means of assisting those who wish to remain in farm work. However, we do not have a large stock of information to draw upon for specific types of work that can be upgraded. One source of information is from employers who have instituted innovative personnel management practices as well as efforts to systematize the work.

Additional programs that have received little attention in agriculture are apprenticeship and other training systems. Research on alternative training systems that might be most beneficial in agriculture would be particularly worthwhile.

CONCLUDING COMMENTS

Seasonal farm labor markets remain largely unstructured, require mainly manual dexterity by workers, and continue to permit extremely free entry and exit by workers. Consequently, many persons apparently find jobs in agriculture when few other avenues of employment are open to them. The employment relationship is typically quite casual. Given this lack of structure and the peak seasonality in many parts of the country during the summer months, it is not surprising that the largest single classification of workers is students. The employment opportunity is obviously beneficial to the students, and the source is timely for employers as well. Without the input by students, the seasonality problem would be far more grave than it has been. By the same token, many problems associated with farm workers are not an issue with students. They are presumably working there while temporarily out of school and are then moving on to some other employment upon the completion of their schooling. (Longitudinal data would provide more confidence in such a statement.) Training programs would presumably be of minimal value for this group; there is no need for special training programs for persons concurrently in school and having every intention of moving on to some other career upon completion of schooling. Moreover, some efforts such as increasing professionalization of farm work would presumably work to their disadvantage.

The nonstudent component of the farm labor force has been the primary focus throughout our discussions. A broad perspective of a labor force with individuals continually moving in and out, but typically poor, is necessary for addressing the problems faced by farm workers. Their poverty is commonly associated with a minimal stock of human capital, severely limiting productivity and potential earning capacity. Increasing the cost of hiring low productivity workers through various programs will definitely raise the productivity level of the employed workers. But it clearly has not benefited those who are not sufficiently productive to meet the increased minimum productivity level, and thus have even more difficulty earning a living.

Within this context, income maintenance programs offer considerable appeal over various programs that are targeted for specific occupational groups. A major consideration is that it permits labor markets to adjust to varying market conditions. Furthermore, the particularly difficult problem of identifying persons who are displaced for one reason or another is eased if the program is available regardless of former occupation.

A major issue, again beyond the farm labor market, is the resolution of the problem of undocumented workers in the United States. Since undocumented workers are believed to be a significant portion of the farm labor force, however the current dilemma is resolved will clearly impact on this market. Similarly, so long as there is a nearly perfectly elastic supply of alien workers for agriculture, it is unreasonable to anticipate many significant changes in the labor market in the near future.

Notes

Chapter 1

1. This section is based upon the analysis of county level 1970 Census of Population data by Calvin Beale, Economic Development Division, ESCS, USDA, whose assistance with this section is gratefully acknowledged.

Chapter 2

1. Although annual man-hours of hired farm labor have declined, the change in annual average man-hours of hired labor per farm is less certain. Estimates of annual man-hours derived by deflating reported expenditures on hired farm labor by the state average wage rate reported by the USDA in *Farm Labor* show a continual decline from one census year to another in annual average man-hours per farm. The decline is 50% between 1969 and 1974. Estimates taken from the USDA publication *The Hired Farm Working Force*, however, show an increase between 1969 and 1974.
2. We are considering annual income differences, and since farm work is seasonal, individuals are permitted to hold other jobs sequentially during the year and to compare the income for the sequence of jobs with the income from occupation 0. To simplify the analysis, it is assumed that wage income is the only characteristic of these other jobs that matters to the workers.
3. Bruce Gardner (1981) and also Poveda (1977) have found in the CPS hired farm work force data that the daily wage rates are much higher for off-farm work than for farm work among workers who report

both types of work in a year. There are several possible explanations. First, workers place a higher marginal value on nonwage aspects of farm than off-farm work. Second, family earnings may be higher when the head works for a wage in agriculture than when he works at nonfarm wage jobs even though his wage rate is higher for a nonfarm job.

4. Sometimes employers or crew leaders directly pay these expenses, but it seems likely to be the workers who ultimately pay in lower earnings than they would otherwise receive. Also, crew leaders are essentially "middle men" between migrants and growers whose function is to monitor labor market conditions and to supply workers to harvest crops at prescribed times.
5. Poveda's and Emerson's Florida studies show that earnings of farm workers initially increase with years of farm work experience for wages, but at a decreasing rate.
6. They do not, however, have any scientific method for classifying jobs. We have argued above that attempts to assess nonwage characteristics of jobs are unlikely to be successful.
7. Some dualists argue that employers use schooling and training for making "irrational" and discriminatory hiring and promotional decisions. Training is viewed as a screening or certification system used to identify pre-existing skills, and the training has no direct effect on a worker's useable skills or productivity (Cain). Griliches shows that schooling has a separate effect on earnings from that of ability. Layard and Psacharopoulos provide evidence against the screening hypothesis of schooling. For instance, they point out that a much less costly method would be developed and used to discover pre-existing skills.
8. Briggs et al. (1977) find considerable sex and race discrimination in Southern rural labor markets. Part of this may be facilitated by labor market disequilibrium, where there is

excess supply of labor at the prevailing wage. Also for some groups, e.g., women and blacks, there may be less reliable information available on their potential job productivity and they may not currently be equal when the type of training and prior job experience are examined for relevancy to current jobs.

Chapter 3

1. The QALS was terminated with the April 1981 survey, subsequent to the writing of this chapter. Starting with July 1982 the survey is to be done annually (editor).

Chapter 4

1. Note that throughout this chapter agricultural employment is meant to include only hired workers. It specifically does not include operators or unpaid family workers. The data throughout this section are from various issues of USDA's *Hired Farm Working Force* publications.
2. This problem is referred to as the identification problem in the econometrics literature. The estimates obtained here would correspond to reduced form estimates rather than structural estimates. Although it is generally a straightforward procedure to obtain estimates of the structure with continuous variable models, the procedure for models with discrete variables such as this become quite involved and are beyond the scope of this chapter.

Chapter 6

1. *Bracero* is Spanish for the "strong-armed one," i.e., a farm worker. There are two classes of legal aliens under the U.S. immigration law: immigrants and nonimmigrants. Those who can stay in the nation for the rest of their lives if they so choose and become citizens, if they apply, are

immigrants. All other aliens legally in the nation are *nonimmigrants*. They may enter only for a precise purpose and stay only as long as permitted. The bracero and the H-2 programs are both nonimmigrant programs.

2. Piece rate pay systems also reduce supervisory needs because they shift (at least part of) the efficiency burden from employers to workers.
3. In the H-2 case, it could be argued that other crops are also harvested by (illegal) aliens. It is probably true that illegal aliens harvest a high proportion of certain crops, but the overwhelming majority of the hired farm work force remains non-Hispanic (and presumably legally resident in the United States) (USDA, *The Hired Farm Working Force* reports).
4. The best example of this strategy is the Coastal Growers (Citrus) Association in California, formed in 1970 to assure an adequate harvest work force and minimize picking costs. About 10% of the 1970 work force now picks a substantially larger crop. This remaining 10% is composed of the "best" pickers--largely prime-age males.
5. In 1979, Florida tomato growers complained that Mexican winter vegetables were being "dumped" in the United States--sold at unfairly low prices. State Department intervention and promises encouraged the Florida growers to withdraw their petition, but the debate illustrates the difficulties inherent in replacing domestic with foreign products even when domestic supplies are limited. (See *Wall Street Journal*, 27 Sept. 1979, p. 34.)

Chapter 7

1. This refers to the choices of the optimal x levels which solve $\max_x EU(\pi_0)$ and $\max_x EU(\pi_1)$.
2. The measure of absolute risk aversion is $r_a = -[U''(\pi)]/[U'(\pi)]$. Decreasing absolute risk aversion implies that $\partial r_a/\partial\pi < 0$.

Chapter 8

1. Since P_2 and P_3 are exogenously determined, the demand for crops from Regions 2 and 3 is perfectly elastic. Thus the area under the demand curve is P × Z.
2. All supply and demand schedules are drawn as straight lines to simplify the diagrams. We acknowledge that statistically estimated labor supply functions are typically nonlinear (Emerson, Chap. 4).
3. Emerson et al. (1976) have argued that for some crops (citrus) the derived demand for labor is perfectly inelastic. The marginal value product schedule "traced" out under the assumption of fixed proportions among inputs will be a stepped curve rather than a smooth one (Dorfman).
4. If the demand for labor is perfectly inelastic, total employment will be the same regardless of migration; the equilibrium wage rates, however, will be lower.

Chapter 9

1. There are hopeful signs that the historical inattention to labor by the Agricultural Extension Service is diminishing. A survey of State Extension Manpower Programs made by David Ruesink of Texas A. & M. University uncovered a few examples in many states of efforts to upgrade, or decasualize farm work, or to improve employer-employee relations in farm work. Unfortunately most of the program activity identified by the survey did not directly relate to upgrading agricultural jobs. The agricultural extension network seems to devote more resources and effort to attempting to eliminate the need for harvest labor through mechanization than it does to upgrading harvest jobs.

Chapter 10

1. Benedict wrote, "The many and evident exceptions to this characterization, as for example the foreign workers of the West Coast states, were largely ignored. . . ." (p. 519).
2. In 1970, however, the USDA began to report wage rates of farm workers identified by job type (field and livestock workers, packinghouse workers, machine operators, etc.) in addition to categories based on method of payment (day, week, month, etc.) (USDA, *Farm Labor*, Apr. 1970, p. 9).

Chapter 11

1. Throughout this discussion terminology from the *Census of Agriculture* will be used. "Regular" workers are defined as those working 150 days or more during the census year for a single employer; "seasonal" workers are those working 25 to 149 days; those working less than 25 days are termed "casual" workers. It should be noted that the number of episodes of employment, rather than the number of farm workers, is compiled using this methodology. Thus if an individual works 150 days for one employer and 15 days each for four other employers, he will be counted 5 times--once as a "regular" worker and again as four "casual" workers. The nature of agricultural payroll records probably prevents any compilation of an unduplicated count of U.S. farm workers.

Chapter 13

1. The Rowe and Smith data came from supplementary questions to the CPS of the Bureau of Census, administered in December 1973 to approximately 47,000 households. The data do not provide information below the regional level, nor infor-

mation on the time of year the work was performed. Furthermore, there is reason to believe that the data underestimate migrants and Mexican workers because of the field collection procedure and the time of the survey interviews (Schlenger, Ondrizek, and Hallan).

2. The eight programs active in fiscal 1979 were: Orange County Manpower Commission ($286,700); CET ($883,200); Proteus Adult Training ($1,555,200); County of Los Angeles ($81,000); Greater California Education Project ($3,643,500); Inland Manpower Association ($477,541); North Bay Human Development Corporation ($1,192,100); and City of Stockton ($564,186).

3. *Federal Register*, Rules and Regulations, May 25, 1979, pp. 30602-30603. Public service employment is not an allowable activity under the Section 303 program. Training applies to "classroom training," "on-the-job training" and "work experience" at outstationed work sites.

4. The CETA was passed into legislation in December 1973 and the USDL's decision to begin funding grants on July 1, 1974 "placed a heavy implementation burden upon both the department and prospective prime sponsors. Within 9 months of December 1973, the program was designed, grants were awarded and the first participants were being enrolled" (*Employment and Training Report of the President* 1976, p. 95). During the brief start-up period, however, procedures for judging alternative organizations and evaluative "machinery" for assessing impacts were not well established. Hence, consultant firms were funded to conduct evaluations. The 1978 CETA Amendments Title III, part B, section 313 (d), require that the secretary of labor prepare and submit to the Congress an annual evaluation plan. The Office of Research and Development of the Office of Policy, Evaluation, and Research, Employment and Training Administration, has overall responsibility for conducting the research experimentation.

References Cited

Abt Associates. 1971. "An Assessment of the Experimental and Demonstration Interstate Program for South Texas Migrants." Final Rep. Cambridge, Mass., Jan.

Alchian, Armen A., and Harold Demsetz. 1972. "Production, Information Costs, and Economic Organization." *Am. Econ. Rev.* 62:777-95.

Arrow, K. J. 1971. *Theory of Risk Bearing.* Englewood Cliffs, N.J.: Prentice-Hall.

---. 1975. "Vertical Integration and Communication." *Bell J. Econ.* 6:173-83.

Baker, B. Kimball. 1967. "Boosting Workers Up Farm Job Ladders." *Worklife* 6:2-6. Employment Train. Adm., USDL.

Barton, Amy E. 1978. *Campesinas: Women Farm Workers in the California Agricultural Labor Force.* Sacramento: Calif. Comm. Status Women.

Batra, R. W., and A. Ullah. 1974. "Competitive Firm and the Theory of Input Demand Under Price Uncertainty." *J. Polit. Econ.* 82:537-48.

Bauder, W. W., J. G. Elterich, R. O. P. Farrish, and J. S. Holt. Jan. 1976. *Impact of Extension of Unemployment Insurance to Agriculture.* Bull. 804. Pa. Agric. Exp. Stn.

Becker, Gary S. 1971. *Economic Theory.* New York: Knopf.

---. 1975. *Human Capital: A Theoretical and Empirical Analysis, with Special Reference to Education.* 2d ed. Human Behavior and Social Institutions 5. New York: Natl. Bur. Econ. Res.

Becket, James W. 1969. "Agricultural Labor Skills--Past, Present, Future." In *Fruit and Vegetable Harvest Mechanization, Manpower Implications*, ed.

B. G. Cargill and G. E. Rossmiller, pp. 257-66. RMC Rep. 17. East Lansing: Rural Manpower Cent., Mich. State Univ.

Bednarzik, Robert W. 1979. "A Micro Model of Labor Supply for Part-Time Workers Using Matched CPS Data." Bur. Labor Stat. Staff Pap. 10. Bur. Labor Stat., USDL.

Belongia, Mike. 1979. "Domestic Food Programs and Their Related Impacts on Retail Food Prices." *Am. J. Agric. Econ.* 61:358-62.

Benedict, Murray. 1953. *Farm Policies of the United States 1790-1950.* New York: Twentieth Century Fund.

Ben-Porath, Y. 1967. "The Production of Human Capital and the Life Cycle of Earnings." *J. Polit. Econ.* 75:352-65.

Binswanger, H. P. 1974. "A Microeconomic Approach to Induced Innovation." *Econ. J.* 84:940-58.

Bishop, C. E., ed. 1967. *Farm Labor in the United States.* New York: Columbia Univ. Press.

Blair, R. D. 1974. "Random Input Prices and the Theory of the Firm." *Econ. Inq.* 12:214-25.

Blau, Peter M., and Otis D. Duncan. 1967. *The American Occupational Structure.* New York: Wiley & Sons.

Briggs, V. M. 1975. "Illegal Immigration and the American Labor Force: The Use of 'Soft' Data for Analysis." Work. Pap. 75-1. Cent. Study Hum. Resour., Univ. Texas.

Briggs, V. M., John Adams, B. Rungeling, and L. Smith. 1977. *Employment, Income and Welfare in the Rural South.* New York: Praeger.

Cain, G. G. 1976. "The Challenge of Segmented Labor Market Theories to Orthodox Theory: A Survey." *J. Econ. Lit.* 14:1215-57.

Cain, Glen G., and Harold W. Watts, ed. 1973. *Income Maintenance and Labor Supply.* Chicago: Rand McNally.

California. Agricultural Labor Relations Board. 1979. *Third Annual Report of the Agricultural Labor Relations Board for the Fiscal Year Ended June 30, 1979.* Sacramento.

California. 1979a. Employment Development Department. *Midmonth Estimates of Employment by Type of Worker*. Rep. 881W. Sacramento.

---.' 1979b. *Occupations in Agriculture 1979*. Sacramento.

---. *Agricultural Employment in California, by Type of Worker: Mid-month Estimates*. Rep. 881M. Various issues.

---. *Farm Labor Report: Employment by Counties*. Rep. 881A. Various issues.

California Commission on the Status of Women. 1978. "Women Farmworkers in the California Agricultural Labor Force." Sacramento, Dec.

California Labor Code. Sections 1140-1166.3 (West).

Carlton, D. W. 1976. "Vertical Integration in Competitive Markets Under Uncertainty." Unpublished, Apr.

Carter, C., D. L. Hueth, J. Mamer, and A. Schmitz. 1981. "Labor Strikes and the Price of Lettuce." *West. J. Agric. Econ.* 6:1-14.

Chiswick, Barry R. 1974. *Income Inequality: Regional Analyses within a Human Capital Framework*. Human Behavior and Social Institutions 4. New York: Natl. Bur. Econ. Res.

Coase, R. H. 1937. "The Nature of the Firm." *Economica* 4:386-405.

Council of Economic Advisers. 1979. *Economic Report of the President*. Washington: GPO.

Covey, C. D. 1980. *Handbook of Regulations Affecting Florida Farm Employers and Employees*. Gainesville: Univ. Fla., Inst. Food Agric. Sci., Fla. Coop. Ext. Serv.

Cox, LaWanda Fenlason. 1942. "Agricultural Labor in the United States 1865-1900 with Special Reference to the South." Ph.D. diss., University of California.

Daberkow, Stan G., and Conrad F. Fritsch. 1979. "Agricultural Workplace Safety: A Perspective on Research Needs." *Am. J. Agric. Econ.* 61:824-35.

Dahlberg, A. 1978. "Changes of Investments in Publicly Owned Social Overhead Capital in Connection with Labor Migration." *J. Reg. Sci.* 18:195-202.

Doeringer, Peter B., and Michael J. Piore. 1971. *Internal Labor Markets and Manpower Analyses*. Lexington, Mass.: D. C. Heath.

Dolp, Franz. 1968. *Decasualization of Seasonal Farm Labor*. Information Series in Agricultural Economics, Rep. 68-1. Berkeley: Univ. Calif. Agric. Exp. Stn.

Dorfman, Robert. 1953. "Mathematical or 'Linear' Programming: A Non-mathematical Exposition." *Am. Econ. Rev.* 43:797-825.

Duloy, John H., and Roger D. Norton. 1973. "CHAC: A Programming Model of Mexican Agriculture." In *Multi-Level Planning: Case Studies in Mexico*, ed. L. Goreux and A. Manne, pp. 291-337. Amsterdam: North-Holland Publ.

---. 1975. "Prices and Incomes in Linear Programming Models." *Am. J. Agric. Econ.* 57:591-600.

Duncan, O. D., and J. D. Cowhig. 1966. "Social Background and Occupational Commitment of Male Wageworkers in Agriculture." *Agric. Econ. Res.* 18:129-35.

Emerson, Robert D. 1975. "The Supply of Hired Farm Workers." Paper presented at winter meetings Econometric Society, Dallas, Texas, Dec.

Emerson, Robert D., and Gustavo J. Arcia. 1979. "Unemployment Insurance and Agricultural Labor Supply." Paper presented at annual meetings Am. Agric. Econ. Assoc., Pullman, Wash., Aug., 1979. Staff Pap. 126, Food Resour. Econ. Dep., Univ. Fla.

Emerson, Robert D., Thomas S. Walker, and Chris O. Andrew. 1976. "The Market for Citrus Harvesting Labor." *Sout. J. Agric. Econ.* 8:149-54.

Employment and Training Report of the President. 1976-1979 ed. (Formerly *Manpower Report of the President*.) Prepared by USDL, Employment Train. Adm. and HEW, Off. Hum. Dev.

Erven, Bernard L., et al. 1978. *Ohio Farm Labor Handbook*. Columbus: Ohio State Univ., Ohio Coop. Ext. Serv.

Fairchild, Gary F. 1975. *Socioeconomic Dimensions of*

Florida Citrus Harvesting Labor. ERD Report 75-2. Econ. Res. Dep., Fla. Dep. Citrus, Univ. Fla., Gainesville.

Feder, G. 1977. "The Impact of Uncertainty on a Class of Objective Functions." *J. Econ. Theory* 16:504-12.

Feldstein, Martin. 1973. "The Economics of the New Unemployment." *Public Interest* 33:3-42.

Finney, D. J. 1971. *Probit Analysis*. 3d ed. Cambridge: Cambridge Univ. Press.

Fischer, S. 1977. "Long Term Contracts, Rational Expectations, and the Optimal Money Supply Rule." *J. Polit. Econ.* 85:191-206.

Fisher, Dennis U. 1975. *Farm Labor Regulations*, Agric. Econ. Ext. Bull. 75-26. Ithaca, N.Y.: Cornell Univ., Dep. Agric. Econ.

Fisher, Lloyd H. 1953. *The Harvest Labor Market in California*. Cambridge, Mass.: Harvard Univ. Press.

Flaim, P. O. 1979. "The Effects of Demographic Changes in the Nation's Unemployment Rates." *Mon. Labor Rev.* 3:13-23.

Fleisher, B. F., and T. J. Kniesner. 1980. *Labor Economics: Evidence and Policy*. 2d ed. Englewood Cliffs, N.J.: Prentice-Hall.

Florida. Department of Commerce. 1977. *1977 Florida Annual Rural Manpower Report*.

Floyd, John E. 1965. "The Effects of Farm Price Supports on the Returns to Land and Labor in Agriculture." *J. Polit. Econ.* 73:148-58.

Friedland, William H., and Amy E. Barton. 1976. "Tomato Technology." *Society* 13:35-42.

Friedland, William H., Amy E. Barton, and Robert J. Thomas. 1981. *Manufacturing Green Gold: Capital, Labor, and Technology in the Lettuce Industry*. New York: Cambridge Univ. Press.

Friedland, William H., and Dorothy Nelkin. 1971. *Migrant: Agricultural Workers in America's Northeast*. New York: Holt, Rinehart and Winston.

Friedman, B. M. 1979. "Optimal Expectations and the

Extreme Information Assumptions of Rational Expectations' Macromodels." *J. Monetary Econ.* 4:23-41.

Fuller, Varden. 1942. "The Supply of Agricultural Labor as a Factor in the Evolution of Farm Organization in California." In *Violations of Free Speech and Rights of Labor,* pp. 19777-19898. Report of Committee on Education and Labor, U.S. Congress, Senate, 76th Cong., 3d sess. 1940.

---. 1960. "Economics of Migrant Labor: Unsolved Social and Economic Problems." *Soc. Order* 10:4-12.

---. 1967. "Farm Manpower Policy." In *Farm Labor in the United States,* ed. C. E. Bishop, pp. 97-114. New York: Columbia Univ. Press.

Fuller, Varden, and Willem Van Vuuren. 1972. "Farm Labor and Labor Markets." In *Size, Structure and Future of Farms,* ed. A. G. Ball and E. O. Heady, pp. 144-70. Ames: Iowa State Univ. Press.

Galarza, Ernesto. 1964. *Merchants of Labor.* San Jose, Calif.: Rosicrucian Press.

Galvin, Dan Castillo. 1977. "Relationship of Education, Age, Sex and Citizenship to the Aspirations of Citrus Harvesters." Ph.D. diss., Texas A&M University, College Station, Dec.

Gardner, Bruce L. 1972. "Minimum Wages and the Farm Labor Market." *Am. J. Agric. Econ.* 54:473-76.

---. 1974. "Farm Population Decline and the Income of Rural Families." *Am. J. Agric. Econ.* 56:600-606.

---. 1981. "What Have Minimum Wages Done in Agriculture?" In *The Economics of Legal Minimum Wages,* ed. Simon Rottenberg, pp. 210-32. Washington, D.C.: Am. Enterp. Inst.

George, P. S., and G. A. King. 1971. *Consumer Demand for Food Commodities in the United States with Projections for 1980.* Giannini Foundation Monogr. 26. Berkeley: Univ. Calif.

Gisser, M. 1965. "Schooling and the Farm Problem." *Econometrica* 33:582-92.

Glover, Robert, and William S. Franklin. 1978. "Hiring Halls as Labor Market Intermediaries."

In *Labor Market Intermediaries*, pp. 255-82. Special Rep. 22. Washington, D.C.: Natl. Comm. Manpower Policy.

Goldberger, Arthur S. 1964. *Econometric Theory*. New York: Wiley & Sons.

Greenwood, Michael J. 1975. "Research on Internal Migration in the United States: A Survey." *J. Econ. Lit.* 13:397-433.

---. 1978. "An Econometric Model of Internal Migration and Regional Economic Growth in Mexico." *J. Reg. Sci.* 18:17-32.

Griliches, Z. 1977. "Estimating the Returns to Schooling: Some Econometric Problems." *Econometrica* 45:1-22.

Haller, Tom. 1979. "A Study of the Employment and Training Needs and Interests of Farmworkers in Yolo and Solano Counties." Prelim. rep. to Interagency Coord. Comm., Rural Econ. Inst., Davis, Calif., 14 June.

Hammonds, T. M., R. Yadav, and C. Vathana. 1973. *The Hired Farm Labor Market: Some Recent Evidence from Oregon*. Tech. Bull. 127. Agric. Exp. Stn., Oreg. State Univ.

Hanushek, Eric A., and John E. Jackson. 1977. *Statistical Methods for Social Scientists*. New York: Academic Press.

Harberger, A. C. 1978. "Basic Needs versus Distributional Weights in Social Cost-Benefit Analysis." Univ. Chicago, May.

Harris, Sara, and Robert F. Allen. 1978. *The Quiet Revolution: The Story of a Small Miracle in American Life*. New York: Rawson Assoc.

Hartfiel, Ann C. 1978. "Evaluation of the Tecnica Peer Training Project." State CETA Off., Sacramento, Calif., Apr.

Hathaway, Dale E., and Brian B. Perkins. 1968. "Occupational Mobility and Migration from Agriculture." In *Rural Poverty in the United States*, pp. 185-237. Pres. Natl. Comm. Rural Poverty. Washington: GPO.

Hathaway, Dale E., and Arley D. Waldo. 1964. *Multiple Jobholding by Farm Operators*. Mich. Agric.

Exp. Stn. Res. Rep. 5. Mich. State Univ., East Lansing.

Hayami, Yujiro, and Vernon W. Ruttan. 1971. *Agricultural Development: An International Perspective*. Baltimore: Johns Hopkins Press.

Hayes, Sue Eileen. 1975. "Seasonal Workers in Extended Employment: Implications for Agricultural Labor Policy." Ph.D. diss., University of California, Berkeley.

---. 1978. "Farm and Non-farm Wages and Fringe Benefits, 1948-1977." In *Technological Change, Farm Mechanization and Agricultural Employment*, pp. 34-72. Publ. 4085, Div. Agric. Sci., Univ. Calif.

---. 1979. *Industry Response to the California Agricultural Labor Relations Act*. Univ. Texas Cent. Study Hum. Resour., Dec.

Hazell, P. B. R. 1971. "A Linear Alternative to Quadratic and Semivariance Programming for Farm Planning under Uncertainty." *Am. J. Agric. Econ.* 53:53-62.

---. 1979. "Endogenous Input Prices in Linear Programming Models." *Am. J. Agric. Econ.* 61:476-81.

Hazell, P. B. R., and P. L. Scandizzo. 1974. "Competitive Demand Structures under Risk in Agricultural Linear Programming Models." *Am. J. Agric. Econ.* 56:235-44.

Heckman, James J. 1979. "Sample Bias as a Specification Error." *Econometrica* 47:153-61.

Hicks, Brian, Susan Whitmore, Mariita Conley, and Ray Marshall. 1976. "Labor Utilization in the South Texas Citrus Harvest Labor Market." Austin: Cent. Study Hum. Resour., Univ. Texas.

Hill, Claude, John Morley, George Middleton, and Brian Shorney. 1974. *Report on a Visit to the Netherlands to Study Forms of Cooperation in Production*. London, Engl.: Cent. Counc. Agric. Hortic. Coop.

Hill, Lowell, and Paul Lau. 1973. "Application of Multivariate Probit to a Threshold Model of Grain Dryer Purchasing Decision." *Am. J. Agric. Econ.* 55:19-27.

Holt, James S. 1979. "Farm Labor and the Structure of Agriculture." In *Structure Issues of American Agriculture*, pp. 143-49. Agric. Econ. Rep. 438. USDA, ESCS.

Holt, James S., Robert D. Emerson, Varden Fuller, Conrad F. Fritsch, and James Garret. 1978. "Toward the Definition and Measurement of Farm Employment." In *Proceedings of Workshop on: Agricultural and Rural Data, May 4-6, 1977*, ser. B, pp. 105-46. Jointly sponsored by Econ. Stat. Comm., AAEA and USDA. Washington: GPO.

Holthausen, D. M. 1976. "Input Choices and Uncertain Demand." *Am. Econ. Rev.* 86:94-103.

Houthakker, H. S. 1967. *Economic Policy for the Farm Sector*. Washington, D.C.: Am. Enterp. Inst.

Huffman, Wallace E. 1977a. "Allocative Efficiency: The Role of Human Capital." *Quar. J. Econ.* 91:59-80.

---. 1977b. "Interactions Between Farm and Nonfarm Labor Markets." *Am. J. Agric. Econ.* 59:1054-61.

---. 1977c. "Off-Farm Work by Farm Families: Some Empirical Results and Policy Implications." *Business and Economic Statistics Section Proceedings of the American Statistical Association Annual Meeting*, pp. 84-92.

---. 1980. "Farm and Off-Farm Work Decisions: The Role of Human Capital." *Rev. Econ. Stat.* 62:14-23.

Huffman, Wallace E., and J. A. Miranowski. 1979. "An Economic Analysis of Expenditures on State Experiment Station Research." Iowa State Univ. Work. Pap. 97. Ames.

Hughes, J. R. T., and Wilbert E. Moore. 1968. "Industrialization." In *International Encyclopedia of the Social Sciences*, ed. David Sills, 7:250-70. New York: Macmillan and Free Press.

Jamieson, Stuart. 1946. *Labor Unionism in American Agriculture*. Bull. 836. USDL. Washington: GPO.

Jenkins, Glenn P., and Chun-Yan Kuo. 1978. "On Measuring the Social Opportunity Cost of Permanent and Temporary Employment." *Can. J. Econ.* 11:220-39.

Jensen, Vernon H. 1964. *Hiring of Dock Workers and Employment Practices in the Ports of New York, Liverpool, London, Rotterdam and Marseilles.* Cambridge, Mass.: Harvard Univ. Press.

---. 1971. *Decasualization and Modernization of Dock Work in London.* Ithaca, N.Y.: N.Y. State Sch. Ind. Labor Relat., Cornell Univ.

Johnston, Bruce. 1970. "Agriculture and Structural Transformation in Developing Countries." *J. Econ. Lit.* 8(June):369-404.

Just, R. E., and R. D. Pope. 1978. "Stochastic Specification of Production Functions and Economic Implications." *J. Economet.* 7:67-86.

Just, R. E., A. Schmitz, and D. Zilberman. 1979. "Technological Change in Agriculture." *Science* 206:1277-80.

Kahn, Laurence M. 1976. "Internal Labor Markets: San Francisco Longshoremen." *Ind. Relat.* 15(Oct.):333-42.

Kelley, J. 1973. "Causal Chain Models for the Socioeconomic Career." *Am. Soc. Rev.* 38:481-93.

King, Allan G. 1978. "Industrial Structure, the Flexibility of Working Hours, and Women's Labor Force Participation." *Rev. Econ. Stat.* 40:388-407.

Kirschner Associates. 1976. "Study of the Rural Manpower Mobility Plan (Annual Worker Plan)." Prepared for Off. Policy, Eval., Res., USDL. Washington, D.C., Aug.

---. 1979. "Longitudinal Study of Effects of Selected Employment and Training Services on Migrant and Other Seasonal Farmworkers." Prepared for Off. Policy, Eval., Res., USDL. Washington, D.C., Jan.

Klein, B., R. Crawford, and A. Alchian. 1978. "Vertical Integration, Appropriable Rents, and the Competitive Contracting Process." *J. Law Econ.* 21:297-326.

Larkin, Timothy. 1974. "Adios to Migrancy." *Manpower* 8:14-22.

Larrowe, Charles P. 1955. *Shape Up and Hiring Hall: A Comparison of Hiring Methods and Labor Relations on the New York and Seattle Waterfronts*. Berkeley: Univ. Calif. Press.

Layard, R., and G. Psacharopoulos. 1974. "The Screening Hypothesis and the Return to Education." *J. Polit. Econ.* 82:985-98.

Lee, John E., Jr. 1965. "Allocating Farm Resources Between Farm and Nonfarm Uses." *Am. J. Agric. Econ.* 46:83-92.

Lee, T. C. 1970. "Estimation of Regression Parameters with Predicted Dependent Variable Restricted in a Certain Range: Comment." *Am. J. Agric. Econ.* 52:613-14.

Leighton, Linda, and Jacob Mincer. 1981. "The Effects of Minimum Wages on Human Capital Formation." In *The Economics of Legal Minimum Wages*, ed. Simon Rottenberg, pp. 155-73. Washington, D.C.: Am. Enterp. Inst.

Levin, Henry M. 1977. "A Decade of Policy Developments in Improving Education and Training for Low-Income Populations." In *A Decade of Federal Antipoverty Programs: Achievements, Failures, and Lessons*, ed. Robert H. Haveman, pp. 123-88. New York: Academic Press.

Levitan, Sar A. 1976. *Programs in Aid of the Poor*. 3d ed. Baltimore: Johns Hopkins Press.

Lianos, T. P. "Impact of Minimum Wages Upon the Level and Composition of Agricultural Employment." *Am. J. Agric. Econ.* 54:477-84.

Lillesand, David, Linda Kravitz, and Joan McClellan. 1977. "An Estimate of the Number of Migrant and Seasonal Farmworkers in the United States and the Commonwealth of Puerto Rico." Rep. prepared for Leg. Serv. Corp., May.

Lowell, Ruth F. 1978. "Testing a Dual Labor Market Classification of Jobs." *J. Reg. Sci.* 18:95-104.

Lucas, R. 1970. "Econometric Testing of the Natural Rate Hypothesis." In *Econometrics of Price Determination*, pp. 50-59. FRB/SSRC Conf., Oct.

McCarl, Bruce A., and Thomas H. Spreen. 1980. "Price Endogenous Mathematical Programming as a Tool for

Sector Analysis." *Am. J. Agric. Econ.* 62:87-102.

MacKinnon, J. G. 1975. "An Algorithm for the Generalized Transportation Problem." *Reg. Sci. Urban Econ.* 5:445-64.

McWilliams, Carey. 1939. *Factories in the Field.* Boston, Mass.: Little, Brown.

Maddala, G. S. 1977. "Identification and Estimation Problems in Limited Dependent Variable Models." In *Natural Resources, Uncertainty, and General Equilibrium Systems: Essays in Memory of Rafael Lusky,* ed. Alan S. Blinder and Philip Friedman, pp. 219-39. New York: Academic Press.

Mamer, John W., and Varden Fuller. 1965. "Labor and the Economic Factors in Fruit and Vegetable Harvest Mechanization." Paper presented at jt. meet. biol. soc. sponsored by Am. Inst. Biol. Sci., Univ. Colo., Boulder, Colo., 23-28 Aug., 1964. Adaptation in *Agric. Sci. Rev.* 3:1-6.

Mamer, John W., and Donald Rosedale. 1980. *The Management of Seasonal Farm Workers Under Collective Bargaining.* Leafl. 21147. Berkeley: Div. Agric. Sci., Univ. Calif.

Marshall, Ray. 1974. *Rural Workers in Rural Labor Markets.* Salt Lake City: Olympus.

Martin, Philip L. 1980. *Guestworker Programs: Lessons from Europe.* USDL.

Martin, Philip, and Candice Hall. 1978. "Labor Displacement and Public Policy." In *Technological Change, Farm Mechanization and Agricultural Employment,* pp. 199-243. Publ. 4085, Div. Agric. Sci., Univ. Calif.

Martin, Philip L., and Marion Houstoun. 1979. "The Future of International Labor Migration." *J. Intern. Aff.* 33:311-33.

Martin, Philip, and Stanley S. Johnson. 1978. "Tobacco Technology and Agricultural Labor." *Am. J. Agric. Econ.* 60:655-60.

Mattila, J. P. 1979. "The Impact of Minimum Wages on School Enrollment and Labor Force Status of Youth." Final Rep. Employment Train. Adm., USDL.

Millen, Bruce H. 1979. "Providing Assistance to

Displaced Workers." *Mon. Labor Rev.* 5(May):17-22.

Mincer, Jacob. 1962. "Labor Force Participation of Married Women." In *Aspects of Labor Economics.* Universities--National Bureau Conference 14. Princeton: Princeton Univ. Press for Natl. Bur. Econ. Res.

---. 1974. *Schooling, Experience, and Earnings.* Human Behavior and Social Institutions 2. New York: Natl. Bur. Econ. Res.

Moore, Charles V., and Gerald W. Dean. 1972. "Industrialized Farming." In *Size, Structure, and Future of Farms,* ed. A. G. Ball and E. O. Heady, pp. 214-31. Ames: Iowa State Univ. Press.

Morewedge, Hosseine. 1970. *The Economics of Casual Labor: A Study of the Longshore Industry.* Berne, Switz.: Herbert Lang.

Muraro, R. P., and Ben Abbitt. 1978. "Budgeting Costs and Returns: Indian River Citrus Production, 1977-78." Econ. Inf. Rep. 91. Food Resour. Econ. Dep., Univ. Fla., Gainesville.

NAACP, Western Region et al., Plaintiffs, v. *Peter J. Brennan, Secretary of Labor, U.S. Department of Labor et al.,* Defendants. 1972. U.S. District Court for the District of Columbia, Civil Action No. 2010-72, filed Aug. 13, 1972.

National Academy of Sciences. 1978. *CETA: Manpower Programs Under Local Control.* Staff Pap. prep. by William Mirengoff and Lester Rindler. Washington, D.C.

National Association of Farmworker Organizations. 1978. *An Analysis of the Department of Labor's Services for Farmworkers.* Washington, D.C., May.

National Commission on Employment and Unemployment Statistics. 1979. *Counting the Labor Force.* Washington: GPO.

Nelkin, Dorothy. 1969. "A Response to Marginality: The Case of Migrant Farm Workers." *Br. J. Soc.* 20:375-89.

North, David. 1979. "Worker Migration: A State-of-the-Arts Review." Unpublished.

O'Rourke, A. Desmond. 1978. *The Changing Dimensions*

of U.S. Agricultural Policy. Englewood Cliffs, N.J.: Prentice-Hall.

Owen, John D. 1978. "Why Part-Time Workers Tend to Be in Low-Wage Jobs." *Mon. Labor Rev.* 6(June):11-14.

Palmer, John L., and Joseph A. Pechman, eds. 1978. *Welfare in Rural Areas: The North Carolina-Iowa Income Maintenance Experiment.* Washington, D.C.: Brookings Institution.

Perry, Stewart E. 1978. *San Francisco Scavengers: Dirty Work and Pride of Ownership.* Berkeley: Univ. Calif. Press.

Polopolus, Leo. 1977. "Farm Labor in Florida." In *Florida's Farmworkers: Toward a Responsible Public Policy,* pp. 3-13. Tallahassee, Fla.: Inst. Soc. Policy Stud., June.

---. 1979. "An Interpretation of the Crew Leader Registration Law." Staff Pap. 133. Dep. Food Resour. Econ., Univ. Fla., Gainesville.

Polopolus, Leo, and Robert D. Emerson. 1975. *Florida Agricultural Labor and Unemployment Insurance.* Bull. 767. Fla. Agric. Exp. Stn.

Polzin, Paul, and Peter MacDonald. 1971. "Off-Farm Work: A Marginal Analysis." *Q. J. Econ.* 85:540-45.

Pool, W. 1976. "Rational Expectations in the Macro Model." *Brookings Pap. Econ. Act.* 2:463-518.

Poveda, Juan A. 1977. "Earnings Differentials among Florida Male Farm Workers." M.S. thesis, University of Florida, Gainesville.

President's Commission on Migratory Labor. 1951. *Migratory Labor in American Agriculture.* Washington: GPO.

Reder, Melvin W. 1963. "The Economic Consequences of Increased Immigration." *Rev. Econ. Stat.* 45:221-30.

Reubens, Edwin P. 1979. *Temporary Admission of Foreign Workers: Dimensions and Policies.* Spec. Rep. 34. Washington, D.C.: Natl. Comm. Employment Policy.

Rochin, R. I. 1977. "New Perspectives on Agricultural Labor Relations in California." *Labor Law J.* 28:395-402.

Rosedale, Donald, and John W. Mamer. 1974. *Labor Management for Seasonal Farm Workers: A Case Study.* Information Series in Agricultural Economics, Rep. 74-1. Berkeley: Univ. Calif., Agric. Exp. Stn.

Ross, Phillip. 1972. "Origins of the Hiring Hall in Construction." *Ind. Relat.* 11:366-79.

Rothschild, M., and J. Stiglitz. 1970. "Increasing Risk I: A Definition." *J. Econ. Theory* 2:225-43.

---. 1971. "Increasing Risk II: Its Economic Consequences." *J. Econ. Theory* 3:66-84.

Rowe, Gene, and Leslie Whitener Smith. 1976. *Households Eligible for a National Farmworker Program Under the Comprehensive Employment and Training Act of 1973.* Agric. Econ. Rep. 324. Econ. Res. Serv., USDA.

Ruesink, David C. 1979. "Survey of State Extension Manpower Programs." College Station: Texas Agric. Ext. Serv., Texas A&M Univ. Syst., Dec.

Rural America. 1977. *Research Report 1: Where Have All the Farm Workers Gone? The Statistical Annihilation of Migrant and Seasonal Farm Workers by Federal Agencies: An Analysis of the Federal Effort to Define and Count Migrant and Seasonal Farm Workers.* Washington, D.C., Sept.

Ruttan, Vernon W. 1962. "The Human Resource Problem in American Agriculture." In *Farming, Farmers, and Markets for Farm Goods.* Suppl. 15. New York: Committee for Economic Development.

Samuelson, Paul A. 1952. "Spatial Price Equilibrium and Linear Programming." *Am. Econ. Rev.* 42:283-303.

Sandmo, A. 1971. "On the Theory of Competitive Firm Under Price Uncertainty." *Am. Econ. Rev.* 61:65-73.

Sargent, T., and N. Wallace. 1976. "Rational Expectations and the Theory of Economic Policy." *J. Monetary Econ.* 2:169-84.

Schlenger, William, L. E. Ondrizek, and J. B. Hallan. 1971. An Examination of Methods Used to Estimate the Number of Migratory Seasonal Farm Workers. Institute of Human Ecology, Raleigh, N.C., Sept. Mimeo.

Schrimper, R. A. 1978. "Food Programs and the Retail Price of Food." *Agric.-Food Policy Rev.* 2:101-8.

Schuh, G. Edward. 1962. "An Econometric Investigation of the Market for Hired Labor in Agriculture." *J. Farm Econ.* 44:307-21.

---. "Comment." 1969. In *The Role of Agriculture in Economic Development*, ed. Erik Thorbecke, pp. 379-85. New York: Columbia Univ. Press for Natl. Bur. Econ. Res.

---. 1974. "The Exchange Rate and U.S. Agriculture." *Am. J. Agric. Econ.* 56:1-13.

---. 1979. "Floating Exchange Rates, International Interdependence, and Agricultural Policy." Paper presented at 17th Intern. Conf., Intern. Assoc. Agric. Econ., Banff, Alberta, Can., 3-12 Sept.

---. 1982. "Out-Migration, Rural Productivity, and the Distribution of Income." In *Migration and the Labor Market in Developing Countries*, ed. R. H. Sabot, pp. 161-90. Boulder, Colo.: Westview Press.

Schultz, Theodore W. 1951. "A Framework for Land Economics: The Long View." *J. Farm Econ.* 33(May):204-15.

---. 1962. "Reflections on Investment in Man." *J. Polit. Econ., Suppl.* 70:1-8.

---. 1971. *Investment in Human Capital.* New York: Free Press.

---. 1975. "The Value of the Ability to Deal with Disequilibria." *J. Econ. Lit.* 13:827-46.

Shapley, Allen E. 1979. *The Law and Michigan Agricultural Labor.* Ext. Bull. E-831. East Lansing: Mich. State Univ., Coop. Ext. Serv.

Sikes, Fred C., and George F. Sorn. 1979. "Statement." Presented to Sel. Comm. Immigr. Refugee Policy at public hearing in Miami, Fla., 4 Dec.

Sjaastad, Larry A. 1962. "The Costs and Returns of

Human Migration." *J. Polit. Econ., Suppl.* 70:80-93.

Smith, Barton, and R. Newman. 1977. "Depressed Wages Along the U.S.-Mexican Border: An Empirical Analysis." *Econ. Inq.* 40:51-66.

Smith, Roy J., Daniel T. Seamount, and Bruce H. Mills. 1965. *Lemon Picking and the Ventura County Tree Production Incentive Wage System.* Calif. Agric. Exp. Stn. Bull. 809, Univ. Calif., Riverside, Jan.

Smith, T. R. 1979. "Migration, Risk Aversion and Regional Differentiation." *J. Reg. Sci.* 19:31-45.

Smith, V. L. 1963. "Minimization of Economic Rent in Spatial Price Equilibrium." *Rev. Econ. Stud.* 30:24-31.

Snedeker, Bonnie B., and David M. Snedeker. 1978. *CETA: Decentralization on Trial.* Salt Lake City: Olympus.

Sosnick, Stephen H. 1978. *Hired Hands: Seasonal Farm Workers in the United States.* Santa Barbara: McNally and Loftin, West.

Steinberg, E. I. 1979. "Labor Mobility in 1960-65 and 1970-75." *Surv. Curr. Bus.* 1:25-27, 36.

Strong, Samuel M. 1973. "An Optimal Control Approach to the Off-Farm Labor Migration Problem." Ph.D. diss., University of Illinois.

Sulton, Paul, and Darryk D. Enos. 1974. "Farming and Farm Labor: A Study in California." Rep. prep. Cent. Urban and Reg. Stud. Claremont Grad. Sch., Calif., June 28. (available from Natl. Tech. Inf. Serv.--DLMA 92-06-72-14-1).

Takayama, T., and G. G. Judge. 1964a. "Equilibrium Among Spatially Separated Markets: A Reformulation." *Econometrica* 32:510-24.

---. 1964b. "An Interregional Activity Analysis Model of the Agricultural Sector." *J. Farm Econ.* 46:349-65.

---. 1971. *Spatial and Temporal Price and Allocation Models.* Amsterdam: North-Holland Publ.

Thompson, Orville E., and R. E. Thomas. 1972. *Func-*

tions and Activities of Agricultural Jobs in California. Davis, Calif.: Dep. Appl. Behav. Sci., Univ. Calif.

Truman, Harry S. 1949-53. Executive Order 10129. June 3, 1950. 3 CFR, 1949-53 Comp., p. 317.

Tweeten, Luther. 1978. "Rural Employment and Unemployment Statistics." Background pap. 4. Washington, D.C.: Natl. Comm. Employment and Unemployment Stat.

---. 1980. "Farm Commodity Prices and Income." In *Consensus and Conflict in U.S. Agriculture: Perspectives from the National Farm Summit, December 1978,* ed. Bruce Gardner and James Richardson. College Station: Texas A&M Univ. Press.

Tyrchniewicz, E. W., and G. E. Schuh. 1966. "Regional Supply of Hired Labor to Agriculture." *J. Farm Econ.* 48:537-56.

---. 1969. "Econometric Analysis of the Agricultural Labor Market." *Am. J. Agric. Econ.* 51:770-87.

U.S., Congress. House. 1976. Committee on Education and Labor. Subcommittee on Agricultural Labor. *Federal and State Statutes Relating to Farmworkers: A Compilation.* 94th Cong. 2d sess. 1976.

---. 1969-70. Hearings before the Subcommittee on Migratory Labor of the Committee on Labor and Public Welfare, on Manpower and Economic Problems. *Migrant and Seasonal Farmworker Powerlessness.* 91st Cong. 1st and 2d sess.

U.S., Congress. Senate. 1978. Committee on the Judiciary, Subcommittee on Immigration. *The West Indies (BWI) Temporary Alien Labor Program: 1943-1977.* 95th Cong. 2d sess.

U.S. Department of Agriculture. 1979. *Noncitrus Fruits and Nuts, 1978 Annual Summary: Production, Use, and Value.* Washington: GPO.

U.S. Department of Agriculture. Economic Research Service. 1978. *Changes in Farm Production and Efficiency.* Washington: GPO.

U.S. Department of Agriculture. Economic Research

Service. Economic Development Division. 1974. *The Hired Farm Working Force of 19--.* Various issues through 1974. Washington: GPO.

---. 1975. *The Hired Farm Working Force of 1975*, by Gene Rowe and Leslie Whitener Smith. Agric. Econ. Rep. 355. Washington: GPO.

U.S. Department of Agriculture. Economics, Statistics, and Cooperatives Service. 1979a. *Status of the Family Farm: Second Annual Report to Congress*, Agric. Econ. Rep. 434. Washington: GPO.

---. 1979b. *Structure Issues of American Agriculture.* Agric. Econ. Rep. 438. Washington: GPO.

U.S. Department of Agriculture. Economics, Statistics, and Cooperatives Service. Crop Reporting Board. *Farm Labor*, various issues. Washington: GPO.

U.S. Department of Agriculture. Economics, Statistics, and Cooperatives Service. Economic Development Division. 1976. *The Hired Farm Working Force of 1976*, by Leslie Whitener Smith and Gene Rowe. Agric. Econ. Rep. 405. Washington: GPO.

---. 1977. *The Hired Farm Working Force of 1977*, by Gene Rowe. Agric. Econ. Rep. 437. Washington: GPO.

---. 1977. *The Hired Farm Working Force*, micro data tape, Dec., CPS Suppl. Washington: GPO.

U.S. Department of Commerce. Bureau of the Census. 1969. *1969 Census of Agriculture*, vol. 2, chap. 4. Washington: GPO.

---. 1974. *1974 Census of Agriculture*, vol. 2, pt. 4. Washington: GPO.

---. 1979. *County Business Patterns, 1974: U.S. Summary.* Washington: GPO.

U.S. Department of Justice. Immigration and Naturalization Service. 1980. *1978 Annual Report of the Immigration and Naturalization Service.* Washington: GPO.

U.S. Department of Labor. 1959. *Farm Labor Fact Book.* Washington: GPO.

U.S. Department of Labor. 1965. *Year of Transi-*

tion: Seasonal Farm Labor, 1965. Report by Secretary of Labor, Willard Wirtz. Washington: GPO.

U.S. Department of Labor. Employment Service. 1977. *Dictionary of Occupational Titles*, 4th ed. Washington: GPO.

U.S. Department of Labor. Employment and Training Administration. 1978a. Unpublished ES-223 Adm. Rep. Washington: GPO.

---. 1978b. *Guide to Farm Jobs* (Eastern States, Gulf to Great Lakes, Intermountain States, Western States). Oct. Washington: GPO.

U.S. Department of Labor. Labor Management Services Administration. 1970. *Exclusive Union Work Referral Systems in the Building Trades*. Washington: GPO.

U.S. Department of Labor. Manpower Administration. Special Review Staff. 1972. *Review of Rural Manpower Service*. Washington: GPO.

U.S. Public Health Service. 1966. *Domestic Agricultural Migrants in the United States*. Public Health Serv. Publ. 540. HEW, Washington, D.C. Rev. Aug.

Wachter, M. 1974. "Primary and Secondary Labor Markets: A Critique of the Dual Approach." *Brookings Pap. Econ. Act.* 3:637-80.

Waldo, Arley D. 1965. "The Impact of Outmigration and Multiple Jobholding upon Income Distribution in Agriculture." *J. Farm Econ.* 47:1235-44.

Wales, T. J., and A. D. Woodland. 1976. "Estimation of Household Utility Functions and Labor Supply Response." *Intern. Econ. Rev.* 17:397-409.

Wallace, T. D., and D. M. Hoover. 1966. "Income Effects of Innovation: The Case of Labor in Agriculture." *J. Farm Econ.* 48:325-36.

Warner, Dennis L. 1979. "An Economic Model of the World Wheat Economy." Ph.D. diss., Princeton University.

Waterfield, Larry. 1979. "FLCRA Seen as 'Toothless Tiger.'" *Packer*, 17 Nov.

Welch, Finis. 1970. "Education in Production." *J. Polit. Econ.* 78:35-59.

Willis, Robert J., and Sherwin Rosen. 1979. "Education and Self-selection." *J. Polit. Econ.* 87, no. 5, pt. 2:S7-S36.

Wise, D. E. 1974. "The Effects of the Bracero on Agricultural Production in California." *Econ. Inq.* 12:547-58.

Witherington, Moffat Patrick, and Cleve E. Willis. 1978. "The Dichotomous Dependent Variable: A Comparison of Probit Analysis and Ordinary Least Squares Procedures by Monte Carlo Analysis." Mass. Agric. Exp. Stn. Res. Bull. 657. Univ. Mass., Amherst.

Yates, M. D. 1978. "The 'Make Whole' Remedy for Employer Refusal to Bargain: Early Experience under the California Agricultural Labor Relations Act." *Labor Law J.* 29:666-76.

Zepp, G. A., and R. L. Simmons. 1979. *Producing Fresh Winter Vegetables in Florida and Mexico: Costs and Competition.* ESCS-72. ESCS, USDA.

Participants

(Affiliations at the time of the conference.)

Darryl Anderson, Counsel, Senate Labor and Human Resource Committee

Burt Barnow, Deputy Director, Office of Research and Development, Employment and Training Administration, U.S. Department of Labor

Richard Bieker, Department of Economics, Delaware State College

Aaron Bodin, Chief, Division of Labor Certification, U.S. Department of Labor

Philip Booth, National Commission on Unemployment, San Diego, California

Harriet Bramble, National Governor's Association, Washington, D.C.

Vernon Briggs, New York State School of Industrial and Labor Relations, Cornell University

Pam Browning, Director of Research, National Association of Farm Worker Organizations, Washington, D.C.

A. F. Cantfil, Director, Office of Labor-Management Policy Development, U.S. Department of Labor, Washington, D.C.

Robert Coltrane, Program Leader, Manpower Studies, Economic Development Division, Economics, Statistics, and Cooperatives Service, U.S. Department of Agriculture

Charles D. Covey, Food and Resource Economics Department, University of Florida

Harry E. Cross, Battelle Memorial Institute, Washington, D.C.

Lynn Daft, Associate Director for Agriculture and

Rural Development, Domestic Policy Staff, White House

Carlton G. Davis, Food and Resource Economics Department, University of Florida

G. Joachim Elterich, Department of Agricultural Economics, University of Delaware

Robert D. Emerson, Food and Resource Economics Department, University of Florida

Bernard L. Erven, Department of Agricultural Economics and Rural Sociology, Ohio State University

Gary Fairchild, Food and Resource Economics Department, University of Florida

Dennis U. Fisher, National Welding Michigan (formerly of Department of Agricultural Economics, Cornell University)

William H. Friedland, Community Studies and Sociology, University of California, Santa Cruz

Conrad F. Fritsch, Consulting Agricultural Economist, Washington, D.C.

Varden Fuller, Department of Agricultural Economics (emeritus), University of California, Davis

Joe Garcia, Farmers Home Administration, U.S. Department of Agriculture, Washington, D.C.

Bruce Gardner, Department of Agricultural Economics, Texas A&M University

Clark Ghiselin, Executive Vice President, Citrus Industrial Council, Lakeland, Florida

Robert W. Glover, Center for the Study of Human Resources, University of Texas, Austin

Terry Glover, Department of Economics, Utah State University

Sue Eileen Hayes, Department of Economics, Sonoma State University, California

James S. Holt, Consulting Agricultural Economist, Washington, D.C.

Wallace E. Huffman, Department of Economics, Iowa State University

Ronald Jones, Office of Research and Development, Employment and Training Administration, U.S. Department of Labor, Washington, D.C.

Richard E. Just, Economics Department, Brigham Young

University, and Department of Agricultural and Resource Economics, University of California, Berkeley (on leave)

Marvin Konyha, Program Coordinator, Rural Community Development, Program Planning Staff, Science and Education Administration, U.S. Department of Agriculture, Maryland

David Lah, Office of Research and Development, Employment and Training Administration, U.S. Department of Labor, Washington, D.C.

William McGreevey, Battelle Memorial Institute, Washington, D.C.

John W. Mamer, Economist, Cooperative Extension, University of California, Berkeley

Philip L. Martin, Department of Agricultural Economics, University of California, Davis

Benjamin N. Matta, Jr., Department of Economics, New Mexico State University

Larry C. Morgan, Department of Agricultural Economics, Texas A & M University

David S. North, Center for Labor and Migration Studies, New Trans Century Foundation

Harland Padfield, Anthropology, Oregon State University

Alfred L. Parks, Department of Agricultural Economics and Rural Sociology, Prairie View A & M University, Texas

Leo Polopolus, Food and Resource Economics Department, University of Florida

Bob Reinsel, Economics, Statistics, and Cooperatives Service, U.S. Department of Agriculture, Washington, D.C.

Refugio I. Rochin, Department of Agricultural Economics, University of California, Davis

Ed Scheopner, U.S. Employment Service, U.S. Department of Labor, Washington, D.C.

G. Edward Schuh, Department of Agricultural and Applied Economics, University of Minnesota

Ellen Sehgal, Office of Research and Development, Employment and Training Administration, U.S. Department of Labor, Washington, D.C.

Allen E. Shapley, Department of Agricultural Economics, Michigan State University

Mary Silva, U.S. Employment Service, U.S. Department of Labor, Washington, D.C.

Thomas H. Spreen, Food and Resource Economics Department, University of Florida

Daniel A. Sumner, Department of Economics, North Carolina State University

Jean Sussman, Department of Agricultural and Applied Economics, University of Minnesota

Merv Tano, Department of Health Education and Welfare, Washington, D.C.

Thomas Till, National Rural Center, Atlanta, Georgia

Fred Thorp, Economics, Statistics, and Cooperatives Service, U.S. Department of Agriculture, Washington, D.C.

Raymond Tremblay, Department of Resource Economics, University of Vermont

Tim Triplett, U.S. Department of Labor, Washington, D.C.

Finis Welch, Department of Economics, University of California, Los Angeles

John W. Wysong, Department of Agricultural and Resource Economics, University of Maryland

David Zilberman, Department of Agricultural and Resource Economics, University of California, Berkeley

Index